Meeting the Foreign in the Middle Ages

Meeting the Foreign in the Middle Ages

Edited by Albrecht Classen

Routledge
New York and London

Published in 2002 by
Routledge
29 West 35th Street
New York, NY 10001

Published in Great Britain by
Routledge
11 New Fetter Lane
London EC4P 4EE

Routledge is an imprint of the Taylor & Francis Group.

Printed in the United States of America on acid-free paper.

10 9 8 7 6 5 4 3 2 1

Cataloging-in-Publication data is available from the Library of Congress.

ISBN 0-415-93002-2

TO CAROLYN AND STEPHAN

Contents

Illustrations

Introduction
The Self, the Other, and Everything in Between: Xenological Phenomenology of the Middle Ages

ALBRECHT CLASSEN

Scholars have traditionally written as if all hermeneutics rely on the binary opposition of self and other. The self does not reach an understanding of itself without the clear demarcation to 'the other' and also through an intricate interaction with 'the other.'[1] Human existence is not something simply given, but needs to be defined and explained. It must be made conscious. According to Martin Heidegger, for instance, our *Dasein* (being-in-the-world) is based on the "primordial signification of the world, where it designates this business of interpreting."[2] Hubert Dreyfus offers the following definition of this phenomenology: "By a double use of the hermeneutic circle, hermeneutic phenomenology strips away our disguises and makes manifest the preontological understanding of being as *unheimlich* which is hidden in each person's awareness and in our public practices, thus revealing the deep truth of our condition."[3] Without the foreign there would be no familiar, and vice versa, as the confrontation of the self with the non-self constitutes identity by way of negotiation and interaction. Consequently, the study of literary and historical texts allows for a critical examination of selfhood in contrast to 'otherness.' To quote İrvin Cemil Schick, "[i]dentity is its own construction, then, and narrative is the medium through which that construction is realized. But the construction of identity is inseparable from that of alterity—indeed, identity itself only makes sense in juxtaposition with alterity."[4] In other words, the categories of distance and differentiation prove to be fundamental for human life, even though it always remains a difficult balancing act to maintain (despite the distance to the other) sufficient contact and exchange as the basis for further developments.[5] Seen negatively and especially from a modern perspective, this leads to a highly dangerous form of xenophobia and hence exclusion of the other, because "[a]nyone who deviates from the official norm, whatever that is, anyone who fails to bear a likeness to the Standard Product, is simply not viewed as fully human, and then becomes at best invisible, at worst a threat to the national security."[6] This realization of one of the crucial conditions of human existence does not, however, only pertain to modern philosophical, theological, literary, and scientific discourse,[7] but equally applies to the investigation of older cultures, such as the Middle Ages when the quest for the self was certainly not yet fully accomplished, and the awareness of other cultures, other peoples, and other languages (not to speak of religions and political systems) was not yet quite developed. At the same time, neither the modern concept of the self or of personal identity nor the idea of "nationhood" was fully in place, although beginning with the twelfth century radical changes can be observed in literature, the visual arts, politics, and religion.[8] Concurrently, the fascination with monster lore (teratology), travelogues about fabulous distant countries, religious accounts of Hell and Purgatory, mystical narratives of visionary revelations, and fantastic tales about giants, dwarfs, strange creatures and peoples were an essential aspect of a medieval mentality, which has, in many strange and bizarre ways, left "an infinity of traces [on us] pertinent to it but without an inventory."[9] In other words, human existence and its development over time is determined by a process of distinguishing the self from the other. Hans-Georg Gadamer describes this phenomenon in the following manner:

> Whatever is being distinguished must be distinguished from something which, in turn, must be distinguished from it. Thus all distinguishing also makes visible that from which something is distinguished. . . . [The prejudices] constitute, then, the horizon of a particular present, for they represent that beyond which it is impossible to see . . . In fact the horizon of the present is being continually formed, in that we have continually to test all our prejudices. An important part of this testing is the encounter with the past and the understanding of the tradition from which we come. Hence the horizon of the present cannot formed without the past . . . Understanding, rather, is always the fusion of these horizons which we imagine to exist by themselves.[10]

Curiously, in many medieval chronicles—which we normally would expect to be realistic, pragmatic, and factual—the world of wonders, of the inexplicable, the strange, and hence of the other also plays a significant role, such as in the German-Austrian rhymed world chronicle by the Viennese Jans Enikel from around 1272, which primarily documents political and historical events.[11] These can be divided, using a system developed by Jacques Le Goff, into *mirabilis*, *magicus*, and *miraculosus*.[12] Surprisingly, Jans Enikel, highly regarded for his mostly accurate historical observations, did not hesitate to incorporate these curious elements in his text. His audience either expected them anyway, or would not have been surprised to be confronted with them, especially as they closely followed a long tradition of the monstrous, miraculous, and magical already present in Biblical accounts, in the many reports of Alexander the Great so popular throughout the entire Middle Ages,[13] and of Caesar (meeting monstrous people), the mysterious

Pope Sylvester, the magician Virgil, and other figures.[14] In contrast to modern historians, but very much in line with his medieval audience's expectations, Jans Enikel peppered his chronological account with many legendary and anecdotal narratives and combined them with his sober sequence of world history.[15] Virgil, for instance, is said to have discovered a glass container in the ground while working in his garden. Many devils were caught in this container like the Arabic Djinni from *One Thousand and One Nights*. They promised to teach him many magical arts if he broke the glass and let them go, which he subsequently did and that is then claimed to be the cause for devils roaming this earth ever since: "zehant die tiufel alle/lêrten in mit schalle/die zouberlist ân arbeit,/als si noch in der kristenheit/allenthalben umbe gât" (23747–751; immediately all the devils noisily and effortlessly taught him all the magical arts that are still practiced everywhere in Christianity). Similarly, Jans Enikel incorporated the miraculous accounts of Alexander the Great and reports, for instance, of the hero's communication with a magical tree which announces to him that he will be murdered soon: "dir wirt vergeben mit swær/von dînem næhsten kamrær" (19637f.; you will be paid back with pain by yours closest servants).[16]

In fact, this curious but not untypical feature of Enikel's chronicle does not come as a surprise because wherever we turn in medieval history, art, and literature there is hardly any area where the familiar is not suddenly confronted with the unfamiliar, the Christian with the pagan, and the human with the non-human. This observation applies both to specific historical aspects and to literary works, as well as to the visual arts, religion, and politics.[17] In Jurgis Baltrušaitis's words, "the Middle Ages have always displayed a noteworthy willingness to renew borrowed forms and to imprint on them their own character. Everything moves and transforms. Blended in the marginal decorations, the Greek-Roman grotesques are completely assimilated to the gothic bizarre world. The arabesques are dragged into the capriciously climbing plants."[18] It will remain uncertain how far medieval artists, writers, and travelers fully understood the implications of the opposition between self and other, but they certainly observed the distance and tried to come to terms with it in many different ways[19]—especially when we consider the image of the noble savage, the threatening monster, travelogues of distant worlds, the history of Jews and Arabs, Mongols and Cathars, miraculous accounts, legends and myths.[20]

Certainly, for a microanalysis we would have to draw clearer distinctions between the early, High, and late Middle Ages, and from an anthropological perspective vast differences would emerge from a comparative investigation involving, for instance, Irish and Welsh cultures on the one hand, and German and Italian on the other, not to mention the Slavic regions, Scandinavia, or Greece.[21] Nevertheless, in order to establish a theoretical and historical platform from which to understand the fundamental contrast between self

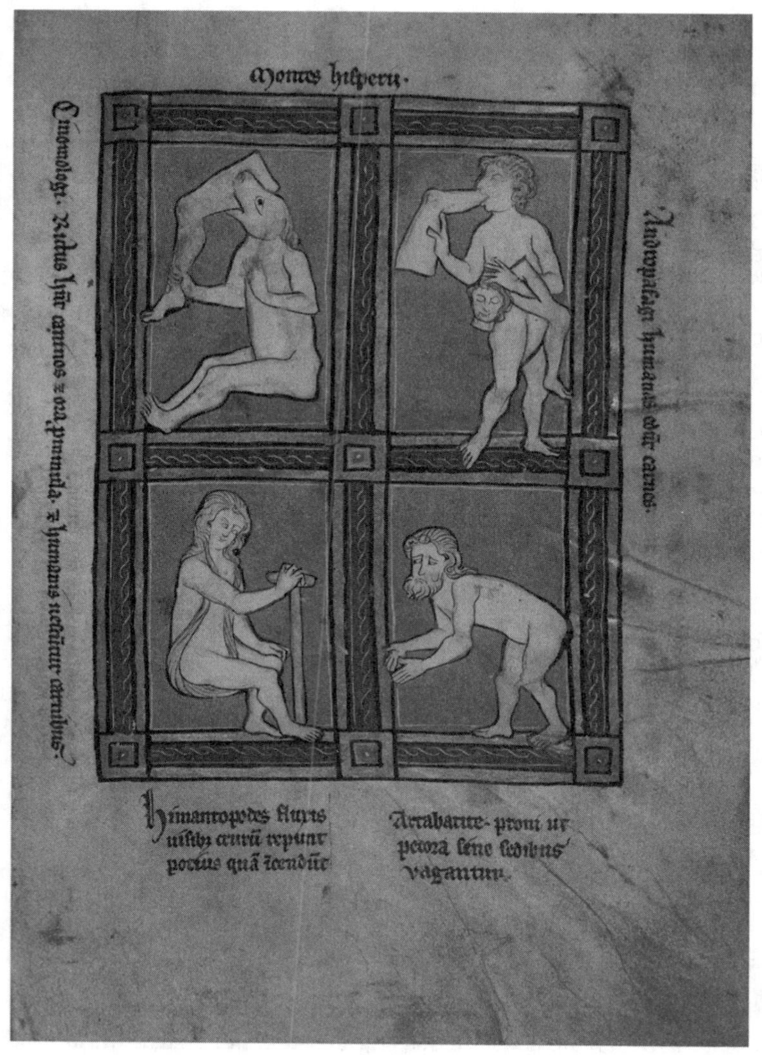

Fig. 1. Images of medieval monster, *Mirabilia mundi*, fol. 117r, c. 1277.

and other, or the familiar and the unfamiliar (macroanalysis), subsequently I will accept a certain level of generalization and discuss medieval culture as a more or less homogenous entity, as one historical-cultural epoch. For instance, we need to consider that, on the one hand, St. Augustine in a way still defended the Jews and their teaching as it "is a great confirmation of our faith that such important testimony is borne by enemies . . . and the unbelief of the Jews increases rather than lessens the authority of these books."[22] On the other hand, when Regino of Prüm composed his *Epistula ad Hathonem archiepiscopum missa* around 900 C.E., he clearly distinguished between the various nations populating this world, using ethnic markers such as "descent, customs, language and law" (*diversae nationes populorum inter se discrepant genere, moribus, lingua, legibus*). Obviously he already had a concise notion of the other in his mind, and even though these markers which separate 'self' from 'other' might have shifted somewhat throughout the centuries, basically the conflicts between Christian Europeans and outsiders, marginalized foreigners, heretics, and imagined monsters remained the same.[23] Some critics even go so far as to argue that the search for identity within Europe has always been a constitutive factor of medieval and modern mentality, which in itself is not to be characterized as negative or positive, instead simply as a factor of all cultural history.[24] Both literary travelogues such as *The Book of John of Mandeville's Travels* and world maps such as the Hereford *mappamundi* provide excellent illustrations for this phenomenon, but also reflect the changing perspectives toward the late Middle Ages when the need for self-identity and the establishment of nationhood also in cultural terms increased tremendously.[25]

Nevertheless, there was a discernible and disturbing trend observable since the late Middle Ages, to erect race barriers, to discriminate against nonconformists, and to expel non-Christians, such as the Jews and Moslems from Spain in 1492.[26] At the end of the fifteenth century, the monstrous became more commodified than ever and turned into a topic of both public and private debates.[27] Not by accident was the catastrophic witchcraze associated with the emergence of modern statehood, and subsequently with the development of modern courts, law systems, and inquisitional organizations.[28] In other words, intolerance might well have been the birthmark of the early modern age, whereas in the Middle Ages the relationship between 'self' and 'other' was still a matter of complex and open-ended negotiations.[29] As a case in point, Albertus Magnus, while commenting on some of the sources for his *de animalibus* (written sometime after 1258), critically remarked that Pliny and Solinus "heed the rumors of common folk rather than offering demonstrable proof of their stories." In a previous chapter he had voiced similar opposition to fabulous accounts which could not be verified: "[T]hese philosophers are much given to falsification and I suspect this to be one of their deceits."[30] This is to say, scholars like Albert also paid close attention to Greek teratology and mythical reports of monstrous creatures, but they began to question the validity of these statements. Nevertheless, the epistemological function of the other for medieval culture cannot be underestimated and seems to have been one of its major components. Even though feared and dreaded, misappropriated for cultural stereotypes, and misused for the justification of military operations and religious offensives, the other was not yet the absolute negative. Even in late-medieval narratives, such as Thüring von Ringoltingen's *Melusine* (1456), and its French source by Couldrette, the appearance of fairies is explained with a reference to the Psalms: "Mirabilis deus in operibus suis" (Ps. 68:36 [Vulgate]), providing a theoretical platform which justified the categorization of all creatures, objects, and phenomena here in this world as emanations of God's will and power.[31] The other was not to be condemned and destroyed, but it was considered as an unusual, surprising, but somehow also acceptable part of divine creation.[32] Intriguingly, the notion of the other within our self was not unknown to medieval people, and the search for the self simply had to take into account that the other—mostly described as a demon or a succubus—represented a challenge to be overcome for the self to find itself. Marie de France deals with this issue in her *lai* "Bisclavret," and we find echoes of it in the Middle English *Sir Gowther* and in the various version of the *Melusine* narrative.[33]

Historians such as David Nirenberg argued both against the idealization of the Middle Ages as a "rose-tinted haven of tolerance" and also against the description of that same period as "a darkening valley of tears."[34] Nevertheless, violence was a pervasive factor of medieval life—but also of many other periods, especially of modern times—and it affected most gruesomely minority groups such as the Jews, lepers, homosexuals, and heretics. One of the many reasons might have been, again in Nirenberg's words, the ever present tension between majority and minority in medieval society: "[e]ven in times of plague and massacre, violence was a central and systemic aspect of the coexistence of majority and minorities. *Convivencia* was predicated upon violence; it was not its peaceful antithesis. Violence drew its meaning from coexistence, not in opposition to it."[35] But even the majority felt threatened by external forces, by unknown elements of nature, and by the impact of myth on everyday life as well as by the actual existence of the minorities whom they assimilated to the monstrous other. *Mappaemundi* and travelogues such as John of Mandeville's famed *Travels* evince a remarkable effort to distinguish from early on the European self from the non-European other, but both documents also reflect a strong concern to use the other simply as a catalyst to identify and characterize the self.[36] Tolerance in the modern sense of the word hardly ever existed in the Middle Ages, but nevertheless there were certain early indications that some individuals espoused a remarkable open mind toward other cultures, other peoples, other religions, and other philosophies.[37] We know of some cases of Christians having converted to

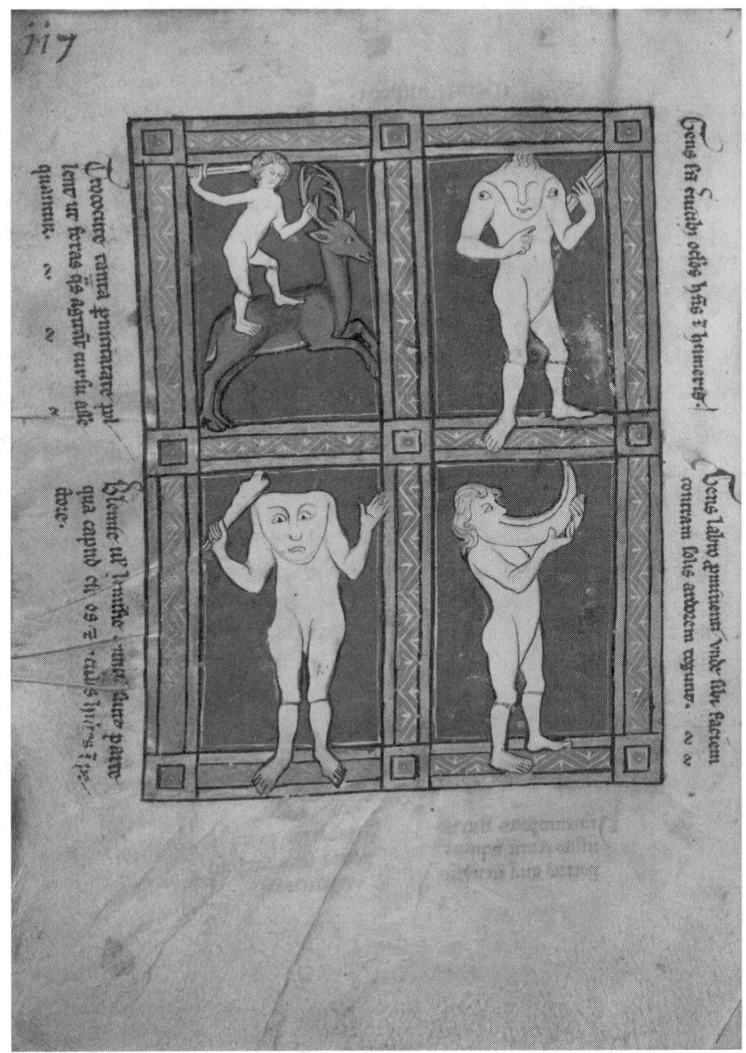

Fig. 2. Images of medieval monster, *Mirabilia mundi*, fol. 117v, c. 1277.

Islam, and of many Christians who openly welcomed Arabic philosophy, medicine, and science.[38] Intolerance, on the other hand, being the dominant public and private attitude also affected the lower social classes (peasants) and women, and hence was not automatically and always linked with race, religion, and culture.

Heroic epics, for instance, always thematize the conflict between the hero and creatures from another world, such as in the case of the Old English *Beowulf* or the *Thidrekssaga*. Courtly romances are basically conditioned by the idea of the knightly quest which takes the protagonist out of the safe haven of King Arthur's court into a world full of dangers, threats, and menaces. Braving these and overcoming their challenges is tantamount to accomplishing the chivalrous deed, which then allows the hero to return to the Round Table and enjoy his fellows' respect and admiration. In this context the appearance of representatives of the "otherworld" serves as a catalyst to launch the narrative, but the foreign or strange creatures also might bring to light "faults in that society which might otherwise go unnoticed and uncorrected."[39] Curiously, at times the knightly hero willy nilly observes that the representatives of the wilderness represent a higher form of culture, or at least seem to live much more in peaceful harmony with nature than the knights do. Before Kâlogrenant in Hartmann von Aue's *Iwein* is about to discover the magic fountain which is ferociously defended by King Ascalon, he encounters a wild man whose behavior and attitude are reminiscent of Paradise, though in appearance he seems more like a monster: "His appearance was otherwise quite wild: / He resembled a Moor, / Was enormous and terrifying / Beyond belief. / His head was truly / Larger than an aurox's. / The brute had / Shaggy hair, the color of soot, / Which was all / Matted together on his beard and head / Right down to the skin."[40] To Kâlogrenant's surprise, however, all the beasts surrounding him keep peace with him and are totally under his command: "My tongue and my threats / Have made it so / That they stand quivering before me / And behave exactly as I wish" (506–10). Once the knight has explained his own nature and purpose in life—"I am in search of adventure" (526)—the wild man informs him about the fountain and points him in the right direction. Kâlogrenant immediately departs and leaves this amazingly peaceful setting behind, but only to experience defeat and disgrace back at court. This underscores the ambiguity of the scene with the wild man (who seems to be a truly wise person) and the knight (who is rash and almost foolish).[41] In other words, in the midst of the dangerous forest the strange person, the other, enjoys peace and order with all animals, whereas in the world outside—where knights battle for fame and glory—violence, fighting, and disorder dominate the court of King Arthur, which he can barely control.[42]

Not surprisingly, the famous lovers Tristan and Isolde in Gottfried von Straßburg's romance find refuge from society's persecution only in the remote grotto of love, and Parzival's mother Herzeloyde in Wolfram von

Eschenbach's grail romance withdraws from the chivalric world into her woodsy solitude Soltâne to protect her young son from the dangers of a military life and to avoid a repeat of her husband Gahmuret's death on the battlefield.[43] Even though medieval people tended to express fear of the dark forests and the dangers lurking there, the wilderness itself often proved to be a safe haven from corrupted society, as the entire history of the Order of the Cistercians suggests.[44]

Medieval manuscripts are as much cluttered with grotesque images, drawings, and drôleries, as are church capitals and sculptures, indicating how much the scribes and illuminators allowed their fantasy free reign, thereby subtly but energetically undermining the rigid theological and intellectual framework established by the Church. However, these images were not simply fantastic creations, but often reflected (if we here disregard for a moment the naive enjoyment of playful and fanciful artwork)[45] deep-seated fears and concrete existential problems which medieval people could not solve, wherefore the artists, among others, resorted to forms of psychological substitution via illustrations, sculptures, and literary texts when dealing with outsiders, namely members of religious, ethnic, racial, and gender minorities. "People with racial or ethnic features different from the majority elicited antipathy too, but attitudes toward them were sometimes ambivalent or contradictory . . . Ambivalence characterized attitudes toward those whose physical appearance had been affected by disease or deformity."[46] Dolores Warwick Frese reaches the same conclusion in her study of the horrifying werewolf theme: "[s]uch fearful adventures in metamorphic reversion were commonly perceived in the Middle Ages as phenomena of daemonic or diabolical possession and had furnished the subject of prior narratives."[47] Apart from threats by military outsiders, people felt endangered by the harsh environment, especially the large medieval woods that had only begun to be partially pushed back in the twelfth and thirteenth centuries to make room for agriculture and city development.[48]

Medieval teratology naturally played a significant role both within the visual arts and in literature, for instance in sculptures, paintings, tapestry, wood carvings, and in courtly romances, heroic epics, and short verse novellas. Jeffrey Jerome Cohen observes,

> The epistemic horizons of the west are populated with fantastic and grotesque creatures who at once repel and entice investigation. Excluded from traditional heuristic systems and incorporated unwillingly into others, the monster always returns to its position at the borders of sanctioned inquiry. . . . The monster is something more than the vehicle of an escapist fantasy here: the certainties of "science" and the ambiguity of the monster must always co-exist because they offer alternative, symbiotic, and supplemental modes of perception.[49]

Irrespective of the undeniable fact that medieval people never really faced monsters as living creatures, they were very much convinced of their existence somewhere at the margins of the European world. Of course, the more medieval travelers explored these margins and entered into hitherto forbidding lands, the more these monsters retreated and were soon only found in great geographic distances and in dreams, making it impossible once again to verify their existence.[50] Not surprisingly, in modern times we only find monsters allegedly living in deep water, in the remote areas of the Arctic and Antartica, in the Himalayas, and in outer space. Medieval fantasy, however, was not limited to the learned tradition of monster lore (which can be traced as far back as to Greek antiquity). Many different documents—visual and literary—reflect upon the curious phenomenon of the "wild man" and the "wild woman," who were often ideal substitutes for repressed sexuality and fear of the unknown.[51] According to Roger Bartra, "[t]he wild man lives in the collective European imagination as a living reminder for Western man that it would have been better for him not to have been born, or, rather, as the vehicle by which man casts doubts on the meaning of life at each turn."[52] Curiously, the various examples of wild men indicate the notion that one could gain salvation and wisdom, but especially pardon from human sin by turning into a beast and living in the woods. "This pagan nucleus is fused with a medieval Christian mythology of sin and penitence, conceiving man as somewhere midway between beasts and angels."[53] Two shocking examples provide ample evidence for this thesis. In Hartmann von Aue's courtly romance *Iwein*, and in his source, Chrétien de Troyes' *Yvain*, the protagonist, having broken his promise to his wife to return from a year of tournaments in time, and hence being expelled from the marriage, becomes mad and roams the woods like a beast until a young lady saves him from his insanity. Bisclavret, the protagonist in Marie de France's famous eponymous lai, leaves his wife for several days every week to transform into a werewolf and later, being betrayed by her, can no longer reassume his human form. Eventually he takes his revenge by biting off her nose before he is given back his clothes that allow him to regain his humanity. In both examples, the experience of total otherness can be related to a form of penitence and salvation, uncannily connecting the familiar world of medieval Christianity with the world of wild nature.[54] Possibly, as Bartra also suggests, the idea of the "wild man" originated in the Celtic cultures and fused with Christian and Greco-Roman mythologies: "medieval wild men were a curious reincarnation of ancient Celtic druids, a powerful network of priests operating from the heart of the forests, who provided some coherence to scattered Celtic tribes."[55] Moreover, ancient myths, superstition, primitive reactions to the teachings of the Church, folk belief, and also the inability to understand natural phenomena led many medieval people to experience encounters with revenants, ghosts, and other spirits who frightened them and forced them to reexamine their

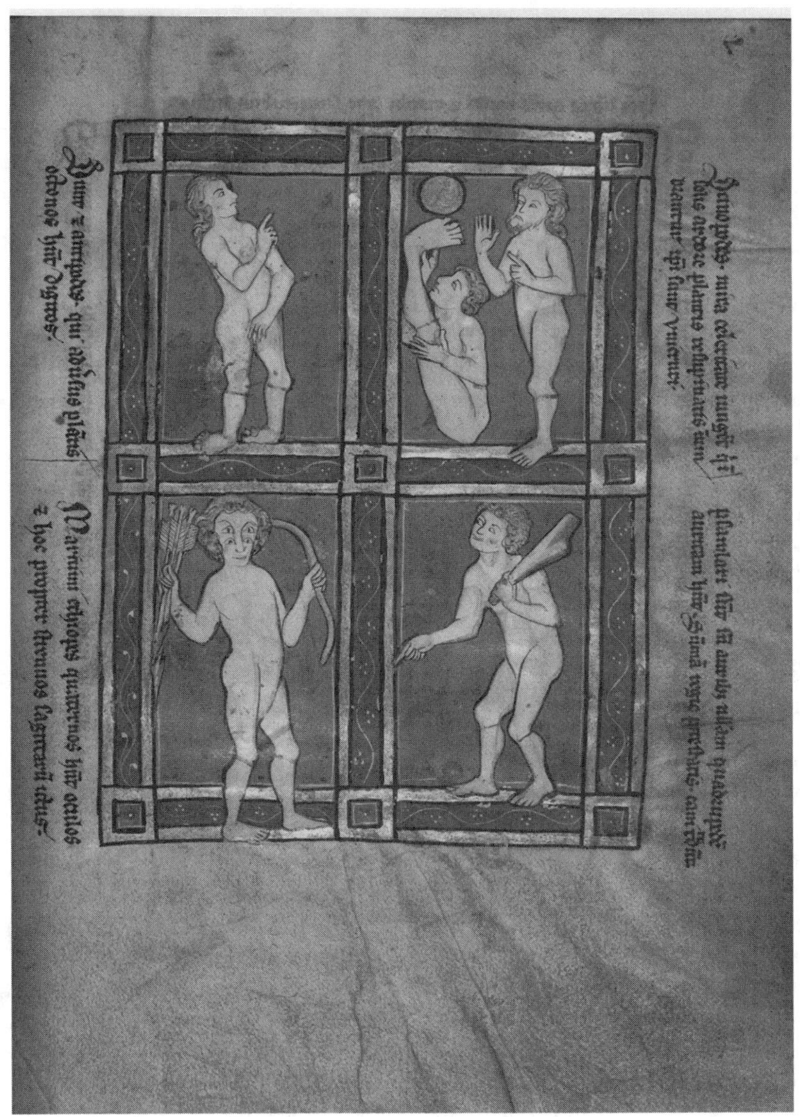

Fig. 3. Images of medieval monster, *Mirabilia mundi*, fol. 118, c. 1277.

identity, their lifestyle, their morality, and perception of the afterlife, as Aline G. Hornaday illustrates in her study on "Visitors from Another Space: The Medieval Revenant as Foreigner."[56]

It seems safe to argue that all cultures at all times have more or less projected an image of self and other, and this would also apply to the Middle Ages which deftly defies, as most recent scholarship has pointed out, modern attempts at homogenizing trends, and instead reflects a surprising and refreshing heterogeneity.[57] This distinction has always served well to establish an identity in contrast to the outside world of the others, whoever they might have been, and allowed the individual and its social group to distinguish itself by excluding others, as it is richly documented in literary texts from the entire Middle Ages.[58] Chroniclers such as Jans Enikel and Ottokar of Styria (Ottokar von Steiermark) specifically targeted other peoples, such as the Hungarians, to portray them as representatives of barbarian or primitive cultures which were not privy to the standard Western European courtly culture and cut very poor figures when they were suddenly confronted with playful jousts and other chivalric entertainment.[59] The many different peoples who can be grouped together as South Slavs, for instance, hardly figured in the minds of Central and Western Europeans, and if so, they were regarded with disrespect, contempt, and sometimes even open hostility, although they were mostly (Eastern and Greek Orthodox) Christians as well. Nevertheless, ever since the great movement from Germany toward the East which started in the twelfth century (age of colonization of Brandenburg, Prussia, East Prussia, and the Baltic lands, and so also of southeastern Europe),[60] cultural conflicts emerged between the native population and the newcomers. "The versatile Slavs possessed the rare quality of being at one and the same time the domestic and external 'other.' In their capacity of 'Wends,' Carniolans, or Carinthians they had been part of the 'German nation' and the Empire . . . The transformation to full 'otherness' was completed in a gradual shift from domestic, in a sense, Germanic, to more distanced 'other,' farther east and south-east."[61] Nevertheless, in many areas of modern Central and Eastern Europe the colonization did not lead to an automatic subjugation of the native population, instead many interesting forms of cohabitation and mutual acceptance can also be observed. In other words, conflicts and sharp racial confrontation certainly raised their ugly heads in the later centuries, but not as markedly during the early centuries—that is, during the period which is the prime object of the present volume.[62] This excludes, tragically, the relationship between Christians and Jews, as demonstrated, for instance, by the Hereford *mappamundi* and *The Book of John of Mandeville's Travels*.[63]

On a literary level, the image of the dwarf fulfilled an important hermeneutic function insofar as it was portrayed, at least from the early through the high Middle Ages, as a representative of a powerful and highly advanced underground world, but in the late Middle Ages the dwarf mostly transmogrified into a dangerous, horrid, mean-spirited, and evil being which deserved to be eliminated.[64] We may deduce from this phenomenon an anthropological constant to demonize others out of fear that they might threaten the establishment of the own self. Primarily medieval Jews suffered from this phenomenon, as did many other minorities, heretics, and sexual deviants such as homosexuals.[65] Recent scholarship has increasingly paid attention to those people who were marginalized and can demonstrate that the study of social borders and efforts to essentialize (that is to say, homogenize) society sheds much more light on the psychic structure, mentality, and ideology of the majority group than ever expected.[66] The absence of a close-knit group ideology and the efforts to cope with this problem often led to the brutal marginalization and then dispossession of Jews and Arabs (Saracens); yet not because of truly religious conflicts, as most Christians knew little about the Koran and the Torah. Instead because they were others, they had to be made really other, giving the Christians a feeling of self at the expense of these minority groups.[67]

We also have to take into account that medieval people were not only expressing sentiments determined by psychological reactions to ideologies and teachings in their almost hysterical opposition against foreigners, but that they were also—in a very realistic and intimidating manner—threatened and attacked from very early on by outsiders conducting themselves with savagery such as the Vikings,[68] the Saracens,[69] and later the Mongols,[70] and perennially endangered by pirates, robbers, thieves, and highwaymen.[71] In other words, the Middle Ages were not a time when people were free of physical threats. Especially during the early centuries they had to struggle hard to survive. They often had good reasons to be afraid of outsiders who arrived as hostile military forces, even though it had been only a few centuries earlier that they themselves had been the feared barbarians attacking a civilized world, the Roman Empire.[72] Certainly, there were periods of famines and periods of affluence, decades and even centuries of misery and warfare, and decades and centuries of prosperity and leisure. Fear, however, remained a major factor for all people throughout Europe for a wide range of reasons which required certain forms of compensation on a regular level.[73]

After the fall of Constantinople to the Turks in 1453, the next wave of external dangers reached the shores of the European continent. Once again both writers and artists produced a wide variety of responses to these foreigners whom they mostly perceived as a devilish threat, but at times also as saviors and peacekeepers in a world torn apart by internecine strife and conflict.[74] Although the Turks represented the infidels, their territory proved to be a safe haven both for Jews from all over Europe (especially from Spain and Portugal), and for international merchants, as reflected, for example, in the German chapbook *Fortunatus*.[75]

This is not to deny that many cultural contacts and exchanges existed, that medieval Europeans tried to understand, for instance, the Islamic world and to profit from the advances in sciences, medicine, and literature which made the Arabs superior for many centuries; yet the notion of the dangerous other and the threatening religious foe remained a dominant feature in the relationship between North and South throughout the entire period, if not, to some extent, even until the present.[76] Surprisingly, as we will see in light of Wolfram von Eschenbach's texts (ca. 1200–1220), exceptions to the rule were possible, and other courtly writers also seem to have transgressed the rigid xenophobic paradigm and opened perspectives toward the heathens which stood in stark contrast to Christian ideology.[77]

The projection of monstrous, ghostly, bizarre, terrifying, and scary beings, and their sometimes playful utilization by poets, painters, sculptors, chroniclers, and musicians mostly served the same purpose, that is, to come to terms with the other, whatever it might have meant for the individual.[78] Almost any body part could be utilized to portray evilness, otherness, and a sense of being excluded from God's own people. Consequently, medieval prejudices targeted those of black skin color, Jewish and other non-Christian religions, and those with physical deformities and terminal diseases, such as lepers. Even people on a socially lower level were easily portrayed as evil and other, such as peasants, although they made up the vast majority of people,[79] and artists used a wide variety of signs "to deprecate those people whom society detested and belittled."[80] Tragically, lepers and other people with a physical handicap also fell into the category of other and were excluded from society.[81] Once the xenological paradigm had been established (see below), stereotyping and "othering" people from different races and religions, it could always be reactivated as soon as the Europeans came into contact with other peoples, so the Sinti and Roma since the late eleventh century—until recently only known under the pejorative term "Gipsies"—and so the American Indians since the late fifteenth century.[82] Many literary texts from the Middle Ages such as the Middle English *Sir Gowther* and the plethora of crusading epics such as Wolfram von Eschenbach's *Willehalm* intriguingly portray the attempts by the Europeans to come to terms with racial, cultural, religious, and political differences.[83]

Modern anthropology, cultural history, sociology, literary studies, ethnology, and political sciences have all realized that the examination of this highly problematic clash between self and other represents a major vehicle to gain deeper insight into a people and its culture. The common denominator of these various approaches to the same object—whether from a modern or from a medieval perspective—has been identified as the fear of the unknown which has always caused major conflicts and tensions throughout history.[84] But whereas xenology—the critical investigation of interculturation, distance, tolerance, and aggression in ethnological, philosophical, and sociological terms—is mainly concerned with exploring how the foreign has been viewed by people and how they have separated themselves from the others, the more important but also more problematic question proves to be whether tolerance has ever been fully realized or whether it played any role in the history of medieval Europe.[85] Any investigation of the other in the Middle Ages requires consideration of both aspects, xenophobia and tolerance.[86]

Obviously, medieval presentations of the other in literature and the visual arts generally do not indicate that such forms of interaction fully existed. Some literary sources, however, indicate that the surviving artifacts and historical documents do not always and exhaustively reflect all relevant aspects of the medieval world. One of the most famous exceptions was Wolfram von Eschenbach's courtly romance *Parzival* and his version of the "chanson de geste," the epic *Willehalm*. Whereas in the first narrative important aspects of interracial exchanges take place, the second contains a monumental speech in defense of heathens, considered to be as much creatures of God as Christians, and hence deserve respect and tolerant treatment, even in the worst war situations.[87] *Willehalm*, composed in 1218 or 1220, deals with the military conflict between the protagonist who defends both his wife, Gyburg, and country, Provence and France, against the Saracens. Gyburg (originally named Arabel), daughter of the heathen king Terramer, had been married to Tybalt. Willehalm had been captured by the Saracens, but soon Arabel fell in love with him, converted to Christianity and followed the escaped prisoner to his home country where she assumed the name Gyburg. Both Tibalt and Terramer attempt to recapture her and to kill her new husband, but eventually, with the help of God and the enormous chivalric bravery of his people, not to mention Willehalm and Gyburg's brother, the young giant Rennewart, the Christians overcome their enemies and drive them back causing enormous bloodshed among them.[88] Nevertheless, during a court council, Gyburg stands up and delivers one of the most important speeches ever given by a woman in medieval literature:

> I hereby remind you princes of the Roman Empire that you will be increasing the honour of Christendom if God so honours you as to allow you to avenge the death of Vivianz in battle against my kinsmen and their army on the field of Alischanz: you will find them formidable fighters. And if you defeat the heathens you should act so that your salvation will be assured. Pay heed to the advice of a foolish woman: spare the creatures of God's Hand!
>
> The first man whom God created was a heathen and you should know for a fact that Elijah and Enoch, heathens though they were, are saved from eternal damnation. Noah, too, who was saved in the Ark, was a heathen, and Job was certainly also one, but God did not cast him down on that account. Think also of the three kings, whose names were Kaspar, Melchior and Balthasar, and whom we must consider as heathens who are not destined

for damnation. God Himself, at His mother's breast, received His first gifts from them. Heathens are not all condemned to perdition. We know it to be a fact that every mother who has borne a child since the time of Eve gave birth to one who was indisputably a heathen, although each child was encircled in the womb by baptism. Baptized women give birth to heathen children, even though baptism may have surrounded the child as it lay there. The Jews have a different custom with regard to baptism, for they perform it through circumcision.

After all, we were all of us heathens once. It pains the person in a state of Grace if the Father has condemned His children to perdition . . .

Whatever the heathens may have done to you, you should allow them to profit from the fact that God Himself forgave those who took His life. Have pity in the battle, if God grants you the victory.[89]

Moreover, Gyburg reminds her audience that she did not leave behind a hated husband, that she was not unhappy where she came from, and that she had lived among people like them all:

[the Christians] believe I brought about this conflict out of desire for human love. It is true that I left love behind me there too and great stores of wealth, and lovely children, with a man of whom I cannot discover that he ever committed any wrongful act since I received a crown from him. Tibalt of Arabi is innocent of any misdeed. I alone bear the guilt, for the sake of the grace of Almighty God, and also to some extent on account of the Marquis who has gained such high renown.[90]

Even if the queen does not harbor the same idea of tolerance as it has surfaced since the age of Enlightenment, no doubt Wolfram has made her his mouthpiece in expressing a powerful message regarding the relationship between Christians and non-Christians.[91] This is not to say that Wolfram undermined the absolute priority and dominance of Christianity; it would also be erroneous to assume that he rejected the idea of the crusades. Nevertheless, Gyburg's powerful speech indicates that the poet harbored tolerant ideas and criticized the harsh, if not barbarous treatment of heathens. These were wrong and misled in their belief, we are told, but the duchess also points out their human quality and the value of all human life![92] The same can be claimed for Wolfram's earlier epic, *Parzival*, composed sometime between 1200 and 1205, where the protagonist's father Gahmuret not only voluntarily joins the forces of the heathen Baruc, but quickly gains the greatest fame as a knight: "his manly vigour won the first place in heathendom, in Persia and Morocco. In other places, too, Damascus and Aleppo, and wherever knights gave battle, in Arabia and under the walls of Araby, his prowess achieved it that none would challenge him in single fight."[93] Moreover, Gahmuret soon falls in love with the black queen Belacane who receives the narrator's highest praise:

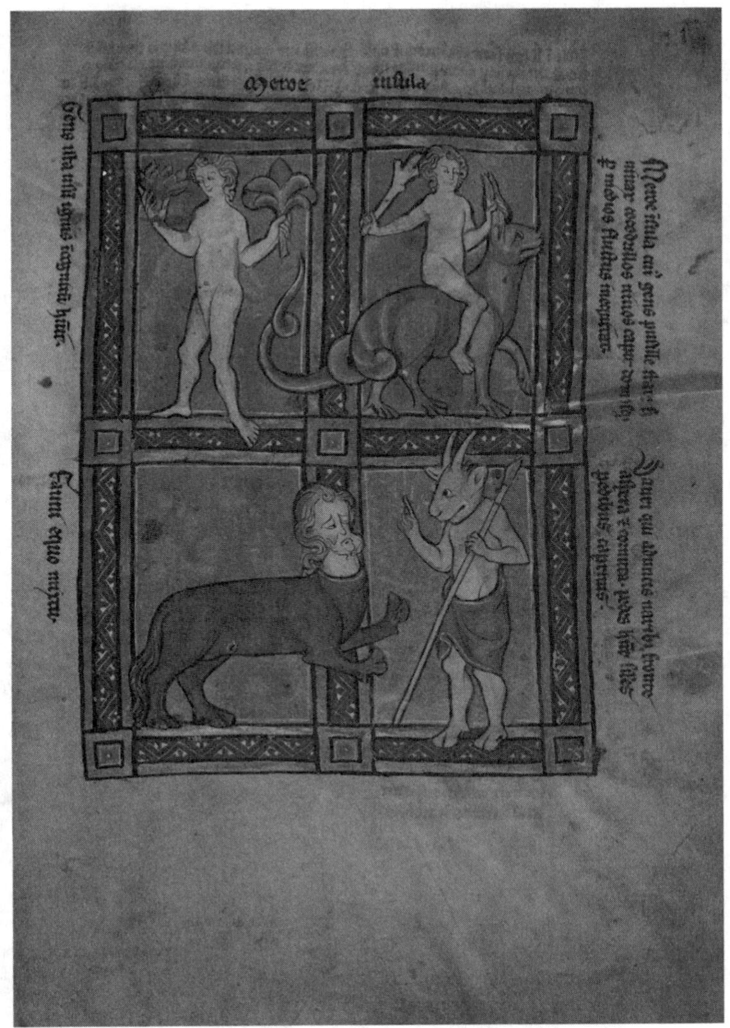

Fig. 4. Images of medieval monster, *Mirabilia mundi*, fol. 119r, c. 1277.

> It seemed to Gahmuret that although she was an infidel, a more affectionate spirit of womanliness had never stolen over a woman's heart. Her modest ways were a pure baptism, as was the rain that fell on her—the flood descending from her eyes down to her sabled breast. Her pleasures in life were devotion to sorrow and grief's true doctrine.[94] (27)

After the hero has defeated Belacane's opponents on the battle field, the two become ardent lovers and experience the most noble feelings: "The Queen yielded to sweet and noble love with Gahmuret, her heart's own darling, little though their skins matched in colour" (34). They marry, as Belacane publicly announces (35), and briefly enjoy their life together until Gahmuret desires new chivalric adventures and experiences a bitter conflict in his soul: "Yet the dusky lady was dearer to him than life. Never was there a woman of comelier form. Her heart, too, was ever mindful of the truly modest woman's ways that were in constant attendance on it" (39). Although Belacane has become pregnant, her husband abandons her, pretending that difference in their religious convictions had forced him to depart, whereas in fact he simply felt burning desire for renewed chivalry, as his French letter to her blatantly reveals (39f.).[95] Even though the narrator explicitly points out their racial and religious differences, he also indicates that these do not matter much at all compared to love, a distinction radically contrary to contemporary attitudes toward other races.[96] The text's message is quite self-evident: Gahmuret loves the black queen irrespective of her blackness and heathen religion, but he abandons her because he is not ready to settle down and lusts for further manly challenges and feats. Tragically, he only would have had to express his wish for her conversion, as she laments after having read his letter: "I will be christened with all speed if only he will come back" (40). In other words, Wolfram ignored the racial difference and thematized, instead, the gender conflict.[97]

Symptomatically, after having married Herzeloyde, Gahmuret also leaves this woman behind to pursue his personal interests in and fascination with knightly combat and tournaments: "if my sorrows ever leave me I should like to go out jousting. If you will not let me go to tournaments I have not forgotten my old trick, how once before I gave my wife the slip," (59); this time, however, he finds his tragic death because of his enemies' treachery. Neither Herzeloyde's whiteness nor her Christianity helped her to keep her husband from departing and hurling himself into knightly combat. Obviously, reflecting back on Belacane, for Wolfram otherness was not a relevant category in his evaluation of people, and in this respect he might well be called the most open-minded poet of the entire Middle Ages.[98]

The confrontation with the other was not only an issue of geo-political dimensions, or of an ethno-anthropological nature, it was also very much the result of ideological, religious, and philosophical conflicts. Both Bogomils,

Cathars, and university critics of the Church were categorized similarly in so far as they were seen as other and had to face persecution and possible elimination.[99] R. I. Moore and Preston King have impressively argued that from a certain perspective one might call medieval society a "Persecuting Society," as it was intolerant of other races and minorities. This radical notion, however, has recently come under heavy attack and is now even described as a caricature which deserves considerable correction and modification.[100] Simultaneously, when the Church attempted to exert universal control over Europe's population, many thinkers and poets valiantly challenged the rigid and overpowering paradigm established by the Christian Church and argued for open-ended discussions, critical assessment of human life and destiny, and for the possible inclusion, of foreigners, strangers, marginal figures, heretical thinkers, and members of other religions.[101] After all, heresy "means choice, and choice implies thought," as R. I. Moore poignantly emphasized.[102] The vast number of heretics throughout the Middle Ages indicates that the Catholic Church did not at all enjoy such solid support as is commonly assumed and constantly had to be on the guard against deviance, opposition, criticism, and outright attack. This was, however, not a typically medieval phenomenon, as "[t]he ancient, the medieval and the modern Churches have all been habitually divided up to and beyond the point of schism by disputes over doctrine which have covered the whole range of intellectual sophistication from the crudest to the most dazzling, and which have given stimulus to, and received it from every conceivable kind of social division, whether between imperialist and particularist, lord and peasant, countryman and townsman, or rich and poor."[103]

In the intellectual field, for example, despite clerical blacklisting of certain texts by Aristotle, philosophers simply did not obey papal rules, and so conflicts continued to erode the Church's absolute authority. Cary Nederman especially points out, "[i]f one examines the historical record, it turns out to be less than surprising that opportunities for and pockets of toleration abounded throughout medieval Europe."[104] In fact, as the testimony of John of Salisbury and Peter of Celle documents, many thinkers embraced diversity even within the Christian universe with its unified faith, and supported coexistence with representatives of other religions from whom the Christians had much to learn.[105]

In many European literary texts the religious theme of the Saracen princess who marries a Christian prince played a significant role, such as in *Willehalm*, the chantefable *Aucassin et Nicolette*, and in *La Prise d'Orange*. Undoubtedly, Sharon Kinoshito is somewhat correct in observing "[t]hat the violence of the military conquest of the religious and cultural Other must be erased in the Saracen woman's willing embrace of the conqueror and all he represents. . . . By casting the epic crusade in the form of an amorous intrigue, tropes of 'courtly love' . . . may be mobilized in the service of an ideology of expansion and conquest."[106] Nevertheless, it would be too simplistic to accept this phenomenon as cultural imperialism—a viewpoint heavily influenced by Edward Said's theory of orientalism, which in turn was based on his interpretation of nineteenth- and twentieth-century literature and cultural artifacts. A number of modifications and corrections need to be taken into account to comprehend the specific medieval conditions.[107] Wolfram von Eschenbach's epic, for instance, contradicts this black-and-white canvas and forces us to perceive gray areas, mixed viewpoints, and clearly an interest in, if not fascination with people from the East, the personified others. The same can be confirmed by considering the Middle High German goliardic epic *Herzog Ernst* and several late-medieval courtly romances such as Johann von Würzburg's *Willhelm von Österreich*.[108]

Gloria Allaire has alerted us to interesting examples in late-medieval Italian literature, such as Lodovico Ariosto's *Orlando*, Andrea da Barberino's *Guerrino*, *Fierabraccia*, and *Aspramonte*, where the pagans are presented not only as despicable heathens, but also as admirable warriors and fighters, brave and even heroic.[109] A clearly noble Saracen can be found in Palomides, who first appears in the thirteenth-century prose *Tristan* cycle in his role as Tristan's rival for Isolt, and in the *Roman de Palamède* (ca. 1230). In almost all versions the Saracen is ultimately baptized, but he demonstrates throughout the narrative his thoroughly good character and virtuosity. According to Nina Dulin-Mallory, "[t]his Saracen's role in the thirteenth-century French and in the fifteenth-century English is entirely literary. Saracens, we discover (though they are required to be baptized) can be good, and Christians, we discover, can be very wicked."[110] In one of the most interesting late thirteenth-century German verse romances, Konrad von Würzburg's *Partonopier und Meliur* (ca. 1270), the Christian protagonist almost loses his struggle to win the love and hand of the Byzantine princess Meliur because his Saracen antagonist displays such outstanding chivalric qualities, rules over vast lands, and is considered by some counselors as a highly dignified, respectable, and hence most worthy successor to the throne.[111]

The same happens with Sir Palomides in Thomas Malory's *Le Morte Darthur* (printed in 1485) where the Saracen is "well cherished with the king and the queen" and recognized as a "noble knight and a mighty man" willing "to be christened for [Isoud's] sake. Thus was there great envy betwixt Tramtrist and Sir Palomides."[112] Even though Palomides overcomes all his knightly opponents in a tournament—"he overthrew many knights, that all the people had marvel of him" (318)—he is eventually defeated by Tramtrist who thus also wins his lady's favor (320f.). Surprisingly, however, Tramtrist is not at all interested in Palomides's religion and in return for sparing his life only requests from him to "forsake my lady La Beale Isoud" and "that ye bear none armour not none harness of war" (320) for one whole year.

Fig. 5. Image from a Gradual, fol. 148v, c. 1460–1480.

On a more abstract level, the notion of a homogenous ideological paradigm dominating the Middle Ages easily proves to be incorrect. In fact, it can be called a "pernicious myth," as the "problematic of the Middle Ages was constituted not by the unity of a single form of life but by the sheer multiplicity and diversity of such forms."[113] Likewise, the barriers between self and other were not as high at these times as they were during later periods. The

Jewish philosopher Maimonides (1135–1204), for instance, radicalized the interpretation of the Torah by using simple logic and rationality, and also a fairly easily understandable Hebrew.[114] Arguing, for example, that the debate about the origin of this world cannot be decided with the help of scientific proof, he suggested that this question should be determined only through a personal approach as a matter of belief. Parallel to Maimonides, Peter Abelard (1079–1142) developed rational concepts for the intellectual debate, particularly in his famous treatise *Sic et Non*; but he also endeavored to explore the conflicts among Christianity, Judaism, and rational philosophy through his intriguing *Dialogue between a Philosopher, a Jew, and a Christian*.[115] In Constant Mews's words, "Abelard shared in this process by which Christian faith was identified as wholly consistent with reason, but he was critical of dogmatic attitudes toward those outside the Christian dispensation. In this sense he did defend values of religious toleration."[116] Many twelfth-century philosophers and theologians such as Albert the Great (Albertus Magnus) and Thomas Aquinas strongly favored drawing a dividing line between a religious and a rational explanation of this world, and hence proposed to view philosophy as an independent science, rather than an *ancilla theologiae* (a maid servant of theology). Of course, Albert did not disregard Christian belief, but he was always considered one of the great theologians of his time who established important scientific foundations for the rational interpretation of this world, firmly convinced that human reason was sufficient for the explanation of the material existence of all things. Likewise, Thomas Aquinas supported the idea of human reason as being an autonomous entity, independent of God's support. Nevertheless, he believed that the discovery of those principles which govern nature was made possible by God as the creator of all life, and so of man. Consequently, belief and scientific knowledge had to be congruent (S. c. g. I, 7).[117] This concept provided philosophical arguments supporting a more critical perception of reality in which people of different races and beliefs existed who were all part of the universal creation. In his *Dialogues against the Jews* (ca. 1108–1110) Petrus Alfonsi argued that all confrontations with foreigners in a critical debate promise fundamental experiences necessary for the learning process on both sides. As a former Jew and adamant critic of his Jewish opponents, however, he does not emerge as a proponent of tolerance—very much on the contrary! Nevertheless Alfonsi, like Gerard of Cremona (1114–1187) and Adelard of Bath (early twelfth century), demonstrates an open-minded attitude and an important level of curiosity and interest in the foreign that might have paved the way at least for future forms of tolerance in principle.[118] Alfonsi can certainly be accused of a severe form of anti-Semitism, but his philosophical approach created, just as in the case of Abelard's *Dialogue between a Philosopher, a Jew and a Christian* (between 1136 and 1139), an epistemological basis for critical debates with people of other religions and convictions.[119]

Finally, after an increasingly discordant development setting the Church and the university apart, in 1277 a major conflict erupted between Tempier, Bishop of Paris, and the professors of the Sorbonne who had, according to Tempier, proven their heretical thinking by advocating ideas such as there was no first man, for humans have always existed; nothing happens by fortuitous circumstance, since everything is conditioned by causal necessity; nothing can be believed unless it is self-evident; the earth is infinite, for there was no point of creation; body and soul cannot be separated, so if the body dies, so does the soul; philosophers are entitled to discuss every kind of question and issue since reason is of highest relevance; theological knowledge cannot be equated with true knowledge; complete sexual continence destroys virtue and humankind; the Christian religion prevents the growth of human knowledge; nothing can be understood of God except that he exists.[120] It will remain uncertain to what extent all these theses had indeed been propounded by the philosophers at the university, but obviously similar thoughts had circulated and led to the violent reaction. The condemnation was a clear backlash to the previous attempts by the philosophers to explore new horizons and concepts of world explanations, that is, tolerance met intolerance, and the latter gained the victory.

John of Salisbury clearly advocated the idea of tolerance, that is, the acceptance of the beliefs and views of others, when he stated in *The Nature of a True Prince*,

> Nevertheless, it is the part of a good and wise man to give a free rein to the liberty of others and to accept with patience the words of free speaking, whatever they may be. Nor does he oppose himself to its works so long as these do not involve the casting away of virtue. For since each virtue shines by its own proper light, the merit of tolerance is resplendent with a very special glory.[121]

Although the connection with Wolfram von Eschenbach seems to be rather far-fetched, ultimately these philosophical issues must be seen in the same light as the statements formulated by this Middle High German poet regarding people of other faiths and races. Although we normally assume that the medieval world represented a strictly homogenous society held together by Christianity and the feudal system, the turmoil caused by the twelfth- and thirteenth-century intellectuals and poets, and the many contacts with foreign peoples and religions in the Asian world clearly indicate that this notion has to be corrected.[122]

Why would artists all over Europe have delighted in creating the most bizarre and grotesque gargoyles, which basically had only the practical purpose of being as a waterspout to lead the rain water away from the stone walls? It might well be that church patrons considered the monstrous images as a useful tool to teach the viewers and pedestrians passing by of the dangers of Hell and the constant threat of the devils' seductiveness, or to ward away evil spirits. But there are too many different types of gargoyles which contradict this claim, and their artistic quality is just too impressive to accept this almost simplistic interpretation. Previously, some scholars held the belief that gargoyles were "meant to scare evils away from the church, to be symbolic of sins forbidden from entering the church, or to represent devils overcome by the church and now made to serve the church as waterspouts."[123] But gargoyles also appear within churches and hence might have been "pagan survivors," or a "pure projector of filth."[124] Janetta Rebold Benton believes that gargoyles reflected medieval nightmares and the fear of Hell causing "visual intimidation. The physical deformations and torments in Hell that were the result of sin were depicted as clearly as possible, the artist sparing no effort to maximize the didactic impact of his images."[125] However, many gargoyles also served entertaining purposes and poked fun at the clerics, ridiculing the human corporeality, inciting the viewers' fantasy and curiosity, ignoring any sense of sin or condemnation. Benton suggests that there was no common denominator in meaning for all gargoyles, rather they reflected "layered meaning."[126] She even goes so far as to suggest that gargoyles simply served as architectural ornaments and as a "sort of signature on [the artists'] work."[127] Bernhard of Clairvaux vehemently criticized the lavish display of animals, monsters, strange bodies, and mythological figures as sculptures, capitals, and gargoyles, warning that these images in stone could tempt people rather to view them out of sheer curiosity, instead of reading in the manuscripts and to meditate upon God.[128] Other theologians such as Alexander Neckam (1157–1217) and Gautier of Coincy (d. 1236) also protested against this dangerous trend, but obviously their words were disregarded, and the artists continued their work. Apparently, the other surreptitiously entered the mental horizon of medieval sculptors and other artists who acknowledged them as important aesthetic elements. In other words, we observe a significant breaking of anthropological barriers beginning to take place already in the High Middle Ages.

Without going further into details, several preliminary conclusions can be drawn regarding this phenomenon and applied to our general concern. The large numbers of gargoyles and related sculptures from the entire Middle Ages make it impossible to identify one exclusive answer to why artists created them. Undoubtedly, gargoyles represented major art work and were officially sanctioned by the Church, for otherwise the sculptors would not have been paid, nor would the gargoyles and similar pieces have been tolerated as ornaments of medieval churches and other buildings. Medieval grotesque art can be interpreted theologically, but it also can be seen anthropologically. To some extent these sculptures warned of Hell and the dangers of afterlife, and of the constant threats by the devils and evil spirits. To some extent, however, they also indicate that medieval people's minds were not entirely dominated by Christianity, and hence were not completely xenophobic, maintaining, at least as far as art is concerned, some interest in the world of the other, powerfully illustrated by stone and wood carvings.[129]

The same phenomenon can be beautifully illustrated in the Middle High German heroic epic *Nibelungenlied* as some of the protagonists directly interact with the otherworld and/or constitute "dark figures" of liminal quality. First written down in about 1200 by an anonymous poet, probably on behalf of the bishop of Passau, Wolfger von Erlau, the heroic epic strangely vacillates between the known and the unknown spheres of human existence.[130] Even though the events take place within Christianity, the protagonist Siegfried appears superhuman and more like a semi-god than as a mortal warrior. Having killed a dragon and bathed in its blood, he has become invulnerable except for a small spot where a leaf had settled during his bath—the metaphorical Achilles' heel. His physical strength is unmatched by any member of the Burgundian court in Worms, and only Brunhild, queen of Iceland and ruler of castle Isenstein, represents a serious threat to him. When King Gunther announces his plans to woo Brunhild, Siegfried advises against it because "[t]his queen has such terrible ways that it costs any man dear who woos her, so that truly you should forgo this journey" (53). Nevertheless, Gunther wants to pursue his plans and relies on Siegfried for help. The latter finally agrees, but recommends leaving behind the entire army of thirty thousand men as "they would all have to die through her arrogance" (54).

Eventually Siegfried succeeds in defeating Brunhild in her competition on behalf of Gunther by means of his secret cloak which makes him invisible and provides him with the strength of twelve extra men. Nevertheless, later during the wedding night Brunhild ridicules her husband and hangs him on a nail until the early morning, demonstrating to him that he has no power over her. Once again, Siegfried is called in to overcome her superhuman strength, but he barely manages to defeat her in this dangerous situation. Only because he feels ashamed and is afraid of being crushed by her, does he summon sufficient power to hold her down and force her to submit to him: " 'Alas,' thought the hero, 'if I now lose my life to a girl, the whole sex will grow uppish with their husbands for ever after, though they would otherwise never behave so' " (92). As soon as he has taken away her belt and her ring, she loses all her previous strength and turns into a submissive wife. Subsequently, Gunther sleeps with her, "and from this intimacy she grew somewhat pale, for at love's coming her vast strength fled so that now she was no stronger than any other woman" (93). The monstrous woman has turned into an integral member of the Burgundian court, and there are no traces left of her former otherness. In Joyce Tally Lionarons's words, "[o]nce she is forced by her loss of virginity to become an active participant in Burgundian power politics, Brünhild's outward appearance no longer matches her inner reality, and it is this more than anything else that is symbolized by her forfeiture of her Otherworldly strength."[131] Siegfried, on the other hand, will be killed by Hagen because his wife Kriemhilt, Gunther's sister, blithely reveals to Hagen the unprotected spot on Siegfried's back. In other words, at the end of the first book, the world of the monstrous has been eliminated, and patriarchy has taken its course. Hagen, whom Edward R. Haymes has called a "liminal character,"[132] then dominates the entire second book without being challenged by any other figure. Despite the clear differences between Siegfried and Brünhild on the one hand, Hagen on the other, the latter nevertheless also maintains contact with the otherworld and calmly faces his own destiny knowing from these contacts that his doom is awaiting him at the end of the Burgundians' visit to Gran where Kriemhilt and her second husband Etzel/Attila rule. Before crossing the Danube—which here assumes the same symbolic function as the river Styx in Greek mythology—Hagen encounters a group of waterfairies whose clothes he removes to force them to foretell his future. Although the first of them, Hadeburg, deceives him by predicting a happy outcome, the second, Sieglind, reveals the truth about the outcome of their journey: "If you ever get to Hungary you will be sadly disappointed. Turn back—there is still time! For, bold knights, you have been invited to Etzel's country in order that you shall die there! All who ride to that land have linked their hands with Death!" (194). The only exception to such a destiny will be the royal chaplain who will return safely to Worms, they tell Hagen. To test the value of their prophecy, he later throws the chaplain overboard against the protest of the entire company while they cross the Danube, and Hagen even pushes the helpless victim further into the water. But when the chaplain reaches the shore and survives: "this brought it home to Hagen that there would be no escaping the fate which the wild nixies had foretold" (198). Consequently, Hagen destroys the ferryboat after they all have crossed the river, knowing all too well that the "knights are doomed to die" (198). Upon the protest of his companions, this astounding warrior declares: "I do it . . . in anticipation that if there is some craven among us that wished to run away, he must die a shameful death in this torrent" (198).

Indeed, both in words and actions Hagen proves to be a liminal character, being part of human society, but also part of the otherworld insofar as he shares its knowledge and, to some extent, its strength as well. Edward Haymes remarks, "Hagen is 'dark' largely because he is a liminal figure, a hero who is at once a mortal and in touch with the other world. He is also dark in his appearance."[133] Even though the intended audience consisted, in all likelihood, of Christians only, the anonymous poet did not hesitate to create this epic with its surprisingly strong allusions to the otherworld where dragons, dwarfs, fairies, and semi-gods ruled, until they were all destroyed by human deception, murder, intrigue, and strategy. But the death of Siegfried, for instance, is not celebrated triumphantly, rather the demise of the otherworld figure par excellence portends badly for human society, for the interaction of the otherworld with the court signaled doom for both.[134] The criticism expressed in the epic, is directed against the inability of both spheres to understand each other; instead of mutual cooperation, the other and the Burgundian court—as representative of the self—collide and eventually destroy each other in a tragic conflict. Nevertheless, the poet, and also the large audience far into the early sixteenth century,[135] responded enthusiastically to this epic as one of the most appealing heroic poems ever composed in the German speaking world. The emergence and eventual defeat of the other undoubtedly played a significant role in this enormous reception process, ending only in the late sixteenth century,[136] but it quickly resumed again and hastened its pace since the late eighteenth century.[137] Curiously, the world of the Hungarians represented in the *Nibelungenlied* indicates that certain forms of tolerance might have been possible, but the arrival of the Burgundians in Gran, King Etzel Cahila's court, signals the end of this harmonious world where people from many different cultures, races, languages, and religions live peacefully together until the final battle starts because of Kriemhilt's hatred of Hagen, leading to an Armageddon, the first victim of which would be the acceptance and even sympathy for the other.[138]

It would be interesting indeed to know the extent to which medieval people had concrete contact with foreigners, the many representatives of the other. This would require an intensive examination of medieval travelogues, world maps, business and political letters, and documents pertaining to world trade. Suffice it here, however, to point out the general phenomenon that international contacts existed throughout the entire Middle Ages, and of course increased during the later period. Merchants encountered Blacks, Arabs, Tatars, and perhaps even Persians, and Chinese. Messengers and ambassadors traveling far and wide reported valuable information about the foreign worlds and foreign people back to their centers.[139] We do not yet know how they communicated or acquired foreign languages, but merchants certainly found ways to interact with their customers even then; hence they had to transcend their linguistic community and acquire some linguistic skills necessary for economic negotiations.[140] Various travelers explored the Asian continent since the twelfth and thirteenth centuries, such as the Franciscans John of Plano Carpini (ca. 1182–ca. 1252) and William of Rubruc (1215/20-ca. 1270). The Venetian Marco Polo (1254–1324) visited the Mongols under Genghis Khan and extensively reported about their empire, culture, political system, and military strategies,[141] The latter even went twice to China out of economic and also general interest, which eventually resulted in his famous *Il Milione* or *Le Divisament dou Monde*.[142] Such travelers either had to rely on translators all the way, or—what seems more likely—managed to acquire some of the foreign languages. At any rate, contacts between Europe and Asia, including the Far East, existed throughout the High and late

Middle Ages, and despite the prevalent notions of monstrous peoples populating those distant regions, in fact, politicians, merchants, travelers, and missionaries knew better. Moreover, the Catholic Church repeatedly made considerable efforts to establish contacts with the Mongols and searched for Christian communities in the Far East. Both Pope Innocent IV (1243–1254) and Urban IV (1261–1264), among others, sent emissaries to Persia and Mongolia and also received Mongolian diplomats. During the Council of Lyon in 1274, for instance, Pope Gregory X met with the representatives of Il-Khan Abaqa because he hoped to receive military help from the Mongols in the crusaders' struggle to fend off the Mameluk forces in Palestine. Other East Asian travelers also found their way to Rome and experienced a friendly welcome, even if this did not mean a true breakdown of stereotypes and enlightened interaction with peoples of different ethnic origin and different religious orientation.[143]

In other words, it would be erroneous to assume that these few cosmopolitan individuals truly fought against pervasive stereotypes or helped to overcome radical notions of otherness, which marginalized all foreigners and excluded them from European society—unfortunately a key aspect of the dominant mentality throughout those times. Otherwise John de Mandeville's (ca. 1300–1372) highly fabricated account of the fabulous East in his *Travels* would not have enjoyed such an enormous popularity far into the early modern age.[144] His alleged "realism was a challenge to an ancient dichotomy between the 'fables' of poets and the 'truth' of science and history which was still seen as nearly identical with the rhetorical opposition of verse and prose."[145] As Mary Campbell points out, "[t]he East remains a convenient screen for imaginative projection, as it was for earlier pilgrims and merchants of our acquaintance."[146] Anthony Grafton suggests, "Mandeville more than anyone else helped to create a sort of vernacular ethnography, one that suggestively transformed the far reaches of the world into a sort of explorer's Club Med, where mild climates, strange but colorful customs, and only the occasional attack of indigestion—in this case, to be sure, caused by the traveler as a dragon ate him—awaited the intrepid tourist."[147] Even Christopher Columbus is claimed to have owned a copy that he studied as a preparation for his exploration of the New World, although other medieval sources such as the French Cardinal Pierre d'Ailly's (1350–1420) *Imago Mundi* provided more than enough fantastic accounts.[148] In other words, the foreign world, the other par excellence, attracted the most attention when presented in a fictionalized manner, titillating the audience's curiosity, feeding on its deep-seated fears and stereotypes, and exciting its interest in the novelty of the unfamiliar world. With regard to Mandeville, Donald R. Howard states, "Mandeville was trying to write a new kind of work, a *summa* of travel lore which combined the authority of learned books and guidebooks with the eyewitness manner of pilgrim and travel writers; combined the pilgrimage to the

Holy Land with the missionary or mercantile voyage into the Orient; and combined the curious and vicarious intentions of some such works with the thoughtful and devotional intentions of others."[149] This was recently confirmed by Klaus Ridder in his extensive study of the German translations of Mandeville's work, where he says: "In bezug auf das Reisen bedeutet dies, daß nicht Unbekanntes entdeckt, sondern immer nur Bekanntes wiedergefunden werden soll, nämlich dort, wo es sich in der kosmologischen Ordnung der Dinge schon immer befand" (With regard to travel this means that the intention was not to discover the unknown, but always the already known, that is, there where it has always been according to the cosmological order of things).[150]

Nevertheless, the literary documents examined above at times indicate the opposite, reveal a curious, if only faint trace of open-mindedness, maybe even a form of tolerance, as the other was not only accepted, but could even be admired as superior to the self. Marie de France's "Bisclavret" would be a case in point, as the wife and her lover prove to be very underdeveloped characters, weak in their ethics, suspicious and fearful of the other, which they can only treat with disrespect and disgust. Instead of trying to understand her husband's true nature, the wife immediately plots to eliminate him, although in his soul he is far more noble than she, as will later be demonstrated through the loss of her nose, a sign of her ignominy even passed on to the next generations.

The same observation might apply to the Middle English *Sir Gawain and the Green Knight* composed sometime in the late fourteenth century,[151] although here we are faced with a much more complex situation of the Arthurian court, confronted by a representative of the otherworld, the Green Knight. At first appearance, the Green Knight stuns all those present at Arthur's Christmas celebration, but he is not portrayed as ugly or devilish, but rather as marvelous and foreign, almost fascinating and impressive: "All standing there studied him and stepped even closer, / With all the wonder in the world at what he would do, / For many marvels had they seen, but such never before" (237–39). Nevertheless, his challenge is highly alienating and threatening, and only Gawain garners enough courage to stand up to him, only to be stunned after having his head chopped off and being reminded of his promise: "To the Green Chapel you must journey, I command you, to get / The dreaded blow you have delivered; you have deserved / To yield after Yule on New Year's morn. / Many men know me, the knight of the Green Chapel; / So you will never fail to find me if you follow my advice" (451–55). When Sir Gawain in fact begins with his search for the Green Knight, he himself turns into a foreigner in a foreign land: "Many cliffs he climbed over in areas strange; / Far removed from his friends, as a foreigner he rides" (713f.). In so many Arthurian tales Gawain is the protagonist who determines the events and proves to be in charge, but here the table has been turned. As the 'foreign' element, the Green Knight, forces Gawain to seek him in his own territory where he will be tested for strength of character, virtuosity, and chivalry. Only too late does Gawain realize that his lust for life was his downfall, if only by a fraction, as Bercilak, the Green Knight, confirms: "But that was not for wild wickedness, nor wooing either, / But because you loved your life; thus the less I blame you" (2367f.). Nevertheless, the experience in the wild, unfamiliar territory both at Castle Hautdesert and the world of magic leaves Gawain confused, ashamed, and humbled because his aunt, Morgan le Fay, had sent Bercilak "[t]o tempt the pride, to perceive if there were truth / In the rumors of renown of the great Round Table" (2457f.).[152] Certainly, Gawain had proven himself, and yet personally he knows that he had failed, as any human being would have failed. The realization of the true meaning of chivalry dawned upon him only when he had left the court of King Arthur behind and had ventured into the wild. Consequently, at the narrative's conclusion, "[w]ild ways in the world Gawain now rides / On Gringolet, after getting the grace to go on with his life" (2479f.). All members of the court join Gawain in wearing the same green band which serves as a token of his sinfulness, or rather human frailty. This is to say, the wild or other has been recognized as complementary to one's own world, the self, and the true hero proves to be the one able to transgress the boundaries between both entities.[153] Magic emerges as a powerful medium to test the validity of courtly values and ideals, and although it belongs to the marginalized territories, its significance is nonetheless noticeable in the center of the Arthurian world because it is not yet associated with the devil or considered a sinful tool by which to acquire knowledge and power.[154]

Quite along the same lines, it seems reasonable to describe Dante Alighieri's grandiose epic *La Divina Commedia* as the ultimate expression of this experience of being suddenly confronted with the 'otherness of death' while still alive in this world. Not by accident the introductory verses with their monumental sense of existential realization of life's limits have been recited throughout the centuries:

Nel mezzo del cammin di nostra vita
mi ritrovai per una selva oscura,
che la diritta via era smarrita.
Ahi quanto a dir qual era è cosa dura
esta selva selvaggia e aspra e forte
che nel pensier rinova la paura!
Tant' è amara che poco è più morte;
ma per trattar del ben ch'i' vi trovai,
dirò de l'altre cose ch'i' v'ho scorte.

[Midway in the journey of our life I found myself in a dark wood, for the straight way was lost. Ah, how hard it is to tell what that wood was, wild, rugged, harsh; the very thought of it renews the fear! It is so bitter that death is hardly more so. But, to treat of the good that I found in it, I will tell of the other things I saw there.][155]

Dante's vision which he so beautifully expressed here was not so unlike that of Sir Gawain, or of the many viewers of medieval gargoyles, or of Beowulf who had to fight Grendel and later Grendel's mother in the cave under the sea. Charles Dahlberg made the pertinent comment concerning this peculiar phenomenon: "we should be aware that likeness and unlikeness are not mutually exclusive contraries, but that unlikeness is a part of likeness, that unlikeness exists only as a consequence of man's likeness to God."[156] In other words, human life gains its full dimension only if confronted with the other as a mirror image of the self.

In fact, if we pursued this topic to its ultimate consequence, we would discover that many, if not most medieval religious thinkers, especially mystics enjoyed just this experience as well. To witness God would indeed be to witness the final otherness, although according to Saint Anselm of Canterbury's (1033–1109) *Proslogion* "God can only be conceived as being without beginning and without end, as being 'inoriginate' and 'imperishable' . . . God is radically other, dwelling 'in light inaccessible,' eluding our senses and our understanding alike."[157] Most radically, the German Dominican Meister Eckhart (ca. 1260–1329) informs us in his "Talks of Instruction," that people must pursue their individual paths to God by "maintaining their own good devotional practice, embracing in it all other ways and thus grasping in their own way all goodness and all ways . . . ; it is not possible for everyone to follow the same way. It is the same with following the severe life-style of such saints. You should love their way and find it appealing, even though you do not have to follow their example."[158] In the same vein, Mechthild von Magdeburg (ca. 1208–1282/97) queries, when she has the handmaid of the soul say to Love: "Now tell me, where is all this leading? You have hunted me, trapped me, bound me, and wounded me so deeply that I shall never be healthy again. You have meted out to me many a cudgel blow. Tell me, am I ever going to recover from you?"[159] Even though these religious authors clearly had in mind the Christian Godhead, their thoughts and revelations indicate an intriguing openness and suggest an individuality in the quest for spirituality which borders on the notion of "tolerance."

The vision of the "unio mystica" strikingly resembles the experience of the total other either in the *Divine Comedy* or in *Sir Gawain and the Green Knight*:

> Under this immense force she loses herself.
> In this most dazzling light she becomes blind in herself.
> And in this utter blindness she sees most clearly.
> In this pure clarity she is both dead and living.
>
> (49)

Apparently, the confrontation with the other represented a major breakthrough in medieval culture, perhaps even being its very touchstone. John the Scot (Eriugena) (ca. 810–877) postulated in his *Periphyseon,* one of the most radical but also clearest notions of God's otherness: " 'All things that are and all things that are not' are modalizations of the divine nothingness, of that 'super-essential nothingness' beyond 'all things that are and are not.'"[160]

Within the earthly dimension, the encounter with foreigners functions like a catalyst, forcing people to reconsider their own culture and to examine its ideological premises. Cultural clashes highlight boundaries, which again necessitate establishing a set of fundamental norms constituting the framework of the self-identity. In this sense all conflicts and encounters with the foreign are ambivalent and ambiguous: they can engender violent and vitriolic forms of hostility, rejection, and fear, and they can also trigger a quest for self-analysis, possibly producing tolerant attitudes. The other could be the concrete foreigners, the military opponents, such as the Mongols, or it could be the symbolic threatening world of the dark forests and dangerous mountains.[161] Furthermore, visionary and mystical experiences also transgressed cultural and religious borders, catapulting the seer into another world, hence confronting him or her with the other in the ultimate sense of the word. In some cases, this experience of the other reflected utopian longings and dreams of fairy lands such as in *Sir Orfeo* where the author provides the following description:

> . . . a fair cuntray,
> As bri$_3$t so sonne on somers day,
> Smoþe & plain & al grene
> – Hille no dale nas þer non y sene.
> Amidde þe lond a castel he si$_3$e,
> Riche & real & wonder hei$_3$e.
> (351–56)[162]

The same utopian world is projected in Marie de France's "Lanval" and in Wolfram von Eschenbach's *Parzival*; it also plays a certain role in many of the innumerable *Alexander* romances[163] and Grail quests.[164]

The general topic discussed in this volume by scholars from many different disciplines has not gone unnoticed in recent years, as the above discussion of various literary, art historical, and historical phenomena has indicated. Xenology within the medieval context, however, continues to be a fairly new consideration which justifies a brief examination of previous contributions to this field. During the winter semester 1985/1986 an interdisciplinary lecture series took place at the University of Düsseldorf, Germany, on the topic "Alternative Worlds in the Middle Ages and Renaissance" at which the contributors explored alterity in general and pragmatic terms. With fairly little interest in the exploration of the theoretical implications of otherness, but interested in concrete cases of alternative cultures, the authors discussed the peculiar case of stylite hermits or pillar saints in late antiquity (Rudolf Hiestand), the tensions between sixteenth-century Russia and Turkey (Hans Hecker), the political and ideological independence of the medieval university (Albrecht Graf Finckenstein), the marginalization of Jews in late-medieval cities (František Graus), the utopian world of courtly love as depicted in Chrétien de Troyes's works (Peter Wunderli), the exterritoriality of utopian spaces in medieval German literature (Gert Kaiser), William Langland's concept of spiritual and material poverty as an alternative to courtly society (Willhelm G. Busse), astrological medicine (Hans Schadewaldt), the *locus amoenus* of the narrative framework for Boccaccio's *Decameron* (Reinhard Klesczewski), and a few utopian concepts in Renaissance literature.[165] Neither the editor nor the contributors to the proceedings, however, fully targeted the idea of otherness as a cultural challenge and oppositional category questioning the identity of the spectator or subjects. The pillar saints were admired by their congregation, and the escape from court into the peaceful idyllic woods as portrayed by Chrétien, Wolfram, and Boccaccio in their respective works do not represent radical difference, but are projections of the self into the margin, even though this margin still forms part of the courtly and Christian universe.

By contrast, investigation of the relationship between Jews and Christians promises to unearth many more important insights in the culturation process of medieval society, as Jews were not always or automatically considered outsiders, foreigners, outcasts, and dangers for the Christian world. The Third Lateran Council (1179) encouraged all Christians to support Jews "pro sola humanitate" (simply out of humanity). In his *Liber contra sectam sive haeresim Saracenorum*, Petrus Venerabilis (1092–1156) recommended viewing all non-Christians as members of the same community based on human reason: "omnis rationabilis mens rerum creatarum veritatem agnoscere cupiat."[166] Unfortunately, this did not exclude later statements of clearly anti-Semitic nature. As Yosef Hayim Yerushalmi underscores: "Medieval Jews by no means always felt themselves strangers in an immediate and personal sense. . . . Above all medieval Jews certainly saw neither virtue nor glamor in alienation, only an abnormal condition that one day must be terminated. To that end they prayed daily for a speedy redemption and, in every age, erupted in messianic movements."[167] This, of course, does not imply that they did not experience violence, persecutions, and pogroms. Quite the contrary, the study of Jewish history particularly profiles the problems and disturbing conflicts which European medieval society experienced in its attempts to cope with and respond to the other simply by suppressing or expelling it.[168] Thomas Aquinas, for instance, argued in favor of tolerating

Jews from a historical and theological perspective, although his reasoning had hardly any impact on the devastation of Jewish culture and life within medieval society which occurred after the twelfth and thirteenth centuries.[169] Nevertheless, confrontation with this non-Christian religion forced theologians, philosophers, and writers to reflect upon this otherness and resolve it in their minds, hence helping them comprehend some aspects of self and other. Georg Wieland has also pointed out the fascinating contributions by Roger Bacon (1214–1292) and Ramon Llull (1232–1316) who both argued in favor of a community where different religions could be represented and no violence would be exerted to force conversion to Christianity, even though this religion undoubtedly was considered the only and true religion.[170]

The topic of the other was also discussed in sessions on the "Dark Figure in Middle High German literature" at the Sixteenth Congress on Medieval Studies at Western Michigan University in Kalamazoo (1981) and at the 1981 meeting of the Midwest Modern Language Association.[171] Although most authors have a fairly clear notion of what such a "dark figure" might be, their papers clearly indicate a level of uncertainty and ambivalence about the proper definition of the other. A sense of liminality, but also of monstrous shape, and absence of social morality is reflected. The dark figure shows up both in the *Rolandslied* by the Pfaffe Konrad (Susan Clark) as well as in the burlesque verse romance *Salman und Morolf* (Maria Dobozy), where the trickster and crafty Morolf displays a dual nature, of being both a goliard and/or a doctor, and being a magical and a normal human being respectively. According to Winder McConnell, the Burgundian queen Kriemhilt emerges as a "death-figure" who threatens and actually realizes the doom of all her relatives because of her husband's murder at their hands. Female figures, particularly Isolde the Fair in Gottfried's *Tristan* can also be identified as "outsiders" or "liminal characters," because she appears as the antimodel of the Virgin Mary and exerts tremendous influence on her male environment (Nancy C. Zak). We might also call the courtly spies, the *gardadors*, *lauzenjadors*, *merkære*, representatives of the outside world where true love does not exist and danger looms for the lovers of the courtly love songs (Stephanie Cain Van D'Elden). Late-medieval literature enjoyed the image of the dark figure more than ever before, such as in *Biterolf und Dietleib* (Franz H. Bäuml), or in Wirnt von Gravenberg's *Wigalois* (Ingeborg Henderson). Apart from some more comical devil figures in The Stricker's verse narratives (Robert E. Lewis), Heinrich von dem Türlin's *Diu Crône* represents the most threatening elements of otherness, as the protagonist Gawain is confronted with a whole panorama of hellish images and scenes which pass in front of his eyes without any explanation (Ernst S. Dick).[172] Particularly in Nordic literature do these dark figures, such as Egill Skalla-Grímsson in the *Egils saga*, lurk where protagonists must struggle to survive under extremely dangerous political conditions, while also revealing traits borrowed from the monster tradition (Jesse Byock).

In the selected papers of a conference held at the University of Minnesota on "Strangers in Medieval Society" (1994) the focus is slightly moved from the mythical to the area of concrete confrontations of people from different cultures during the Middle Ages. F. R. P. Akehurst and Stephanie Cain Van D'Elden here define the strangers as "those persons who have their own community and culture, and who come into a new environment. They are within the law, they tend not to be parasites, and they may be very beneficial in their new milieu."[173] This puts a slightly different emphasis on the topic, as here we learn about the role of merchants in the Mediterranean (Kathryn L. Reyerson); merchants and missionaries in Asia during the late Middle Ages (William D. Phillips Jr.); international merchants in fourteenth-century London (Derek Pearsall); the situation of Jews in fourteenth-century France (William Chester Jordan); the role of minstrels as outsiders within the courtly context (Maria Dobozy); conflicts within feudal society as illustrated by *Renaut de Montauban* (William Calin); and about the narrative function of disguise and deception in medieval and Renaissance comic literature (Janet L. Solberg). Susan Crane concentrates on fourteenth-century knights in disguise as a form of self-dramatization,[174] whereas Edward R. Haymes explores the sexual quest in Wolfram's *Parzival* as a form of otherness.

Unfortunately, at times there is also a tendency to use the term otherness as convenient substitute for hermeneutics. This is the case with a volume containing the proceedings of a conference which took place in Pack Forest near Seattle (November 1993), and those of a conference organized in Kloster Ottobeuren/Germany (July 1995) where most contributors presented papers on a wide range of German medieval narratives under the heading of "Fremdes wahrnehmen—fremdes Wahrnehmen" (to perceive the foreign—alienated perception). However, with the exception of Alexandra Stein's hardly innovative investigation of the goliardic epic *Herzog Ernst* and the conflicts of communication between Duke Ernst and foreign peoples on the one hand, and Ute von Bloh's study on aspects such as amazement, astonishment, and fear in the fifteenth-century chapbook *Herzog Herpin* on the other, none of the authors really deals with the actual confrontation with the other in existential, cultural, and sociological terms.[175] Interpretations of the ordeal-scene in Gottfried von Straßburg's *Tristan* (Kelly Kucaba), of the concept of heroism in the epic *Kudrun* (Mark Pearson), or of the conflict between courtiers and farmers in Neidhart's songs (Herfried Vögel), for instance, prove insightful, but they do not shed light on the actual topic addressed by the book's title. Udo Friedrich argues that the author of the *Strassburger Alexander* (ca. 1170) explored the relationship between civilization and nature as a basis of self-identification, which indeed might be an important reflection of the narrative's basic strategy. It does not inform us at all, however, about otherness as a cultural aspect, essentially defining the identity of center and margin.[176]

The contributors to a volume with the proceedings from a conference on *Monde oriental et monde occidental dans la culture médiévale* held in Ajaccio, Corsica (1996), approach the topic in more concrete fashion. Here we are informed about the role of Saracen women in medieval German literature (Danielle Buschinger); the role of Alexander and Ulysses in the Middle Ages (Martine Di Febo), the presentation of the Occident in medieval maps (Angelika Groß); the foreign world of the Huns as depicted in the *Nibelungenlied* (Marc Moser); Saracens in the chronicle of the fourteenth-century Villani family in Florence (Guiseppe Porta); and Christian theology in pagan context within the famous legendary tale of *Barlaam und Josaphat* by Rudolf von Ems (Françoise Salvan-Renucci). In addition, Wolfgang Spiewok explores the experience of the orient in German byzantine romances such as *König Rother*, *König Oswald*, *Orendel*, and *Salman und Morolf*; Colette Stévanovitch discusses the image of the Muslim in the Middle English *King of Tars*; and John V. Tolan examines the conflicts and interactions between Christians and Arabs in ninth-century Spain. Unfortunately, the contributions are mostly limited to straightforward descriptions of literary and historical facts, whereas the critical examination of the other as a phenomenological challenge to medieval European elite culture finds hardly any consideration.

Obviously, much work in the field of medieval xenology remains to be done, both in theoretical and very basic editorial terms. The concept of the other needs to be explored much more in detail, as the terms "liminal," "ambivalent," "strange," and "outsider" do not do full justice to the complex interaction between self and other. In addition, many important literary and historical texts which inform us about the conflicts between center and margin, the enclosed and the excluded, are still awaiting critical editions, not to speak of modern translations. At least Michael Goodich's valuable anthology provides a first comprehensive overview, even though he limits his volume to the perceptions of Jews, apostates, and sexual nonconformists. Goodich points out that although many groups, such as the Cathars, were radically marginalized and attempts were made to eliminate them altogether, they "established their own subcultures, each characterized by its own rules of honor, meeting places, garments, skills, jargon, and signs of group identity."[177] In other words, when we talk about strangers, foreigners, outsiders, or others, we must also consider in greater detail the basic power structure of a specific society which was largely based on the concept of a homogenous majority to the disadvantage of the suppressed or marginalized minority.

Perhaps postcolonial theory might illuminate some curious aspect of a rather heterogenous world in the Middle Ages which we today might view through lenses shaped by "epistemological colonizations of time."[178] In light of the writings of Giraldus Cambrensis dealing with English/Welsh borderland issues, Jeffrey Jerome Cohen argues that the medieval world did not represent a homogeneity imposed on it by modern thinkers, instead was almost always faced by outsiders, foreigners, hence the other.[179] This troublesome constellation could even include women and peasants who "were often institutionally marginalized by the clerical elite, even though they were regarded as members of the body of Christ."[180] Almost the same observation was made by Friedrich Heer who had grouped Jews and women together: "for although during the 'open' Middle Ages Jews and women made a positive contribution to culture and to society, both were later relegated to the life of the Ghetto, and it was they who suffered most when society closed its ranks during the later Middle Ages." Heer even went one step further in his argument: "Witch-mania was a catching malady in a world made schizophrenic by masculine anxieties and masculine fears,"[181] an observation recently fully confirmed by Ronnie Po-chia Hsia.[182] On the other hand, Jewish cultures survived many difficult periods of persecutions, even in the late Middle Ages, which had not only something to do with the Jews' resilience and ability to fight back, but also with the general social context in which certain forms of tolerance and mutual respect were possible, or where pragmatic, economic, and social reasons overruled xenophobia and hatred of non-Christians.[183] The situation of the Jewish community in Worms/Germany illustrates the complex situation well. Whereas in 1348 Emperor Charles IV had implicitly permitted the city to carry out a pogrom against the Jews, a new Jewish community established itself there in the fifteenth century. In 1484 and 1558 attempts to carry out new pogroms and to expel all Jews failed as the authorities did not side with the mob and protected the minority. In 1614 the Christian citizens staged a riot against the Jews whom they all made to leave, but the Emperor forced them to allow the Jews' return in 1616 who were then even protected by the soldiers sent by the Duke of the Palatinate.[184] Historical investigations of ethnic constellations in central and eastern European countries during the High Middle Ages also confirm that in political terms the concept of selfhood, nationhood, political entity, independence, and the like were still very much a matter of negotiations, leaving surprisingly extensive room for integration, mutual acceptance, and respect, such as in the case of Hungarians, the Eastern Slavs, the Cumians, and the Russians.[185] Quite naturally, however, the same constellations also led to many bitter conflicts and military strife.

In general, however, as Alexander Patschovsky has noted in summarizing the contributions to a conference on tolerance in the Middle Ages (Regensburg, October 1994), the roots of the modern concept of tolerance—specifically developed not before the eighteenth century—go as far back as the twelfth century. They might have constituted a very feeble, endangered beginning, but roots they were after all. Our search for tolerant attitudes in the Middle Ages must, however, target individuals, not collectives, as many writers, artists, philosophers, statesmen, and theologians demonstrated. Nevertheless, these islands of open attitudes toward the other existed in a sea of intolerance and violence against them.[186]

This is to say, there were intriguing outlets and vents which prevented the total closing-up of medieval society always faced by individuals who deliberately excluded themselves from the majority, such as heretics and mystics, but also pilgrims, journeymen, Gipsies (Sinti and Roma), goliards, and vast numbers of the poor.[187] Surprisingly large numbers of people were forced to live an unstable life, to be on the move all the time, and hence had to abandon the security of the traditional community. Whereas royalties and itinerant preachers and monks (Franciscans and Dominicans, primarily) deliberately gave up on the idea of *stabilitas loci* for very specific reasons, many people had no choice and had to go begging and so constituted *de facto* foreigners and outsiders.[188] Some of the best known individuals who did not blend in and resisted conformity I have referred to above, and many more deserve mention here, such as William of Tyrus, Pope Innocent III, and St. Francis of Assisi.[189] Peter the Venerable and Robert of Ketton even went so far as to consult Muslim scholars for the Latin translation of the Qur'an, perhaps not out of a true interest in Islam, but certainly out of the understanding that the other had to be dealt with from a critical, especially well-informed platform.[190]

Obviously the most feasible avenue to reach out of the narrow-minded paradigm of feudal and Christian society proved to be the search for the divine, the mystical, and the visionary. Although mysticism is certainly unrelated to the confrontation between Christianity and Islam, for instance, it was as much concerned with otherness as the concrete political and religious tensions between the European center and its margins. Our first important example was Mechthild of Magdeburg (see above), but many others from all over Europe could be cited as confirmation, be it Hildegard of Bingen, Hadewijch of Brabant, St. Clare of Assisi, Birgitta of Sweden, Julian of Norwich, or Marguerite Porete. After all, as Elizabeth Alvilda Petroff has stated, "[f]or women who were sensitive to the emotional content of traditional images of masculine and feminine, the participation in the crucifixion became enormously liberating, for the opposites of passive and active, female and male, were reconciled in this single act."[191] This does not qualify mystical women better than mystical men for the interaction with the other. Rather, the visionary experience as such forced the individual to confront a distinctly other in the form of the Godhead and to discard the self, at least during the time while the revelation lasted.[192] This is to say that the witnessing of the other in medieval times produced many different facets and created a multiplicity of intercultural situations. But the more medieval people discovered the individual, the more they realized the need to set boundaries and to distinguish themselves from the others as a means of self-definition.[193] A radical and quite surprising alternative proved to be the declaration, found in the *Gesta Romanorum* (late fourteenth century), "Deus est mortuus," expressing a deep sense of frustration over the downfall of Christianity which did not provide hope for society's resurrection even with God's help.[194]

Consequently, the stereotypical projection of the enemy Muslim in practically all crusade chronicles and similar types of texts "enabled Western Christians to define themselves in religio-ethnic terms, whereas some authors of crusade epics reified and devalued them to the level of animals who could be used as foodstuff for the crusaders.[195] Indeed, the Muslim became, so to speak, a photographic negative of the self-perception of an ideal Christian self-image that portrayed Europeans as brave, virtuous believers in the one true God and the one true faith."[196] In Hrotsvit of Gandersheim's play *Pelagius* the Muslim/Saracen provides, through his violent actions against the martyr, a vehicle for the Christian to establish their religious community, as Lisa Weston now observes: "In engaging with that textual body, readers of Hrotsvit's *Pelagius* define themselves through the twin processes of identifying with but inevitably distinguishing themselves from the foreignness of both the martyr and his persecutor."[197] Nevertheless, according to Wolfram von Eschenbach and many other late-medieval writers and philosophers such as Peter Abelard, John of Salisbury, and Peter of Celle, at least within the literary and philosophical arena,[198] both the Muslim and the Jew could also at certain times and under certain circumstances be viewed in quite a different light, as they were then accepted more or less as equals among equals.[199] We know, for instance, that Emperor Frederick II conducted a nonmilitary, nonviolent "crusade" to the Holy Land in 1228–1229 and proved how successful more or less tolerant diplomacy could be in a world of religious hostile confrontations. Moreover, when Frederick established a Saracen colony at Lucera in northern Apulia in 1224, almost in the immediate vicinity of Rome, he thus increased the Pope's hatred against him. To make sure that the transfer of these Saracens from Sicily to a region then known as Capitanea would not lead to political unrest and military strife, Frederick exempted them from all royal taxes, granted them religious freedom, and allowed them a considerable degree of self-government. In addition, at his court the Emperor entertained many people from different cultures and religions, and it was at this location where—in the context of thirteenth-century Europe at least—possibly the most advanced approach toward the other was taken.[200] Representatives of all three world religions contributed to the emergence of a truly international cultural center where various languages were spoken, ideas were exchanged without the danger of being accused of hereticism, and literary and scientific advances from Northern Europe and Italy merged with those from the Arabic world.[201] It would probably be more correct, however, to ascribe an even higher degree of tolerant attitude to Frederick's predecessors, the Norman rulers Roger II (1101–1154), William I, and William II (1154–1189), even if their idealization in turn would be tantamount to mythologizing them. Tragically, the multicultural community in southern Italy and Sicily eventually could not maintain a balance of ethnic distribution and economic and cultural equality, leading to the absolute dominance of the Latinate culture under the Hohenstaufen rulers.[202] Similar pockets of open-minded societies could be found elsewhere as well, such as in early-medieval Catalonia, twelfth-century Toledo/Spain, and, surprisingly, in some of the Crusader states.[203] In a way this new anthropological concept is well outlined in Wolfram von Eschenbach's *Parzival*, where Gahmuret's love of the Black Queen Belacane implies, as David Tinsley argues, the development of a new set of cultural norms, or courtliness, which serves to transcend the traditional boundaries of kingdom, race, lineage, and, as I would add, religion.[204]

Depending on perspectives and source materials, one might find the Middle Ages either highly xenophobic, or displaying, in stark contrast, surprising elements of open-mindedness, if not tolerance almost in the modern sense of the word.[205] Unfortunately, the personal contacts, intellectual debates, material exchanges, and to some extent even interreligious marriages did not influence society as much as the crusades, warfares, the Inquisition, and other forms of violent oppression and aggression.[206] Only rarely do we hear what the ordinary people believed, what they thought about other cultures and religions, but those witnesses which are available to us often paint quite a different picture than the official documents. More often than not their testimonies indicate that the confrontation with the other was not considered a threat, but instead as an enrichment.[207] Thus, it would be erroneous to equate medieval with intolerant, just as it would be utterly false to equate modern with tolerant.

The German dramatist, essayist, and writer Gotthold Ephraim Lessing was not the first to use the famous ring parable in his play *Nathan der Weise* (1779; *Nathan the Wise*) in which he formulated an unmistakenly enlightened concept of tolerance, borrowed from Boccaccio's *Decameron* (ca. 1350) (possibly also from the *Gesta Romanorum* [late thirteenth/early fourteenth century], but there the ring parable pursues a very Christian teaching). Here in the third story of the first day a Jew named Melchisedech answers the Saladin's question regarding the truth of the three world religions—Christianity, Islam, and Judaism—by means of a parable: "it is the same with the three Laws given by God our Father to three peoples, concerning which you have questioned me. Each of them thinks it has the inheritance, the true Law, and carries out His Commandments; but which does have it is a question as far from being settled as that of the rings."[208] Nevertheless, the other continued to be an epistemological problem for people in the Middle Ages—as it has even more so for people of later epochs—and the majority of them tended to reject it, expunge it, and attempted to eradicate it from their mental horizon. The contributions to this volume will shed light on the multiple approaches and perspectives espoused in medieval times and will indicate the vast complexity of this issue pertaining to *The*

Foreign in the Middle Ages which has direct impact on our present lives as we struggle to come to terms with the other in its multiple manifestations. Many studies have recently focused on this xenological phenomenon, as the late twentieth and early twenty-first centuries have witnessed an enormous growth of interculturation due to massive movements of populations worldwide. In light of these observations it seems very appropriate also to investigate the historical roots of encounters with the foreign.[209] Even though this volume is concerned with literary and historical material, the ultimate premise of all the contributions rests in the belief that the gap between 'us' and 'them,' or between 'self' and 'other' can and must be overcome if the human race is to survive. In Loring Danforth's highly insightful words, "the goal of a truly humanistic anthropology can be achieved . . . [if we accept] the full realization that both 'we' and 'they' share a common humanity. . . . Any serious inquiry into another culture, therefore, leads to a greater understanding of one's own culture. An investigation of the Other involves an exploration of the Self as well."[210]

I would like to express my thanks to the many contributors to this volume whose articles I cannot introduce here individually. Their patience and collaboration were essential in achieving the desired scholarly quality of this volume. Many of their contributions were presented in the form of short conference papers both in the United States and in England, but they were all thoroughly revised and expanded for this volume. I have taken note of their thoughts and observations throughout this introductory essay. May this volume reach many readers and have an impact on our thinking and outlook as our world continues to struggle against intolerance and conflicts between races, religions, cultures, and genders. The teachings from the past are not all pleasant—quite on the contrary—but they are necessary both for the present and the future. Likewise, the past was not always a dark age and can provide significant epistemological models for the modern world.

Notes

I would like to express my thanks to Lourdes Maria Alvarez, Alan Bernstein, and Jean Jost for reading this introductory article and for giving their valuable comments and suggestions.

1. Helmut Plessner, "Mit anderen Augen," H. Plessner, *Gesammelte Schriften*, ed. G. Dux, Otto Marquard, and E. Ströker, vol. 8 (Frankfurt a.M.: Suhrkamp, 1983), 88–104; here 93–99, 102; see also Otto Friedrich, *Studien zur Hermeneutik*, Alber-Broschur Philosophie (Freiburg: K. Alber, 1982), 95.
2. Wendell V. Harris, *Dictionary of Concepts in Literary Criticism and Theory*, Reference Sources for the Social Sciences and Humanities, 12 (New York, Westport, CT, and London: Greenwood Press, 1992), 133.

3. Hubert Dreyfus, "Beyond Hermeneutics: Interpretation in Late Heidegger and Recent Foucault," *Hermeneutics: Questions and Prospects*, ed. Gary Shapiro and Alan Sica (Amherst: University of Massachusetts Press, 1984), 73; for a comprehensive overview of hermeneutics, see W. V. Harris, *Dictionary*, 129–38.
4. İrvin Cemil Schick, *The Erotic Margin: Sexuality and Spatiality in Alteritist Discourse* (London and New York: Verso, 1999), 21.
5. Frithjof Rodi, "Das Nahe-Bringen von Überlieferung. Über die kulturellen Lebensbezüge der 'Vertrautheit' und 'Fremdheit'," *Philosophisch-theologische Grenzfragen : Festschrift für Richard Schaeffler zur Vollendung des 60. Lebensjahres*, ed. Richard Schaeffler, Julie Kirchberg, and Johannes Muther (Essen: Ludgerus, 1986), 291ff.; here 229.
6. Giles Gunn, *The Interpretation of Otherness: Literature, Religion, and the American Imagination* (New York: Oxford University Press, 1979), 177.
7. Orrin F. Summerell, "Introduction: When God is not Deity," *The Otherness of God*, ed. Orrin F. Summerell, Studies in Religion and Culture (Charlottesville and London: University Press of Virginia, 1998), 1–13; provides an extensive bibliography on recent studies dealing with otherness.
8. Robert Hanning, *The Individual in Twelfth-Century Romance* (New Haven and London: Yale University Press, 1977); John Benton, "Consciousness of Self and Perceptions of Individuality," in *Renaissance and Renewal in the Twelfth Century,* ed. Robert Benson and Giles Constable, (Cambridge, Mass.: Harvard University Press, 1982), 263–95; Caroline Bynum, "Did the Twelfth Century Discover the Individual?," *Jesus as Mother: Studies in the Spirituality of the High Middle Ages*, Publications of the Center for Medieval and Renaissance Studies, UCLA, 16 (Berkeley and Los Angeles: University of California Press, 1972), ch. 3; Lee Patterson, *Negotiating the Past* (Madison: University of Wisconsin Press, 1987), 182–84.
9. Antonio Gramsci, *The Prison Notebooks: Selections*, trans. and ed. Quintin Hoare and Geoffrey Nowell-Smith (New York: International Publishers, 1971), 324.
10. Quoted from *The Hermeneutic Reader: Texts of the German Tradition from the Enlightenment to the Present*, ed., Kurt Mueller-Vollmer (New York: Continuum, 1985), 272.
11. Philipp Strauch, ed., *Jansen Enikels Werke*, Monumenta Germaniae Historica. Deutsche Chroniken und andere Geschichtsbücher des Mittelalters 3, unchanged reprint (1900; Munich: Monumenta Germaniae Historica, 1980); cf. Leopold Hellmuth, "Zur Entstehungszeit der Weltchronik des Jans Enikel," *Österreich in Geschichte und Literatur* 29 (1985): 163–170.
12. Jacques Les Goff, "Le merveilleux dans l'Occident médiévale," ibid., *L'imaginaire médiévale*, Bibliotheque des histoires (1985; Paris: Gallimard, 1991), 22–29.
13. Scot McKendrick, *The History of Alexander the Great: An Illuminated Manuscript of Vasco da Lucena's French. Translation of the Ancient Text by Quintus Curtius Rufus*, Getty Museum Monographs on Illuminated Manuscripts (Los Angeles: The J. Paul Getty Museum, 1996).

14. Simona Leonardi, "I 'Wunder' nella 'Weltchronik' di Jans Enikel: Relazione tra testo narrativo e testo iconico," *Medioevo e Rinascimento* XIII/ns. X (1999): 103–28.
15. Helmut de Boor, *Die deutsche Literatur im späten Mittelalter*. Part One: *1250–1350*. 5th ed. Neubearbeitet von Johannes Janota, Geschichte der deutschen Literatur von den Anfängen bis zur Gegenwart III/1 (1962; Munich: Beck, 1997), 168–70.
16. Along the same lines, in the Middle High German *Alexanderlied* by the Pfaffe Lamprecht (ca. 1170) the protagonist and his men meet, among many other miraculous and wondrous creatures, a host of delightful young maidens who happily join them in lovemaking and spend a long time with them until they suddenly pass away as flowers always do, causing the men great pain and sorrow; Irene Ruttmann, *Das Alexanderlied des Pfaffen Lamprecht (Strassburger Alexander)*. Text, Nacherzählung, Worterklärungen (Darmstadt: Wissenschaftliche Buchgesellschaft, 1974), 5193–358.
17. Michael Camille, *Image on the Edge: The Margins of Medieval Art* (Cambridge, Mass.: Harvard University Press, 1992), 78–84.
18. Jurgis Baltrušaitis, *Il Medioevo fantastico: Antichità ed esotismi nell'arte gotica*, trad. di F. Zuliani e F. Bovoli (1972; Milan: Adelphi Edizioni, 1973), 278: "Il Medioevo ha sempre avuto una notevole attitudine a rinnovare le forme prese a prestito e a imprimere loro il proprio carattere. Tutto si muove e si muta. Mescolate alle decorazioni dei margini, le grottesche greco-romane sono completamente assimilate alla bizzarria gotica. Gli arabeschi sono trascinati nei capricci delle piante rampicanti completamente."
19. Modern anthropology is called upon to investigate this very opposition and to utilize it as an epistemological tool. Loring M. Danfort, *The Death Rituals of Rural Greece* (Princeton: Princeton University Press, 1982), 5f., argues: "Anthropology inevitably involves an encounter with the Other. All too often, however, the ethnographic distance that separates the reader of anthropological texts and the anthropologist himself from the Other is rigidly maintained and at times even artificially exaggerated. In many cases this distancing leads to an exclusive focus on the Other as primitive, bizarre, and exotic. The gap between a familiar 'we' and an exotic 'they' is a major obstacle to a meaningful understanding of the Other, an obstacle that can only be overcome through some form of participation in the world of the Other." See also Dietrich Krusche, *Literatur und Fremde. Zur Hermeneutik kulturräumlicher Distanz* (Munich: iudicium, 1985); *Das Fremde und das Eigene. Prolegomena zu einer interkulturellen Germanistik*, ed. Alois Wierlacher, Publikationen der Gesellschaft für Interkulturelle Germanistik 1 (Munich: iudicium, 1985).
20. Götz Pochat, *Das Fremde im Mittelalter: Darstellung in Kunst und Literatur* (Würzburg: Echter, 1997).
21. For a case study involving the British and the Welsh, see the article by Michael Goodich in this volume.
22. *Contra Faustus manichaeum*, xvi, 21; here quoted from Paula Fredriksen, "Divine Justice and Human Freedom: Augustine on Jews and Judaism, 392–398," *From Witness to Witchcraft: Jews and Judaism in Medieval*

Christian Thought, ed. Jeremy Cohen. Wolfenbütteler Mittelalter-Studien 11 (Wiesbaden: Harrassowitz, 1996), 29–54; here 49.

23. Robert Bartlett, *The Making of Europe: Conquest, Colonization, and Cultural Change, 950–1350* (Princeton: Princeton University Press, 1993), 197.
24. Bo Stråth, ed., *Europe and the Other and Europe as the Other*. Multiple Europes, 10 (Brussels, Bern, Berlin, et al.: Peter Lang, 2000). Although the contributors to this volume focus mostly on the period from the eighteenth to the twentieth century, their theoretical conclusions significantly contribute to our understanding of medieval Europe as well.
25. See the contribution to this volume by David B. Leshock, "Religious Geography: Designating Jews and Muslims as 'Foreigners' in Medieval England."
26. Winfried Frey, in his contribution to this volume, "The Intimate Other: The Dialogue between 'A Christian and a Jew' by Hans Folz," discusses the devastating consequences of Folz's literary strategies to incite the population of Nuremberg to a radical and violent form of anti-Semitism.
27. Philip M. Soergel, "Portraying Monstrous Birth in Early Modern Germany," *The Future of the Middle Ages and the Renaissance: Problems, Trends, and Opportunities for Research*, ed. Roger Dahood, Arizona Studies in the Middle Ages and the Renaissance 2 (Brepols: Turnhout, 1998), 129–50.
28. *Ketzer, Zauberer, Hexen: Die Anfänge der europäischen Hexenverfolgungen*, ed. Andreas Blauert, edition suhrkamp, 1577 (Frankfurt a.M.: Suhrkamp, 1990); see especially Blauert's introductory article, "Die Erforschung der Anfänge der europäischen Hexenverfolgungen," 11–42.
29. Bartlett, *The Making*, 240–42; in his conclusion, Bartlett goes one step further, however: "It has been shown, reasonably conclusively, how the mental habits and institutions of European racism and colonialism were born in the medieval world: the conquerors of Mexico knew the problem of the Mudejars; the planters of Virginia had already been planters of Ireland." He continues: "There is no doubt that the Catholic societies of Europe had deep experience of colonialist enterprise prior to 1492 . . . Both ecologically and historically the medieval Latin world was contiguous and often continuous with the neighbouring cultures and societies. Nevertheless, from the Iberian peninsula in a wide arc east across the Mediterranean and north to the Arctic Circle, Catholic Europe did have a frontier and, from the tenth century, a frontier that was moving outwards" (313).
30. Albert the Great, *Man and the Beast: de animalibus (Books 22–26)*, trans. James J. Scanlan, Medieval & Renaissance Texts & Studies (Binghamton, NY: Medieval & Renaissance Texts & Studies, 1987), 23.24 and 25.26; see the introduction, 17f.
31. *Romane des 15. und 16. Jahrhunderts. Nach den Erstdrucken mit sämtlichen Holzschnitten*, ed. Jan-Dirk Müller, Bibliothek der frühen Neuzeit 1 (Frankfurt a.M.: Deutscher Klassiker Verlag, 1990), 12; see also the commentary by Müller, 1044. Thüring quoted incorrectly, as it should say: "Mirabilis deus in sanctis suis." Cf. also Ps. 138:14: "mirabilia opera tua." These observations in Thüring's chapbook point the way toward early-modern metaphysical studies, such as practiced by Paracelsus.

32. Götz Pochat, *Das Fremde* (1997), 44, points out that the ninth-century philosopher John Scotus Eriugena argued for the inclusion of the "dissimilia signa" in the divine universe, as even the monstrous and the ugly had its divinely-willed function.
33. See Michael Uebel's study "The Foreigner Within: The Subject of Abjection in *Sir Gowther*" and also Jesus A. Montaño's contribution "*Sir Gowther*: Imagining Race in Late Medieval England," both in this volume.
34. David Nirenberg, *Communities of Violence: Persecution of Minorities in the Middle Ages* (Princeton: Princeton University Press, 1996), 9.
35. Nirenberg, *Communities of Violence*, 245.
36. See the contribution by David Leshook, "Religious Geography: Designating Jews and Muslims as 'Foreigners' in Medieval England," to this volume.
37. See the extraordinary articles collected in *Das Licht der Vernunft: Die Anfänge der Aufklärung im Mittelalter,* ed. Kurt Flasch and Udo Reinhold Jeck, (Munich: Beck, 1997).
38. See, for example, the case of the fourteenth-century Majorcan Anselm Turmeda, here discussed by Lourdes María Alvarez.
39. Jeff Rider, "The Other Worlds of Romance," *The Cambridge Companion to Medieval Romance*, ed. Roberta L. Krueger, Cambridge Companions to Culture (Cambridge: Cambridge University Press, 2000), 115–31; here 118.
40. Hartmann von Aue, *Iwein*, ed. and trans. Patrick M. McConeghy, Garland Library of Medieval Literature, Series A 19 (New York and London: Garland Publishing, 1984), 426–36.
41. In Chrétien's version, *The Knight with the Lion*, the wild man is called a "churl" who exerts sheer physical force to subjugate the wild animals; still, Chrétien projects a scene of almost paradisiac nature, here quoted from *The Complete Romances of Chrétien de Troyes*, trans. David Staines (Bloomington and Indianapolis: Indiana University Press, 1990), 260f.
42. For the thirteenth-century illustrations of this epic narrative, see Volker Schupp and Hans Szklenar, *Ywain auf Schloß Rodenegg: Eine Bildergeschichte nach dem 'Iwein' Hartmanns von Aue* (Sigmaringen: Jan Thorbecke Verlag, 1996); especially the depiction of the wild man is highly impressive and represents probably the best piece of the huge wall fresco; Hartmut Bleumer, "*Das wilde wîp:* Überlegungen zum Krisenmotiv im Artusroman und im 'Wolfdietrich' B," *Natur und Kultur in der deutschen Literatur des Mittelalters*, ed. Alan Robertshaw and Gerhard Wolf (Tübingen: Niemeyer, 1999), 77–89; here 81f., suggests that the forester represents the congruence of the self with 'the other.' Bleumer does not see, however, the superior character of the wild man whose calm and peaceful manner sharply contrasts with Kalogrenant's failure as a knight; the same applies to Iwein in Hartmann's eponymous romance; see also the recent study by Dorothy Yamamoto, *The Boundaries of the Human in Medieval English Literature* (Oxford: Oxford University Press, 2000), 144–224.
43. Will Hasty, *Adventure as Social Performance: A Study of the German Court Epic*, Untersuchungen zur deutschen Literaturgeschichte 52 (Tübingen: Niemeyer, 1990), points out that many wounded and disappointed heroes such as Helmbrecht in Wernher the Gardener's *Meier Helmbrecht* and—as I

would add—Bertschi Triefnas in Heinrich Wittenwiler's early fifteenth-century *Ring* retire into the woods and try to find an hermitage as a form of "Paradise lost," or utopia. Hasty concludes: "In this study the relationship of complicity between court society and the *outside* has been characterized by paradox, transgression, and love. This complicity has at times seemed to indicate the inevitability of violence, alienation and servitude as aspects of the human condition. However, if we do not regard them as 'natural' aspects of an unchangeable universe, but rather as results of an ongoing *performance* of society that constantly involves alternative possibilities, paradox, transgression and love may allow us to perceive another order—one whose integrity would not necessarily depend on the displacement of its own insufficiencies and/or on the violent suppression or integration of alternative world-views." (138)

44. Heinz-Dieter Heimann, "Der Wald in der städtischen Kulturentfaltung und Landschaftswahrnehmung: Zur Problematik des kulturellen Naturverhältnisses als Teil einer Umwelt- und Gesellschaftsgeschichte des Mittelalters und der frühen Neuzeit," *Mensch und Natur im Mittelalter*, 2. Halbband. ed. Albert Zimmermann and Andreas Speer, Miscellanea Mediaevalia 21/2 (Berlin and New York: de Gruyter, 1992), 866–81; regarding the Cistercians' escape from civilization, see Peter Dinzelbacher, *Bernhard von Clairvaux: Leben und Werk des berühmten Zisterziensers* (Darmstadt: Primus Verlag, 1998), 31–37; David H. Williams, *The Cistercians in the Early Middle Ages: Written to Commemorate the Nine Hundredth Anniversary of Foundation of the Order at Citeaux in 1098* (Leominster: Gracewing, 1998).
45. See, for instance, Jane Backhouse, *The Sherborne Missal* (London, Toronto, and Buffalo: The British Library–University of Toronto Press, 1999), the scenes with wild men on the bottom margin on p. 216 or the almost cute dragon facing St. Sylvester on the bottom of p. 395.
46. Ruth Mellinkoff, *Outcasts: Signs of Otherness in Northern European Art of the Late Middle Ages*, Volume One: *Text* (Berkeley, Los Angeles, and Oxford: University of California Press, 1993), LI.
47. Dolores Warwick Frese, "The Marriage of Woman and Werewolf: Poetics of Estrangement in Marie de France's 'Bisclavret,' " *Vox intexta: Orality and Textuality in the Middle Ages*, ed. A. N. Doane and Carol Braun Pasternack (Madison: The University of Wisconsin Press, 1991), 183–202; here 186f.
48. Josef Semmler, ed., *Der Wald in Mittelalter und Renaissance*. Studia humaniora 17 (Düsseldorf: Droste, 1991). Summarizing the discussion by Marcella Roddewig, he comments: "Der Wald an der Grenze zwischen *Purgatorium* und *Paradiso* hält die Schrecknisse des Erdenlebens parat, läßt jedoch bereits die Fülle der Gnadensonne erahnen, die dem aufgeht, der auf seiner Erdenwanderung alle Anfechtungen überstand und würdig ist, in den Wald des Paradieses einzutreten"(13)
49. Jeffrey Jerome Cohen, "The Limits of Knowing: Monsters and the Regulation of Medieval Popular Culture," *Medieval Folklore* III (1994): 1–37; here 1; see also his *Of Giants: Sex, Monsters, and the Middle Ages* (Minneapolis: University of Minnesota Press, 1999).

50. Rudolf Wittkower, "Marvels of the East: A Study in the History of Monsters," *The Journal of the Warburg and Courtauld Institutes* V (1942): 159–97; John Block Friedman, *The Montrous Races in Medieval Art and Thought* (Cambridge, Mass.: Harvard University Press, 1981); Jean Céard, *La nature et les prodiges: l'insolité au 16e siècle, en France*, Travaux d'humanisme et Renaissance 158 (Geneva: Droz, 1977); Mary Campbell, *The Witness and the Other World: Exotic European Travel Writing, 400–1600* (Ithaca and London: Cornell University Press, 1988); Claude Lecouteux, *Les monstres dans la pensée médiévale européenne: essai de presentation.* Cultures et civilisations médiévales 10 (Paris: Presses de l'Universite de Paris-Sorbonne, 1995).
51. Malcolm Jones, "Wild Man" (1037–1041); Lorraine K. Stock, "Wild Woman" (1041–044), *Medieval Folklore: An Encyclopedia of Myths, Legends, Tales, Beliefs, and Customs,* Carl Lindahl, John McNamara, John Lindow, eds. 2 vols. C Santa Barbara, Denver, and Oxford [England]: ABC-Clio, 2000.
52. Roger Bartra, *Wild Men in the Looking Glass: The Mythic Origins of European Otherness*, trans. Carl T. Berrisford (Ann Arbor: The University of Michigan Press, 1994), 204; see also the classical study on this topic by Richard Bernheimer, *Wild Men in the Middle Ages: A Study in Art, Sentiment, and Demonology* (Cambridge, Mass.: Harvard University Press, 1952); Timothy Husband, *The Wild Man: Medieval Myth and Symbolism* (New York: Metropolitan Museum of Art, 1980); see also Jeffrey Jerome Cohen, ed., *Monster Theory: Reading Culture* (Minneapolis: University of Minnesota Press, 1996).
53. Bartra, *Wild Men*, 77.
54. Albrecht Classen, "Die guten Monster im Orient und in Europa: Konfrontation mit dem 'Fremden' als anthropologische Erfahrung im Mittelalter," *Mediaevistik* 9 (1997): 11–37.
55. Bartra, *Wild Men*, 79.
56. See her contribution to this volume.
57. Jeffrey Jerome Cohen, "Introduction," *The Postcolonial Middle Ages*, ed. Jeffrey Jerome Cohen, The New Middle Ages (New York: St. Martin's Press, 2000), 1–17; here 8, goes so far as to suggest "that 'Europe' as a unifying concept is a fairly recent fiction that travels back in time problematically." Considering the unity of the Christian Church, the pervasive and all-dominating system of feudalism and the all-encompassing social order of the three classes, the significant role played by Latin as a universal language, and the shared chivalric culture epitomized by King Arthur, however, Cohen's thesis would require a considerable reassessment. See also the collection of articles, *Europe and the Other and Europe as the Other*, ed. Bo Stråth 2000.
58. See Jean Jost's contribution to this volume, "Margins in Middle English Romance: Culture and Characterization in *Awntyrs off Arthure at the Terne Wathelyne* and *The Wedding of Sir Gawain and Dame Ragnell*."
59. András Vizkelety, " 'Du bist ein alter Hunne, unmäßig schlau . . .' Das Ungarnbild im deutschen Mittelalter," *Das Ungarnbild in Deutschland und*

das Deutschlandbild in Ungarn: Materialien des wissenschaftlichen Symposiums am 26. und 27. Mai 1995 in Hamburg, ed. Holger Fischer, Aus der Südosteuropa-Forschung 6 (Munich: Südosteuropa-Gesellschaft, 1996), 11–21; see also the contribution by Alexander Sager to this volume, "Hungarians as *vremde* in Medieval Germany."

60. Friedrich Heer, *The Medieval World: Europe 1100–1350*. Trans. from the German by Janet Sondheimer (1961; New York and Toronto: The New American Library, 1962), 44–47; Robert Bartlett, *The Making of Europe*, 1993.
61. Kiril Petkov, *Infidels, Turks and Women: The South Slavs in the German Mind, ca. 1400–1600* (Frankfurt a.M., Berlin, Bern, et al.: Peter Lang, 1997), 19f.
62. Josef Joachim Menzel, "Die Akzeptanz des Fremden in der mittelalterlichen deutschen Ostsiedlung," *Toleranz im Mittelalter*, ed. Alexander Patschovsky and Harald Zimmermann, Vorträge und Forschungen XLV (Sigmaringen: Thorbecke, 1998), 207–19.
63. See the contribution by David B. Leshock to this volume.
64. Albrecht Classen, "Außenseiter der Gesellschaft im späthöfischen Roman, Volksbuch und Volkslied: Eine literar-soziologische und ethnologische Untersuchung," *Europäische Ethnologie und Folklore im internationalen Kontext. Festschrift für Leander Petzoldt zum 65. Geburtstag*, ed. Ingo Schneider (Frankfurt a.M., Berlin, et al.: Peter Lang, 1999), 351–66.
65. Leonard B. Glick, *Abraham's Heirs: Jews and Christians in Medieval Europe* (Syracuse: Syracuse University Press, 1999); John Boswell, *Christianity, Social Tolerance, and Homosexuality: Gay People in Western Europe from the Beginning of the Christian Era to the Fourteenth Century* (Chicago: University of Chicago Press, 1980); ibid., *Same-Sex Unions in Premodern Europe* (New York: Villard Books, 1994); Caroline Walker Bynum, *Fragmentation and Redemption: Essays on Gender and the Human Body in Medieval Religion* (New York: Zone Books, 1991); Joan M. Ferrante, *To the Glory of Her Sex: Women's Roles in the Composition of Medieval Texts*, Women of Letters (Bloomington and Indianapolis: Indiana University Press, 1997); Malcolm Lambert, *The Cathars* (Oxford and Malden, Mass.: Blackwell Publishers, 1998).
66. *Europäische Mentalitätsgeschichte: Hauptthemen in Einzeldarstellungen*, ed. Peter Dinzelbacher, Kröners Taschenausgabe 469 (Stuttgart: Alfred Kröner, 1993). See, in particular, the chapters on "Ängste und Hoffnungen," "Kommunikation," and "Das Fremde und das Eigene." See also the recent study by Peter Dinzelbacher, *Angst im Mittelalter. Teufels-, Todes- und Gotteserfahrung: Mentalitätsgeschichte und Ikonographie* (Paderborn, Munich, Vienna, and Zurich: Ferdinand Schöningh, 1996). Cf. Jean Delumeau, *Le péche et la peur: la culpabilisation en Occident XIIIe-XVIIIe siècles* (Paris: Fayard, 1983).
67. Dominique Barthélemy, *L'an mil et la paix de Dieu: La France chrétienne et féodale 980–1060* (Paris: Fayard, 1999), 184–90.
68. Michael Hasloch Kirkby, *The Vikings* (Oxford: Phaidon; New York: Dutton, 1977); Gwyn Jones, *A History of the Vikings* (London, New York, et al.: Oxford

University Press, 1968); R. I. Page, *Chronicles of the Vikings: Records, Memorials and Myths* (Toronto and Buffalo: University of Toronto Press, 1995).

69. David R. Blanks, "Western Views of Islam in the Premodern Period: A Brief History of Past Approaches," *Western Views of Islam in Medieval and Early Modern Europe: Perception of Other*, ed. David R. Blanks and Michael Frassetto (New York: St. Martin's Press, 1999), 11–53. For a review of this volume and its lasting contribution to Medieval Studies, see Kurt Villads Jensen's review in *The Medieval Review* (internet) TMR 00.07.10 (www.hti.umich.edu).
70. Leo de Hartog, *Genghis Khan: Conqueror of the World* (1979; London and New York: I. B. Tauris, 1999);
71. John Haywood, *Dark Age Naval Power: A Re-Assessment of Frankish and Anglo-Saxon Seafaring Activity* (London and New York: Routledge, 1991); Archibald R. Lewis and Timothy J. Runyan, *European Naval and Maritime History, 300–1500* (1985; Bloomington: Indiana University Press, 1990); for the figure of the highwayman and robber, see *Medieval Outlaws: Ten Tales in Modern English*, ed. Thomas H. Ohlgren (Thrupp–Stroud, Gloucestershire: Sutton Publishing, 1998).
72. Michael Richter, *The Formation of the Medieval West: Studies in the Oral Culture of the Barbarians* (New York: St. Martin's Press, 1994), 3–26.
73. For further explorations of this topic, see Bo Stråth, ed., *Europe and the Other and Europe as the Other*, 2000.
74. *Europa und die Türken in der Renaissance*, ed. Bodo Guthmüller and Wilhelm Kühlmann, Frühe Neuzeit 54 (Tübingen: Niemeyer, 2000); Carl Göllner, *Turcica*. Vols. I and II: *Die europäischen Türkendrucke des 16. Jahrhunderts*. Vol. III: *Die Türkenfrage in der öffentlichen Meinung Europas im 16. Jahrhundert*, Bibliotheca Bibliographica Aureliana 23/70 (1968; Baden–Baden: Valentin Koerner, 1978).
75. *Romane des 15. und 16. Jahrhunderts*, 1990; Albrecht Classen, "Die Welt eines spätmittelalterlichen Kaufmannsreisenden: Ein mentalitätsgeschichtliches Dokument der Frühneuzeit: *Fortunatus*," *Monatshefte* 86, 1 (1994): 22–44.
76. *The Meeting of Two Worlds: Cultural Exchanges between East and West during the Period of the Crusades*, ed. Vladimir P. Goss, Christine Verzár Bornstein, Studies in Medieval Culture XXI (Kalamazoo, MI: Medieval Institute Publications, 1986).
77. See, for example, Wirnt von Gravenberg's *Wigalois* where both heathens and magic are well received and viewed with considerable sympathy; Stephan Maksymiuk, *The Court Magician in Medieval German Romance*, Beiträge zur Literaturwissenschaft und Bedeutungsforschung 44 (Frankfurt a.M, Berlin, et al.: Peter Lang, 1992), 127f.
78. Albrecht Classen, " 'The Other' in Medieval Narratives and Epics: The Encounter with Monsters, Devils, Giants, and other Creatures," *Canon and Canon Transgression in Medieval German Literature*, ed. Albrecht Classen, Göppinger Arbeiten zur Germanistik 573 (Göppingen: Kümmerle, 1993), 83–121.
79. Paul Freedman, Images of the Medieval Peasant: Figurae: Reading Medieval Culture (Stanford: Stanford University Press, 1999); for a

review, see S. H. Rigby in *The Medieval Review* (internet) 29 Mar 2000 08:11:36.

80. R. Mellinkoff, *Outcasts*, 229. She outlines in great detail the various means by which artists marginalized minorities and outcasts; see also Ernst Schubert, *Fahrendes Volk im Mittelalter* (Bielefeld: Verlag für Regionalgeschichte, 1995).
81. The best example for this phenomenon can be found in Hartmann von Aue's "Der arme Heinrich," where the lord, struck by "miselsuht," that is, leprosy, withdraws from society and awaits his death far away in the countryside. Nobody wants to stay with him, except a farmer's young daughter who later will be the catalyst for his rescue. Hartmann von Aue, *Der arme Heinrich*, ed. Hermann Paul, 16th, newly prepared ed. by Kurt Gärnter, Altdeutsche Textbibliothek 3 (Tübingen: Niemeyer, 1996).
82. Reimar Gilsenbach, *Weltchronik der Zigeuner: 2000 Ereignisse aus der Geschichte der Roma und Sinti, der Gypsies und Gitanos und aller anderen Minderheiten, die "Zigeuner" genannt werden*. Part One: *Von den Anfängen bis 1599*. 2., korrigierte und ergänzte Aufl., Studien zur Tsiganologie und Folkloristik 10 (1994; Frankfurt a.M., Berlin, Bern, et al.: Peter Lang, 1997).
83. See, for instance, the contributions to this volume by Michael Uebel, Jesus Montaño, and David F. Tinsley.
84. *Kulturthema Fremdheit. Leitbegriffe und Problemfelder kulturwissenschaftlicher Fremdheitsforschung*, ed. Alois Wierlacher, Kulturthemen 1 (Munich: iudicium, 1993), 39–53, et passim.
85. *Kulturthema Toleranz: Zur Grundlegung einer interdisziplinären Toleranzforschung*, ed. Alois Wierlacher, Kulturthemen 2 (Munich: iudicium, 1996).
86. Further discussion of this issue will be provided in Cary J. Nederman's monograph *Worlds of Difference: European Discourses of Toleration, c.1100–c.1550* (University Park: Pennsylvania State University Press, 2000); see also Michael Goodich's contribution to this volume, "Foreigner, Foe and Neighbor: the Religious Cult as a Forum for Political Reconciliation."
87. Ulrich Müller, "Toleranz zwischen Christen und Muslimen im Mittelalter? Zur Archäologie der Beziehungen zwischen dem christlich-lateinischen Okzident und dem islamischen Orient," *Kulturthema Toleranz* (1996) 307–53.
88. For a brief synopsis and critical assessment, see Marion E. Gibbs and Sidney M. Johnson, *Medieval German Literature: A Companion*, Garland Reference Library of the Humanities 1774 (New York and London: Garland, 1997), 194–202.
89. Wolfram von Eschenbach, *Willehalm*, trans. Marion E. Gibbs and Sidney M. Johnson (Harmondsworth, Middlesex: Penguin, 1984), 155f. (Book VI).
90. *Willehalm*, 157.
91. Karl Bertau, "Das Recht des Andern: Über den Ursprung der Vorstellung von einer Schonung der Irrgläubigen bei Wolfram von Eschenbach," ibid., *Wolfram von Eschenbach. Neun Versuche über Subjektivität und Ursprünglichkeit in der Geschichte* (Munich: Beck, 1983), 241–58; Carl Lofmark, "Das Problem des Unglaubens im 'Willehalm'," *Studien zu Wolfram von Eschenbach: Festschrift für Werner Schröder zum 75. Geburtstag*,

ed. Kurt Gärtner and Joachim Heinzle (Tübingen: Niemeyer, 1989), 399–413; Klaus Kirchert, "Heidenkrieg und christliche Schonung des Feindes. Widersprüchliches im 'Willehalm' Wolframs von Eschenbach," *Archiv für das Studium der neueren Sprachen und Literaturen* 146 (1994): 258–70.

92. Joachim Heinzle, "Noch einmal: Die Heiden als Kinder Gottes in Wolframs 'Willehalm'," *Zeitschrift für Deutsche Philologie* 117 (1998): 75–86.
93. Wolfram von Eschenbach, *Parzival*, trans. by A. T. Hatto (London: Penguin, 1980), 21.
94. For further aspects in recent Wolfram research, see *A Companion to Wolfram's Parzival*, ed. Will Hasty, Studies in German Literature, Linguistics, and Culture (Columbia, S.C.: Camden House, 1999).
95. Most recently, Waltraud Fritsch-Rößler, *Finis Amoris: Ende, Gefährdung und Wandel von Liebe im hochmittelalterlichen deutschen Roman*, Mannheimer Beiträge zur Sprach- und Literaturwissenschaft 42 (Tübingen: Narr, 1999), 184–86, argued that Wolfram left this passage deliberately vague, as Gahmuret's reasons could both be the ending of his love for Belacane—though very unlikely—or his religious compunctions—equally unreasonable. Instead, Fritsch-Rößler thinks that Gahmuret could not return to his beloved for a number of circumstantial reasons, even though he wanted, which is not a very convincing interpretation either. See my review forthcoming in *Mediaevistik*.
96. Dione Flühler-Kreis, "Er ist ein Schwarzer, daran ist kein Zweifel: Zur Darstellung des Mohren und zum Toleranzbegriff im Mittelalter," *Bild und Abbild vom Menschen im Mittelalter. Akten der Akademie Friesach "Stadt und Kultur im Mittelalter" Friesach (Kärnten), 9.–13. September 1998*, ed. Elisabeth Vavra, Schriftenreihe der Akademie Friesach 6 (Klagenfurt: Wieser, 1999), 147–72; here 153–55; for further references regarding Blacks in medieval art and literature, see there.
97. For a further investigation of this text and its underlying humanistic ideals, see David F. Tinsley's contribution to this volume, "The Face of the Foreigner in Medieval German Courtly Literature."
98. Andreas Mielke, *Nigra sum et formosa: Afrikanerinnen in der deutschen Literatur des Mittelalters: Texte und Kontexte zum Bild des Afrikaners in der literarischen Imagologie*, Helfant Texte T 11 (Stuttgart: helfant edition, 1992), 103f.
99. *Les Cathares en Occitanie*. A l'initiative de Robert Lafont: avec la collaboration de Paul Labal, et al. (Paris: Fayard, 1982).
100. Robert Ian Moore, *The Formation of a Persecuting Society: Power and Deviance in Western Europe, 950–1250* (Oxford: Blackwell, 1987); Preston King, *Toleration* (London: Allen and Unwin, 1976); see also Henry Kamen, *The Rise of Toleration* (New York: McGraw-Hill, 1967); Jeffrey Richards, *Sex, Dissonance and Damnation: Minority Groups in the Middle Ages* (London: Routledge, 1990); David Nirenberg, *Communities of Violence: Persecution of Minorities in the Middle Ages* (Princeton: Princeton University Press, 1996).
101. Art Kleiner, *The Age of Heretics: Heroes, Outlaws, and the Forerunners of Corporate Change* (New York: Currency Doubleday, 1996); more from a

historical perspective, see Arno Borst, *Medieval Worlds: Barbarians, Heretics, and Artists in the Middle Ages* (Cambridge and Oxford: Polity Press, in association with B. Blackwell, 1991); Walter Nigg, *The Heretics* (New York: Dorsett Press, 1990); Chas Clifton, *Encyclopedia of Heresies and Heretics* (Santa Barbara: ABC-CLIO, 1992).

102. R. I. Moore, *The Birth of Popular Heresy*, Medieval Academy Reprints for Teaching 33 (1975; Toronto, Buffalo, and London: University of Toronto Press, in association with the Medieval Academy of America, 1995), vii.
103. R. I. Moore, *The Birth of Popular Heresy*, 6.
104. Cary J. Nederman, "Introduction: Discourses and Contexts of Tolerance in Medieval Europe," *Beyond the Persecuting Society: Religious Toleration Before the Enlightenment*, ed. John Christian Laursen and Cary J. Nederman (Philadelphia: University of Pennsylvania Press, 1998), 13–24l; here 15.
105. See the contribution by Cary J. Nederman to this volume.
106. Sharon Kinoshita, "The Politics of Courtly Love: *La Prise d'Orange* and the Conversion of the Saracen Queen," *Romance Review* 86, 2 (1995): 265–87.
107. Edward Said, *Orientalism* (1978; Harmondsworth: Penguin, 1995).
108. Albrecht Classen, "Multiculturalism in the German Middle Ages? The Rediscovery of a Modern Concept in the Past: The Case of *Herzog Ernst*," *Multiculturalism and Representation: Selected Essays*, ed. John Rieder, Larry E. Smith, Literary Studies East and West 10 (Honolulu: College of Languages, Linguistics and Literatures, University of Hawaii, 1996), 198–219; ibid., "Confrontation with the Foreign World of the East: Saracen Princesses in Medieval German Narratives," *Orbis Litterarum* 53 (1998): 277–95.
109. Gloria Allaire, "Noble Saracen or Muslim Enemy? The Changing Image of the Saracen in Late Medieval Italian Literature," *Western Views of Islam*, 173–84.
110. Nina Dulin-Mallory, " 'Seven trewe bataylis for Jesus sake': The Long-Suffering Saracen Palomides," *Western Views of Islam*, 165–72; here 172.
111. At the end, of course, the Christian hero wins against all odds and defeats the Persian king. Nevertheless, Konrad did not hesitate to portray the heathen as an highly idealized figure; see my contribution to this volume.
112. Sir Thomas Malory, *Le Morte D'Arthur*, ed. Janet Cowen. With an Introduction by John Lawlor (1969; Harmondsworth, Middlesex: Penguin, 1979), 317f. (book VIII, 9).
113. Cary J. Nederman, "Liberty, Community, and Toleration: Freedom and Function in Medieval Political Thought," *Difference and Dissent: Theories of Toleration in Medieval and Early Modern Europe*, ed. Cary J. Nederman and John Christian Laursen (Lanham, Boulder, et al.: Rowman & Littlefield, 1996), 17–37; here 18; see also Alasdair MacIntyre, *After Virtue*. 2nd ed. (London: Duckworth, 1981), 165; Constantin Fasolt, *Council and Hierarchy* (Chicago: University of Chicago Press, 1991), 103.
114. Marvin Fox, *Interpreting Maimonides: Studies in Methodology, Metaphysics, and Moral Philosophy*, Chicago Studies in the History of Judaism (Chicago: University of Chicago Press, 1990).
115. John Marenbon, *The Philosophy of Peter Abelard* (Cambridge [England] and New York : Cambridge University Press, 1997).

116. Constant J. Mews, "Peter Abelard and the Enigma of Dialogue," *Beyond the Persecuting Society*, 25–52; here 45.
117. *Medieval Culture and Society*, ed. David Herlihy (1968; Prospect Heights, IL: Waveland Press, 1993), 158–65; Heinrich Fichtenau, *Heretics and Scholars in the High Middle Ages: 1000–1200*, trans. Denise A. Kaiser (1992; University Park: The Pennsylvania State University Press, 1998), 215ff. et passim. Fichtenau emphasizes, 223: "This ratiocinative mode of thought emerged slowly from the shadow of spirituality. There now arose a speculative theology, at home ever less in the monastic community and ever more in the academic one." See also Giles Constable, *The Reformation of the Twelfth Century* (1996; Cambridge: Cambridge University Press, 1998), 141–47.
118. Ruedi Imbach, "Selbsterkenntnis und Dialog: Aspekte des philosophischen Denkens im 12. Jahrhundert," *Aspekte des 12. Jahrhunderts. Freisinger Kolloquium 1998*, ed. Wolfgang Haubrichs, Eckhart C. Lutz, Gisela Vollmann-Profe. Wolfram-Studien XVI (Berlin: Schmidt, 2000), 11–28, here 25–28; see also John Tolan, *Petrus Alfonsi and His Medieval Readers* (Gainesville, Tallahassee, et al.: University Press of Florida, 1993), 19, takes a more negative stand: "Despite the calm, polite tone of Peter's and Moses' arguments, the *Dialogi* present a radically new attack on Judaism, far more negative than the Latin works of the Augustinian tradition. Judaism for Alfonsi is a conspiratorial, anti-Christian sect." And: "Alfonsi was the first Latin writer of anti-Jewish polemic to assert that the Jews were guilty of deicide. . . ."
119. Peter Abelard, *Ethical Writings: His Ethics or "Know Yourself" and His Dialogue between a Philosopher, a Jew and a Christian*, trans. Paul Vincent Spade. With an Introduction by Marilyn McCord Adams (Indianapolis: Hackett Publishing, 1995), xi: "The interlocutors thus display semi-enlightend tolerance."
120. *Aufklärung im Mittelalter? Die Verurteilung von 1277*. Das Dokument des Bischofs von Paris eingeleitet, übersetzt und erklärt von Kurt Flasch, excerpta classica VI (Mainz: Dieterich'sche Verlagsbuchhandlung, 1989); see also Ralph McInerny, *Aquinas against the Averroists. On There Being Only One Intellect* (West Lafayette: Purdue University Press, 1993); *Das Licht der Vernunft,* ed. Kurt Flasch, Udo Reinhold Jeck, 1997.
121. Quoted from *The Portable Medieval Reader*, ed., James Bruce Ross and Mary Martin McLaughlin (1949; New York: The Viking Press, 1960), 257; for a more recent translation, see John of Salisbury, *Policraticus: of the Frivolities of Courtiers and the Footprints of Philosophers*, ed. and trans. Cary J. Nederman, Cambridge Texts in the History of Political Thought (Cambridge [England] and New York: Cambridge University Press, 1990). For a particularly interesting but also exceptional case, see the history of medieval Lithuania and its slow conversion to Christianity which could not be enforced by the Western Church. In 1323, King Gediminias (1316–41), declared publicly: "I permit any man to live in my land according to his customs and his Faith." Quoted from Rasa Mazeika, "Bargaining for Baptism. Lithuanian Negotiations for Conversions, 1250–1358," *Varieties of Religious Conversion in the Middle Ages*, ed. James Muldoon (Gainesville, Tallahassee, et al.: University

Press of Florida, 1997), 131–45; here 140. For a critical assessment of John of Salisbury's notion of tolerance, see Cary J. Nederman, "Toleration, Skepticism, and the 'Clash of Ideas': Principles of Liberty in the Writings of John of Salisbury," *Beyond the Persecuting Society*, 53–70.

122. See the valuable contributions to *Die Begegnung des Westens mit dem Osten. Kongressakten des 4: Symposions des Mediävistenverbandes in Köln 1991 aus Anlass des 1000: Todesjahres der Kaiserin Theophanu*, ed. Odilo Engels and Peter Schreiner (Sigmaringen: Thorbecke, 1993); Franco Hilario, "La construction d'une utopie: l'Empire de Pretre Jean," *Journal of Medieval History* 23 (1997): 211–225.

123. Janetta Rebold Benton, "Gargoyles: Animal Imagery and Artistic Individuality in Medieval Art,"*Animals in the Middle Ages: A Book of Essays*, ed. Nona C. Flores, Garland Medieval Casebooks 13 (New York and London: Garland, 1996), 147–65; here 157.

124. Janetta Rebold Benton, "Gargoyles," 157.

125. Janetta Rebold Benton, "Gargoyles," 159.

126. Janetta Rebold Benton, "Gargoyles," 160.

127. Janetta Rebold Benton, "Gargoyles," 163; see also Michael Camille, *Image on the Edge: The Margins of Medieval Art* (Cambridge, Mass.: Harvard University Press, 1992), 78–84; cf. also the vast number of wood and stone carvings, not to forget the infinite drôleries in medieval manuscripts, see Anthony Weir and James Jerman, *Images of Lust: Sexual Carvings on Medieval Churches* (London: B. T. Batsford, 1986); consult also Nurith Kenaan-Kedar, "The Margins of Society in Marginal Romanesque Sculpture," *Gesta* 31 (1992): 15–24; Peter Dinzelbacher, "Monster und Dämonen am Kirchenbau," in *Dämonen, Monster, Fabelwesen*, ed. Ulrich Müller, Werner Wunderlich, Mittelalter Mythen 2 (St. Gallen: UVK. Fachverlag für Wissenschaft und Studium, 1999), 103–26.

128. Bernhard of Clairvaux, *Apologia*, 12, 29, *Opera*, ed. Jean Leclercq et al. (Rome: Editiones Cistercienses, 1957), vol. III, 106.

129. Katrin Kröll, "Der schalkhaft beredsame Leib als Medium verborgener Wahrheit," Katrin Kröll, Hugo Steger, eds., *Mein ganzer Körper ist Gesicht. Groteske Darstellungen in der europäischen Kunst und Literatur des Mittelalters*, Rombach Wissenschaft. Reihe Litterae 26 (Freiburg: Rombach, 1994), 239–94; Albrecht Classen, "Gargoyles—Wasserspeier: Phantasieprodukte des Mittelalters und der Moderne," *Dämonen, Monster, Fabelwesen*, 1999, 127–33.

130. *The Nibelungenlied*. A New Translation by A. T. Hatto (1965; Harmondsworth, Middlesex: Penguin, 1979); see also Winder McConnell, *The Nibelungenlied*, Twayne's World Authors Series, TWAS 712 (Boston: Twayne Publishers, 1984); Otfrid Ehrismann, *Nibelungenlied. Epoche—Werk—Wirkung*, Arbeitsbücher zur Literaturgeschichte (Munich: Beck, 1987); Theodore M. Andersson, *A Preface to the Nibelungenlied* (Stanford: Stanford University Pres, 1987); Gottfried Weber, *Nibelungenlied*. 6., überarbeitete und erw. Aufl. des Bandes *Nibelungenlied* by Werner Hoffmann, Sammlung Metzler 7. (Stuttgart: Metzler, 1992); Edward Haymes, *The Nibelungenlied: History and Interpretation*, Illinois Medieval Monographs 2 (Urbana: University of Illinois Press, 1986).

131. Joyce Tally Lionarons, "The Otherworld and its Inhabitants in the *Nibelungenlied*," *A Companion to the Nibelungenlied*, ed. Winder McConnell, Studies in German Literature, Linguistics, and Culture (Columbia, S.C.: Camden House, 1998), 153–71; here 167.
132. Edward R. Haymes, "Preface," *The Dark Figure in Medieval German and Germanic Literature*, ed. E. R. Haymes and Stephanie Cain Van D'Elden, Göppinger Arbeiten zur Germanistik 448 (Göppingen: Kümmerle, 1986), iii–vi; here iv.
133. Haymes, "Preface," vi.; see also Holger Homann, "The Hagen Figure in the Nibelungenlied: Know Him by His Lies," *Modern Language Notes* 97 (1982): 759–769; Peter Wapnewski, "Hagen: ein Gegenspieler?," *Gegenspieler*, ed. Thomas Cramer and Werner Dahlheim. Dichtung und Sprache 12 (Munich: Carl Hanser, 1993), 62–73; Albrecht Classen, "Das heroische Element im *Nibelungenlied*—Ideal oder Fluch?," *Ir sult sprechen willekomen. Grenzenlose Mediävistik. Festschrift für Helmut Birkhan zum 60. Geburtstag*, ed. Christa Tuczay, Ulrike Hirhager, and Karin Lichtblau (Bern, Berlin, Frankfurt a.M., et al.: Peter Lang, 1998), 673–92.
134. Strangely, Walter Haug, "Mündlichkeit, Schriftlichkeit und Fiktionalität," *Modernes Mittelalter: Neue Bilder einer populären Epoche*, ed. Joachim Heinzle (Frankfurt a.M.: Insel, 1994), 376–97; here 396f., argues that many of the events which take place in the *Nibelungenlied* remain inexplicable, irrational, and unmotivated. "Die sich im ersten Teil als sinnlos (sic!) darstellende heroische Vergangenheit aufersteht als Sinnlosigkeit menschlichen Verhaltens . . . Man versucht, die heroische Welt zu überwinden; es gelingt nicht, vielmehr erfährt man, indem man sich auf sie einläßt, ihre Sinnlosigkeit am Ende als Macht der eigenen Seele" (397) [The heroic past presented in the first part emerges as a metaphor of the meaninglessness of human behavior . . . The characters try to overcome the heroic world, but it does not work. On the contrary, they learn that when they plunge into it at the end meaninglessness turns out to be a force of the own soul]. This in itself is a meaningless statement and does not offer any significant insight in the *Nibelungenlied*.
135. Joachim Heinzle, "The Manuscripts of the Nibelungenlied," *A Companion to the Nibelungenlied*, 105–126; see also Joachim Bumke, *Die vier Fassungen der 'Nibelungenklage.' Untersuchungen zur Überlieferungsgeschichte und Textkritik der höfischen Epik im 13. Jahrhundert*, Quellen und Forschungen zur Literatur- und Kulturgeschichte 8 (242) (Berlin and New York: de Gruyter, 1996).
136. If we include the "Lied vom hürnen Seyfrid," a balladic derivation of the *Nibelungenlied*, which was first printed around 1530—we do not have any handwritten copies—then the reception process really never came to an end; see Bodo Gotzkowsky, *"Volksbücher." Prosaromane, Renaissancenovellen, Versdichtungen und Schwankbücher: Bibliographie der deutschen Drucke*. Part One: *Drucke des 15. und 16. Jahrhunderts*, Bibliotheca Bibliographica Aureliana CXXV (Baden-Baden: Verlag Valentin Koerner, 1991), 335–47; see also Albrecht Classen, *The German Volksbuch. A Critical History of a Late-Medieval Genre*, Studies in German Language and Literature 15

(Lewiston, Queenston, and Lampeter: The Edwin Mellen Press, 1995), 1, 5, 24f., 33, et passim.

137. Siegfried Grosse, Ursula Rautenberg, *Die Rezeption mittelalterlicher deutscher Dichtung: Eine Bibliographie ihrer Übersetzungen und Bearbeitungen seit der Mitte des 18. Jahrhunderts* (Tübingen: Niemeyer, 1989), 166–230; Werner Hoffmann, "The Reception of the *Nibelungenlied* in the Twentieth Century," *A Companion to the Nibelungenlied*, 127–152.
138. See Alexander Sager's contribution to this volume, "Hungarians as *vremde* in Medieval Germany."
139. See, for example, Donald E. Queller, *The Office of Ambassador in the Middle Ages* (Princeton: Princeton University Press, 1967); Heinz-Dieter Heimann, Ivan Hlavác^*ek, eds., Kommunikationspraxis und Korrespondenzwesen im Mittelalter und in der Renaissance* (Paderborn: Ferdinand Schöningh, 1998); Jacques Merceron, *Le message et sa fiction: La communication par messager dans la littérature française des XII*[e] *et XIII*[e] *siècles*, University of California Publications in Modern Philology 128 (Berkeley, Los Angeles, and London: University of California Press, 1998); *New Approaches to Medieval Communication*, ed. Marco Mostert, with an Introduction by Michael Clanchy, Utrecht Studies in Medieval Literacy 1 (Turnhout: Brepols, 1999).
140. Most recently, Verio Santoro has discovered a German-Arabic dictionary from before 1477, " 'Teustzß uss saracenisse gedolmetzt'. Il lexicon Germanico-Arabicum della Biblioteca Apostolica Vaticana, Pal. lat. 607 (ff. 2r–4r)," *Medioevo e Rinascimento* XIII/ns. X (1999): 271–92.
141. de Hartog, *Genghis Khan*, 1999, 186–90; Ulrich Müller, "Dschinghis Khan und die Dschingisiden: 'Der Kaiser aller Menschen', die Mongolen und Mogule," in *Herrscher, Helden Heilige,* Ulrich Müller, Werner Wunderlich, Mittelalter Mythen 1 (St. Gallen: UVK Fachverlag für Wissenschaft und Studium, 1996), 173–96.
142. Albrecht Classen, "Marco Polos Iil Milione / Le Divisament dou Monde: Der Mythos vom Osten," *Herrscher, Helden, Heilige*, 1996, 423–36.
143. Wilhelm Baum, *Die Verwandlungen des Mythos vom Reich des Priesterkönigs Johannes: Rom, Byzanz und die Christen des Orients im Mittelalter* (Klagenfurt: Verlag Kitab, 1999), 177–87. For further references to contacts between medieval Europe and Asia, see his extensive bibliography; see also Wilhelm Baum, Raimund Senoner, *Indien und Europa im Mittelalter: Die Eingliederung des Kontinents in das europäische Bewußtsein bis ins 15. Jahrhundert* (Klagenfurt: Kitab, 2000); the most solid treatment of this topic can now be found in Marina Münkler, *Erfahrung des Fremden. Die Beschreibung Ostasiens in den Augenzeugenberichten des 13, und 14, Jahrhunderts* (Berlin: Akademie-Verlag, 2000).
144. See David Leshock's contribution to this volume.
145. M. Campbell, *The Witness and the Other World*, 123.
146. M. Campbell, *The Witness and the Other World*, 153.
147. Anthony Grafton, with April Shelford and Nancy Siraisi, *New Worlds, Ancient Texts: The Power of Tradition and the Shock of Discovery* (Cambridge, Mass., and London: The Belknap Press of Harvard University Press, 1992), 71.

148. Valerie I. J. Flint, *The Imaginative Landscape of Christopher Columbus* (Princeton: Princeton University Press, 1992), 53f., 99f.
149. Donald R. Howard, *Writers and Pilgrims: Medieval Pilgrimage Narratives and Their Posterity* (Berkeley, Los Angeles, and London: The University of California Press, 1980), 58; see also his "The World of Mandeville's Travels," *Yearbook of English Studies* 1 (1971): 1–17.
150. Klaus Ridder, *Jean de Mandevilles Reisen: Studien zur Überlieferungsgeschichte der deutschen Übersetzung des Otto von Diemeringen*, Münchener Texte und Untersuchungen zur deutschen Literatur des Mittelalters 99 (Tübingen: Niemeyer, 1991), 9.
151. *Sir Gawain and the Green Knight: A Dual-Language Version*, ed. and trans. William Vantuono (New York and London: Garland Publishing, 1991).
152. Richard H. Osberg, "Rewriting Romance: From *Sir Gawain* to *The Green Knight*," *The Future of the Middle Ages and the Renaissance: Problems, Trends, and Opportunities for Research*, ed. Roger Dahood, Arizona Studies in the Middle Ages and the Renaissance 2 (Turnhout: Brepols, 1998), 93–108.
153. For the relevant comments of modern scholarship on *Sir Gawain and the Green Knight*, see W. Vantuono; now also see Robert J. Blanch and Julian N. Wasserman, *From Pearl to Gawain: Forme to Fynisment* (Gainesville, Tallahassee, et al.: University Press of Florida, 1995), 9, especially 33–43.
154. Richard Kieckhefer, *Magic in the Middle* Ages (Cambridge: Cambridge University Press, 1990); Le *merveilleux et la magie dans la littérature*, ed. by Gérard Chandès. Cermeil, 2 (Amsterdam and Atlanta: Editions Rodopi, 1992); regarding the emerging new culture of magic and occultism in the early-modern age, see Gerhild Scholz Williams, *Defining Dominion. The Discourse of Magic and Witchcraft in Early Modern France and Germany*, Studies in Medieval and Early Modern Civilization (Ann Arbor: The University of Michigan Press, 1995).
155. Dante Alighieri, *The Divine Comedy*, trans., Charles S. Singleton. *Inferno.* 1: *Italian Text and Translation*, Bollingen Series LXXX (Princeton: Princeton University Press, 1970), Canto 1, 1–9.
156. Charles Dahlberg, *The Literature of Unlikeness* (Hanover and London: University Press of New England, 1988), 3.
157. John Clayton, "The Otherness of Anselm," *The Otherness of God*, ed. Orrin F. Summerell. Studies in Religion and Culture (Charlottesville and London: University Press of Virginia, 1998), 14–34; here 14f.
158. Meister Eckhart, *Selected Writings*, sel. and trans. Oliver Davies (London: Penguin, 1994), 29.
159. Mechthild of Magdeburg, *The Flowing Light of the Godhead*, trans. Frank Tobin, pre. Margot Schmid, The Classics of Western Spirituality 91 (Mahwah, N.J.: Paulist Press, 1998), 42.
160. Ray L. Hart, "God and Creature in the Eternity and Time of Nonbeing (or Nothing): AfterThinking Meister Eckhart," *The Otherness of God*, 35–59; here 37.
161. Josef Semmler, ed., *Der Wald in Mittelalter und Renaissance*, 1991. The various contributions to this volume indicate that the forest could either be

used as a metaphor of religious refuge, or as a dangerous location where robbers and wild animals roamed.

162. Here quoted from Jeff Rider, "The Other Worlds of Romance," 2000, 122.
163. *Alexanderdichtungen im Mittelalter: Kulturelle Selbstbestimmung im Kontext literarischer Beziehungen*, ed. Jan Cölln, Susanne Friede, and Hartmut Wulfram, together with Ruth Finckh, Veröffentlichungen aus dem Göttinger Sonderforschungsbereich 529 "Internationalität nationaler Literaturen 1 (Göttingen: Wallstein Verlag, 2000).
164. J. W. Thomas, "The Other Kingdom in the Arthurian Romances of Medieval Germany and the Motif of Departure and Return," *Germanic Notes and Reviews* 25 (1994): 3–5; Jeff Rider, "Marvels and the Marvelous," Norris J. Lacy, ed., *The Arthurian Encyclopedia*, 2nd ed. (New York: Garland, 1991), 311–13; see also the still valuable study by Howard Rollin Patch, *The Other World According to Descriptions in Medieval Literature*, Smith College Studies in Modern Languages, New Series (Cambridge, Mass.: Harvard University Press, 1950).
165. Ludwig Schrader, ed., *Alternative Welten in Mittelalter und Renaissance*, Studia humaniora 10 (Düsseldorf: Droste, 1988).
166. Georg Wieland, "Das Eigene und das Andere. Theoretische Elemente zum Begriff der Toleranz im hohen und späten Mittelalter," *Toleranz im Mittelalter*, 1998, 11–25; here 14.
167. Yosef Hayim Yerushalmi, "Medieval Jewry: From Within and From Without," *Aspects of Jewish Culture in the Middle Ages*, ed. Paul E. Szarmach (Albany: State University of New York Press, 1979), 1–26; here 24; Albrecht Classen, "Jüdisch-deutsche Literatur des Mittelalters und der Frühneuzeit als Dokumente des Kulturaustauschs: Mit besonderer Beachtung jüdisch-deutscher Volkslieder des 16. Jahrhunderts," *Amsterdamer Beiträge zur älteren Germanistik* 50 (1998): 185–207.
168. Leonard B. Glick's observation, "[t]he reason for their survival, of course, was that they were useful—often all but indispensable—as sources of liquid capital. But once that usefulness declined, they were doomed" (*Abraham's Heirs*, 274), is certainly one-sided and too negative, even though it contains a significant kernel of truth. See also Sara Lipton, *Images of Intolerance: the Representation of Jews and Judaism in the Bible moralisée*, The S. Mark Taper Foundation Imprint in Jewish Studies (Berkeley and London: University of California Press, 1999). But there were also many, heretofore unaccounted examples of cultural interaction, exchange, and cooperation, so when a Freiburg manuscript (Hs. 163, f. 96^{v}) refers to a Jewish painter: "littera curiosior directa pictori iudeo," quoted from Christian Kiening, *Schwierige Modernität. Der* >Ackermann< des Johannes von Tepl und die Ambiguität historischen Wandels, Münchener Texte und Untersuchungen zur deutschen Literatur des Mittelalters 113 (Tübingen: Niemeyer, 1998), 58; see also Gavin Langmuir, *History, Religion and Antisemitism* (Berkeley: University of California Press, 1990); in clear contradistinction to him, Anna Sapir Abulafia, "Twelfth-Century Renaissance Theology and the Jews," *From Witness to Witchcraft*, 125–39; see also Jeremy Cohen, "The Muslim Connection or On the Changing Role of Jews in High Medieval Theology," ibid., 141–62.

169. John Y. B. Hood, *Aquinas and the Jews*, Middle Ages Series (Philadelphia: University of Pennsylvania Press, 1995), 110: "The cornerstone of medieval toleration was the notion that it was somehow beneficial to Christians that Jews continue to exist in their midst. Aquinas and others continued to support this view, but in terms of social reality their arguments had ceased to make sense."
170. Wieland, "Das Eigene und das Andere," 20f.
171. *The Dark Figure*, ed. Edward R. Haymes and Stephanie Cain Van D'Elden, 1986.
172. Although very little known by literary scholarship, Heinrich's *Diu Crône* offers fascinating and almost disturbing concepts of how the world of the 'self' can be challenged by 'the other.' Heinrich von dem Türlin, *The Crown. A Tale of Sir Gawein and King Arthur's Court*. Trans. and with an Introduction by J. W. Thomas (Lincoln and London: University of Nebraska Press, 1989); Hartmut Bleumer's *Die >Crône< Heinrichs von dem Türlin. Form-Erfahrung und Konzeption eines späten Artusromans*, Münchener Texte und Untersuchungen zur deutschen Literatur des Mittelalters 112 (Tübingen: Niemeyer, 1997), proves to be disappointing as he limits his investigation of the "Wunderketten" to a theological interpretation where the miracles are seen as religious symbols only, whereas the novelty of Heinrich's romance is described as a simple experiment with the figure constellation; see my review in *Seminar* XXXV, 4 (1999), 345–47.
173. *The Stranger in Medieval Society*, ed. F. R. P. Akehurst and Stephanie Cain Van D'Elden, Medieval Cultures 12 (Minneapolis and London: University of Minneapolis Press, 1997), vii.
174. Unfortunately she does not even mention the most famous knight in disguise, the thirteenth-century Styrian knight Ulrich von Liechtenstein who authored the well-known *Frauendienst*, ed. Franz Viktor Spechtler, Göppinger Arbeiten zur Germanistik 485 (Göppingen: Kümmerle, 1987).
175. *Fremdes wahrnehmen–fremdes Wahrnehmen: Studien zur Geschichte der Wahrnehmung und zur Begegnung von Kulturen in Mittelalter und früher Neuzeit*, ed. Wolfgang Harms and C. Stephen Jaeger, together with Alexandra Stein (Stuttgart and Leipzig: S. Hirzel, 1997); see also my review in *Leuvense Bijdragen* 87 (1998): 259–63.
176. Alexander's adventures in the east and his encounters with monsters served Ulrich von Etzenbach to explore the construction of gender and sexuality in his eponymous romance, composed sometime between 1270 and 1286. Kerstin Schmitt, "Minne, Monster, Mutationen: Geschlechterkonstruktionen im 'Alexanderroman' Ulrichs von Etzenbach," *Natur und Kultur in der deutschen Literatur des Mittelalters*, 1999, 151–62; here 162, points out: "Im Monstrum verwischen sich die Eindeutigkeiten des geschlechtlichen Körpers (*sex*): sie oszillieren zwischen Mann und Frau wie bei den bärtigen Frauen, werden zu monströsen Gegenbildern, wie bei den schweineartigen Frauen, oder vermischen sich, wie bei den *konocefalî*, so mit ihren tierischen Anteilen, daß sie kein Geschlecht mehr zulassen."
177. *Other Middle Ages: Witnesses at the Margins of Medieval Society*, ed. Michael Goodich, The Middle Ages Series (Philadelphia: University of Pennsylvania Press, 1998), 3.

178. Jeffrey Jerome Cohen, "Introduction," *The Postcolonial Middle Ages*, 2000, 5.
179. Jeffrey Jerome Cohen, "Hybrids, Monsters, Borderlands: The Bodies of Gerald of Wales," *The Postcolonial Middle Ages* (2000), 85–104; here 98; see also Michael Goodich's contribution to this volume.
180. Goodich, ed., *Witnesses*, 4.
181. Friedrich Heer, *The Medieval World*, 309.
182. "Witchcraft, Magic, and the Jews in Late Medieval and Early Modern Germany," *From Witness to Witchcraft*, 419–33.
183. L. B. Glick, *Abraham's Heirs*, 1999, 270, argues to the opposite: "Not much needs to be said about the period between about 1350 and 1500, for these were terminal years for western European Jewry, years characterized for the most part by steady decline in population and very difficult social circumstances." Most historians would agree with him, but examples illustrating the opposite case can often be cited. The famous German *Meistersänger* Hans Sachs refers to a rich Jew in his comedy "Die jung witfraw Francisca" (1560), who had been murdered by a (Christian) merchant. When two night watchmen believe to have identified the latter, they make every effort to apprehend him, because otherwise they would face a severe penalty by the authorities. To be sure, Sachs does not harbor any specific sympathy for the Jew, but he nevertheless calls the merchant a murderer and implies that he needs to be thrown into prison and brought to justice. *Hans Sachs*, ed. A. v. Keller and E. Goetze, vol. 20 (1892; Hildesheim: Georg Olms, 1964), A 5, 2, 225a, 47–63.
184. Christopher R. Friedrichs, "Anti-Jewish Politics in Early Modern Germany: The Uprising in Worms, 1613–17," *Central European History* 23 (1990): 91–152; Ronnie Po-chia Hsia, "Bürgeraufstand in Worms 1614: Judenprivilegien und Bürgerrechte in der frühen Neuzeit: ein Widerspruch?," *Aussenseiter zwischen Mittelalter und Neuzeit: Festschrift für Hans-Jürgen Goertz zum 60. Geburtstag*, ed. Norbert Fischer and Marion Kobelt-Groch, Studies in Medieval and Reformation Thought LXI (Leiden, New York, and Cologne: Brill, 1997), 101–110.
185. See, for instance, Márta Font, "On the Frontiers of West and East: The Hungarian Kingdom and the Galician Principality Between the Eleventh and Thirteenth Centuries," *Annual of Medieval Studies at CEU* 6 (2000), ed. Katalin Szende and Marcell Sebök (Budapest: Central European University, Department of Medieval Studies, 2000), 171–80; cf. also the other contributions to this volume.
186. Alexander Patschovsky, "Toleranz im Mittelalter: Idee und Wirklichkeit," *Toleranz im Mittelalter* (1998), 391–402.
187. See the excellent discussion of this enormously complex situation by Bob Scribner, "Wie wird man Aussenseiter? Ein- und Ausgrenzung im frühneuzeitlichen Deutschland," *Aussenseiter zwischen Mittelalter und Neuzeit*, 21–46; see also Erich Goode, Nachman Ben-Yehuda, *Moral Panics. The Social Construction of Deviance* (Cambridge, Mass.: Blackwell, 1994); for a history of the goliards, see Wolfgang Hartung, *Die Spielleute. Eine Randgruppe in der Gesellschaft des Mittelalters*, Vierteljahresschrift für Sozial- und Wirtschaftsgeschichte. Beihefte 72 (Wiesbaden: Steiner, 1982).

188. E. Schubert, *Fahrendes Volk im Mittelalter*, 1995, 31, emphasizes: "Mobilität gehört zur Vitalsituation des mittelalterlichen Menschen" (mobility characterizes the vital situation of medieval people). He also points out that merchants regularly left their home community to trade with people in different lands, hence transgressed communal barriers and communicated with 'the other' via their profession. See also Helen Waddell, *The Wandering Scholars*. 3rd ed. (1900; Boston: Houghton Mifflin, 1927), and Michel Mollat, *The Poor in the Middle Ages: an Essay in Social History* (1978; New Haven: Yale University Press, 1986).
189. Karl Bertau, "Das Recht des Andern," 1983; Rainer Christoph Schwinges, *Kreuzzugsideologie und Toleranz: Studien zu Wilhelm von Tyrus*, Monographien zur Geschichte des Mittelalters 15 (Stuttgart: Hiersemann, 1977); R. W. Southern, *Western Views of Islam in the Middle Ages* (1962; Cambrigde, Mass.: Harvard University Press, 1978); Rainer Christoph Schwinges, "Die Wahrnehmung des Anderen durch Geschichtsschreibung: Muslime und Christen im Spiegel der Werke Wilhelms von Tyrus († 1186) und Rodrigo Ximénez de Rada († 1247)," *Toleranz im Mittelalter* (1998), 101–127.
190. Blanks and Frassetto, "Introduction," *Western Views of Islam*, 4; see also David Knowles, "Arabian and Jewish Philosophy," ibid., *The Evolution of Medieval Thought*. 2nd ed. D. E. Luscombe, C[hristopher] N[ugent] L[awrence] Brooke (1962; New York: Longman, 1988), 175–86; Michael Haren, *Medieval Thought: The Western Intellectual Tradition from Antiquity to the Thirteenth Century*. 2nd ed. (1985; Toronto and Buffalo: University of Toronto Press, 1992), 118–37.
191. Elizabeth Alvilda Petroff, *Medieval Women's Visionary Literature* (New York and Oxford: Oxford University Press, 1986), 14; see also Peter Dinzelbacher, *Mittelalterliche Frauenmystik* (Paderborn, Munich, et al.: Ferdinand Schöningh, 1992).
192. Albrecht Classen, "Flowing Light of the Godhead. Binary Oppositions of Self and God in Mechthild von Magdeburg," *Studies in Spirituality* 7 (1997): 79–98.
193. See the now almost classical study by Colin Morris, *The Discovery of the Individual: 1050–1200* (London: Society for Promoting Christian Knowledge, 1972); George Duby, Philippe Braunstein, "The Emergence of the Individual," *A History of Private Life*. II: *Revelations of the Medieval World*, ed. Georges Duby, trans. Arthur Goldhammer (Cambridge, Mass., London: The Belknap Press of Harvard University Press, 1988), 507–630.
194. Olaf Pluta, " 'Deus est mortuus.'—Nietzsches Parole 'Gott ist tot!' in einer Geschichte der *Gesta Romanorum* vom Ende des 14. Jahrhunderts," *Atheismus in Mittelalter und in der Renaissance*, ed. Friedrich Niewöhner and Olaf Pluta, Wolfenbütteler Mittelalter-Studien, 12 (Wiesbaden: Harrassowitz, 1999), 239–70.
195. See Leona F. Cordery's contribution to this volume, "Cannibal Diplomacy: Otherness in the Middle English Text *Richard Coer de Lion*."
196. David R. Blanks and Michael Frassetto, "Introduction," *Western Views of Islam*, 1–9; here 3.

197. Quoted from the conclusion of her contribution to this volume, "The Saracen and the Martyr: Embracing the Foreign in Hrotsvit's *Pelagius*."
198. See the critical analysis of John of Salisbury's *Policraticus* and Peter of Celle's *The School of the Cloister* in Cary J. Nederman's contribution to this volume, "Social Bodies and the Non-Christian 'Other' in the Twelfth Century: John of Salisbury and Peter of Celle."
199. Albrecht Classen, "Emergence of Tolerance: An Unsuspected Medieval Phenomenon. Studies on Wolfram von Eschenbach's *Willehalm*, Ulrich von Etzenbach's *Wilhelm von Wenden*, and Johann von Würzburg's *Wilhelm von Österreich*," *Neophilologus* 76 (1992): 586–99; Harry Kühnel, "Das Fremde und das Eigene: Mittelalter," *Europäische Mentalitätsgeschichte: Hauptthemen in Einzeldarstellungen*, ed. Peter Dinzelbacher, Kröners Taschenausgabe 469 (Stuttgart: Kröner, 1993), 415–28.
200. John Phillip Lomax, "Frederick II, His Saracens, and the Papacy," *Medieval Christian Perceptions of Islam: A Book of Essays*, ed. John Victor Tolan, Garland Reference Library of the Humanities, 1768 (New York and London: Garland Publishing, 1996), 175–97; see also Francesco Gabrieli, "Friedrich II. und die Kultur des Islam," *Stupor mundi: Zur Geschichte Friedrichs II. von Hohenstaufen*, ed. Gunther Wolf, Wege der Forschung 101 (Darmstadt: Wissenschaftliche Buchgesellschaft, 1966), 270–88.
201. Hans Niese, "Zur Geschichte des geistigen Lebens am Hofe Kaiser Friedrichs II.," *Historische Zeitschrift* 108 (1912): 473–540; Ernst Kantorowicz, *Kaiser Friedrich der Zweite*. 3rd. ed., Werke aus dem Kreis der Blätter für die Kunst. Geschichtliche Reihe (1927; Berlin: Bondi, 1931), 285–339; Horst Eberhard, *Der Sultan von Lucera: Friedrich II. und der Islam*, Herder Spektrum 4453 (Freiburg: Herder, 1997); David Abulafia, *Frederick II. A Medieval Emperor* (London: Penguin, 1988), questions most of the praise heaped upon the emperor, but even he cannot deny that Frederick's court was amazingly open-minded and receptive to many different ideas.
202. Walter Koller, "Toleranz im Königreich Sizilien zur Zeit der Nomannen," *Toleranz im Mittelalter* (1998), 159–85; further references can be found here.
203. Ulrich Müller, "Toleranz zwischen Christen und Muslimen im Mittelalter?," 1996; see also Lourdes María Alvarez's contribution to this volume, "Anselm Turmeda: The Visionary Humanism of a Muslim Convert and Catalan Prophet."
204. See David F. Tinsley's contribution to this volume, "The Face of the Foreigner in Medieval German Courtly Literature."
205. Odilo Engels, Peter Schreiner, eds., *Die Begegnung des Westens mit dem Osten: Kongreßakten des 4: Symposions des Mediävistenverbandes in Köln 1991 aus Anlaß des 100. Todesjahres der Kaiserin Theophanu* (Sigmaringen: Thorbecke, 1993).
206. Heinrich Fichtenau, *Heretics and Scholars*, 256f.
207. Carlo Ginzburg, *The Cheese and the Worms: The Cosmos of a Sixteenth-Century Miller*, trans. John and Anne Tedeschi (1976; Baltimore: The Johns Hopkins University Press, 1992), 49f., points out that the poor miller

Menocchio admitted to the inquisitor in 1599 that "God the Father has various children whom he loves, such as Christians, Turks, and Jews and to each of them he has given the will to live by his own law, and we do not know which is the right one." This is a clear reference to Boccaccio's *Decameron*, as Menocchio himself indicated a month later.

208. Giovanni Boccaccio, *The Decameron*, trans. Richard Aldington (1930; New York: Dell Publishing, 1970), 61; see also Giovanni Boccaccio, *Decamerone*. Edizione critica secondo l'autografo hamiltoniano, a cura di Vittore Branca (Firenze: Accademia della Crusca, 1976).

209. See, for example, Stefan Rieger, Schamma Schahadat, Manfred Weinberg, eds., *Interkulturalität: Zwischen Inszenierung und Archiv*, Literatur und Anthropologie 6 (Tübingen: Narr, 1999); the theoretical basis and fundamental concepts of modern xenology, at least from a German perspective, have been established by Alois Wierlacher, ed., *Kulturthema Fremdheit. Leitbegriffe und Problemfelder kulturwissenschaftlicher Fremdheitsforschung*, Kulturthemen 1 (Munich: iudicium, 1993); see also *Communicating Across Cultures For What?: a Symposium on Humane Responsibility in Intercultural Communication,* ed. John C. Condon and Miksuko Saito (Tokyo: Simul Press; [Forest Grove, OR; distributed by ISBS], 1976); Katharina Bremer, *Achieving Understanding: Discourse in Intercultural Encounters*, Language in Social Life Series (London: Longman, 1996); Anindita Niyogi Balslev, *Cross-Cultural Conversation: Initiation*, American Academy of Religion Cultural Criticism Series 5 (Atlanta: Scholars Press, 1996).

210. Loring M. Danforth, *The Death Rituals of Rural Greece* (Princeton: Princeton University Press, 1982), 6.

1

The Saracen and the Martyr:

Embracing the Foreign in Hrotsvit's *Pelagius*

LISA WESTON

All saints are foreigners of a sort among other, less holy human beings. However potently they may model correct behavior and subjectivity, their perfection ultimately exceeds imitation. If not, that is, literally foreigners in the national or ethnic sense, they incorporate the distinction as they straddle the boundary between the human Same and the transcendent Other. As Thomas Heffernan has argued, the meaning of saints for their communities arises from exactly this collision, the collision and the conflation of the imperfect earthly and perfect heavenly significations and identities.[1] In this respect martyrs prove especially problematic: as the martyr suffers at the hands of persecutors who are more explicitly and simplistically foreign (in the sense of outside the community which reveres the saint's memory) he or she draws from the faithful responses not only of emulation, affection, and desire, but also of awe, horror, and pathos. And yet, the tortures these foreign persecutors enact upon the martyr's body are precisely what establish the martyr's sanctity—and therefore ironically create the saint's cult. In some measure, then, the persecutors, however foreign, respond to the saint by acting out passions and desires which those who most revere the saint both recognize and refuse.[2] Produced within and serving the needs of a cultic community, hagiographic narrative enacts this inherent negotiation of licit and illicit desires, and the subsequent formation of boundaries between "us" (the saint's community) and "them" (the persecutors and other non-believers) upon the textual body of the saint.

Making manifest the difference of sanctity in a perfect (and adamantly defended) corporeal integrity, the bodies, both physical and textual, of a virgin martyr constitute a particular and provocative focus for such boundary formation. Such is particularly the case in the *Pelagius* of Hrotsvit of Gandersheim (c.935–c.975), a poetic legend in which paradoxical attractions and disavowals bind martyr, murderer, and cult followers within a complex economy of desire and horror, of identification and denial which ultimately troubles and undermines categories like "foreign," "different" and "same." Throughout the corpus of her works, saintly Christian bodies, whether subjected to martyrdom or to the rigors of extreme monastic eremitism, become the site of moral struggle, of literally or metaphorically violent distinction between corporeal integrity and pollution, truth and falsehood, good and evil.[3] The majority of the legends and plays remove the setting of the struggle to the distant, quasi-mythological past of the Age of Martyrs. By contrast, although it deploys similar rhetorical tropes and follows similar narrative structures, Hrotsvit's *Pelagius* related a contemporary tenth-century martyrdom based on eyewitness accounts rather than written sources. Chronological proximity renders interaction with the explicitly foreign persecuting agents more immanent a political possibility for Hrotsvit and her audience, and issues of identification with the foreigner—whether martyr or persecutor—more urgent. The Islamic Spain of the legend constitutes not only a more "realistic" site for definition by religious difference, but also—as the setting is deployed in Hrotsvit's poem—a locus for other contemporary, local cultural anxieties about gender and sexuality.

Although the persecutor of the tale enjoys the same combination of lust and political power as any Dulcitius—to draw an example from one of Hrotsvit's better known dramas—and although the virginal hero resists as adamantly chaste as any Agape, Chionia, or Hirena, Pelagius *is* male. And his gender matters. Granted, male virginity is by no means unknown in medieval hagiography; indeed, in many ways virginity as a construct defies and confounds gender distinction. Hagiographic trials of male virginity rarely, however, involve explicit same-sex desire, seduction, and/or assault. In fact, the text's overt invocation—and subsequent refusal—of same-sex desire characterizes its engagement with the foreign. As Mark Jordan notes, Hrotsvit's text depicts same-sex desire "not as something present within the Christian world, but as alien, repulsive, imposed from without," a relegation in which the "sodomitic vices" of the persecutor are localized and eventually exorcized by being "confine[d] . . . to a single, sinning soul," that of the Saracen king.[4]

That explicit disavowal of illicit, foreign desire stands, however, as but one part of a more complex rhetoric of gender and sexual difference. From the first lines, the narrating Hrotsvit's relation to the saint and especially his body—the beauty of which, physical and/or spiritual, effectively stimulates both licit and illicit desire—is uneasy. In an eleven-line prefatory prayer she addresses the saint as "Glorious Pelagius, most valiant martyr of Christ and soldier of the King who reigns forever."[5] His status as martyr thus equates here with a male identity as soldier of Christ; his virginity is not an issue. Hrotsvit by contrast is his "obedient handmaid."[6] The conjunction of power and gender difference between the soldier and the handmaid underscores the particular (hetero)sexual model for poetic inspiration implicit in her subsequent request that the saint "refresh the dim cave of her understanding with dew from heaven."[7] That metaphorical fecundation creates a worthy song, a new and proper textual body. It also reifies and enacts a heteroeroticism perhaps problematic in a monastic woman like Hrotsvit, and certainly at issue in her other narrations of (female) virgin martyrs.[8]

The gender difference between the saint and the hagiographer and the heterosexuality of the hagiographic process prefaces a narrative set within a virtually complete male homosocial world. From the moment the victorious Saracen king "defiled the ancient mother of pure faith [Cordoba] with barbarian rites,"[9] until such time as the Christian community, explicitly "persons of both sexes,"[10] gather to sing hymns as Pelagius's relics are tested for sanctity, an anxious lack of gender difference pervades the poem. During this time Cordoba is void of songs such as those the learned Hrotsvit might have created; what songs are attempted—by, significantly, "just men who burned to compose sweet songs to Christ and to rebuke in words foolosh idols"[11]—are silenced by martyrdom.

The result of the metaphorical "rape" of Christian Cordoba is a kingdom in which difference both exists and does not exist. That is, the text and its narrator clearly distinguish the Christians and their defeated king from the rather overdetermined barbarous, violent pagan forces and their first leader: the "perfidious race of Saracens," "the leader of a barbarian people," "a man perverse and profane," "a perverse tyrant."[12] Within the text's depicted Cordoba, however, these foreigners co-exist with Christians despite their barbaric customs and religious difference within a *status quo* marked by integration and tolerance. And while tolerance may be a virtue for modern audiences, within Hrotsvit's text it constitutes a paradoxically dangerous erasure of distinction and of the (appropriate) heterosociality from which devotion and reverence arise. After the conquest "pagans are mingled with righteous inhabitants in order to persuade them to discard the customs of their fathers and corrupt themselves."[13] Although initially desiring to erase the difference of Christianity entirely, the conqueror pragmatically issues an unjust decree (unjust in that it eliminates the distinction of just Christians from unjust pagans): Christians are free to follow their religion so long as they do not blaspheme the rites of their Islamic overlords. A peace, albeit a false one, of denial of difference quiets the conquered nation, despite the presence of a now marginalized group of Christians led by saintly zeal to break this mandate by composing songs.

Within the usurped Cordoba of the text, a place of carnivalesque reversals, excesses, and failures of discrimination, these self-determined martyrs represent an element of ironic foreignness which both disrupts civil peace and (at least for Hrotsvit and her audience) seeks by that disruption to recreate true peace. Within that Cordoba the second Saracen king, Abderrahman, the villain of the legend, is rightful heir and dutiful son but also, the text tells us, inferior to his paternal line.[14] Metaphorically if not literally Abderrahman is the product of intermarriage between Christian Cordoba and her Saracen conqueror. In the narrative logic of the legend it is the miscegenation and erasure of ethnic and religious difference which creates him a man "stained with carnal luxury" and sullied (as is later made explicit) by "sodomitical vices."[15] That is, the genesis of his sodomitical desires, his individualized refusal to discriminate between licit and illicit sexualities, is Cordoba's previous lack or denial of difference, her surrender to the embrace of the foreigner.[16]

The fullest evidence of Abderrahman's sin is his decision to make war on Christian Galicia, for if Abderrahman is defined as the paradoxically rightful son of an unrighteous foreign line, Galicia and its rulers are both foreign, marginal to Cordoba as the center of political and cultural power—it is a remote place[17]—and the rightful inheritors of the older Cordoba: like the ancient, pre-conquest Cordoba Galicia is proudly warlike as well as staunchly Christian. Indeed it is a more vigilant Cordoba, for while the city was noted for its many pleasures, and perhaps therefore susceptible to Saracen luxury and false peace, Galicia is robustly zealous and single-minded in its devotion.[18]

The battle between the Christian Galicia and the Saracen Cordoba narratively restages the earlier conquest with a different ending. It is even more allegorically overdetermined: in this psychomachia-like struggle against temptation, the Christian province fights an overtly satanic Abderrahman who "burn[s] with demonic ire, bearing in his heart the Serpent's ancient bile."[19] The leader of the Galicians, Pelagius's father (in earlier legend his uncle, a bishop) doubles the defeated king of Cordoba displaced by Abderrahman's father. Pelagius as his heir thus doubles both Abderrahman and, in the sexual threat of his martyrdom, the compliant raped Cordoba. (He also allegorically echoes Christ in his role as ransom for a soul captured by the devil.)

Within Abderrahman's court, to which Pelagius comes as a marginalized foreigner, a prisoner, Christian and Galician, the body of the saint, and the differing ways that body is read inside and outside the text, becomes the narrative focus. Pelagius is the only character for whom Hrotsvit provides an extended physical description, and the only character whose physical appearance becomes the object of variously desiring gazes. Read correctly, from outside the text, his corporeal beauty is appropriately emblematic of inner spiritual beauty. Noble in birth and character, Pelagius is "handsome in every part of his physical form, beautiful in the splendor of his body and prudent in counsel, shining with goodness, in the first flower of his youth."[20] Seen as an outward sign of inner goodness, his beauty provokes moral desire, emulation and devotion; it occasions, for instance, Hrotsvit's own poetic expression of that chaste, licit desire. Within the legend, however, other erroneous readings of Pelagius's body are played out. The body of the virgin martyr becomes a locus of difference and distinction: the way its beauty and the significance of that beauty is acknowledged and interpreted defines and distinguishes the narrative's internal audiences.

Once Pelagius, the "glorious friend of Christ,"[21] is incarcerated in the dark dungeons of Cordoba he is subject first to the pitying interpretation of Abderrahman's courtiers who respond to his beauty and his eloquence in ways which echo Hrotsvit's own descriptions, if in an overly literal fashion. They see his physical beauty and "taste the words of his sweet mouth, flowing with the honey of rhetoric" and desire his liberation from the shackles that hold him. Their appeal to Abderrahman repeats the same words: if only the king "could see his exceptional beauty and taste his honey speech," he could not but long to make him part of the royal court, to reward him with the military rank he ironically already possesses in Christ's court.[22] Thus far, their reaction is approved and validated by the text. What calls their judgment into question is their consequent well-meaning and pragmatic but undifferentiating acknowledgment and acceptance of the their king's desires: "they knew the proud ruler of the rich city to be corrupted by sodomitic vices, to love ardently beautiful youths, [and] to wish to unite himself with them in friendship."[23] Their thinking, expressed in these lines, confounds negatives (*vitiis Sodomitis*) and positives (*amicitia, amare*) in ways that *should* be seen as ironically inappropriate. In the interim, however, in the moment of reading, since it is Pelagius's beauty—both physical and spiritual—to which both Hrotsvit and her readers (on the one hand) and the courtiers and especially Abderrahman (on the other) are attracted, the text might be said to provoke, even require, identification with foreign, sodomitical desire for what is not distinguished as different. The confusion perhaps reveals an anxiety about the limits of licit affection in *amicitia*, an anxiety especially resonant in a homosocial community such as that of Hrotsvit's Gandersheim. While in her dramas of imperiled female virginity the loving homosocial (wholly feminine) choir of virgins represents utopian space, here the dangers and temptations of such a space appear deflected and distanced from female into male, and contained within the purified heterosociality of the text.[24]

Abderrahman's lustful gaze and the attempted rape it instigates invert, yet in some ways presage the desires which finally unite Christ and Pelagius, his *miles* and *amicus*. Within Abderrahman's court, Pelagius fascinates with both physical beauty and rhetorical eloquence.[25] At first glance/taste the Saracen king "burns with desire for his beauty.[26] He orders Pelagius to be seated with him on the throne in carnivalesque anticipation of the way Christ will seat the martyr with honor, and attempts to embrace him, to taste (literally) the lips whose honeyed eloquence he desires immoderately. While Abderrahman's command anxiously presages Pelagius's later reception in heaven (a similarly homosocial world in this text) there is, however, one obvious and crucial difference: the carnality, the literalness of this earthly king's misreading of Pelagius's body. As Hrotsvit's initial prayer and the later depiction of his reception into that other heavenly court, Pelagius is already Christ's *miles* and *amicus*. Similarly, when Abderrahman has Pelagius literally bathed of the stains of imprisonment the wording literalizes earlier metaphorical baths of baptism and martyrdom.[27] The gem-studded collar with which he is adorned doubles both the chains of his imprisonment and the laurel of his reception into heaven.

Pelagius's response to Abderrahman's advances aligns itself with the text's ridicule of the earthly king's carnivalesque lack of distinction: the saint treats it as a joke.[28] He denies the lips Abderrahman has attempted to taste, though not his words, which repeat the courtiers' earlier pleas: *Non decet ergo,* they had argued, "it was not fitting" for a great king to deny himself a courtier of Pelagius's beauty; "it is not fitting," Pelagius argues, for a Christian "to bow his chaste neck within a barbarian embrace."[29] Nor, he adds, reversing active and passive roles, for a Christian to seize a kiss from the servant of the Devil. Reinstating difference, Pelagius restricts Abderrahman's embraces to those similar to him in idolatry, that is (within the text) his undiscriminating devotion to false, foolish gods.

In Hrotsvit's text Pelagius is, at this point, a lovable youth (*ephebum . . . amandum,* 140.251); for Abderrahman he is a silly, petulant boy (*lascive puer,* 252) who fails to acknowledge the laws which govern and threaten him. His ironically mock fatherly advice and appeal to Pelagius's reverence and piety all echo Pelagius's own speeches of persuasion to his father. The blow which Pelagius strikes Abderrahman is expressed in words which recall the previous martyrdom of Christians, *sanguis. . . . madeficit* (141.274f.) As a silly boy Pelagius exasperates and finally enrages the king by striking him; the blow soaks the ruler's beard with blood just as previous martyrdoms of zealous Christians had soaked the soil of the city. Abderrahman's final response to the teasing, denied virginal body is to order its mutilation and destruction. Pelagius is catapulted over the city walls, and then, when this miraculously fails to disfigure the body's beauty, decapitated. It is as *ephebum amandum*, by contrast, as well as *miles*, that Pelagius is received into heaven, rewarded with "the victory prize of fervent love" and "joined with the throng" of martyrs and virgins around Christ's throne.[30] It is at this point that the text specifically mentions Pelagius's virginity, perhaps because only in heaven can the virgin's implicit denial of gender difference be beyond danger of misreading.

"Amen," Hrotsvit adds, bringing the legend to an initial conclusion—though the poem does not end there. And neither do the problematics of Pelagius's body as a locus for difference, even if its beauty is in decapitation and death seemingly devoid of overt sexual danger.

Fishermen who ply the literal river encircling Cordoba—as opposed to the allegorical seven rivers of learning which graced the preconquest city—find the bloody, disjointed body. They do not initially recognize Pelagius or notice his beauty; that happens only after they have reunited the head with the body, restoring some measure of his virginal, physical integrity. If their gaze carries mercenary rather than sexual desire, the body remains the site of other anxieties and provocative of other necessary distinctions. Like Abderrahman's courtiers, the fishermen both read and misread Pelagius's body as a commodity, literal and/or allegorical ransom. They recognize (that is, they read correctly) the signs of an executed Christian; but they see (that is, misread) in these signs the possibility of making a profit by selling the corpse as the relics of a martyr.

The Christians who buy the body—at a literally high price, as the text repeats several times, appropriate to its spiritual worth and its future value as the instigator of free miracles of healing—inhabit a landscape which seems suddenly and inexplicably free of non-Christian overlords. After Pelagius's martyrdom Abderrahman and his court disappear from the text; this textual erasure of their literal foreignness substitutes for the divine retribution and/or mass conversions which often conclude a martyrdom legend. (Of course, this erasure, like the appearance of an active market in relics, also negotiates the historical and political realities of an anomalously contemporary legend.) The paradoxical need to both reaffirm and dissolve difference, however, remains within the text; and thus the Christian congregation which purchases the body, which welcomes the relics with (significantly) sweet hymns and which buries Pelagius in an earthly tomb appropriate to his heavenly glory, eventually subjects the body (or at least the head) to a second martyrdom of sorts in order to prove the validity of its miraculous power—to prove, that is, its difference from most corpses. If their motivation differs—licit rather than illicit desire, reverence rather than anger and pique—the result of their immersion of the saint's head in the furnace replicates that of Abderrahman's attempt to destroy Pelagius. (In an ironic reversal its literal fire echoes the metaphorical fire of the, usually overly literal, king's desire and wrath; it also reifies the fire of Christian zeal earlier in the poem.) In neither case is the physical body injured; indeed, in this second trial the head is as if it were refined until it shines more dazzlingly than gold.

At the same time, the process of their test also involves the congregation, one which specifically unites men and women in a reaffirmation of heterosociality similarly refined, purified, and devoid of the possible dangers of gender difference, in a corporate imitation of the martyr. Of their own free will they fast—a discipline which recalls the detail of the saint's hunger while imprisoned—as well as singing sweet hymns and praying, that is, committing the "crimes" of both Pelagius and previous Christian martyrs. Nevertheless, when all is said and done, they remain human beings on earth who revere and attempt but ultimately fail to emulate Pelagius completely. At best they are those Christians of lower merit whose bodies could not survive the furnace without some slight injury at least.

What the text produces, finally, and what the body of Pelagius comes to signify, is a negotiation of the dangers of both difference and lack of difference. Hrotsvit's text requires difference, requires something of the foreign, the Other, to establish the identity of both the saint and the community. That is, masculine sanctity such as that of the *miles* Pelagius is constituted in opposition to the femininity of his human hagiographer, even as his virginity and moral integrity are established in their defense against sexuality. Christians are most clearly defined in their zealous struggle against pagans. The dangers contingent upon the coexistence of opposites, the tensions arising from the foreigner's presence, generate the drama enacted within and upon the body of the martyr. An illicit religious heterosociality which mingles the Christian with the foreign, pagan Other creates Abderrahman's sodomitic regime in which lack of religious distinction implies both sexuality and the obliteration (or at least conflation) of gender difference. That dangerous homosociality is ultimately replaced by a licitly heterosocial community, explicitly male and female, Christians clearly distinguished from non-Christians. It constitutes a renewed virginal body politic, as it were, cleansed like Pelagius's corporeal form, and purified of sexuality and the variable sexual temptations implicit in both gender difference and indifference. This purification occurs through the narrative and rhetorical erasure of foreign pollution in the figure of the Saracen king. If Abderrahman must disappear textually, however, he can do so only after he fulfills his function as the designated foreigner, a scapegoat of sorts. As his persecution proves the martyr's sanctity in ways which ironically prefigure the Christian community's test of the martyr's relics, he establishes the limits of the community's desire for the saint.

As for Pelagius, the double ending of Hrotsvit's hagiographic narrative illustrates the similar paradox of his foreignness. His death, his sacrifice is also required, and his acceptance into Heaven (the reward and sign of his sanctity) coincides with the creation both of a Christian cultic community focused on his relics and a textual body which can function as a model of inimitable moral perfection. In engaging with that textual body, readers of Hrotsvit's *Pelagius* define themselves through the twin processes of identifying with, but inevitably distinguishing themselves from, the foreignness of both the martyr and his persecutor. The text thus vividly enacts the necessary process of validating difference by embracing the foreign even while disavowing the foreigner.

Notes

1. Thomas Heffernan, *Sacred Biography: Saints and their Biographers in the Middle Ages* (Oxford and New York: Oxford University Press, 1988), 9. My interpretation of sanctity and hagiographic narrative throughout this essay depends to some measure on Heffernan's work, as well as that of Peter Brown, *The Cult of the Saints: Its Rise and Function in Latin Christianity.* Haskell Lectures on History of Religions, New Ser. 2 (Chicago: The University of Chicago Press, 1981) and *Society and the Holy in Late Antiquity* (Berkeley: University of California Press, 1982); and John S. Hawley, *Saints*

and Virtues. Comparative Studies in Religion and Society 2 (Berkeley: University of California Press, 1987).

2. On the foundational function of sacred violence, see René Girard, *Violence and the Sacred* (Baltimore and London: John Hopkins University Press, 1977), *The Scapegoat* (Baltimore: Johns Hopkins University Press, 1986) and *Violent Origins* (Stanford: Stanford University Press, 1987), as well as Mary Douglas, *Purity and Danger* (London: Routledge & K. Paul, 1966).
3. For overviews and analyses of Hrotsvit's work, see Marcelle Thiébaux, *The Writings of Medieval Women*. The Garland Library of Medieval Literature: a Critical Study of Texts from Perpetua († 203) to Marguerite Porete († 1310) (New York and London: Garland, 1994), Peter Dronke, *Women Writers of the Middle Ages* (Cambridge: Cambridge University Press, 1984), as well as Katherina Wilson, *Hrotsvit of Gandersheim: A Florilegium of her Works* (Woodbridge, Suffolk, and Rochester, NY: D.S. Brewer, 1998) and especially *Hrotsvit of Gandersheim: "Rara Avis in Saxonia"?* A Collection of Essays comp. and ed. by Katharina M. Wison (Ann Arbor: Marc Publishing, 1987).
4. Mark D. Jordan, *The Invention of Sodomy in Christian Theology* (Chicago: The University of Chicago Press, 1997), 20. For medieval conflation of the Muslim and the homosexual, see also Steven F. Kruger, "Racial/Religious and Sexual Queerness in the Middle Ages," *Medieval Feminist Newsletter* 16 [Fall 1993], 32–36. R. I. Moore also details the ways in which various kinds of "foreigners," including homosexuals and Muslims along with Jews and witches, are subject to similar rhetorics in *The Formation of a Persecuting Society: Power and Deviance in Western Europe 950–1250* (Oxford: Basil Blackwell, 1987).
5. Inclite Pelagi, martir fortissime Christi / et bone regnantis miles per saecula regis. H. Homeyer, ed., *Hrotsvithae Opera* (Munich, Paderborn and Vienna: Ferdinand Schöningh, 1970), 130.1–2.
6. Subjectam . . . famellam. Homeyer, 130.4.
7. Exigui supero de rore rigari / Pectoris obscuram iam mis clementius antrum. Homeyer, 130.6–7.
8. See, for example, the Praefatio to her dramatic works, in which even reading Terence's plays of seduction is posed as a temptation, a textual seduction, of the virgin reader (Homeyer, 233–234).
9. Polluit et veterem purae fidei genetricem / Barbaricu ritu. Homeyer, 132.37–38.
10. Personae sexus . . . utriusque. Homeyer, 145.377.
11. Iustorum . . . virorum . . . Qui Christo laudes ardebant pangere dulces/ Ipsius et stultos verbis reprehendere divos. Homeyer 134.82–84.
12. Perfida . . . Saracenorum gens; Ductor barbaricae gentis; vir sat perversus . . . profanus; perversi . . . tyranni. Homeyer, 131.24; 131.32; 132.33; 132.43.
13. Paganos iustis intermiscendo colonis, / Quo sibi suaderent patrios dissolvere mores . . . [et] secum sordere. Homeyer 132.39–41.
14. De gemine regi; Deterior patribus. Homeyer, 133.71; 133.73.
15. Luxu carnis maculatus; vitiis . . . Sodomitis. Homeyer, 133.73; 138.205.
16. As Steven F. Kruger notes in his discussion of non-Christian bodies and medieval anxieties about religious conversion, "sex that transgressed the lines of religious distinction was associated with both 'bestiality' and 'sodomy.' "

"Conversion and Medieval Sexual, Religious, and Racial Categories," in *Constructing Medieval Sexuality*, ed. Karma Lochrie, Peggy McCracken, and James A. Schultz, Medieval Cultures 11 (Minneapolis: University of Minnesota Press, 1997), 158–179; here 169. Cf. also Karma Lochrie, *Covert Operations*. The Middle Ages Series (Philadelphia: University of Pennsylvania Press, 1999), especially Chapter 5, "Sodomy and Other Female Perversions," and Allen J. Frantzen, *Before the Closet: Same-Sex Love from Beowulf to Angels in America* (Chicago: The University of Chicago Press, 1998) as well as Jordan for other discussions of "sodomy" as a category implying gender conflation: "Homosexuality, Luxuria, and Textual Abuse" in *Constructing Medieval Sexuality*, ed. Karma Lochrie, Peggy McCracken, and James A. Schultz, (1997), 24–39.

17. Locis . . . remotis. Homeyer, 134.92.
18. On the connection between luxury and illicit sexuality, see especially Mark D. Jordan, "Homosexuality," 1997, 24–39.
19. Fervebat daemonis ira, / Corde gerens veterem serpentis denique bilem. Homeyer, 134.97–98.
20. Omni praenitida compostus corpore forma, . . . formae splendore decorus, / Consilio prudens, tota bonitate refulgens, . . . primos flores iuvenilis. Homeyer, 136. 144–148.
21. Egregium Christi . . . amicum. Homeyer, 137.190.
22. Eius praenitidam velles si cernere formam / Et tam mellitam saltem gustare loquelam, / Quam cuperes iuvenem tibimet coniungere talem / Gradu militiae necnon assumere primae, / Corpore candidulo tibi quo serviret in aula. Homeyer 139.213–217.
23. Ipsum felicis certe summum caput urbis / Corruptum vitiis cognoscebant Sodomitis / Formosos facie iuvenes ardenter amare / Hos et amicitiae propriae coniungere velle. Homeyer, 138.204–207.
24. Cf. Jordan, *Invention*, especially pp. 22–28, for a discussion of this anxiety as expressed in the liturgical veneration of St. Pelagius. I consider Hrotsvit's definition of chaste female homosociality in "Gender Without Sexuality: Hrotsvitha's Imagining of a Chaste Female Community," in *The Community, The Family and the Saint: Patterns of Power in Early Medieval Europe: Selected Proceedings of the International Medieval Congress, University of Leeds, 4–7 July 1994, 10–13 July 1995*, ed. Joyce Hill and Mary Swan, (Turnhout: Brepols,1998), 127–142.
25. Tum faciem iuvenis, tum dulcia verbula fantis. Homeyer, 139.230.
26. Ardebat formam . . . amandum. Homeyer, 139.232.
27. Lavacro corpus detergere puro / lotaque. Homeyer, 139.220–221. Compare descriptions of Cordoba's rightful Christian king as baptismate lotum (Homeyer, 131.27) and previous zealous martyrs as: sanguine lotae (Homeyer, 133.68).
28. Ludens; magno ridicule. Homeyer 140.240–241.
29. Sobria barbarico complexu subdere colla. Homeyer, 140.244.
30. Ferventis bravio . . . amoris; Adiunctus turmis caelisti sede receptis. Homeyer, 142.305; 142.311. Compare Abderrahman's desire: iuvenum coniungere; sibi sedulo iunctus (Homeyer, 139.215; 139.235).

2

Foreigner, Foe, and Neighbor:

The Religious Cult as a Forum for Political Reconciliation

MICHAEL GOODICH

In his study of biblical miracles, Howard Clarke Kee has noted that in early Christianity the miracle often served the functional role of redefining the community of the covenant and as divine sign that heralded the impending rule of God. Those persons who had either experienced a miracle or witnessed its performance established a permanent community of believers bound together by their common faith and experience of the sacred and were to serve as the kernel of a religious cult in support of a particular saint. Following the Christianization of the Roman Empire in the fourth century, the paraphernalia of the saint's cult (including relic worship, miracles, processions, feast days, etc.) clearly served as a sacred means of spiritually defining the village, urban, and national community within a geographic space occupied by a defined group of people; and of reconciling former enemies within the framework of a religious cult.[1] Cult and miracle became a socially and religiously legitimate agency for the expression of familial and communal pride and cohesion. It has been amply demonstrated by Fustel de Coulanges, Peyer, Brown, and others that in the late Roman and early medieval periods the episcopal saint posthumously took on many of the features of the pagan protective deity and the Roman magistrate, as both defender of the city's liberty and protector of its inhabitants.[2] The patron saint was credited with putting an end to plague, drought, or other natural catastrophe, defeating enemy armies, and reinforcing the sometimes fragile unity of the tribe, city, or state. At the same time, as the patron of a cosmopolitan city populated by persons drawn from different tribal and social backgrounds, the saint's cult served as an institution which drew such people together and helped to overcome their 'foreignness.' The processions that highlighted the saint's day included members of all social classes, professional guilds, laity and clergy, often strategically placed close to the saint's relics according to their proximity to political power. The theft or removal of a saint's relic from one city to another was often an important stage in a continuing political or economic battle between two political powers. The victorious side viewed the acquisition of its enemy's sacred relics as confirmation of its prestige and power.[3]

This unifying role of the episcopal saint and his cult as a mediator between warring factions and a medium for the reconciliation of social conflict has been amply demonstrated for the early Middle Ages. It has been less fully shown for the later medieval period, when the bishop often continued to serve both during his lifetime and posthumously as an intermediary between conflicting political, social, tribal, and even national groups; many reports of the bishop helping to settle conflicts over feudal property or mediating between warring factions in the medieval commune survive. As one of the observers of the canonization trial of Archbishop Philip of Bourges (d. 1261) remarked (1265/66), "He happily restored concord and peace to quarrels and conflicts."[4] In the cult of Bishop Thomas of Hereford (d. 1282), who was canonized in 1320 by Pope John XXII, many miracles illustrate the reconciliation of such ethnic groups as the English, Irish, Welsh, and Normans. The bishopric of Hereford was situated on the border of the Welsh marches, which faced both a campaign of conquest and colonization and efforts at integration during the reign of Edward I in the late thirteenth century.[5] The religious cult, which expressed a unity that transcended familial or ethnic loyalties, could thus stand alongside such diplomatic efforts as truce, mediation, parleys, and arbitration as a means of accommodating two societies at war.[6] Thomas's canonization records reflect the conflict between the Welsh and English on the political and military level, while at the same time illustrating areas of cooperation and even reconciliation between the two communities both during his lifetime and in his posthumous career. This is documented in the testimony presented at the extensive canonization trial held at London and Hereford between July 13 and November 13, 1307. More than three hundred miracles allegedly occurred between about 1287 and 1299 due to Thomas's intervention, some reported with a brief statement recorded by local clerics at the site of the saint's tomb in Hereford, others by a large number of witnesses at the canonization hearing. For the purpose of this paper, due to the imperfections of the Bollandist version found in the *Acta sanctorum*, which was rewritten in narrative form rather than as a direct transcription, I have consulted the original manuscript of the trial, Vat. Lat. Ms. 4015.[7] This is supplemented by four other manuscripts: Paris B.N. Lat. Ms. 5373A, fols. 1r–65^{r}, Exeter College (Oxford) Ms. 158 and Bibliotheca Alexandrina Ms. 99, which contain the summarized versions of the proceedings used by Pope John XXII and the cardinals in their curia discussion of the case, including a study of twenty-six selected miracles; and Vat. Cod. Otto. Ms. 25.16, fols. 44^{r}–46^{v}, which contains material related to the case's consideration under Pope Clement V on May 11 to 15, 1313. The hearings were conducted in 1307 during the pontificate of Pope Clement V by a commission composed of the influential theologian William Durand, bishop of Mende (in southern France), the papal nuncio in England, William of Festa, and Ralph Baldock, bishop of London, and represent perhaps the fullest surviving medieval canonization dossier, including letters of postulation supporting the candidate's sainthood, a long digression dealing with Thomas's excommunication in 1282 (just before his death) by John Pecham, archbishop of Canterbury, and other related documents.[8] Thomas's case may be seen in the context of papal efforts to mollify the English king following a period of sharp conflict with Rome under Pope Boniface VIII. His chief "defender" or postulator was Henry de Schorne, canon and archdeacon (1303–1318) of Hereford cathedral, prebendary of Warham (1303–?) and Oxford doctor of canon law.[9] Although the testimony presented by the clergy was largely in Latin (as is the protocol itself), the lay aristocracy testified in French, and the common folk in English or Welsh, illustrating the linguistic patchwork of the region bordering England and Wales.[10] The commissioners were assisted by a host of proctors, notaries, and translators who edited and rendered the text into the inquisitorial form demanded by Rome, which had been refined and adapted for both heresy and canonization trials during the pontificate of Pope Innocent III (d. 1216) and his successors.[11] The witnesses were permitted to correct their testimony on a later occasion if necessary.[12]

Although on the administrative and political levels distinctions might remain between Welsh and English, native and immigrant settler, this religious cult could become the focus for the reconciliation of the two communities, who maintained a very precarious peace in the late thirteenth century, during which Welsh resistance remained close to the surface. In order to illustrate the creation of a new community of faith in which several "national" groups converge, the case of the Welshman William Cragh[13] of Llanrhidian (situated about eleven miles south of Swansea) in the Gower peninsula, the son of Rhys ap Wilym Swanith, deserves highlighting. Despite the extensive protocol, his case does not appear among those miracles examined by the curia for possible inclusion in the final canonization bull, since it presumably did not conform to the minimum medical and judicial standards established to verify supernatural intervention.[14] Such a miracle might also reopen some of the political wounds that the new cult was intended to heal. Cragh had allegedly been miraculously saved from death by hanging in 1290 due to the posthumous intervention of Thomas of Hereford at a time when Wales was experiencing the baleful effects of forced colonization and Anglicization. The testimony concerning Cragh's case was delivered largely in Welsh and was translated with the aid of two Welsh Franciscans of Hereford;[15] although the other witnesses spoke in French or English. Eight other persons testified, including Lord William de Braose (in variant forms, de Breos or de Brewes) the Younger (d. 1326) of Gower, whose father, William (d. 1290), the second lord, was probably no longer alive at the time of William Cragh's capture and abortive execution; the younger lord's stepmother Maria de Roos (d. 1326), third wife of the former lord, who had given up the lordship to her stepson; John de Bageham (or Laggeham or Berham, at various points in the manuscript), seneschal to William de Braose; William of Codminton (or Codminster or Codmeston), rector of the church of Findon in the diocese of Chichester and chaplain to the Braose family; and others, both lay and clergy, who were present at the abortive hanging and its aftermath. Braose, his stepmother and the chaplain testified at St. Paul's chapel in London on July 14 and 15, 1307; the others at St. Catherine's chapel at Hereford Cathedral on November 6 and 9, 1307. The Braose family, derived from Falaise in Normandy, was active in Scotland and Ireland and was granted the Gower lordship in 1203 by King John, numbering among the leading lord marchers and landowners in the region. It boasted twenty-six knights' fees, including ten in Sussex and Gower, and two of its members had recently served as bishops of Hereford and Llandaff.[16] Braose the Younger had himself fought during the Welsh wars at the siege of Einlyn in December 1287 and January 1288 and at the presumed time of the miracle was serving in the area of Hereford, which in many ways served as the focus of royal and episcopal activity for western Wales, which explains the popularity of Thomas's cult not only in his diocese, but also in Wales and areas of England and Ireland bordering on the Irish sea.[17] The Braose clan was itself related to the Cantilupes, Thomas's family, who also possessed lands on the Welsh side of the border, which may further explain the encouragement of Thomas's cult by the Braose family and their clients.

Since the Cragh case deals with the capital crime of treason, it should be noted that the legal and jurisdictional situation in the area of Wales and its border region under King Edward I was not entirely clear. In principle, persons were judged according to their own national law, whether English or Welsh, but the separation between Welsh and English law was not always practical or observed. Archbishop Pecham had regarded traditional Welsh law as both contrary to reason and the laws of both the Old and New Testaments. It is also reported that the Welsh prince David Llewelyn (d. 1246) had abolished *galanas*, that is, compensatory family fines in cases of homicide. Royal power was growing at the expense of the local lords and cases of treason would have been reserved for royal courts. Such an unsettled situation characterized by unclear jurisdiction and occasional vigilantism would readily lend itself to calls for divine intervention to secure justice. Braose was regarded as a rather improvident lord, who had lost many of his lands and privileges as a result of the complaints lodged against him by the men of Gower. The younger Braose was to suffer public humiliation in a royal court in 1305 because of contempt of court.[18] After 1284, royal power increased considerably and the traditional Welsh system of justice in which compurgation and blood feud law founded on the principle of the collective responsibility of the kindred was quickly being replaced by the use of the jury and inquest.[19] Royal interference in marcher (holding jurisdiction over the border region) courts also quickened after about 1290, following the accession of the younger Braose to the lordship.[20] In 1306, as a result of complaints lodged against him in the royal court, Braose was forced to introduce the jury system for both the English and Welsh in felony cases in the English county of Gower, and the burghers of Swansea were granted a charter of rights.[21] As R.R. Davis has noted regarding the situation in Gower under Braose the Younger:

> All in all, there was ample opportunity of the king of England or the prince of Wales to intervene in the affairs of Gower and to do so in a fashion which seemed to undermine its Marcher status. The king's court could act as an appellate tribunal to hear the grievances of the men of Gower against their lord; royal commissions were established to investigate the malpractices of seigniorial officials, lands alienated there without royal licence were confiscated; and even the lordship was seized into royal lands for default of justice. It was a catalogue of royal intervention which must have sent shivers down the spine of any self-respecting Marcher lord.[22]

This suggests the considerable disorder prevailing in the region.

In 1306, in the course of the considerable litigation and conflict concerning the legitimacy of the rule of Braose the Younger, in addition to certain economic rights, the burgesses of Swansea were granted the following liberties: bail was to be allowed in many cases, the burgesses were not to be fined without the judgment of their peers, the lord's bailiffs were not to hold court without permission, when the lord's chancery was opened writs were to be drawn up as required, the hearing of cases was not be to adjourned or prolonged from one court session to another, forced military service was to cease, and burgesses were not to be forced to travel beyond the borders of Gower.[23] Until such rights were granted, the draconian punishments generally meted out even for rather minor infractions are reflected in Thomas of Hereford's protocol. It is reported, for example, that a certain Cristina Cragh of the parish of Wellington in the diocese of Hereford was hanged in 1292 or 1294 (along with perhaps ten others, although the figures differ) for stealing a pig and then selling it, although a vow to Thomas had saved her.[24] Cristina had the same family name as our *miraculé* William Cragh, and they may have therefore been related. It was common for whole families to become devotees of a particular patron saint. It is stated that she was a member of the fraternity of the hospital of St. John of Jerusalem, which also had a house in William's native town in Wales, Llanridian. A house connected to the order of St. John was situated a short distance from the parish of Wellington, which was itself adjacent to the village of Marden, where some of the most well-known miracles attributed to Thomas had taken place.[25] After her liberation from the gallows, Cristina fled to the church of St. Martin, and didn't dare to leave for three weeks, lest she be retaken and again condemned to hang.

The miraculous liberation of the rebel William Cragh reflects the conflict and reconciliation of Welsh and English within the context of a shared religious cult. It is difficult to determine whether Cragh's trial is related to political and military events in Wales in 1287, because of the continuing conflict during this period.[26] Nevertheless, at the time of the miracle the victim was in his early twenties. Witnesses at the canonization trial, recalling events that had occurred nearly twenty years earlier, provide various dates for the time of his hanging and miraculous liberation. They suggest dates between 1289 and 1292. William de Braose recalled that Cragh's miracle occurred in 1289 during his service in Gower, while another witness, the priest William of Codmeston, suggested 1291.[27] But the Exeter College manuscript records that a delegation of pilgrims including Braose himself arrived at Thomas's tomb on Friday, December 2, 1290 and reported that the attempted hanging had taken place on Saturday, November 26, 1290.[28] According to the evidence drawn largely from the canonization trial, William Cragh, son of ap Rees of the parish of Llanrhidian[29] in the diocese of St. David's, had been apprehended at Swansea along with one Trahern ap Howell (or Hywel) of Grwyne-Vechan or Gryne-Vawr in South Wales and several comrades-in-arms as "malefactors" or rebels active in the local rebellions against royal control of Gower and were taken to Swansea prison. According to the chaplain William of Codmeston, Cragh and Trahern were the leaders of the Welsh "thieves."[30] The lands of a certain Trahern ap Hywel at Catheiniog, who may perhaps be identified with this beadle (a law court official) of Maenordeilo, were delivered to the burgesses of Dryslwyn by 1307–08 rebel (although the repetition of the same names attached to different persons in contemporary sources often makes clear identification difficult).[31] Since Trahern is described in the Hereford canonization record as a "*nobilis*" and ringleader of the rebels, in all likelihood he may be identified with this same Trahern ap Hywel of Catheiniog.[32] Cragh was forty-five at the time of his testimony in 1307 and would therefore have been twenty-five when he had taken part in the siege and razing of the strategically important manor of Oystermouth in June, 1287, presumably under Rhys ap Maredudd of Dryslwyn, a former ally of Edward I in earlier campaigns who had now turned against the king.[33] It is reported that neither women nor children were spared during the siege, which had followed the raising of Swansea castle.[34] Maredudd had been opposed by a force under the leadership of the earls of Gloucester and Glamorgan and other marchers appointed by Mortimer on July 2, 1287.

Maredudd was to be captured in 1291 and the revolt would then have collapsed. Some of the former rebels were to petition for the acceptance of the English jury law and of inquest, while giving up their afforested woods in order to keep their pastures and other lands. This development undoubtedly led to the intermingling of Welsh and English in Welsh Gower.[35] In order to pacify the region, a royal order had further provided that Welshmen who had been involved in the insurrection would be received into the king's peace, Maredudd's lands were to be confiscated, and a relief force of 1200–1300 Welsh foot soldiers would be created. On February 8, 1289, the elder Braose had been ordered to guarantee that no one in Gower receive or aid Maredudd, and in 1291 the younger Braose was to be among those entrusted with the pacification of Wales.[36] The jail deliveries heard at Hereford by the royal justiciar Robert Malet in 1291–93, for example, recorded in a court roll at the Public Records Office contain a considerable number of cases of Welsh murderers, thieves, and other malefactors (whose activities may represent acts of rebellion rather than crime). Jail deliveries concerning Swansea have not been found, so that given the chaotic state of justice and the incomplete records, it may not be possible to uncover criminal records of Cragh's case.[37] By his own testimony, Cragh was a poor (*pauper*) but free man (*liber*) who was subject to the jurisdiction of William de Braose.[38] Cragh had been accused of killing thirteen men. He claimed innocence of any of the crimes of which he stood accused, which would presumably lay the groundwork for his eventual redemption, since his arrest, conviction, and attempted execution could thus be regarded as illegitimate and would warrant the appeal for supernatural assistance.

The accused had been apprehended between the feasts of St. Michael (October 16) and All Saints (Nov. 1), 1290. It is known that the younger Braose had apprehended fourteen rebels, of whom twelve were freed, while Cragh and Trahern were imprisoned. Although the year is not specified in the papal trial, as noted above, the Exeter College manuscript clearly refers to 1289. He was held for fifteen days. He was tried and found guilty on the feast of St. Martin, (November 11) and was scheduled to be executed on the following Monday at 3 P.M. along with three others at the order of William de Braose.[39] The Exeter College source, however, notes that the execution had occurred on November 26. This document contains an on-the-spot record made by the clerks of Hereford cathedral of those persons who appeared as pilgrims at Thomas's tomb. Their names, the ex-voto offering, and the reason for their pilgrimage are here recorded, and because this information was taken down at the time of the event, it may be more reliable than the impaired memories of witnesses nearly twenty years later. The discrepancy concerning the amount of time that elapsed between the trial and the execution date may stem from the faulty memories of the interlocutors. The *presbyter* Thomas Marshall said this occurred around noon; an acquaintance named John ap Howel said it was in the early evening, after nones, since he had just eaten dinner.[40] The accused were escorted by ten mounted soldiers about a quarter of a mile from Swansea castle to the site of the hanging, along with their kin and several Franciscan friars. According to Cragh, the accused were hanged serially. Ythel Fachan, one of the onlookers, attached to William's neck a knotted heavy rope of the kind worn by Franciscan friars. After the ladder had been removed, Cragh was hanged twice following a mishap the first time round, and remained hanging on the gibbet until vespers, that is, late afternoon or early evening. In the case of his fellow rebel Trahern, no family or friends looked after the disposal of the body, which was removed by the local butchers after superfluities had exited from his lower parts. The absence of kin or friends may stem from the fear of being too closely identified with the leader of the rebels. Lord William de Braose noted that under Welsh law the guilty could be redeemed for a fine. Cragh's kin and friends had provided a hundred cows as a ransom for his freedom.[41] But this was apparently deemed insufficient, since under traditional Welsh law one hundred and six cows and one bull were required in capital cases. It is more likely that due to the introduction of the inquest and jury system, such a system no longer applied.

In the course of his own testimony during the canonization proceeding, Cragh noted that, although he himself had no full recollection of the events, he understood that the rope had broken, and he had fallen down. He had awoken the next day and reported a vision that he had experienced on the morning of the hanging while asleep in prison after cockcrow. It is not clear whether the apparition had been seen by the thirteen other persons detained with him. In contemporary dream theory, sunrise was regarded as the optimum time for the receipt of visions, and the closer the vision occurs to sunrise, the more proximate its fulfillment.[42] Cragh's vision is highly reminiscent of a tried and true hagiographical *topos* found in the case of prisoners released due to divine intervention with which the interlocutor might have been acquainted; miraculous intervention to save persons "unjustly" hanged also conforms to a hagiographical *topos*.[43] A similar vision occurred on June 6, 1293 to the imprisoned William Talgar, who also testified at the canonization hearing.[44] Suffering an injured arm during his harsh imprisonment, Talgar saw Thomas of Hereford in a vision asking the Virgin for mercy; his arm was healed and he was freed from prison. Cragh himself reported having seen the Virgin Mary dressed in a white robe decked with precious jewels on her head, bearing the Christ child just as Cragh had himself admitted having seen in images. The image of the Virgin and the infant Jesus was a popular theme in thirteenth century piety and is reflected in many contemporary written and visual hagiographical sources. She was accompanied by a man she identified as Thomas of Hereford, who was later to free him. As a result, even prior to the event, Cragh anticipated being rescued by Thomas, although he claimed no prior acquaintance with the saint.[45] The Virgin instructed the detainees to climb down a ladder that stood beside her. They all did so and were freed from prison—at least in his dream. Cragh (who kept on his person the bent penny which would serve as an ex-voto at Thomas of Hereford's tomb) had asked the Virgin what would happen to the ringleader of the rebels, Trahern ap Howell, and she replied, "Forget about him." Trahern was in fact hanged and died, while all the others were freed. Such supernatural intervention would serve to bolster and legitimize the willingness to accept Edward I's solution of reconciling minor rebels like Cragh in return for the sacrifice of such ringleaders as the ill-fated non-collaborator Trahern.

Cragh's confession prior to the hanging was made to the priest Madoc, a rural dean of Gower, to whom he had confided the vision, and who was probably influential in publicizing this miracle.[46] Cragh knew that the saint he had seen was neither Thomas the Apostle nor Thomas Becket because he had earlier visited Thomas's tomb as a pilgrim, which suggests prior devotion to the cult. On the day of his capture he had bent a silver penny in Thomas's honor in order to be freed, which he carried on the way to his execution.[47] This was to be cited as a peculiarly English devotional practice in the subsequent curial examination of Thomas's miracles. Cragh had taken this coin with him to the execution, had thought about the saint and called upon others to invoke him. The importance of frequent churchgoing and exposure to the religious images found in sculpture, stained glass, fresco, or the minor arts for the education of the laity and the identification of the saint is here clearly illustrated. Such common exposure within the same community created a shared treasury of symbols and images that drew believers together and reinforced religious discourse.

When Cragh had been taken down from the gibbet, the seneschal John de Bageham confirmed his death and returned to Swansea castle to deliver his report. Cragh was taken for dead. Much attention is given in the protocol to the clear signs of death in order to establish that his revival constituted a miracle. The precision of the witnesses suggests either a wide acquaintance with the symptoms of death or that they had been prompted beforehand by officers of the court.[48] Maria de Braose, the mistress of Swansea castle, had asked that he be taken to a cemetery for burial. Maria's kindness to Cragh may have been the result of her own close ties to Gower, the region from which Cragh had come. She ordered the seneschal to use some twine from her daughter Margaret's purse in order to measure Cragh for Thomas of Hereford. This was in accordance with another English custom that was to be discussed in the subsequent curial examination of selected miracles of Thomas prior to his canonization. Cragh's body—carried on the execution ladder, which served as a bier—was then taken to a house belonging to one Thomas Matheus situated near the church of St. Mary, which nearly abutted the castle. Those who were present—perhaps a hundred persons—beseeched the aid of God and Thomas, reciting the *Te Deum*, *Paternoster* and *Ave Maria*. Within a short time, he revived between nones (about 3 P.M.) and sunset. Despite the seneschal's claim that Cragh was an evil man, Maria and her daughter measured his body. This conformed with the English custom of providing an ex-voto candle whose wick was the length of the body of the person seeking divine assistance. The lord's stepmother therefore seems to have played a central role in this new community of faith, that is, the cult of Thomas of Hereford. The next day she prepared almond broth in order to hasten his recovery. When he was revived (the seneschal said a month after the hanging, which conflicts with other evidence),[49] the victim undertook a three-day pilgrimage joined by the lord and his wife and the members of his household (*familia*), reaching Hereford on Friday, December 2, taking along as ex-voto offerings a waxen chain, an image of the victim, and the rope with which he had been hanged.[50] He promised to reform his life. The fact that he kept to his vow was confirmed nearly twenty years later at the time of Thomas's canonization trial.[51] The presence of the local English lord in the retinue undertaking pilgrimage indicates the collective nature of this miracle, which thus served as a forum for the meeting of persons of varying social and ethnic origins and the reconciliation of political foes.

A second miracle in this collection that illustrates the integration of the English and Welsh populations concerns a babbling orphan named John who had appeared at Thomas's tomb in 1292 when he was twenty-six. He had appeared to have been born with a stump for a tongue and could only grunt. His case was based on the testimony of seven persons. Here again, a vision played a decisive role. This young man had dreamed that his tongue had been put back, and when he awoke, suddenly began to speak, praising Thomas in English. Since it soon became clear that he also knew Welsh, it was apparent to the witnesses that he had learned this language as a native tongue from his parents.[52] He had lived in Hereford for three years, and his transformation was reported by many people in both the city and its surrounding region. On the other hand, since his family does not appear to have been present, this may suggest that he was one of the homeless victims of the war between English and Welsh. Like the case of William Cragh, this miracle provides stark evidence of the way that Thomas of Hereford's cult served as a forum for the reconciliation of the English, French, and Welsh.

Although the case of William Cragh may illustrate the cooperation of English and Welsh in achieving reconciliation through a posthumous cult, there is also evidence that during his lifetime Thomas of Hereford did not always act as an impartial figure. When three Welsh *vills* (manors), which represented (according to Robert de Woodford, constable of the Ledbury castle) one third of the income of the bishopric, were harried by a large band of armed Welshmen, the bishop promptly excommunicated and anathematized them. As a result some other Welsh residents allied themselves with the English.[53] Thomas had visited the area, but was forced to preach through an interpreter, since he didn't speak Welsh.[54] After his death, clearly most of those wounded soldiers aided through invocation of the saint were Englishmen fighting against the Welsh.[55] Another canonization witness, a fishmonger of Hereford, reported that the saint's humble and honest manner of speaking extended to all but the Jews. He actively supported the royal attempt to expel them from the kingdom and deprive them of their property, and rejected the attempt of fifty Jews to end this persecution through payment of a fine. He insisted that he would only attempt to convert them, because they are "enemies of God and rebels against the faith."[56]

Nevertheless, this microhistorical reconstruction of this attempted hanging of William Cragh in 1290 is a vivid illustration of the power of the faith and of a newly created religious cult to bring warring groups together. Despite the destruction inflicted on Swansea and South Wales shortly before (in which William had taken part), the spectators, including members of the court which had found him guilty of grave crimes, accepted the authenticity of this miracle. Witnesses took note of the deep hatred nourished by the justiciars and William de Braose for Cragh, so they would not have colluded in the falsification of a miracle.[57] One witness even noted that those who had seen the execution and believed that Cragh was dead, had rejoiced because he had been among the leaders of the "malefactors."[58] The subsequent three-day journey to Thomas's shrine at Hereford in the company of the local lord and his *familia* may be viewed as a public act of reconciliation between the Welsh and the English. Before this miracle, the cult of Thomas of Hereford does not appear to have been active in Wales. It was probably via the English- and French-speaking residents of Swansea that it gained a new adherent in the person of the Welshman William Cragh and his kinsmen and friends.

Wales was the uneasy meeting ground of two peoples, the Welsh and the English (with a strong Norman presence), whose integration was accompanied by severe dislocations, particularly under Edward I: rebellions, local wars, an occupying army, colonization, the introduction of new laws and the suppression of the old. Focusing on the individual case of William Cragh graphically illustrates the impact of such changes in the area of Wales most strongly influenced by English power. Despite the animosity that still clearly characterized relations between the two communities, the cult of Thomas of Hereford represented a more amenable forum in which enemies could join together in a common enterprise. The lord's stepmother Maria de Roos appears to have played a central mediating role in the reconciliation which brought a convicted Welsh rebel together with his English lord. The joint pilgrimage to Thomas's shrine at Hereford represented public recognition of a shared religious faith which could overcome political differences.

Notes

1. Howard Clarke Kee, *Miracle in the Early Christian World: A Study in Sociohistorical Method* (New Haven: Yale University Press, 1983). Part of this

paper was presented at the conference "Saints and Communities" held in Groningen in July, 2000. I would like to thank the participants for their valuable comments.

2. Peter Brown, *The Cult of the Saints: Its Rise and Function in Latin Christianity* (Chicago: University of Chicago Press, 1981); Nicole Hermann-Mascard, *Les reliques des saints* (Paris: Klinksieck, 1975); Numa-Denis Fustel de Coulanges, *The Ancient City*, trans. Willard Small, 3rd ed. (Garden City, N.J.: Doubleday, 1954); John H. Corbett, "The Saint as Patron in the Work of Gregory of Tours," *Journal of Medieval History* 7.1 (1981): 1–13.
3. See for example, Hermann-Mascard, *loc. cit.*; Patrick Geary, *Furta sacra* (Princeton: Princeton University Press, 1978) for examples of relic theft.
4. B.N. Lat. 5373A, *Processus super vita et miraculis Phillipi*, fol. 52r.
5. Vat. Lat. 4015, 138^{r} tells of a ship carrying wool and skins from St. Ives in Cornwall to Gascony which contained a crew of mixed backgrounds. See *Miracula ex processu, Acta sanctorum*, ed. Socii Bollandina, 68 vols. to date (Paris: V. Palme, 1863–1940) 3 October I: 610–96; here 657.
6. Rees Davies, "Frontier Arrangements in Fragmented Societies: Ireland and Wales," Robert Bartlett and Angus MacKay, *Medieval Frontier Societies* (Oxford: Clarendon, 1989), 77–100; here 87.
7. Patrick Daly, "The Process of Canonization in the Thirteenth and Fourteenth Centuries," in *St. Thomas Cantilupe Bishop of Hereford: Essays in his Honour* ed. Meryl Jancey, (Hereford: Friends of Hereford Cathedral Publications Committee for the Dean and Chapter, 1982), 125–35, contains a summary of the documentary sources. See Vat. Lat. 4015, fol. 7^{r} ff. for the testimony. I understand that Susan Ridyard is editing the documents connected to Thomas of Hereford's case for publication.
8. Ronald C. Finucane, "The Cantilupe-Pecham Controversy," in *Jancey, op. cit.*, 103–123.
9. John Le Neve, *Fasti Ecclesiae Anglicanae, 1300–1541*, ed. Joyce M. Horn (London: Institute of Historical Research, 1962), II. Hereford Diocese, 5, 48.
10. Vat. Lat. 4015, fol. 219^{v}–220^{v} on the Welsh-speaking friars who translated the testimony of those who knew neither French nor Latin.
11. Eric Waldram Kemp, *Canonisation and Authority in the Western* Church (Oxford: Oxford University Press, 1948); D.J. Blaher, *The Ordinary Causes in Processes of Beatification and Canonization* (Washington: Catholic University of America, 1949); Stephan Kuttner, "La réserve papale du droit de canonisation," *Revue historique de droit français et étranger* N.S. 17 (1938): 172–228; here 206–12; see also Kuttner's later remarks in "Retractatio VI" in idem, *The History of Ideas and Doctrines of Canon Law in the Middle Ages* (London: Variorum, 1980), 7–11; Renate Klauser, "Zur Entwicklung des Heiligsprechungverfahrens bis zum 13: Jahrhundert," *Zeitschrift der Savigny-Stiftung für Rechtsgeschichte: Kanonistische Abteilung* 40(1954):85–101; here 101; Wilhelm Imkamp, *Das Kirchenbild Innozenz' III. (1198–1216)* (Stuttgart: Hiersemann, 1983), 273–89 on Innocent's role; André Vauchez, *Sainthood in the Later Middle Ages*, trans. Jean Birrell (Cambridge: Cambridge University Press, 1997), 22–57; Roberto Paciocco, "*Sublimia negotia." Le canonizzazione dei santi nella curia papale e il ordine dei frati*

minori (Padua: Centro studi antoniani, 1996), 17–39. A thorough account of one precedent setting case under Innocent III is Jürgen Petersohn, "Die Litterae Papst Innozenz' III. zur Heiligsprechung der Kaiserin Kunigunde (1200)," *Jahrbuch für Landesforschung* 37 (1977): 1–25.

12. Vat. Lat. 4015, fol. 220r contains further details concerning the parents of one of the *miraculé*, William Cragh, which were added by "Willelmus ap Rees alias dictus Crah" at a later date. Two sessions were held in which Cragh was interviewed, which gave him an opportunity to amend his remarks. The manuscript contains many marginal additions, some in a different hand, which suggests revisions of the *miraculé's* testimony.
13. In Exeter College (Oxford) 58, fol. 19r he is called Crawe. I wish to thank Peter Brown for drawing my attention to two important articles which deal with this case, Michael Richter, "Waliser und Wundermänner um 1300," in *Spannungen und Widersprüche: Gedenkschrift für František Graus* ed. Susanna Burghartz et al. (Sigmaringen: Jan Thorbeke Verlag, 1992): 23–36; and idem, "William ap Rees, William de Braose and the Lordship of Gower, 1289 and 1307," *Studia celtica* 32 (1998): 189–209, which is a transcription of the relevant text from Vat. Lat. Ms. 4015. I would like to thank Robert Bartlett for allowing me to read his manuscript *The Hanged Man: A Story of Miracle, Memory and Colonialism in the Middle Ages,* which deals with this case.
14. Vauchez, *op. cit.,* 540–54 for the transcript of the curial discussion.
15. The order of St. John of Jerusalem appears to have been particularly active in the region, possessing a burgage in Llanridian and a hospital in Swansea. See William Rees, *The Hospital of St. John of Jerusalem in Wales or on the Welsh Borders* (Cardiff: University of Wales Press, 1967), 22n, 29.
16. John E. Morris, *The Welsh Wars of Edward I* (Oxford: Clarendon, 1901), 60–63. For the family tree, see appendix, 6.
17. Vat. Lat. 4015, fol. 10r ff. for his testimony.
18. Ralph A. Griffiths, *The Principality of Wales in the Later Middle Ages: The Structure of Government I. South Wales, 1277–1536* (Cardiff: University of Wales Press, 1972), 265.
19. T. Jones Pierce, *Medieval Welsh Society. Selected Essays*, ed. Beverley Smith (Cardiff: University of Wales Press, 1972), 289–308. The 'oath-helpers' were traditionally drawn 2/3 from the paternal line and 1/3 from the maternal.
20. Rees R. Davies, *Lordship and Society in the March of Wales, 1282–1400* (Oxford: Clarendon, 1978), 30; Griffiths, *Principality,* 252–53, 263–65, 315.
21. George Thomas Clark et al., eds., *Carte et munimenta quae ad dominium de Glamorgancia pertinent*, 6 vols., III (Cardiff: William Lewis, 1910), 990–1000.
22. Davies, *Lordship*, 30.
23. See for example, Edith Evans, *Swansea Castle and Its Medieval Town* (Swansea: Swansea City Council, 1983), 10.
24. Vat. Lat. 4015, fol. 235r ff.
25. Le Neve, *op. cit.*, 50.
26. Glanmor Williams, ed., *Glamorgan County History*, 6 vols. to date (Cardiff: W. Lewis, 1936–88), II, ed. Thomas Brynmor Pugh, 229–30 on local rebellions.

On February 8, 1289, William de Braose the Elder issued an order in Gower forbidding anyone from receiving or aiding the rebel Rhys ap Maredudd, who undertook a surprise attack on Swansea, but was captured in 1291.

27. Vat. Lat. 4015, fol. 10ʳ, testimony delivered at London.
28. Exeter College 58, fol. 20ʳ.
29. West of Swansea (Rhidianton in English). For place names, see John E. Southall, *Wales and her Language* (Newport: D. Nutt, 1892); Thomas Morgan, *Place Names in Wales*, 2nd ed. (Newport: J. E. Southall, 1912); Samuel Lewis, *A Typographical Dictionary of Wales*, 4th ed., 2 vols. (London: S. Lewis, 1840), II, n.p.
30. William de Braose says (fol. 11ʳ) he was a "malefactor qui in dicta guerra erat de rebellibus dicti domini Regis" (i.e., Edward I). John ap Howell (fol. 227r) described him as a "ductor multorum malefactorum," while Maria de Roos (fol. 8r) called him a "latro famosus." William of Codmeston (fol. 13ʳ) says, "erant duo famosi latrones et malefactores in terra . . . et unus ex dictis malefactoribus vocabitur Willelmus Cragh et alius Traharn ap Howel."
31. Griffiths, *Principality*, 376.
32. See the testimony of John ap Howel, Vat. Lat. 4015, 227ᵛ: "qui erat nobilis . . ."
33. J.B. Smith, "The Origins of the Revolt of Rhys ap Maredudd," *Bulletin of the Board of Celtic Studies* 22.2 (1965): 151–63.
34. Public Records Office (PRO), E. 164/1, fol. 238ʳ; Clark, *Carte*, III, 860 extract from the *Annals of Glamorgan*: "1287. Hoc anno III. Idus Junii [10 June] villam de Sweynese combussit et predavit et V. kal. Julii [26 June] castrum de Ostremew cepit et incendit." See also William Henry Jones, *History of Swansea and of the Lordship of Gower* (Carmathen: [n.d.], 1920), 265–66; Ian Soulsby, *The Towns of Medieval Wales* (Chichester: Phillimore, 1983), 242–47. The only witness to specifically link Cragh to the siege of Oystermouth was the chaplain John de Bageham (fol. 223ᵛ), but his statement seems plausible.
35. Williams, *Glamorgan*, III, 231–32.
36. *Placitorum in domo capitulari Westmonasteriensi asservatorum abbrevatio. Temporibus regum Ric. I, Johannnis, Henr. III, Edw.I, Edw. III* (London: G. Eyre & A. Strahan, 1811), 227.
37. PRO, Just. 3/89.1.2.
38. Vat. Lat. 4015, fol. 220ʳ: "estimat se esse xlv annorum et quod moratur sub temporale domino . . . Wilhelmi de Brewes baronis."
39. The most detailed witness concerning the hanging was William of Braose's seneschal, John de Bageham. See fol. 223ᵛ.
40. Vat. Lat. 4015, fol. 222ᵛ, 227ʳ.
41. Vat. Lat. 4015, fol. 12ʳ⁻ᵛ; Richter, "Waliser," 26; R.R. Davies, "The Twilight of Welsh Law, 1284–1534," *History* 51 (1966): 143–64; here 148.
42. For some bibliography on this subject, see Michael Goodich, "Jüdische und christliche Traumanalyse im zwölften Jahrhundert," *Psychologie und Geschichte* 3.1 (1991): 77–82; Steven Kruger, *Dreaming in the Middle Ages*

(Cambridge: Cambridge University Press, 1992); Tullio Gregory, ed., *I sogni nel medioevo* (Rome: Edizioni dell' Ateneo, 1985); Albrecht Classen, "Die narrative Funktion des Traumes in mittelhochdeutscher Literatur," *Mediaevistik* 5 (1992): 11–37; idem, "Transpositions of Dreams to Reality in Middle High German Narratives," *Shifts and Transpositions in Medieval Narrative. A Festschrift for Dr Elspeth Kennedy*, ed. Karen Pratt (Cambridge: D. S. Brewer, 1994), 109–120.

43. Baudouin de Gaiffier, "Un theme hagiographique: Le pendu miraculeusement sauvé," *études critiques d'hagiographie et d'iconologie* (Brussels: Société des Bollandistes, 1967), 194–226; idem, "Liberatus a suspendio," in ibid., 227–32. On the procedures of medieval execution, see Esther Cohen, *The Crossroads of Justice: Law and Culture in Late Medieval France* (Leiden: Brill, 1993), 181–203. For other cases, see Michael Goodich, *Violence and Miracle in the Fourteenth Century: Public Grief and Public Salvation* (Chicago: University of Chicago Press, 1995), 51–57. On hagiographical *topoi*, see Peter Toldo, "Leben und Wunder der Heiligen im Mittelalter," *Studien zur vergleichenden Litteraturgeschichte* 1 (1901): 20–35; 2 (1902): 87–103, 304–53; 4 (1904): 49–100; 5 (1905): 337–53; 6 (1906): 289–333; 8 (1908): 18–74; 9 (1909): 451–60. See also Jacques-Paul Migne, *Index de miraculis*, in *Patrologia cursus completus: Series latina*, 222 vols. (Paris: J. P. Migne, 1844–1902), vol. 219: 332–62.
44. Vat. Lat. 4015, fol. 291^{v}; Exeter College 58, 27^{v}, 28^{r}.
45. Ibid., fol. 221^{r}. The witness was asked how he knew the apparition was neither Thomas the Apostle nor Thomas Becket.
46. Ibid., fol. 221^{v}.
47. He said that this was an English custom and was presumably also found in Wales.
48. William Braose (fol. 11^{r}) says: "lingua dicti Willelmi pendebat extra os suum quasi in longa est digitus manus hominis longior et dicti lingua erat nigra tota et inflata et ita grossa cum sanguine." See for example, Ronald C. Finucane, *The Rescue of Innocents: Endangered Children in Medieval Miracles* (New York: St. Martin's Press, 1997), passim; Christian Krötzl, "Evidentissima signa mortis. Zu Tod und Todesfeststellung in mittelalterlichen Mirakelberichten," *Symbole des Alltags, Alltag der Symbole. Festschrift für Harry Kühnel zum 65. Geburtstag*, ed. Gertud Blaschitz (Graz: Akademische Druck- und Verlagsanstalt, 1992): 765–75, on the signs of death.
49. Vat. Lat. 4015, fol. 284^{r}.
50. The de Braose family seems to have often undertaken pilgrimages. On March 12, 1282, the elder de Braose reportedly received protection until Michaelmas due to a pilgrimage to Santiago de Compostela (i.e., he could not be sued in a court of law). See Williams, *op. cit.*, 619, n. 147.
51. Vat. Lat. 4015, fol. 227^{v}: "et ex tunc dictus Willelmus cessavit malefacere."
52. B.N. Lat. 5373A, fol. 115^{v} (testimony of cleric *Johannes* de Brampton etc.), 186^{r}.
53. Vat. Lat. 4015, fol. 22^{v}.

54. Ibid., fol. 58[v].
55. Ibid., 267[r].
56. Ibid., fol. 88[r]. For Thomas's views concerning the Jews and his support for their expulsion from England, see fol. 104[r].
57. Vat. Lat. 4015, fol. 14[r]: "dictus dominus de Breuse et eius iusticiarii officiales et ministri multum odiebant dictum Willelum Cragh et multum gaudebant de suspendio et morte eiusdem et dicti ministri et iusticiarii interfuerant in suspendio supradicto." Exeter College 38, fol. 25[r].
58. Vat. Lat. 4015, fol. 227[r]: "et valde gaudebant quod dictus Willelmus fuerat frequenter ductor multorum malefactorum."

3

Hungarians as *vremde* in Medieval Germany

ALEXANDER SAGER

I. "Die Hungrigen"

When the first western European authors became aware of the Hungarians, just before their *honfoglalás* (i.e., conquest of the Carpathian basin, after 880),[1] they literally did not know what to make of them. The earliest sources register the vanguard raiding parties as "hostes antea inexperti" (enemies unknown before), "gens retro ante seculis inaudita quia nec nominata" (a people unheard of in past ages, never having been named), "qui modo in novissimo temporum apparuerunt" (newly appeared on the scene).[2] For an early medieval author or audience, the notion of an "unknown" and "unnamed" *gens* was more than a mere admission of ignorance. This was the age of the *origo gentis*, the narrative roots of national historiography, in which the status of a people was measured by the identifiability and prestige of its ancient patrimony.[3] Ultimately, the lists of the descendants of Noah in Genesis 10 were thought to cover all nations (or their ancestors) on earth. An important agendum of medieval ethnography—considered part of theology since Latin-Christian late antiquity[4]—was to trace the genealogies of contemporary *gentes* back to a scion of Noah. Thus to claim that the Hungarians were "unheard of" was to insinuate that they were outside of and foreign to the divine order of the world.[5]

The *honfoglalás* after 880 and their ensuing, large-scale raids far to the west and south transformed the Magyars from a threat on the margins of European society to a potential disaster in its very center. This occasioned a sudden fearful obsession with finding the newcomers a tangible place in history. Scholars set to work, producing a variety of biblical, pseudohistorical, and learned identifications. Remigius of Auxerre (d. 908) mentions that many came to believe the Hungarians to be *Gog* and *Magog*, the "invaders from the north" whom Ezekiel prophesied would descend upon and destroy Israel.[6] Gog and Magog also appear among the allies of Satan in the book of Revelation.[7] This was, indeed, a popular ascription with a long and flexible history. The Goths, Scyths, Huns, and various other barbarians and invaders—especially from the continental east, which to Mediterranean antiquity and the early Middle Ages was the north—were all identified at one time or another with Gog and Magog.[8] The Magyars were simply the latest invaders from that direction.

Remigius himself disputed this association, however, and produced a more idiosyncratic explanation. He claimed that "fame quam patiebantur Hungri vocati sunt" (the Hungarians received their name from the famine they suffered) during their nomadic peregrinations.[9] To be sure, once one realizes that behind *fames* lies the German word *Hunger* (*Hungri* = "die Hungrigen," "the hungry ones"), Remigius's solution seems nothing more than the kind of linguistic determinism familiar from Isidore of Seville's (d. 636) *Etymologies,* indeed characteristic of the medieval period as a whole.[10] Still, Isidore's etymologies were based in Latin. His assumption that the nomenclature of the world derived from Latin roots could be justified, in a sense, by that language's continuing prestige as the universal medium of communication in the Roman empire, the *orbis latinus*. Remigius, by modulating Isidorean technique into German, implicitly elevates his provincial idiom to the status of an imperial language with Adamic powers of naming.

The effects of this onomastic move on its object are even more remarkable. Not only do the Hungarians assume, for Remigius, a German-conditioned identity; their "hunger" is that of a corporeal condition transformed into a *völkish* essence—an essence paradoxically based on lack, on deprivation. Remigius provides, literally in one word, a quasi-anthropologic explanation for the Magyar invasions, as if the deprivation constitutive of Hungarian nature has led perforce to the depredations of their war bands in Europe.

The association of Hungarians with hunger and appetite also played a part in another major theory concerning their origins, first advanced by Regino of Prüm (d. 915) in the early tenth century. According to Regino, the Hungarians, a "gens ferocissima, omni belua crudelior" (very fierce people, more cruel than any monsters), came from "Scythicis regnis," specifically from "paludibus, quas Thanais sua refusione in inmensum porrigit" (the Scythian kingdoms, from the immense swamps of the Don estuary.)[11] With this thesis the German bishop shifted from theology/eschatology to Greco-Roman ethnography, linking the Hungarians with that people whom the ancient world had considered the barbarian *par excellence*, the "absolute embodiment of cultural otherness": the Scythians.[12]

Regino provides a lengthy description of the location of Scythia and the customs of the Scythians. The land "includitur . . . tergo Asia" (borders on Asia at its far end); it is a huge and ethnopolitically undifferentiated country: "hominibus hanc inhabitantibus inter se nulli fines, perraro enim agrum exercent, nec domus illis ulla aut tectum vel sedes est, armenta et pecora semper pascentibus et per incultas solitudines errare solitis" (The people who dwell there have no borders among themselves, for they hardly ever cultivate the fields, have no houses of any kind, but wander throughout the uncultivated wastes grazing their animals).[13] Demographic factors come into play: on one hand Scythia, despite being a wasteland, is nonetheless highly productive, for the cold north (*septemtrionalis plaga*) is "tanto salubrior corporibus hominum et propagantis gentibus coaptata" (healthy for the human body and fit for the propagation of peoples).[14] On the other hand, however, the land cannot support the great numbers it brings forth—for some strange reason the climate is not equally healthy for the game animal body! Therefore Scythia's inhabitants frequently emigrate, and especially tend to invade neighboring Europe.[15]

It is true that Regino borrows—common practice throughout all of medieval historiography—much from earlier Roman and Germanic sources for this excursus. "Scythia" had long since become a literary topos of the near continental east, a "magic box" from which, like a secular equivalent of the Gog and Magog topos, any number of nomadic peoples were thought to spring.[16] Still, his historiographic technique shows more subtlety and independence than he has generally been given credit.

First of all, despite the inherited vagueness and atemporality of the Scythian topos, Regino approaches the Hungarian/Scythian relationship historically. He explicitly mentions that he is quoting from previous historians, a move certainly not *de rigeur* in the early medieval period.[17] More important, in sharp contrast to the tendency of eschatologically-informed ethnography,[18] nowhere does Regino simply conflate the two peoples. He seems to have solid empiricist scruples concerning the relationship between the latter-day Hungarians, "unknown in previous ages" and the Scythians, described in his source as "gens antiquissima semper habitata" (the most ancient people that ever existed).[19] In his comparison he ostentatiously marks the Hungarians as the "gens memorata" (the people I was talking about previously),[20] impeding any direct elision with his Scythian information.

Secondly, Regino's development of the hunger motif explains the Hungarian invasions in terms of a certain anthropologic rationalism, one more sophisticated than Remigius's etymologizing wordplay. Motifs of population growth and starvation alluded to in Remigius's letter are both worked out in more detail and given a more general theoretical grounding. Regino's Hungarians, despite their "ferocity" and "cruelty," their habit of eating raw flesh, and their cannibalist proclivities, are not agents of devilish malice, but themselves victims of the demographic rigors of their homeland. Regino's Scythia, able to produce but unable to nourish great multitudes, is a causal engine of aggressive exterritorialization. This explanatory model is thoroughly secular, which for the early Middle Ages may be considered an achievement, especially for a bishop. Nowhere in his excursus does he lapse into the transcendental causal mode so familiar in discussions of heathen otherness throughout the period. His Hungarians may be fierce and cruel, but he eschews Remigian expressions such as "gens Deo odibilis" (people hateful to God) and avoids the hackneyed discourse of the "flagellum Dei" (scourge of God), whereby troubles with pagans and invaders are explained as God's punishment for Christian sins.[21]

Finally, Regino's Scythian/Hungarian compilation had a lasting effect on the later medieval invention of Hungarian tradition. It was one of the major sources of the first Hungarian historical chronicles. To analyze this transmission goes beyond the scope of this essay. However, I would like to suggest that the historicism and secularism of Regino's approach was one of the major reasons for his text's appeal to the early Hungarian chroniclers. It enabled them to appropriate, justify, and recuperate their own problematic and alien "Scythian heritage" in secular, historicist terms. This was largely their own achievement, but Regino provided a congenial point of departure.[22]

II. *Ostarliut*

German heroic epics developed an imagology of the Huns and Hungarians that diverged sharply from the Latin ecclesiastical tradition. Representations of the steppe nomads (as well as other east European peoples, such as the Slavs) are unique to heroic literature, the epic geographies of which looked eastward from the earliest times. They hardly appear in Arthurian romance and crusading epic, both of which were influenced primarily by French models.[23]

Indeed, the earliest surviving example of heroic poetry in Germany, the *Hildebrandslied*-fragment (mid–ninth century), represents, in a sense, the appropriation of a "foreign," indeed an east European literature, very much in the same way French narratives of Arthur appropriated the foreign *matière de Bretagne*. Although the precise transmission of the *Hildebrandslied* is anything but clear, its narrative material is clearly East Germanic (Gothic or Lombardic) in origin, presuming as its basis sagas of king Theoderic the Great (Dietrich von Bern in the vernacular), his exile from Italy and his sojourn among the Huns.[24] These sagas were, in turn, predicated on historical constellations in fifth-century southeastern Europe, where several groups of Goths (led by the Amali, Theoderic's clan) entered into alliance with the Huns of Attila.[25] Let us look more closely at the *Hildebrandslied*, for in it we already find all the elements that later characterize the Dietrich-cycle as a whole.

Hildebrand meets Hadubrand in single combat between two opposing forces. In the parley before battle, Hildebrand asks Hadubrand who his father and relatives are. Hadubrand relates that his father, Hildebrand, abandoned his family long ago and headed east into exile in the company of Theoderic, fleeing the hatred of Odoacer. Hadubrand now believes his father to be dead. Hildebrand attempts to convince his son otherwise, and proffers a gift of reconciliation, a golden armband that the Lord of the Huns gave him. Hadubrand accuses his opponent of subterfuge, calling him a treacherous old Hun and claiming to know from sailors on the western seas that his father died in battle. Hildebrand laments that his thirty-year exile has to end in such a fashion, but realizes that combat is unavoidable if he doesn't wish to be known as a coward among the easterners. The warriors arm themselves and the battle begins [here the text breaks off].

As is clear from this synopsis, the *Hildebrandslied* shows remarkable attention to the "east," the *ōsten*. Reflecting on his father's departure years ago, Hadubrand seems fixated on the direction of Hildebrand's flight: twice we hear "he went east" within a few lines.[26] Within the tight discursive regime of alliterative poetry, such repetition underscores the importance of the motif, especially since the east seems only marginally relevant to Hildebrand's question "uuer sin fater uuari" (who his father was). Hildebrand, for his part, justifies the ultimate necessity of combat in terms of his reputation among the *ostar-liut* (easterners).[27]

What is meant by the "east" in this text? Jennifer Williams writes that "[t]he land in the East need not be synonymous with the land of the Huns since the Huns' kingdom presumably lay to the north or northeast of Italy. The use of two different designations, 'East' and 'Huns' would also suggest separate places."[28] There are two problems with this interpretation. First, it is difficult to imagine who the "easterners" could be, other than the Huns. The armband implies that Hildebrand is in the service of the Hunnish lord; consequently, it is among that folk that his military (i.e., social) reputation matters.[29] For this reason I disagree with William's suggestion of the *ōsten* as the "eastern Empire," that is, Byzantium. Secondly, it need not follow from the assumption that Italy is the scene of the action that the Hunnish kingdom lay to the "north or northeast." I suggest we read *Lombardic* as northern Italy, where (as Williams herself points out) a respected branch of scholarship would localize the text's origins anyway. Directly east from there (modern day Slovenia and southern Hungary) lay the westernmost extension of the Hunnic empire, which had shifted considerably to the southwest in the fifth century under Attila—that is, from north Pontic Scythia to Pannonia and northern Illyricum.[30] Thus, I see no problem with identifying the "east" with the Huns, if we accept the thesis that the *Hildebrandslied* preserves a fifth-century geographic imagination.

But what if it does not? After all, with the possible exception of its proper names, the poem bears no linguistic trace of its putative East Germanic heritage. It is preserved only in a strangely hybrid Upper/Lower German adaptation. It is possible that the transmission involved changes in content as well as language. In any case, even if we presume that the term "east" remained in the text along its entire migration route from northern Italy to Bavaria/Swabia to Fulda, in the German geography of its reception the "east" and "easterners" will have suggested something completely different than in Italy. It could have implied a wide range of lands along the whole length of the Carolingian *marchae orientalis* from Slovenia to the Wendish territorries east of Saxony in the ninth century. If that be the case, then while the internal economy of the text will doubtless still have kept the *ostarliut* firmly linked with the Huns, the geographic imagination of its transalpine audience could have read the Huns as the masters of the entire East from the Baltic to the Adriatic. As we shall see, the *Hiunenland* of the later German epics is precisely such a generalized east European space under the rule of the Huns.

What about the *Hildebrandslied*'s image of "the foreigner," "the Other"? As we have noted, Hadubrand, refusing to believe Hildebrand to be his father, calls him a "treacherous old Hun" ([ummet spaher] alter hun). András Vizkelety writes of this passage: "Der junge Mann wurde so erzogen, daβ dem, der aus dem Osten kommt, nicht zu trauen ist" (The young man was raised to mistrust anyone from the east), and further: "die Klischees für die Beurteilung der Hunnen haben sowohl die mündlich tradierte epische Erinnerung als auch die gelehrte lateinische Historiographie konserviert" (Both oral epic tradition and scholarly Latin historiography preserved the pejorative clichés concerning the Huns).[31] Jennifer Williams finds that "[t]he regime in Hiltibrant's native land clearly views the Huns with some animosity."[32]

Both Williams's and Vizkelety's analyses remain at the level of historiographical inventory, failing to address adequately how the poem's image of the "easterner" functions within the central literary problematic of Hildebrand's exile and alienation from his family and native land. For after all, Hadubrand's animosity and mistrust are manifestly *in error*, hindering the reunion of father and son. The tragic core of the poem is the inability (or refusal) to perceive the "own" in the "other," even the most intimate own (the father) in the guise of the most extremely other (the Hun). Depending on the degree to which we wish to read the text's heroic-age pathos in later medieval, Christian-ethical terms, we might say that the *Hildebrandslied* offers critical commentary on the "xenologic phenomenology" typical of late antique/early medieval west European views of the steppe nomads. As Vizkelety stresses throughout his article, the Huns and Hungarians were long considered inhuman or subhuman in the Middle Ages. Surely one of the lessons of the *Hildebrandslied*'s tragedy of misrecognition lies in the refutation of this—of Hildebrand's—view of the Hun. Indeed, it provokes us to the counterthesis that "even he who comes out of the East is human, too."

The flight of Germanic heroes to Hunnic eastern Europe and their exile at the Hunnic court became part of the *Kernfabel* of an entire medieval German epic cycle, that of Dietrich von Bern (Dietrich of Verona).[33] The relationship between the Dietrich of "literature" and the Theoderic of "history" is complicated,[34] and few generalizations apply across the board.[35] What is important here is that the core narrative represents a threefold historical revision of the east European space vis-à-vis the biography of Theoderic: first, vernacular epics represent Dietrich and Etzel, king of the Huns, as contemporaries, indeed as companions, whereas the lives of their historical counterparts did not overlap, much less intertwine.[36] Second, in making Italy Dietrich's homeland and the Land of the Huns his place of exile, the sagas reverse the east/west relationship in Theoderic's career, which began in Greece and ended in Italy.[37] This brings us to the third, in its historical remodeling most striking point: whereas Theoderic ruled Italy successfully for thirty years, Dietrich spends thirty years in exile, fruitlessly attempting to regain his lost kingdom, yet forsaking the chance even when it presents itself and forever returning to the court of his host and single benefactor, Etzel.[38]

The exile thematic, which is also to be found in other German epics such as the *Waltharius* and *Nibelungenlied*, enabled German literature, in contrast to other west European literatures, to develop a positive imagology of the steppe nomads and their settled successors, and, in a larger sense, of the "pagan invader" in general. French epics revised the complex historical experience of the Islamic wars into a straightforward, manichean imagology of good vs. evil, of Christian vs. heathen, of "us" vs. "them." In contrast, the German epic refigured Hungarian history of the ninth and tenth centuries into the Hunnic/Germanic entanglements of the Dietrich tradition, which not only disallowed the facile sundering of own from other, of native from foreigner, but, through the motif-complex of Germanic exile, fostered the representation of their interaction, collaboration, and mutual dependence, as well as their conflict. This Germanic-Hunnic/Hungarian enmeshment is most evident in the picture of Hungary in the *Nibelungenlied*.

III. Hiunenland

There has long been a tendency in the scholarship (especially that written in English) to regard the Hiunenland of the *Nibelungenlied* as a realm of pure otherness. In the words of A.T. Hatto, the Burgundians are "drawn away into a distant past" as they approach Etzel's Hungary, "a place grown shadowy and remote."[39] For Stephen Wailes Hiunenland is a mythic "Otherworld," and Etzel is the "fiend" who rules there, "presiding" over the destruction of the Burgundians.[40] Joyce Lionarons writes: "[A]lthough at first glance Etzel's Hungary may seem to have more in common with the historical world of Burgundy and Xanten than with the Otherworld of Isenstein or Nibelungenland, its poetic representation as a literal kingdom of the dead places it firmly in the realm of the otherworldly."[41]

An elaborate and sophisticated network of historical references and contemporary allusions to Hungary in the text, however, militates against such a vague, mythic conception of otherness, be it as a "kingdom of the dead" or as a realm of ethnologic alterity.[42] Historians have noted, for example, that Rüdiger's Hunnic margraviate in the west of Etzel's kingdom reflects German/Hungarian territorial relations in the tenth century, the only period the Hungarians managed to control Lower Austria east of the river Enns (the old Carolingian *Ostmark*).[43] At the same time, however, the nations subject to Etzel show a remarkable conformity to the early thirteenth-century ethnic makeup of Hungary, especially the western frontier zone with which Bavarians and Austrians would have been familiar. Russians, Greeks, Poles, Vlachs, and Pechenegs appear often in contemporaneous records.[44] The figure and character of Etzel strongly resembles not only representations of Géza, the last pagan ruler of Hungary, but also the image of the Christian Hungarian king in contemporaneous German historical texts.[45] The reference to "German guests" (*tiutsche geste*) at the Hunnic court reflects the presence of Germanic aristocrats—the so-called *hospites teutonici*—among the vassals of the Hungarian kings, a presence continuous throughout the medieval period, but especially important at the turn of the thirteenth century.[46] Many more connections could be pointed out.[47] In addition, the *Nibelungenlied*'s east completely lacks the teratological otherness of its north; Hiunenland numbers no dwarves, dragons, supernaturally-endowed amazons, or legions of shadow-warriors among its denizens.

Thus Hiunenland is quite the opposite of what Lionarons claims, an "otherworldly" locus on a par with the septentrional world of Isenstein and Nibelungenland. Its representation seems to be more a product of assimilation to (from an Austrian or Bavarian point of view) local and familiar Hungary than abjection into a vague, shadowy, mythic alterity. On the imagological level, I see no reason to ascribe to the *vremdheit* of Etzel's kingdom anything more than the local color of the Austro-Hungarian border in the early thirteenth century.

The foreignness of Hiunenland must be approached differently, from the point of view of Kriemhild and the Burgundians. When, in the twenty-second adventure, Kriemhild crosses the Traisen river into the Hunnic empire, she beholds a spectacle of cultural plurality and *vremdheit*:

Von vil maniger sprâche sah man ûf den wegen
vor Etzelen rîten manigen küenen degen,
von kristen und von heiden vil manige wîte schar.
dâ si die vrouwen funden, si kômen hêrlichen dar.

Von Riuzen und von Kriechen reit dâ vil manic man.
den Pœlân unt den Walachen sach man swinde gân
ir ross diu vil guoten, dâ sie mit kreften riten.
swaz si site hêten, der wart vil wênic vermiten.

Von dem lande ze Kiewen reit dâ vil manic degen,
unt die wilden Petschenære. dâ wart vil gepflegen

mit dem bogen schiezen zen vogeln die dâ flugen.
die pfîle si vil sêre zuo den wenden vaste zugen.

Ein stat bî Tuonouwe lît in Ôsterlant,
diu ist geheizen Tulne dâ wart [Kriemhilt] bekant
vil manic site vremede, den si ê nie gesach.
si enpfiengen dâ genuoge, den sît leit von ir geschach.[48]

[In front of Etzel one could see numbers of bold knights of many different languages riding along the roads, great companies past counting of both Christians and heathens who were marching in splendid array to where they found the ladies. Many men from Greece and Russia were riding there, and the good horses of the Poles and Wallachians passed swiftly by as their riders spurred them with vigor, while they all freely comported themselves according to their native customs. From the land of Kiev, too, many a knight was riding there, not to mention the wild Petchenegs who, laying the arrow to the bow at full stretch, shot at birds on the wing with zest. There is a town in Ôsterlant on the Danube called Tulln, where Kriemhild saw many strange customs that she had never encountered before. Many people received her there whom she was later to cause great harm.]

"Die östliche Völkerwelt mit erlebter Fremdartigkeit tut sich . . . auf" (The world of eastern peoples reveals itself, mediated through the experience of foreignness) wrote Karl Bartsch/Helmut de Boor concerning these passages in the footnotes to the (still) standard edition of the text.[49] Shortly later, commenting upon the single appearance of the term "German" (*tiutsch*) in the *Nibelungenlied*, the editors outline a fundamental ethnocultural dichotomy: "Gegenüber dem fremden Völkergemisch des Hunnenreiches faβt der Dichter Kriemhilds burgundische Begleiter, Rüedegers Mannen und Dietrichs Goten zu dieser Einheit zusammen" (The poet unites Kriemhild's Burgundian escort, Rudiger's troops, and Dietrich's Goths in this term [*tiutsch*] by way of contrast to the foreign mix of peoples in the Hunnic kingdom).[50]

The belief in German "unity" vs. a "foreign mix of [east European] peoples" doubtless has more to do with twentieth-century nationalist sentiments than with medieval literature. Bartsch/de Boor's comments have not gone without criticism, as might be expected from a scholarship committed to exposing the abuses the *Nibelungenlied* suffered as a "German national epic" in the nineteenth and twentieth centuries.[51] In one sense, however, Bartsch/de Boor's view was not only justified, but also remarkably insightful for a period in literary criticism lacking a theory of (or interest in) visuality in narrative. The *Nibelungenlied* does not present the "foreignness" of the east European world as such, but rather as *experienced* foreignness ("*erlebte* Fremdartigkeit").[52] The textual approach to the Land of the Huns is governed entirely by Kriemhild's personal approach, mediated through her first uneasy gaze upon Etzel's multigentilic retinues as they come riding along the Austrian roads to receive and integrate her into Hiunenland.

Even though the first part of the narrative has moved through many lands (the Rhineland, the Netherlands, Hessen, Saxony, Iceland, Swabia, Bavaria, and Austria) it is, surprisingly, only now that we hear any mention of ethnocultural otherness, "different languages," "native customs," "strange customs," and the like. In Iceland, for example, there is no reference to the *vremde site* of the Icelanders as a whole, but only about the individual nasty habits (*vreislîche sit*) of Brunhild.[53] As Brunhild journeys down the Rhine from the north and enters Burgundy as Gunther's bride, we get no sense that she is being received and integrated into another, a foreign world, or that she herself is foreign in any way.

Until the borders of Hiunenland are reached the non-issue of ethnocultural *vremdheit* is not at all conspicuous. We simply presume to be moving about a typical heroic world of passive cultural and linguistic sameness, one in which difference in communicative media is not important, being suspended or universalized in order to streamline the representation of character and conflict. Yet such media-transparency suddenly comes to an end as Kriemhild looks upon the strange customs and hears the strange tongues of her new home. Simultaneously, the latter undergoes a retrospective revision. With the sharp focus on east European difference, what seemed a passive sameness of language/culture in the lands previously traversed is foregrounded as a unity. Not a "German" or "Germanic" unity, as Bartsch/de Boor suggest, but a quasi "western" uniformity of everything prior to Hunnic "eastern" Europe.

Ominously, Kriemhild's first experience of east European otherness is underwritten by a premonition of disaster: the practitioners of the "many strange customs" are linked to the "many people" in Hiunenland fated to come to harm through her agency (st. 1341, 3–4). This passage adumbrates what will become a central problem of Kriemhild's new life in Hiunenland, her persistent feeling of being a foreigner in exile (*ellende*) and a concomitant inability or refusal to integrate: "ich hœre mîn die liute niuwan für ellende jehen" (I always hear the people saying that I am like a foreigner in exile), she complains years later to Etzel. While Kriemhild's *ellende* is more a result of her unwillingness to forget the murder of Siegfried, her inability to cope with Hunnish otherness plays a part in her fateful decision to invite the Burgundians to Hiunenland:

Ez lag ir an den herzen spât unde vruo,
wie man si âne schulde bræhte dar zuo,
daz si muose minnen einen heidenischen man.
die nôt die het ir Hagene unde Gunther getân.[54]

[She was constantly preoccupied with the thought that she had been forced to marry a heathen. Hagen and Gunther bore the blame for this.]

Scholars have considered this passage a "foolish addition"of religious discourse to the text, one having no relation to the reality of Kriemhild's marriage to Etzel nor to her true agenda of revenge for Siegfried's murder.[55] It is certainly true that Kriemhild not only chose willingly to marry a heathen, but also that Hagen was very much against letting her do so. Until this point we hear nothing to suggest she is unhappy with Etzel. Still, Kriemhild's religious scruples are not complete pretense. They are forshadowed not only in her initial unease in the face of Hunnish foreignness, but also in an earlier passage in which the narrator describes the multireligious character of Etzel's kingdom:

> . . . die küensten recken von den ie wart vernommen
> under kristen und under heiden: die wâren mit im alle komen.
>
> Bî im was z'allen zîten — daz wætlîch mêr ergê—
> kristenlîcher orden unt ouch der heiden ê.
> in swie getânem lebene sich ietslîcher truoc,
> daz schuof des küniges milte daz man in allen gap genuoc.[56]
>
> [The most fearless warriors ever known among Christians and heathens alike had all joined him. The Christian and the heathen way of life existed side by side in [Etzel's kingdom]. That could hardly even happen again. Whatever rite one followed, the king's largesse provided amply for all.]

This passage immediately precedes Kriemhild's entrance into Hiunenland. In effect, Etzel's new Burgundian bride enters Etzel's kingdom as the harbinger of destruction for its multicultural idyll. Her religious scruples, despite the superficiality of their causal role, intimate that peaceful Christian-heathen cohabitation will come to an end through her agency.

Kriemhild is not the only exile; Hiunenland is replete with "western" European heroes and ladies living there in the condition of *ellende*: Rudiger, Dietrich, Hildebrant, Irinc, Irnfried, Hawart, and Herrat. When they arrive, the Burgundians, too, are *ellende.* In his recent book, Jan-Dirk Müller proposes *ellende* as the central organizational category of Etzel's kingdom:

> Alle an Etzels Hof sind *ellende,* das heißt, aus dem sozialen Zusammenhang gelöst, in den sie hineingeboren wurden. . . . Die entscheidenden letzten Kämpfe finden nur noch zwischen *ellenden* statt, den Amelungen . . . und den *ellenden* burgondischen [*sic*] Überlebenden. Sie sind aus der geordneten politischen Welt herausgefallen. . . . So schafft Etzels exterritorialer Hof die Bedingungen eines Laboratoriums, aus dem politische Strukturen ausgeblendet sind, damit alle nur noch Helden sein können.[57]
>
> [Everybody at Etzel's court is *ellende*; that is, separated from the social context into which they were born. . . . The decisive last battles take place

> exclusively between *ellenden*, the Amelungs [i.e., Dietrich and his men] . . . and the Burgundian survivors. They have all been alienated from the ordered political world. . . . Etzel's exterratorial court is like a laboratory in which, under controlled conditions, political structures have been eliminated so that everybody can simply be a hero.]

Ellende is the condition of heroic anomy, the opposite of the elaborate feudal structures of lordship and loyalty characteristic of Burgundy and the Netherlands. In Hiunenland, overarching political structures dissolve in the regression to naked violence.[58] Violence, however, is not a phenomenon immanent to Hiunenland, which rests in a "strange stasis" devoid of battles for power and dominance.[59]

Using Müller's insights, I propose quasi-Conradian terms for the Germanic-Hunnic entanglements of the *Nibelungenlied*: highly organized and civilized (courtly) Europeans (Germanic heroes) encounter each other in a foreign zone (Hiunenland) far from the centers of civilization (courtly Rhineland). Free from the limitations and constraints of the ordered political and social world (hierarchical, courtly feudal society), they regress to violence and brutality (pure heroism), deploying contingents of "natives" (Huns) as grist in private wars against each other (Kriemhild and her Hunnish vassals vs. the Burgundians). The "otherness" of Hiunenland is secondary, a mere catalyst enabling the desublimation and emergence of the courtly world's real antithesis and Other: the Germanic hero.

The old theme of Germanic exile in eastern Europe complicated the representation of the eastern foreigner, preventing the emergence of any clear ethical, much less national or proto-national, distinction between the own and the other in the German heroic epic tradition. As we have seen, this was not the case in French epics, which tolerated no great zone of ambivalence in the representations of Muslims vis-à-vis Christians. Yet we must keep in mind strongly differing historical and cultural contexts. French epics thematize the contemporaneous crusade and reconquest of Spain, waged against an enemy with a religion and social system that could compete with Christianity on all levels. The Hungarian invasions, in contrast, were comparatively short-lived, far less destructive, and, since the Magyars did not have a highly developed religion or social system, ended in swift conversion and acculturation to the west. By the time main texts in the German heroic tradition were written, Hungary had already been a fully-fledged member of Christian Europe for well more than a century.

Still, these differences only became clear in long historical retrospective. As Otto of Freising's notorious comments (c. 1150) on the Hungarians demonstrate, the memories of the tenth century invasions and pagan savagery could continue exercising a negative influence on Hungarian "public relations" many generations after the fact.[60] It was not until the late thirteenth century that Hungary and the Hungarians were seen by contemporaries as fully-fledged members of western *christianitas*.[61] Against this background, the relatively positive and open imagology of the steppe nomads in vernacular German epic poetry is striking indeed.

Notes

1. Literally "occupation of the homeland," a linguistic construction of curious and untranslatable tautology.
2. *Annales Bertiniani*, in Monumenta Germaniae Historica Scriptores (Hannover: Hahn, 1826), vol. 1, 458 (for the year 862); Regino of Prüm, *Chronicon*, in Monumenta Germaniae Historica Scriptores rerum germanicarum in usum scholarum (Hannover: Hahn, 1989), 131 (for the year 889); Remigius Antissiodorensis, *Epsiola ad D. episcopum virdunensem*, in Patrologia Latina (Paris: J. P. Migne, 1853), vol. 131, col. 966c. See also Szabolcs de Vajay, *Der Eintritt des ungarischen Stammbundes in die europäische Geschichte* (Mainz: Hase & Koehler, 1968), 11; Balint Hóman, *A magyar hún-hagyomány és a hún-monda* (Budapest: Studium, 1925), 33–34.
3. Jenö Szücs, *Nation und Geschichte* (Cologne, Vienna: Böhlau Verlag, 1981), 285.
4. Arno Borst, *Der Turmbau von Babel: Geschichte der Meinungen über Ursprung und Vielfalt der Sprachen und Völker* (Munich: Deutscher Taschenbuchverlag, 1995), v. II/1, 373.
5. See Borst, *Der Turmbau*, 569, 578.
6. Remigius, col. 966b: "opinio[] . . . quae innumeros tam in vestra quam in nostra regione pervasit . . . putatur Deo odibilis gens Hungrorum esse Gog et Magog . . ."
7. Remigius, col. 966b. Borst, *Der Turmbau*, 531. Ezekiel 38: 10–14; Rev. 20: 7–10. See also Jeremiah 1:14.
8. See Andrew Alexander, *Alexander's Gate, Gog and Magog, and the Enclosed Nations* (Cambridge, Mass.: Waverly Press, 1932), 5.
9. Remigius, col. 968a. See Borst, *Der Turmbau*, 531.
10. András Vizkelety, " 'Du bist ein alter Hunne, unmäßig schlau . . ." in *Das Ungarnbild in Deutschland und das Deutschlandbild in Ungarn: Materialien des wissenschaftlichen Symposiums am 26. und 27. Mai 1995 in Hamburg*, ed. Holger Fischer (Munich: Südosteuropa-Gesellschaft, 1996), 11–21; here 13.
11. Regino, 131.
12. François Hartog, *The Mirror of Herodotus: the Representation of the Other in the Writing of History*, trans. Janet Lloyd (Berkeley: University of California Press, 1988), 30. The Scythians, in fact, provide a link between theology and ethnography, since they themselves were often (since Josephus) considered to be Gog and Magog. See István Vásáry, "Medieval Theories Concerning the Primordial Homeland of the Huns" (Spoleto: Centro italiano de studi sull'alto Medioevo, 1988), 218–19.

13. Regino, 131.
14. Regino, 132.
15. Regino, 132.
16. Vásáry, 223. See also Maximilian Georg Kellner, *Die Ungarneinfälle im Bild der Quellen bis 1150. Von der "Gens detestanda" zur "Gens ad fidem Christi conversa"* (Munich: Verlag Ungarisches Institut, 1997), 77–78.
17. Regino, 131: "non superfluum videatur, si de Scythiae situ et Scytharumque moribus historiographarum dicta sequentes aliquid commemorenus."
18. See note 6: "putatur . . . gens Hungrorum . . . *esse* Gog und Magog."
19. Justin Junianus, *Epitoma historiarum Philippicarum Pompei Trogi*, quoted from Kellner, 78. Significantly, this remark is not quoted by Regino, although it is to be found in the same sections of Justin from which he derives his other passages. Still, it seems to have conditioned his view.
20. Regino, 131.
21. See Remigius, col. 968a: "Nunc justo Dei judicio in nostris grassantur cervicibus. . . . Deo se per talia hominum monstra [i.e the Hungarians] ulciscente de nobis. . . ."
22. Compare the early thirteenth century Anonymus Belae Regis Notarius, *Gesta Hungarorum* (*Die "Gesta Hungarorum" des anonymen Notars*), ed. Gabriel Silagi (Sigmaringen: Thorbecke Verlag, 1991), 32–35, 138–39 ("De Scythia"). See also József Deér, "Szkitia leírása a Gesta Ungarorumban," *Magyar Könyvszemle* 37 (1930): 246–252.
23. In fact, the German *Rolandslied* adopts from the *Chanson de Roland* the contradictory allegiances of the Hungarians, who are both subjects of Charlemagne (1771, 5210, 6846) and part of Baligan's heathen army (8101).
24. Dieter Kartschoke, *Geschichte der deutschen Literatur im frühen Mittelalter* (Munich: Deutscher Taschenbuchverlag, 1994), 125. The debate over the text's Gothic or Langobardic origins/ transmission is summarized by Jennifer Williams, *Etzel der rîche: the Depiction of Attila the Hun in the Literature of Medieval Germany, with Rreference to Rrelated Byzantine, Italic, Gallic, Scandinavian and Hungarian sources (450–1300)*. European University Studies, Series I, German Language and Literature 364 (Bern: Peter Lang, 1981), 127–130.
25. On these "New Goths" or "Hunnic Goths" see Herwig Wolfram, *History of the Goths* (Berkeley: University of California Press, 1990), 248–58.
26. forn her ostar giueit   floh her otachres nid
hina mit theotrihhe   enti sinero degano filu.
her fur-laet in lante   luttila sitten
prut in bure   barn unuuahsan
arbeo laosa   her raet ostar hina. (18–22)
"[Hildebrand] went east a long time ago, fleeing the hatred of Odoacer with Dietrich and many of his companions. He abandoned his young wife at home, and left his ungrown son without any inheritance. He rode off east." Quoted from *Althochdeutsche poetische Texte*, ed. Karl Wipf (Stuttgart: Reclam, 1992), 150.
27. der si doch nu argosto"   "ostar-liuto
der dir nu uuiges uuarne   nu dih es so uuel lustit." (56–58)

"He who would refuse to fight one so eager for combat would truly be considered a coward among the easterners, said Hildebrant." Quoted from Wipf, ed., 154.

28. Williams, 126.
29. Wolfram offers some interesting comments about the bonds of loyalty between the Huns and the "Hunnish Goths" that can perhaps be applied to Hildebrand's concern for his reputation among the *ostarliut*: "[These Goths] had adopted the Hunnic attitude that emigration and separation from the main tribe were serious crimes. Whoever ran away from the Huns showed his contempt for the Goths and lost his Amal identity, which was even more highly regarded than Attila's nobility. . . . The Goths were bound to the Huns by oath and loyally devoted to them." *History of the Goths,* 257.
30. Wolfram, *History of the Goths*, 254; *The Roman Empire and its Germanic Peoples* (Berkeley: University of California Press, 1997), 127.
31. Vizkelety, 11.
32. Williams, 126.
33. Joachim Heinzle, *Einführung in die mittelhochdeutsche Dietrichepik* (Berlin and New York: Walter de Gruyter, 1999), 2.
34. I write quotes around "history" and "literature" less from a postmodern viewpoint, with its radical reduction of all historical empirica to representation and "fiction," as from the now fairly traditional thesis that heroic literature could have been understood by its practitioners and audience to be "real" history. See Karl Hauck, "Heldendichtung und Heldensage als Geschichtsbewusstsein," in *Alteuropa und die moderne Gesellschaft: Festschrift für Otto Brunner*, ed. Alexander Bergengruen and Ludwig Deike (Göttingen: Vandenhoeck and Ruprecht, 1963), 122–24; and Walter Haug, "Andreas Heuslers Heldensagenmodell: Prämissen, Kritik und Gegenentwurf," *Zeitschrift für deutsches Altertum* 104 (1975): 273–292.
35. The most recent detailed study is Joachim Heinzle, *Einführung in die mittelhochdeutsche Dietrichepik* (see footnote 33); Roswitha Wisniewski's *Mittelalterliche Dietrichdichtung* (Stuttgart: J. B. Metzler, 1986) is broader in textual basis and more speculative in its conclusions.
36. Attila died in 451; Theoderic was born in 450.
37. See Wisniewski, 52.
38. The extent to which the *Hildebrandslied* "prefigures" these features of later epic is contested. There is, as Williams points out, (1) no explicit mention of Etzel/Attila in the *Hildebrandslied*, but only of a "lord of the Huns"; (2) nothing said about Dietrich at the Hunnish court, but only of Hildebrand himself; (3) no reference to Dietrich's exile, but only of Hildebrand's. One's point of view depend on the degree to which one presumes the existence of a more developed (oral) Dietrich saga by the ninth century (of which the *Hildebrandslied* would be merely one example), in which Dietrich's exile at Etzel's court is "understood." Helmut de Boor, *Das Attilabild in Geschichte, Legende und heroischer Dichtung* (Darmstadt: Wissenschaftliche Buchgesellschaft, 1963), 10, and Dieter Kartschoke, 125, make this presumption, and I agree with them. Jennifer Williams refuses to make any extra-textual assumptions at all (see her critique of de Boor, 125). Ultimately—as in so many arguments

about the relationship between oral and written traditions—the matter cannot be ultimately resolved.

39. A. T. Hatto, trans., *The Nibelungenlied* (Harmondsworth: Penguin Books, 1966), 399.
40. Stephen Wailes, "The *Nibelungenlied* as Heroic Epic," in *Heroic Epic and Saga*, ed. Felix J. Oinas (Bloomington: Indiana University Press, 1978), 138.
41. Joyce Tally Lionarons, "The Otherworld and its Inhabitants in the *Nibelungenlied*," in *A Companion to the Nibelungenlied*, ed. Winder McConnell. Studies in German Literature, Linguistics, and Culture (Columbia, S. C.: Camden House, 1998), 153–71; here 171.
42. To be sure, there is no explicit identification of the Huns with the Hungarians in the *Nibelungenlied*. Ms. B has—most of all the ms.—only two references to "Hungary": *Ungerland* (1373, 1) and *Ungern* (1162, 1). The latter is, strictly speaking, a dative plural of the ethnic name "Hungarians," but its usage here is—as in modern German—purely geographical, as is clear from the lack of a preposition ("*zen Ungern*"). In fact, "Hungarian" never appears as an ethnic name in German heroic poetry; the terms "Hun," "Hunnic," and "Land of the Huns" have a veritable onomastic monopoly. See George Gillespie, *A Catalogue of Persons Named in German Heroic Literature (700–1600) Including Named Animals and Objects and Ethnic Names* (Oxford: Clarendon Press, 1973), 79–80, 132. Thus, Williams's belief that "[b]y the twelfth century the Hun-Hungarian identification is complete and Etzel appears in German vernacular poetry as both Hun and Hungarian" (265) is too conditioned by contemporary Latin historiography. I follow Árpád Berczik, "Vermutliche ungarische Spuren im Nibelungenlied," in *Akten des V. internationalen Germanisten-Kongresses Cambridge 1975*, ed. L. Forster and H.-G. Roloff, *Jahrbuch für internationale Germanistik,* Reihe A, II (Bern/Frankfurt a. M.,1976), 383–88; here 385, who finds "no allusion to the relationship between Huns and Hungarians."
43. See Fritz Peter Knapp, "Neue Spekulationen über alter Rüdiger-Lieder," in *Pöchlarner Heldenliedgespräch: Das Nibelungenlied und der mittlere Donauraum,* ed. Klaus Zatloukal (Vienna: Fassbaender, 1990), 47–58; here 48–49, 51–52.
44. *Das Nibelungenlied,* ed. Karl Bartsch and Helmut de Boor, trans. Siegfried Grosse (Stuttgart: Reclam, 1997), st. 1339–40. See Konrad Schünemann, "Ungarische Hilfsvölker in der Literatur des deutschen Mittelalters," *Ungarische Jahrbücher* 4 (1924): 99–101, 114; Hansgerd Göckenjahn, *Hilfsvölker und Grenzwächter im mittelalterlichen Ungarn* (Wiesbaden: Franz Steiner Verlag, 1972).
45. Aloys Schröfl, *Der Urdichter des Liedes von der Nibelunge Nôt und die Lösung der Nibelungenfrage* (Munich: J. B. Hohenester Verlag, 1927), 79–80; Friedrich Panzer, "Nibelungische Problematik," *Sitzungsberichte der Heidelberger Akademie der Wissenschaften: Philosophisch-historische Klasse*, no. 3 (1954): 23–24, 26. The epic passage in question is the representation of Etzel as harsh with his own subjects and generous with foreigners (st. 1895–97) vis-à-vis the *Vita St Stephani*'s picture of "Geiza, severus quidem et crudelis veluti potentialiter agens in suos, misericors autem et liberalis

in alienos" (*Vita St Stephani*, in Monumanta Germaniae Historica, Scriptores, v. 11, ed. D. W. Wattenbach [Hannover: Hahn, 1867], 230: "Géza could be harsh, cruel and violent with his own folk, but was compassionate and generous with foreigners"). Etzel's non-participation in combat reflects Ottokar von Steiermark's (early 1300s) observation that "ez ist der Unger gewonheit und jehent ouch offenbare, ir kunic si in zahtbære darzuo, daz er sulle striten" (*Österreichische Reimchronik*, in Monumenta Germaniae Historica Deutsche Chroniken, vol. 5, part 1, ed. Joseph Seemüller [Hannover: Hahn, 1890], vv. 16,126–29: "It is the custom of the Hungarians, which they openly admit, that they consider their king too honorable to participate in battle himself"). The same motif appears in Thomas Ebendorfer's *Chronicon Austriacum*, in Scriptores rerum Austriacarum, vol. II, ed. Hieronymus Pez [Leipzig: J. F. Gleditschius and Sons, 1725], 739: "Ungarorum mos habet, ut rex propria in persona bellum intrare non debeat" ["It is the custom of the Hungarians that the king himself never enter battle"].

46. *Nibelungenlied,* st. 1354. Heinz Thomas, "Dichtung und Politik um 1200: Das Nibelungenlied," in *Pöchlarner Heldenliedgespräch*: *Das Nibelungenlied und der mittlere Donauraum,* ed. Klaus Zatloukal (Vienna: Fassbaender, 1990), 103–29; here 109 with note 20.
47. See also Bálint Hóman, "Geschichtliches im Nibelungenlied" (Berlin, Leipzig: Walter de Gruyter and Co., 1924). There has been, however, a tendency to overinterpret the impact of Hungarian history on the *Nibelungenlied.* Despite many interesting points, Péter Simon's "A Nibelungének magyar vonatkozásai" goes too far in claiming the epic's plot to be modeled directly on eleventh-century Hungarian dynastic conflicts (322–24). Aloys Schröfl (note 45) saw the "solution" of practically every conundrum the *Nibelungenlied* has to offer in terms of a putative tenth-century vernacular German original written by bishop Pilgrim of Passau for the purpose of converting the Magyars to Christianity.
48. *Nibelungenlied*, st.1338–41.
49. Karl Bartsch and Helmut de Boor, eds, *Das Nibelungenlied.* 22nd edition (Mannheim, F.A. Brockhaus, 1988), 216.
50. Bartsch/de Boor, 218.
51. See Thomas, 109.
52. Dezsö Dümmerth has recently proposed an interesting theory regarding Tulne (st. 1341, 3). Not the Austrian city of Tulln north of Vienna was the original model for Tulna, he claims, but rather Hungarian Tolna (about 100 miles south of Budapest). He concludes that the *Nibelungenlied* probably drew upon the same written Hungarian sources as Simon of Kézai for the *Gesta Hungarorum* (c. 1282). Dümmerth's evidence is that, when Kriemhild reaches Tulne, "the country suddenly becomes completely Hunnish" (lesz egyserre "hunná" a táj). However, he neglects to note that the event described is simply a typical epic royal reception whereby the host rides a good distance to meet his arriving guests. Not the "country" is Hunnish at Tulne, but rather Etzel's multigentilic retinues, who have come several days westward into Austria to receive Kriemhild. Dezsö Dümmerth, *Az Árpádok nyomában* (Budapest: Franklin Nyomda, 1987), 63–72, esp. 71.

53. *Nibelungenlied*, st. 330, 2.
54. *Nibelungenlied*, st. 1395.
55. Bartsch/de Boor, 224.
56. *Nibelungenlied*, st. 1334, 3–4 –1335, 1–4.
57. Jan-Dirk Müller, *Spieleregeln für den Untergang. Die Welt des Nibelungenliedes* (Tübingen: Max Niemeyer Verlag, 1998), 183–185.
58. Müller, 183.
59. Müller, 184.
60. Otto von Freising, *Gesta Friderici*, ed. Franz-Joseph Schmale (Berlin: Deutscher Verlag der Wissenschaften), I, ch. 33: "Sunt . . . Ungari facie tetri, profundis oculis, statura humiles, moribus et lingua barbari et feroces, ut iure fortuna culpanda vel potius divina pacientia sit admiranda, quae, ne dicam hominibus, sed talibus hominum monstris tam delectabilem exposuit terram." [The Hungarians are swarthy of face, with deep-set eyes, short in stature, and have wild, barbaric customs and language. One seems justified in blaming fortune, or rather in marveling at divine patience, that has exposed such a delightful land to such—I will not say men, but caricatures of men.]
61. A French Dominican proclaimed at a church synod in Lyon in 1274: "Barbari non comparent praeter Tartaros . . . . Nam Wandali qui et Poloni, et Huni qui et Hungari, Gothi qui et Daci sunt effecti Catholici . . . ." [There are no more barbarians, with the exception of the Tartars . . . . For the Poles, who were once the Vandals, the Hungarians, once the Huns, and the Danes, once the Goths, have all been made into Catholics.] Joannes Dominicus Mansi, *Sacrorum conciliorum nova et amplissima collectio* XXIV, 110. Quoted from Szücs, 268, 282, 320.

4

The Face of the Foreigner in Medieval German Courtly Literature

DAVID F. TINSLEY

Nu ir sît sô küene, als mir ist geseit,
sone ruoch ich, ist daz iemen liep oder leit:
ich wil an iu ertwingen, swaz ir muget hân:
lant und bürge, da so mir werden undertân
(110)[1]

[Now since (as they tell me) you are brave—and I do not care who minds—I will wrest from you by force all that you possess! Your lands and your castles shall all be subject to me.]

I. Medieval Notion of the Foreign

Siegfried issues this seemingly suicidal challenge only moments after he and his twelve retainers have been received at the wealthy court of the powerful Burgundian kings in Worms. The stage has been carefully set. The medieval audience knows that Siegfried has undertaken the journey in order to win the hand of Kriemhild, requiring the consent of her brother-kings and adherence to additional preconditions, agreements, and taboos. Sigmund, his father, has warned him sternly not to rely upon force to win his bride. Hagen who plays the loyal retainer and wise counselor in the first part of the epic, has reported of Siegfried's heroic childhood deeds. Siegfried is an arriving foreigner, whose survival under normal circumstances would rest upon his ability to follow elaborate courtly protocols. Instead he throws down a gauntlet to Gunther and his liege men. This moment thus contains the potential for the kind of unfathomable carnage that the narrator has predicted since the opening stanza. Yet, as many commentators have noted, nothing happens.[2] The Burgundians offer vague promises in response. Siegfried, mollified for whatever reason, begins the extended visit that will end with his brutal murder. Yet it is clear we cannot even begin to speculate about this moment without knowing what customs prevail at the Burgundian courts and what expectations govern the conduct of visitors. In order to understand perhaps the most puzzling passage in the first half of the *Nibelungenlied*, it is therefore essential to comprehend the foreign in all of its dimensions.

Defining foreignness is challenging for any culture, but it is particularly complicated in the case of medieval literature. In circumscribing the notion of the foreign, as depicted in the *Nibelungenlied* and in Wolfram von Eschenbach's *Parzival,*[3] I shall utilize categories associated with the notion of "Mentalitäten," conceived by the *annales* school in France[4] and defined by František Graus as "der gemeinsame Tonus längerfristiger Verhaltensformen und Meinungen von Individuen innerhalb von Gruppen."[5] Graus stresses that "Mentalitäten" may never be described directly, but rather must emerge through comparative studies of utterances and patterns of behavior of a particular group: "Sie sind nie einheitlich, oft widersprüchlich, bilden spezifische 'verinnerlichte Muster' " [They are never uniform, often contradictory and [tend to] form specific patterns of internalization].[6] Although Graus uses medieval attitudes toward death to illustrate the methodology of reconstructing particular "Mentalitäten," it is striking how fundamental the notion of the foreign or the foreigner is to his theoretical construct. For Graus, the experiences of a visitor abroad best illustrate how the apprehension of difference, whether in the reactions of the host culture or in the realization of one's own incompatibility, underlies awareness of "Mentalitäten."[7] The challenge, both for Graus and for the author of this article, is to transcend the immediate awareness of otherness in order to reconstruct upper Rhenish and transalpine medieval aristocratic "Mentalitäten." Analyzing "Meinungen und Verhaltensformen" associated with the notion of the foreign, however, is fraught with difficulties and complexities, some of which I shall survey in the following paragraphs.

It is illuminating, for example, to observe how little light is shed by an etymological foray into Middle High German notions of the foreign. The word-fields associated with "vremde" or "vrömede" yield by far the richest treasury of signifiers, with meaning distributed fairly evenly among semantic contrasts to "home" and connotations of the unknown or the strange.[8] This mirrors the semantic distribution of the modern German word "fremd" between "fremdländisch," or foreign in the sense of geography and/or culture, and "fremdartig," which connotes unconventional appearance or behavior.[9] Both connotations play a key role in Gahmuret's adventures in the opening book of Wolfram von Eschenbach's *Parzival*, as we shall see in greater detail below, but the point of reference is always that of the "Heimat," that is, foreignness is rooted in unconventional behaviors usually associated with visits from foreign cultures and registered in the reactions of the indigenous or the initiated. A second, equally complex dimension of foreignness inhabits adjectival and nominal variants of the Middle High German word "ellende," which connotes persons who have been banned or exiled from their own society, the foreign cultures in which they must seek to survive, or the life one must live under such conditions.[10] Here the initiated are forcibly separated from the indigenous culture; the underlying perspective is that of the displaced, the exiled, of strangers in a strange land who experience their own otherness in contrast to the different customs that surround them or in the separation from social integration. Precisely this quality of "ellende" is explored in the fate of Rüdiger of Pöchlarn at the conclusion to the *Nibelungenlied*.

We cannot, in any case, associate "vremede" or "ellende" with Germany in its modern sense. Clearly, Germanness had meaning for the Middle Ages. The adjectives "diutisch," "diutsch" and the noun "diutsch" are amply attested in Middle High German sources, the former modifying "lant," "lite," "rîch," "ritterschaft," and "künne."[11] Yet the semantic limits of "diutsch" are determined culturally rather than geopolitically, by custom and language. Germany did not come into existence as a national state until 1871;[12] German as a lingua franca for the German-speaking principalities did not evolve significantly until the sixteenth century.[13] This status as "verspätete Nation" has two consequences for medievalists working with notions of foreignness. First, the noun "fremdeheit" connotes difference from the "heim" or "Heimat" in modern German, that is, strangeness in custom, based on the customs of the "heim," which was the city, the principality, or the castle, not the country. "Heimat" can find its basis in lineage, family, or feudal ties, but not in nation.[14] Second, the medieval dimensions of "Heimat" shape the authorial or narratorial perspective accordingly. Most authors writing in Middle High German are incapable of adopting the judgmental self-confidence of a Tacitus (ca. 55 C.E.–ca. 120 C.E.), which arises in Roman hegemony, nor the didactic earnestness of a Thomasin von Zerclaere (ca. 1186–ca.1235), which arises in his courtly sophistication. Their sense of place is too limited, their sense of nation too nascent.

The interpreter's task is further complicated by the fact that medieval authors were working with different notions of subjectivity. As Carolyn Walker Bynum reminds us, "When we speak of 'the development of the individual,' we mean a particular self, something open-ended. In contrast, as John Benton has noted, the twelfth century regarded the discovery of *homo interior*, or *seipsum*, as the discovery within oneself of human nature made in the image of God, *an imago Dei,* that is the same for all human beings."[15] This means that no matter how humble or flawed the outer shell, the focus will remain on the developing soul. Benton and Bynum agree, moreover, that the exterior human being's conduct in this life was shaped by expectations surrounding his or her social position. Bynum reminds us further that "all the basic concerns of early twelfth-century spirituality—poverty and preaching, withdrawal and community, love of neighbor and love of God—were expressed in terms of models."[16] If identity is born in the recurring interaction of the individual, the social group, and the exemplar, notions of the foreigner are inevitably shaped by social expectations surrounding conduct, dress, and obligation. Constant reexamination, as called for in the newly adopted requirements for confession, and the influence of exemplars, who in their violation of social norms exhibit the potential of the foreign, ensure that the process of defining and identifying the foreigner remains dynamic. The social group whose values and interests sparked the adaptation of Old French romances like *Parzival* and Germanic epics like the *Nibelungenlied* was the provincial nobility of the Rhine and Upper German provinces. Moreover, such socially determined subjectivity also guarantees the creation of indigenous foreigners, based on notions of social group and exemplars. For the nobility, for instance, commoners are foreigners by blood and peasants are slightly more than animals; for clerics, the laity constitute the "Other"; men proclaim their physical and moral superiority to women; whereas in the cities foreignness comes to reside ever more outside one's particular guild or profession.

In addition to the dynamic dimensions of subjectivity, one must also take into account the aesthetic peculiarities of romance landscapes.[17] When we turn our attention to Wolfram's *Parzival*, it will be with the knowledge that Arthurian and grail romances have their own landscapes, centered upon Arthur's court, and always containing the potential to mirror the psychological state of the knight/hero. In his desire to transcend and universalize the courtly ideal, Wolfram transforms the Arthurian landscape to include not only the dark forests and ravines of *aventiure*, but also the exotic lands of heathen kings and queens. The *Nibelungenlied* consistently defines "Heimat" according to kingdom. One can trace the path of the Nibelungen, with one notable exception, from the Rhenish court of Worms to Etzel's court on the Danube.[18] But even here, the boundaries are set by the limits of ruling power, not by linguistic or national barriers.

In composing or adapting Arthurian romances from Old French or Low German sources, an author like Wolfram knew from the beginning that his chosen genre originated in another language and culture. This meant he composed in anticipation of his audience's (and his patron's) expectations, which had been shaped by reading or hearing heroic epics and songs. The burgeoning interest in the new courtly culture made authors like Wolfram and Hartmann into de facto cultural ambassadors. In one sense, Wolfram is a kind of Siegfried, approaching the mighty with the goal of wooing their patronage, and his extended commentaries, all but absent in Chrétien, serve to assimilate Wolfram's audience into the foreign literary culture of Minnesang and romance. For example, Wolfram feels compelled to explain primogeniture to his audience and does so by comparing northern Italian and German law (I, 4,26–30). Otherwise they would not understand Gahmuret's dilemma as the second son, nor would they appreciate the *triuwe* inherent in Galoes's offer of a place at court. Conversely, the author of the *Nibelungenlied* must fuse the literary conventions of the past, that is, of oral heroic poetry with the emerging courtly conventions of his time. The act of authorship itself presupposed in the thirteenth century intensive interaction with the foreign. Authorship was viewed as a craft, like carpentry, and it was the task of Wolfram and the *Nibelungendichter* to give familiar shape to what was, in essence, foreign material. When viewed from a modern perspective, the act of composition is informed by the desire for assimilation.

II. "Ritterschaft in fremdiu lant": The Courtly and the Foreign in *Parzival*

When Gahmuret refuses his older brother Galoes's generous offer of a place at court and announces: "ich wil kêren in die lant" (I, 8,8) [I am off to see the world (18)], we witness the first description of foreign territory. "Die lant" connote all lands outside of Anjou. The lure of these lands is the prospect of errantry, which could be called both the means and the essence of Gahmuret's virtue.[19] The world of Book I, therefore, is the world of the questing knight, consisting of kingdoms which extend beyond the borders of the Roman Empire, from Scotland to Babylon and from Denmark to North Africa. The Arthurian court does not assume its role as the center of the universe until Book III, and then only temporarily. In fact, Gahmuret takes service with a heathen emperor, the Baruch of Baldac, and his feats are celebrated from Morocco to Persia and back to Damascus. He earns particular fame before the gates of Alexandria, where he is responsible for defending the Baruch's army against the Babylonian onslaught. It is important to note that this varied geography must be understood in literal and tropological terms. The catalogue of foreign lands is meant to convey the magnitude of Gahmuret's deeds, as well as the exotic nature of the locales in which he performs them. It is not only an itinerary in the modern or (medieval/literal) sense; it is a catalogue of fame earned in storied but distant lands.[20] Thus Wolfram alerts his audience to a world which will transcend the Celtic forest and thus does he anticipate the meeting of Parzival and Feirefiz in Book XV and the subsequent joining of the heathen with the Christian worlds inherent in Feirefiz's lust-driven conversion and marriage to Repanse de Schoye.[21]

Even more striking here is the notion that courtly service is distinct from religious conviction. Gahmuret is not the typical Arthurian knight. He is certainly not the prototypical knight of Christ.[22] Gahmuret moves easily between realms ruled by Christians and kingdoms proudly governed by the servants of Mohammed. Knighthood and courtly service can apparently be performed anywhere, so long as there exist noble and beautiful ladies and the possibility of serving them in individual combat between assembled armies.[23] The fact that twelve Saracen pages ride in Gahmuret's train is even offered as evidence of ideal courtliness (I, 18,29–30). So, as we have seen, "Heimat" in this part of *Parzival* is one's kingdom. Foreigners live in other kingdoms. Whether Christian or heathen, it is possible to serve ladies and kings in any of the "lant" into which Gahmuret rides, or, in the case of Zazamanc, sails.

The first news that Wolfram gives us of Zazamanc evokes a courtly world much like Anjou. The people are mourning the death of Isenhart, "der den lîp in dienste vlôs um ein wîp" (I, 16,5–6) [who had lost his life in the service of a lady (22)], which sounds conventional enough. The audience also hears the name of the lady, Belacane, and they know she is "süeze falsches âne," [sweet and constant(22)], a description generic enough to cover the charms of Enite or Laudine. The narrator then discloses that Belacane's kingdom is beleaguered by the armies of Isenhart's uncle, Vridebrant of Scotland, because she had refused to give Isenhart her love and thereby caused his death. These descriptions could pertain to any castle or walled city in the Arthurian world and are meant to underscore the courtly ethos that governs the conduct of besiegers and besieged.[24]

When Gahmuret disembarks, his herald is begged by the people to intervene on Belacane's behalf, and Gahmuret offers to serve "umbe guot" [for hire (22)][25] Only at this point does Wolfram introduce notions of foreignness. Gahmuret notices that all residents of Zazamanc are black, "vinster sô diu nâht" (I, 17,24) [as dark as night (22)]. Despite some fears that his lodgings may be substandard or at least not conducive to "hoher muot," ("bî den ducht in diu wîle lanc" (I, 17,26) [he had had enough of their company (22)]),[26] Gahmuret rides into the city. In the scenes that follow, Wolfram repeatedly evokes the dark skin of his hosts, but now his goal seems to be to mitigate the sense of strangeness. For example, the introductory words "Moere und Moerinne was beidiu wîp unde man" (I, 19,19–20) [All the inhabitants were Moors, every man and woman of them (23)] precede an extensive passage in which the wounds suffered by the defenders are catalogued with no less sympathy than is the starvation of the besieged in Condwiramur's city (IV, 184–185,8). Gahmuret is struck by the darkness of the ladies who surround him ("manege tunkele frouwen sach er bîdenthalben sîn; nâch rabens varwe was ir schîn" (I, 20,4–6) [He saw many dusky ladies on either side of him whose colour resembled the raven's (23)]), yet Wolfram reveals that his hero is greeted by the Burggraf in proper courtly fashion (I, 20,20), and Gahmuret salutes the bravery of the wounded and beaten knights who accompany their lord (I, 20,17–18). Although Wolfram doubts that Gahmuret enjoys the greeting kiss of the Burggraf's wife (I, 20,25–6), this is only meant to create a contrast with Gahmuret's feelings after he makes the Queen's acquaintance.[27]

When Gahmuret and Belacane actually meet, Belacane is the first to fall under Amor's sway:

> der Künneginne rîche
> ir ougen fuogten hôhen pîn,

dô si gesach den Anschevîn.
der was sô minnecliche gevar,
daz er entslôz ihr herze gar,
ez waere ir liep oder leit:
daz beslôz dâ vor ir wîpheit.
(I, 23, 23–29)

[As they lit on the Angevin, the Queen's eyes did great hurt to her. He looked so winsome that, irresistibly, he unlocked her heart which until that time her feminity had kept locked fast. (25)]

Her response could not be courtlier. Minne finds its way into her heart "ex visu," just the way it should. Her quick response is in no way connected to her foreignness. The question is only whether Gahmuret will remain immune, as did Eneas, whose relationship with Dido would have come to the audience's mind.[28] The queen's beauty is then contrasted with the shining white bed on which the two sit. Her crown of rubies glows against the blackness of her skin, and the effect is dazzling. Gahmuret's response is to pledge service to her, come what may:

ich pin niht wan einec man:
swer iu tuot od hât getân
dâ biut ich gegen mînen schilt.
(I, 24, 25–29)

[I am but one man, but if any has wronged you, or wrongs you still, I interpose my shield. (25)]

Belacane then confesses her awful Minne-transgression to Gahmuret ("dô ich sîn dienst nâch minne enphienc, deiz im nâch fröuden niht ergienc. des muoz ich immer jâmer tragen" (I, 26,27–29) [As a woman I betrayed myself to let him serve me for love without his bringing it to a happy consummation, so that I must forever rue it. (26)]), even as she praises the knightly virtues of Isenhart.

sîn lîp was tugend ein bernde rîs.
der helt was küene unde wîs,
der triwe ein recht belibeniu fruht:
sîn zuht wac für alle zuht.
er was noch kiuscher denne ein wîp.
(I, 26, 11–15)

[Fine qualities burgeoned on him like blossoms on a spray. This knight was brave and discerning. Loyalty bore fruit in him nourished from deep roots. His breeding excelled all breeding. He was more modest than a woman (26).]

Here Belacane invokes the courtly value Wolfram elevates to a cardinal virtue: "triuwe."[29] Even more striking is the mention of Isenhart's skin color in the same breath as additional praise ("er was gein valscher fuore ein tôr, in swarzer varwe als ich ein Môr" (I, 26,21–23) [He was untutored in the ways of perfidy (26)]).[30] Wolfram clearly means to stress that courtliness transcends skin color.

As Belacane breaks down into tears while continuing her story, Gahmuret proves himself not impervious to Minne's siren song:

> Gahmureten dîuhte sân,
> swie sie waere ein heidenin,
> mit triwen wîplîcher sin
> in wîbes herze nie geslouf.
> ir kiusche was ein reiner touf,
> und och der regen der sie begôz,
> der wîac der von ir ougen flôz
> ûf ir zobel und an ir brust.
> riwen phlege was ir gelust,
> und rehtiu jâmers lêre.
>
> (I, 28,10–19)

> [It seemed to Gahmuret that although she was an infidel, a more affectionate spirit of womanliness had never stolen over a woman's heart. Her modest ways were a pure baptism, as was the rain that fell on her—the flood descending from her eyes down to her sabled breast. Her pleasures in life were devotion to sorrow and grief's true doctrine (27).]

The fact that she is a heathen is mitigated in Gahmuret's mind and heart by her "triwe," as here again Wolfram's cardinal virtue is invoked, her virginity, which the narrator sees as a kind of baptism, and, finally, her weeping, which anyone familiar with Enite's mourning scene in Hartmann's Erec knows can take on spiritual connotations.[31] As a black woman, a heathen, and the queen of Zazamanc, Belacane is a foreigner in the physical, religious, and geopolitical terms of the text. But her beauty, virtue, "triwe" and passion transcend the above categories and grant her not only status as a proper lady for Gahmuret to love and serve, but also hint at a higher spirituality which will eventually be realized through her son, Feirefiz.[32]

Wolfram then puts himself in the heathen's sandals by having his audience imagine what it must have been like for Belacane to fall in love with a light-skinned non-believer. Between sobs, she steals a glance at Gahmuret and realizes that he, too, is good looking. Wolfram explains: "sie kunde ouch liehte varwe spehen: wan sie het och ê gesehen manegen liehten heiden" (I, 29,3–5 [She was a judge of fair complexions, too, since before this she had seen many a fair-skinned heathen (27)]). I mention this passage because it documents the author's sensitivity to foreignness. He does not paint love in courtly colors merely because he knows no other idiom, but rather in the full knowledge that he is bringing together a black, heathen queen with the Angevîn father of his future hero.[33]

The stage is now set for love, but for proper love involving patience and sacrifice. The feelings are mutual and as strong as Minne can make them, yet pure, "getriulîch":

> aldâ wart undr in beiden
> ein vil getriulîchiu ger:
> sie sach dar, und er sach her
> (I, 29, 6–8)

> [With this there was born between them a steadfast longing—she gazed at him and he at her (27).]

They are one (I, 29,14). Her dinner service to him kneeling is a sign of devotion. She, too pledges her service to him (I, 21–22). Yet consummation cannot come before service. Despite what it costs them, the two retire to separate chambers for the night. Gahmuret spends a sleepless night torn between the joy that the great honors have brought to him and the distress that Minne has engendered in his heart:

> den helt verdrôz
> daz sô lanc was diu naht.
> in brâhte dicke in unmacht
> die swarze Moerinne,
> des landes küneginne
> (I, 35, 20–22)

> [The hero lost his patience with the night for dragging on so. With thoughts of the dusky Moorish Queen he fell from swoon to swoon (30).]

The next morning Gahmuret rides out to battle and meets Hiuteger, one of Vridebrant of Scotland's barons, who comments on the multicultural milieu of this courtly battle:

> wenne oder wie
> kom dirre Franzois in diz lant?
> het ich den für einen Môr,
> sô waer mîn bester sin ein tôr.
> (I, 37,16–20)

> ["How and when did this Frenchman arrive in the country," he mused, "if I took him for a Moor I'd be a fool at best" (31).]

Noteworthy in the battle scenes is the fact that Gahmuret's victories are quickly won and fairly fought, whether against European (I, 38,1) or Moor (I, 41,24–25). Black and white knights fight on both sides. As we already saw in the descriptions of the besieged, chivalry and bravery transcend the boundaries of kingdoms, the schism of creed, and the color of skin. This same pattern is sustained in the negotiations that follow. Gahmuret displays true "milte" in his allocation of spoils and placation of the vanquished and victors (I, 52,1–16). The Moors and the Christians are beneficiaries of his greatness, without favor to either side.

In matters of love, Belacane does not recidivate. No sooner does Gahmuret ride through her gates, than she dismisses her court and has him brought to her bedchamber. The union of the two lovers transcends mere physical consummation, and stands in stark contrast to the blackness and whiteness of their hues:

> dô phlac diu küniginne
> einer werden süezer minne,
> und Gahmuret ihr herzen trût,
> ungelîch was doch ir zweier hût.
> (I, 44,27–30)

> [The queen yielded to sweet and noble love with Gahmuret, her heart's own darling, little though their skins matched in colour (34).]

The product of this union is Feirefiz, on whom, as the narrator comments "got wunders wart enein" (I, 57,37) [It had pleased God to make a marvel of him (40)]. His skin is mottled, and she kisses his white spots as a sign of her devotion to his father. Feirefiz will distinguish himself in battle. As for his mother, her emblem is the turtledove, a medieval sign of devotion. She will suffer terribly but never relent in her love. In this willingness to suffer she embodies "triwe" and prefigures the fate of Sigune, who later becomes a teacher and an exemplum for Parzival:

> diu het ie den selben muot:
> swenne ir an trûtscheft gebrast,
> ir triwe kôs den dürren ast.
> (I, 57,12–14)

> [They (turtledoves) keep such faith that when they lose their mates they never fail to seek the withered bough (40).]

When Gahmuret evokes Belacane's heathen status, he is disguising his true motives. This is signaled by her willingness to convert, which prefigures that of her mottled son.

The issue of taking a heathen courtly lover is revisited and clarified in Book II by means of Gahmuret's conflicting obligations to Belacane, Ampflise, and Herzeloyde.[34] There Herzeloyde is completely frank with her reluctant lover:

> Ir sult die Moerinne
> lân durch mîn minne.
> des toufes segen hât bezzer kraft.
> nu ânet iuch der heidenschaft,
> und minnet mich nâch unser ê.
> (I, 94, 11–15)

> ["You must give up the Mooress in favor of my love," said she. "In the Sacrament of Baptism there is greater virtue. Now divorce yourself from heathenry and love me as our rites enjoin" (57).]

Herzeloyde wishes Gahmuret's affirmation that courtly love between Christians should take precedence over courtly devotion to a heathen. Yet once again the issue of Belacane's foreignness is mitigated by the fact that she is just one of Herzeloyde's concerns. At the same time she demands clarification of Gahmuret's relationship with Ampflîse, his "domina." Wolfram is inordinately careful to maintain the balance between the two worlds; there is also a Christian rival. The truth finally emerges when Gahmuret answers frankness with frankness:

> lât ir niht turnieren mich,
> sô kan ich noch den alten slich,
> als dô ich mînem wîbe entran,
> die ich ouch mit rîterschaft gewan.
> dô si mich ûf von strîte bant,
> ich liez ir liute unde lant.
> (I, 96,29–30–97,1–4)

> [If you will not let me go to tournaments I have not forgotten my old trick, how once before I gave my wife the slip. Her too I won by deeds of arms. When she tied me up to keep me from fighting I left her land and people (59).]

Now the audience knows for certain that the restless quest for knightly prowess is what motivates Gahmuret to leave both women, heathen and Christian. Indeed, he reminds Herzeloyde that she is a prize won in battle and therefore Belacane's equal. Even here Herzeloyde's Christian status is no help. Errantry and knightly deeds determine the essence of proper conduct. As the narrator already confided to his audience in Book I: "daz er niht rîterschefte vant, des was sîn freude sorgen phant" (I, 54,17–20) [till finding no help. Errantry and knightly deeds determine the essence of proper conduct. As the narrator already confided to his audience in Book I: "daz er niht rîterschefte vant, des was sîn freude sorgen phant" (I, 54,17–20) [till finding no deeds of arms to perform he began to pine and fret, so that his happiness turned to sorrow (39)].[35]

We have seen how Wolfram defines foreignness in Book I by means of geopolitical, racial, and religious criteria. Belacane is Queen of Zazamanc, she is a Moor, and she is a heathen. But we have also seen how ideals of knighthood and courtly love serve to transcend all three divisions. Knights may serve heathen kings and queens and even accept the fealty of heathens, so long as they comport themselves properly. "In die lant" makes no distinction between Zazamanc and Spâne. Scottish and Moorish princes attack Belacane; an Angevin defends her. Second, the courtly (and spiritual) virtue of "triwe" serves to transcend the gulf separating heathens and Christians. It is, as Wolfram asserts, a kind of baptism. Unquestionably, Herzeloyde is accorded higher status; as the mourning widow she is associated with images of the Virgin Mary. But Belacane is the turtledove in her devotion, also a very powerful image associated with Mary. Ultimately the fates of these two women and their sons serve to unite Wolfram's world under the auspices of the Grail Society.[36]

III. "Wir sin ouch ellende als Rüedeger der degen": Exile and the Foreigner in the *Nibelungenlied*

We now shift our focus from the amorous quests and conquests of Gahmuret to the dark and bloody demise of the Nibelungs in order to explore how the courtly and the foreign shape the heroic ethos at the conclusion of the *Nibelungenlied*. To measure the interaction of the courtly with the foreign, one must define these terms as they govern the conduct of Kriemhild and Hagen.[37] Medievalists have long recognized that the actions of Siegfried and the Burgundians may be judged according to two value systems, the heroic and the courtly.[38] An example of heroic values is offered by the "Atlakvita" from the *Edda*.[39] The virtues are *triuwe* to the family or clan, *milte* to the household, and *êre* which is determined by one's prowess in battle and demonstrated by courage that transcends fear of death and the obligation to avenge wrongs done to one's family. Trickery and deception (*list*) are virtues and may be used at any time to overcome one's enemies. One also shows prowess in detecting and overcoming deception. Gúnnar and Högni epitomize such courage in their willingness to travel unarmed to the land of the Huns, even though Gúdrún has warned them that it will bring their deaths. Högni displays prowess in killing eight Hun warriors. Gúnnar falls victim to deception when he is imprisoned in the Tower of Serpents, but later is able to injuries suffered by the family or clan is embodied by Gúdrún, who not only is willing to kill and serve her own sons as Atli's dinner course, but also finally murders him and burns down his hall, perishing in the process.

Courtly values, which find full flower in Arthurian and grail romances, mark the shift in notions of identity from shame to guilt culture and from outer obligation to inner development.[40] The hero's initial failure is transcended through what he learns in the course of his questing. *Triuwe* remains a paramount virtue, but is directed toward the *domina* or lady, whom the hero must be prepared to serve through devotion and in battle, regardless of what reward he might receive. *Milte* is realized by the king's generosity, not only to his liegemen but also to his questing guests. *Ere* is realized through the hero's development, with divine help, as is the case with Yvain's lion or Parzival's encounters with Sigune and Trevrizent. The knight's inner development mirrors inexactly the soul's progress toward the divine. A courtly virtue unknown to the Atlivita is *zucht,* mastery of the elaborate conventions and proper social actions demanded of courtiers. *List* is permitted only when the knight and lady seek to conceal their secret love. Battle takes place according to precise rules and rarely ends in death, so long as the opponent is another knight of equal station.

The conflict between these competing value systems is especially evident in the Siegfried episodes of the *Nibelungenlied.* The two most commonly cited examples are found in the parallel courtships of Kriemhild and Brünhild. As Haymes notes, Siegfried's courtship of Kriemhild "is completely dependent on the language and images of *Minnesang*."[41] Siegfried is content to wait an entire year before seeing his beloved, and ceremonies featuring unbelievable wealth and extravagance accompany each step of the courtship. Gunther's winning of Brünhild, on the other hand, could be included in any heroic song. Brünhild is a queen of superhuman strength who fights with her suitors on equal terms. Whosoever overcomes her wins her hand. Losers die ignominiously. Brünhild is finally overcome by *list,* Siegfried using a cloak of invisibility to win her without her knowledge on Gunther's behalf. Some commentators speak of the education of Siegfried in the first part. When he first appears in Worms, he announces his intentions to best the Burgundians in battle and to take Kriemhild as his prize. In the course of an extended visit, he is "tamed" by Minne, and learns to conduct himself properly, that is, according to courtly expectations. In this view, then, the roots of Siegfried's murder and death lie in the incompatibility of the two systems. While all strive to maintain *zucht* in the public sphere, Siegfried must again resort to *list* and a second trial of strength with Brünhild in her bedchamber in order that Gunther consummate his marriage. His "heroic" act of taking Brünhild's belt and ring and bestowing them on Kriemhild brings about his destruction, as Kriemhild uses her knowledge to humiliate Brünhild in public and Hagen desires to avenge the honor of his queen.

Haymes recognizes that the actions of the characters may not be explained by reference to two value systems, and proposes a third value system, what he calls "aristocratic" values drawn from the courtship plots of the *Spielmannsepik*, which feature elaborate descriptions of ceremonies similar to those in the *Nibelungenlied*. Otfrid Ehrismann disagrees. He would abandon the use of value systems altogether as anachronistic constructions in favor of an ethos of narrative:

> Die Ethik des Nibelungenliedes folgt dem Gesetz epischen Handelns, sie entfaltet sich situationsbedingt, einmal höfisch, einmal heroisch, einmal modernisierend, einmal archaisierend. Es ist eine fiktionale (phantasierte) Ethik, die ihre Wirklichkeit für die Zeit der *alten maeren* behauptet.[42]
>
> [The ethos of the Nibelungenlied follows the dictates of epic narrative; it unfolds according to the demands of each situation, sometimes reflecting courtly values, sometimes heroic values, sometimes contemporary, sometimes archaic. It is a fictional construct imposing itself on the time of epic poetry that it purports to evoke.]

Let us consider this question in light of the only figure who moves freely among the heroic and the courtly scenes of the *Nibelungenlied*: Rüdiger of Pöchlarn. Rüdiger enjoys universal respect, as confirmed by the protagonists of the second part: Kriemhild and Hagen. The grieving Kriemhild agrees to hear Etzel's petition only after she hears that Rüdiger is the messenger:

> ich ensehe gerne den Rüedegêres lîp
> durch sîne manege tugende. waere ér niht her gesant,
> swerz ander boten waere, dem waere ich immer umbekant. (1221)
>
> [I will not deny that I shall be pleased to see Rüdiger for the sake of his many fine qualities," answered the highborn lady. "Had any other than he been sent I should not have admitted the ambassador, whoever he was." (158)]

The friendship of Hagen and Rüdiger dates back to Hagen's time at Etzel's court (1180).[43] The grim "küene degen" who is willing to murder a chaplain without a second thought (1576) and who urges his men to nurture themselves on the blood of their enemies (2114), is moved to declare to Rüdiger: "Got sol daz gebiuten, daz ir tugent immer lebe" (2199) [God grant that your fine qualities abide on earth forever (271)]. Anyone who enjoys the friendship of both Hagen and Kriemhild is worthy of critical attention.

Rüdiger casts a wide net. His virtues transcend the courtly and heroic worlds of the *Nibelungenlied*. He unites the warring factions, he brings together the grieving widow Kriemhild with the grieving widower Etzel. He serves his liegelord faithfully while treating the visiting Burgundians with honor. His generous spirit is defined by his hospitality. Yet, when the time comes to fight, he comports himself like a hero, dying in the act of killing Gernôt. Thus, Rüdiger is comfortable in all milieus, whether they be courtly, heroic, or aristocratic, as Haymes defines them. His actions also reflect in their vacillation the "narrative ethos" espoused by Ehrisman, Rüdiger is "einmal höfisch, einmal heroisch."[44]

In the process of ceremony and negotiation, Rüdiger is also forced to assume a network of filial and feudal obligations which eventually bring about his downfall.[45] He holds his lands through marriage to Gotelind and feudal obligation to Etzel. This feudal obligation motivates his journey to Worms on Etzel's behalf. His desire to serve Etzel motivates in turn his oath of personal fealty to Kriemhild (1257). His generosity and attention to his obligations as host motivate the marriage of his daughter to Giselher and the gift of the shield to Hagen. When Hagen murders Ortliep, thus bringing Etzel's desire for revenge in line with that of Kriemhild, Rüdiger's position becomes untenable.

Hans Naumann authored the classic interpretation of Rüdiger's conflicting obligations.[46] As Naumann sees it, Rüdiger has no choice. On the one hand, he is obligated as a liegeman of Etzel's to fight on the Hun's behalf. He is obligated by his oath to Kriemhild to avenge any wrong done to her. On the other hand, he is obligated by his duties as host to honor the Burgundians, not to murder them. He is obligated by marriage to defend his son in law, Giselher, not to slaughter him. He gives voice to this desperation in responding to Kriemhild:

> ich swuor iu, edel wîp,
> daz ich durch iuch wâgte êre und ouch den lîp.
> daz ich die sîele verliese, des enhân ich niht gesworn.
> zur dirre hôchgezîte brâhte ich die fürsten wol geborn.
> (1250)

> [There is no denying it, noble lady, that I swore to risk my life and position for you: but that I would lose my soul I never swore! (266)]

Rüdiger confirms his courage and generosity by bestowing the means of his destruction, his own shield, upon a potential destroyer, Hagen.[47] Small wonder that the Nibelungs, even Hagen, are moved to tears (2197). The narrator underscores the tragedy of Rüdiger's position, again and again invoking the words "edel Rüedegêr." Thus it is understandable that Rüdiger has been eulogized by medievalists as the "perfect knight" whose virtues cannot overcome the web of lies and treachery woven by Hagen and Kriemhild.[48]

I would like to argue that the medieval audience would have seen Rüdiger in a completely different light. The obvious cue to do so informs Hildebrand's elegiac words, "wir sîn ouch ellende als Rüedegér der degen" (2263)

[Like valiant Rüdiger, we too are wretched exiles (279)], but a close reading reveals repeated references to exile, stretching back even to the idyll of the Burgundian sojourn in Pöchlarn.[49] Let us now examine the Rüdiger episodes in light of what the audience might have understood. After Rüdiger and his men have been slaughtered, the men of Dietrich's household appear on the scene, led by Hildebrand. Only now does the audience learn of the fierce veneration that Dietrich's household has for the dead Pöchlarn. One after another, weeping, Dietrich's warriors praise him: Sigestab, the Duke of Verona, calls him the "freude ellender diete,"[50] that is, their only source of happiness in long years of exile. Wolfwin compares the loss to that of his own father (2259). Wolfhart laments the loss of Rüdiger's leadership in battle (2260). Wolfbrand, Helpfrich, and Helmnot chime in with heartfelt laments. This surprising show of reverence by the household of the greatest Germanic hero has been largely ignored by commentators, but a medieval audience would not have missed its significance. One presumes the vassals of Verona are thinking back to Dietrich's flight into exile and arrival in Pöchlarn, where they experienced the same hospitality and *milte* that Gotelind and Rüdiger accord the Burgundians in the twenty-seventh adventure. Hildebrand makes explicit the connection that Dietrich's household feels: "wir sîn ouch ellende als Rüedegér der degen" (2263). Hildebrand wishes to justify his request that the Burgundians surrender Rüdiger's corpse, but the audience was meant to focus on Rüdiger's fate in exile. Rüdiger is so generous to guests because he himself is, as Lexer puts it, "der(jenige), der in oder aus einem fremden Lande, fremd, oder in der Fremde ist" [someone who is either in or who is from a foreign country, either foreign or in foreign lands].[51] Like Dietrich, like Hildebrand, Rüdiger must live "verbannt," which had always taken on connotations of misery and loneliness in the Germanic tradition.

Viewing Rüdiger as an exile allows the audience to see the events of the second part in retrospective, imparting new insights and the shock of recognition for which Wolfram is justly famous. Three scenes in particular deserve mention. First, we realize that Rüdiger's position at Etzel's court is a great deal less secure than is generally supposed. This is evident in the charges the anonymous Hun makes in response to Rüdiger's inactivity:

> Dô sah ein Hiunen recke Rüedegêren stân
> Mit weinenden ougen, unde hetes vil getân.
> Der sprach zer küneginne: "nu seht ir, wie er stât,
> Der doch gewalt den meisten hie bî Etzelen hât,
> (2138)
>
> Und dem ez allez dienet, liut unde lant.
> Wie ist sô vil der bürge an Rüedegêr gewant,
> Der er von dem künege vil manege haben mac!
> Er gesluoc in disen stürmen noch nie lobelîchen slac."
> (2139)

[At this point a Hunnish warrior noticed Rüdiger standing there with tears in his eyes—Rüdiger had been weeping copiously—and he said to the Queen: "Just look at Rüdiger, the way he stands there, the man who has the greatest power here under Etzel, and to whom lands and people owe allegiance! Think of the castles that have been made over to him and in what numbers he has received them from the King! Yet in these battles he has not struck an honourable blow!" (265)]

These words represent the view of the "Hun on the street," the view of the people of the "Heimat" that I discussed in the introduction. Here the jealousy of the Huns is palpable. No matter how loyal past service has been, one recognizes that an exile is vulnerable. As the Huns of Etzel's court see it, Rüdiger is not a tragic hero, but rather a foreigner who has assumed a position of power at court based upon the *milte* of his host. The expectation is that Rüdiger must defend Etzel's interests and those of his queen at any cost. When the Hun openly questions Rüdiger's honor, Rüdiger kills him with a single blow. Commentators who idealize Rüdiger in the context of courtliness have great difficulty explaining this seeming fall into barbarousness, but if one knows that Rüdiger is an exile, then his vulnerability justifies any action against those who would threaten his position at court.[52]

Rüdiger's position also explains Volker's fatalistic jibe "an uns wil dienen Rüedegêr sîne bürge und sîniu lant" (2173) [Rüdiger means to earn his land and castles from us (269)], which is a clear reference to the fact that Rüdiger holds Pöchlarn only at the behest of Etzel. This remark certainly reflects the conflict of obligations already analyzed by Naumann and Wapnewski, but it also represents the perspective of the foreigner, who finds himself in a hopeless position and who is reflecting upon whether Rüdiger will hold to his pledge of safe conduct to his guests or choose rather to defend his own power and interests by supporting Etzel and his queen.

Rüdiger's offer to forsake all of his obligations and to retreat into exile now appears doubly tragic.[53] Rüdiger is already in exile. He has succeeded in creating a position of some security among the Huns. His threat to leave exile in order to go into exile is simply not an option in the traditional literary world of Dietrich and Hildebrand. We must therefore read his words as a sign of despair. They distort a heroic motif beyond recognition, thereby creating a narrative device which shows the true hopelessness of Rüdiger's position.

Even the idyll of Pöchlarn now takes on a darker aspect. As Margrave, Rüdiger's lands and wealth are dependent upon his marriage and his defense of Etzel's borders. His power does not rest upon his lineage. This fact is underscored in the figure of Gotelind, whose autonomy is comparable only to that of the virgin Brünhild and the widow Kriemhild. While lying in bed, Gotelind and Rüdiger discuss on equal terms the question of who should be Helche's successor (1168). The "rîche Gotelind" controls the wealth. He must ask her permission before rewarding his followers (1171). During the sojourn of the Nibelungs in Bechalâren, Volker's praise of the "minneclîche," "edele," and "guot" daughter of Rüdiger and Gotelind is presented as a hypothetical marriage proposal. If he were a king, he asserts, he would marry her immediately (1675). Rüdiger protests, answering: "wir sîn hie ellende, beide ich und mîn wîp: waz hülfe grôziu schoene der guoten juncfrouwen lîp?" (1676) [My wife and I both live in exile here. What advantage could great beauty bring the good young lady? (208)]. Under normal circumstances, one would assume, Rüdiger would have no hope of marrying off his daughter to someone of kingly status.[54] Indeed, this is precisely the situation to which Brünhild thinks she is objecting when she is mortified by the marriage of Kriemhild to Siegfried. Hagen then steps in and arranges the marriage with Giselher, "als ez wol künege gezam" (1679) [In the manner befitting a king (209)], based on Gotelind's lineage, not Rüdiger's, "ez ist sô hôher mâge, der marcgrâvinne lîp," (1678) [The young Margravine is of such high lineage (209)]. This unheard-of honor brings poor Rüdiger even more embarrassment, as he is forced to acknowledge that he has no lands for a dowry and must give gifts of mere silver and gold (1681–82).[55]

The audience is meant to see Rüdiger not only as a noble margrave, but also as "ellende," as an exile with limited status and prospects. Granting this, one may assume the author wished for them to ponder Dietrich's fate, as told in heroic songs like the *Hildebrandslied* and in contemporary versions of historical Dietrich epics like the *Buch von Bern* and the *Rabenschlacht*.[56] In these versions of Dietrich's life, he is driven into exile by the usurper Ermrich and finds refuge at the court of Etzel, where Rüdiger is especially hospitable to him. Dietrich eventually kills Ermrich and takes back his kingdom, but only at the cost of many retainers' lives, most of whom step forward to eulogize Rüdiger in the *Nibelungenlied.* Dietrich's warriors so sympathize with Rüdiger because he is "ellende," a stranger in a strange land, who survives by serving a foreign lord, in this case, Etzel.

The *Hildebrandslied* dramatizes the consequences of such separation.[57] When Hildebrand must fight to the death against Hadubrand, his own son, this signifies the complete breakdown of family and clan ties that were essential to identity in Germanic society. Since the hero can only live on through the celebration of his prowess in song, this battle has transcendent consequences for father and son. The death of Hadubrand means that Hildebrand's family line and all possibilities of future honor have been snuffed out. For Hadubrand, who has already endured a miserable existence as a fatherless boy in a culture where the father's lineage is all-determining, the victory over his father brings him essential recognition, but at the cost of severing the tie his own culture holds most dear.

Thus the desperate courage of Rüdiger as he attacks the Burgundians evokes the fatalism of Hildebrand as he realizes no reconciliation is possible with his own son. The tragedy of Rüdiger's fate lies therefore less in the demise of an ideal knight and courtier than in the heroic death of an exile, of a landless Margrave totally dependent upon the largess of Etzel who swears an oath of personal fealty to Kriemhild in order to realize the marriage plans of his lord, of a vassal married to a wealthy and much more noble lady who seeks to better his daughter's status through marriage, and of a hero of lesser rank, who is courageous but nevertheless not in the league of warriors such as Hagen, much less superheroes such as Dietrich of Bern. Seen from this perspective, then, the tragedy of Rüdiger lies in his status as an outlander. His command of courtliness, his nobility of character, his adeptness at diplomacy, his legendary largesse, and even his absolute adherence to feudal obligations cannot transcend his *fremdecheit.*[58]

IV. The Foreign and the Courtly

I hope to have demonstrated in the preceding pages just how essential the notion of the foreign is to the understanding of *Parzival* and the *Nibelungenlied.* The Gahmuret episodes not only serve to document the hero's lineage, they also prepare the audience to accept a new world in which traditional measures of foreignness—nationality, lineage, and race—will be transcended under the banners of the Grail king. The Rüdiger episodes explore the tragedy of exile and the question of whether *triuwe* and *zuht* are sufficient to overcome the perils of reestablishing oneself far from the protections of home and clan. In each case, the traditional view of the hero is transformed by our understanding of his foreignness. Gahmuret is no longer the knight errant, whose amorous and chivalrous exploits comprise an entertaining but thematically meaningless prelude to the tale of Parzival's fall and redemption. Wolfram's audience was meant to see him as Parzival's allegorical counterpart, Moses to Parzival's Christ, whose unceasing quests in search of *prîs* prefigure the unceasing yet blind quests of his son for forgiveness. Rüdiger is no longer the tragic courtier, but rather Dietrich's thematic twin, whose fate is death in exile, despite the status he tries to achieve through hospitality, service, and the marriage of his daughter to Giselher.

Equally interesting is the need for a universal value system which permits both Wolfram and the Nibelungenpoet to assimilate the "foreign" literatures they were presenting to their patrons, in the former case, the grail romance, and in the latter case, the still popular heroic songs and epics of courtship (*Spielmannsepen*). The ideals of courtliness, as imported from Old French and Lower German sources, serve to transcend the foreign boundaries of kingdom, race, and lineage. Gahmuret is a disinherited second son, he is an Angevin, and he is a Christian, yet the might of Minne and the force of his arms allow him to emerge as King of Zazamanc and the legitimate lover of a Moorish heathen queen, whose claims to Gahmuret are presented as equal to those of Ampflise and Herzeloyde. The battle and reconciliation of Parzival and Feirifiz should have brought the heathen and Christian worlds together, if Wolfram had dared to risk such a bold conclusion. In the *Nibelungenlied* courtliness is set against the dangers and challenges of exile. If, as I have argued, the tragedy of Rüdiger lies in his status as an outlander, then the message of the Rüdiger episodes is that command of courtliness, nobility of character, adeptness at diplomacy, superhuman largesse, and even absolute adherence to feudal obligations, cannot transcend *fremdecheit*.

It is, of course, too early to reach a conclusion regarding the "Mentalitäten" of the Rhenish, upper-German, and transalpine nobility who constituted the patrons and the audience for the works just analyzed. At the level of reception, however, it is interesting to note that, at least for the provinces of the Holy Roman Empire, foreign cultures are the source for the new literary genres that transform the aesthetic enterprises of the provincial courts. The first "Golden Age" of German literature follows a period of interaction and confrontation between East and West during the Crusades. It is no accident, finally, that the cities, where the largest degree of cultural and social assimilation was achieved, become the centers for collection and preservation of these genres in the fourteenth and fifteenth centuries. Ultimately, we are forced to ask whether a foreign encounter—the German nobility's assimilation of courtly values as celebrated in vernacular literatures—constitutes the roots of modernity.

Notes

1. All quotations from the *Nibelungenlied* are from Rosemary Wisniewski, ed., *Das Nibelungenlied*, Deutsche Klassiker des Mittelalters (Wiesbaden: Brockhaus, 1979). As is customary, quotations will be annotated by strophe. All translations are from *The Nibelungenlied*, trans. from the Middle High German by A.T. Hatto, Penguin Classics (Baltimore, Md.: Penguin Books, 1969).
2. Werner Hoffmann, *Das Siegfriedbild in der Forschung bis 1978* (Darmstadt: Wissenschaftliche Buchgesellschaft, 1979), surveys the older secondary literature on this confrontation. Otfrid Ehrismann, *Nibelungenlied. Epoche—Werk—Wirkung*, Arbeitsbücher zur Literaturgeschichte (Munich: Beck, 1987), 117 summarizes the views of all recent commentators on the subject.
3. All quotations from *Parzival* are from Karl Lachmann, ed., *Wolfram von Eschenbach*, 6th ed., (Berlin and Leipzig: Walter De Gruyter, 1965). Quotations will be annotated by strophe and line. All translations are from Wolfram von Eschenbach, *Parzival*, trans. from the Middle High German by A.T. Hatto, Penguin Classics (New York: Penguin Books, 1980).
4. Jean-Claude Schmitt, *Ghosts in the Middle Ages: The Living and the Dead in Medieval Society*. Trans. from the French by Teresa Fagan (Chicago: University of Chicago Press, 1998), offers a recent, compelling study using this methodology with a complete bibliography of French sources.
5. The underlying tone of longer-lasting patterns of behavior and opinion as demonstrated by individuals in group settings. See František Graus, ed., "Mentalität—Versuch einer Begriffsbestimmung," *Mentalitäten im Mittelal-*

ter. Methodische und inhaltliche Probleme, Vorträge und Forschungen 35 (Sigmaringen: Jan Thorbecke Verlag, 1987), 9–48; here 17. Unless otherwise indicated, all translations from modern German are my own.

6. See Graus, 17.
7. Graus, 12–13.
8. Matthias Lexer, *Mittelhochdeutsches Handwörterbuch*, 3 Volumes (Stuttgart: Hirzel, 1992), here III, Sp. 500–502.
9. Interestingly, many synonyms of the modern noun "Fremder," which means "stranger" or "foreigner" still carry pejorative connotations in modern German. This may explain why the Center for Medieval Studies at the University of Minnesota entitled its 1994 conference "Strangers in Medieval Society," defining "strangers" as "those persons who have their own community and culture, and who come into a new environment." See F.R.P. Akehurst and Stephanie Cain Van D'Elden, eds., *The Stranger in Medieval Society*, Medieval Cultures 12 (Minneapolis and London: University of Minnesota Press, 1998); here vii.
10. Lexer I, Sp. 539–541.
11. Lexer I, Sp. 443–444.
12. A rich sourcebook for questions of German political and cultural unity is *"Was ist des Deutschen Vaterland*, ed. Peter Longerich, Serie Piper 1269 (Munich: Piper, 1990).
13. Peter von Polenz, *Die Geschichte der deutschen Sprache*. 9th ed. (Berlin: de Gruyter, 1978), 117, depicts a process of assimilation lasting three centuries, but beginning in the sixteenth century.
14. "Der angeblich formende 'Nationalcharakter' ist ein *Postulat* des Nationalismus, stark durch Stereotypen und Vorurteile belastet, für die historische Forschung ist er als Ausgangspunkt irreführend." Graus, 19.
15. Carolyn Walker Bynam, "Did the Twelfth Century Discover the Individual?," *Jesus as Mother: Studies in the Spirituality of of the High Middle Ages* (Berkeley: University of California Press, 1982), 82–109; here 87. See also John F. Benton, "Consciousness of Self and Perceptions of Individuality," *Renaissance and Renewal in the Twelfth Century*, ed. Robert L. Benson and Giles Constable (Cambridge, Mass.: Harvard University Press, 1982), 263–298.
16. Bynum, 103.
17. Erich Auerbach, "The Knight Sets Forth," *Mimesis: The Representation of Reality in Western Literature* (Princeton: Princeton University Press, 1968), was among the first to recognize the essential function of landscape in depicting the hero's inner development.
18. See Friedrich Panzer, "Der Weg der Nibelungen," *Erbe der Vergangenheit: Festschrift für Karl Helm zum 80. Geburtstag, 19. Mai 1951* (Tübingen: Niemeyer, 1951), 83–107; and Karl Weller, "Die Nibelungenstraße," *Zeitschrift für deutsches Altertum* 70 (1933): 49–66.
19. For a comprehensive listing of the older literature on the Gahmuret books, see Joachim Bumke, *Wolfram von Eschenbach*, Sammlung Metzler 36 (Stuttgart: Metzler, 1981), 102–103. The following interpretation will reflect the perspective first advanced systematically by Christa Ortmann, "Ritterschaft: Zur Frage nach der Bedeutung der Gahmuret-Geschichte im Parzival Wolframs

von Eschenbach," *Deutsche Vierteljahresschrift fur Literaturwissenschaft und Geistesgeschichte* 47 (1973): 664–710, to wit, that the Gahmuret books are worthy of serious attention, that Wolfram intended the fate of the father to prefigure the fate of his sons, and that any total interpretation of *Parzival* must integrate the themes of the Gahmuret books with the Parzival and Gawain sagas. See also Dennis H. Green, "Der Auszug Gahmurets," *Wolfram-Studien* 1 (1970): 62–86; here 62–63; and Eleanor Kutz, "The Story of the Parents in Wolfram von Eschenbach's *Parzival*," *Monatshefte* 70 (1978): 364–374.

20. Green, 83, draws parallels to medieval Celtic literature and to Arthurian romance.
21. As Ortmann notes, "Wolfram hat das Thema des 'Perceval': Der Weg des ritterlichen Menschen durch Schuld und Läuterung zum Gral . . . ausgeweitet auf den ganzen heidnisch-christlichen Bereich" (665). This view was advanced early on by Walter J. Schröder, "Der dichterische Plan des Parzival Romans,"*Beiträge zur Geschichte der deutschen Sprache und Literatur* (Tübingen) 74 (1952): 160–192.
22. Green, 65, warns with some justification against the idealization of Gahmuret as an Arthurian knight. I will argue, following Ortmann, that Gahmuret is meant to epitomize a different ideal of knighthood.
23. Ortmann concisely summarizes the ethos of knighthood at work in the first two books: "Ritterschaft . . . motiviert so die Ausfahrt als teleologische Bestimmung des *art*, dem die wertbegriffliche Norm des *prîs* in Kampf und Minne immanent ist und der durch die eben darin sich ausdrückende Konformität mit dem gesellschaftlichen Ideal auch im Einklang steht mit den beiden Exponenten dieser Wertwelt, mit *got* und mit dem gelücke" (669).
24. Bumke speaks for the commentators who devalue the Gahmuret episodes when he observes "*diu strenge minne* (35,3), von der Gahmuret geplagt wird, ist kaum etwas anderes als seine sinnliche Begierde nach der schönen Negerkönigin, die ihm mit ihrem Körper auch ihre Herrschaft schenkt" (65). Henry Kratz, *Wolfram von Eschenbach's Parzival. An Attempt at a Total Evaluation*, Biblioteca Germanica 15 (Bern: Francke, 1973), 173–203; here 194, also doubts that Gahmuret loves Belacane. More germane, in my view, is the fact that Gahmuret is no more devoted to Belacane than he is to Herzeloyde or Ampflise. Such views ignore the evidence presented in this article and elsewhere, which documents Wolfram's efforts to present the Christian and heathen worlds as both embracing *ritterschaft*.
25. For Bumke this is just another "transaction" in Gahmuret's curiously mercantile kind of knighthood: "Die Ritterwelt des ersten Buchs ist ohne die übliche ideologische Verbrämung gezeichnet: es geht nicht um hohe Werte, sondern nur um den eigenen Vorteil" (65). Ortmann relates this arrangement to the ideal of *prîs* as follows: "Im Stichwort *helfe* sind Kampf und Minnedienst, die beiden Hauptmotive ritterlicher Tätigkeit, kausal miteinander verbunden" (676). Green, 66–67, reminds us that Gahmuret's generosity and lack of concern with material reward are underscored especially in the scenes following his defeat of the besiegers and reward of Belacane's defenders.

26. See Holger Noltze, " 'bî den dûht in diu wile lang'—Warum langweilt sich Gahmuret bei den Môren?," *bickelwort* und *wildiu maere: Festschrift für Eberhard Nellmann zum 65. Geburtstag*, Göppinger Arbeiten zur Germanistik 618 (Göppingen: Kümmerle, 1995), 109–119.
27. The shared values of the black besieged and the white hero are further reflected in their preparations for the meeting. In hopes of attaining Gahmuret's help, Belacane is advised to have her nobles dress as richly as possible (I, 22,19–20); Gahmuret adorns himself in similar fashion (I, 22,30–23,1).
28. Petrus Tax explores the parallels between *Parzival* and the Middle High German versions of the *Aeneid* in his "Gahmuret zwischen Aneas und Parzival: Zur Struktur der Vorgeschichte von Wolframs 'Parzival,' " *Zeitschrift für Deutsche Philologie* 92 (1973): 24–37. See also Green, 76–78.
29. Loyalty or fidelity in the Arthurian pantheon of values. Wolfram universalizes this quality to the point of making it synonymous with *caritas*, thus evoking the dichotomy divine love—despair, which accompanies Parzival's arduous inner journey to the Grail kingship.
30. Here I disagree with Hatto's decision to use the term "blackamoor," a racist designation, even for the Middle Ages, which is later used by the ship's captain to denigrate the citizens of Zazamanc. I would propose the following, more neutral translation: "He was a bastion against improper conduct and in color black as I, a Moor." Noltze, 114, refuses to rule out racism as one of Gahmuret's motives for leaving Belacane, but I fail to see how Gahmuret's sleepless night may be seen as illustrating "indifference."
31. As Kurt Ruh, *Höfische Epik des deutschen Mittelalters*, vol. 1, Grundlage der Germanistik 7 (Berlin: Schmidt, 1977), 129, notes: "Es geht vielmehr um einen höhern, den höchsten Grad der Treue: völlige Demut, Opferbereitschaft bis zum Tode—die Treue, wie sie die Märchenfigur der Griseldis zu bewähren hat."
32. Ortmann, 678, cites her "triuwe," "wîplicher sin," and "kiusche."
33. See Green, 80–81 for a summary of the parallels between the way of the son and the way of the father.
34. As Gahmuret rides into the tournament, Ortmann imagines the audience being aware of the three conflicting courtly obligations under which he must fight: "Er steckt im Harnisch Belacanes, er wird um Minnedienst von Amphlise umworben, er kämpft in einem Turnier, in dem es erklärtermaßen um den Besitz Herzeloydes geht" (683). Ortmann sees Gahmuret beholding to three aspects of the knightly code, for Belacane, the right of Minne in marriage, for Amphlise, the right of courtly service (Minnedienst), and for Herzeloyde, the right of possession through knightly prowess. See Ortmann, 684.
35. Reading Gahmuret anachronistically as a heartless cad completely misses Wolfram's point, which is simply that a knight who sets forth in search of *prîs* may never cease his questing without losing his honor. As Ortmann comments: "*Werdekeit* kann nur durch *ritterschaft* real werden, d.h. sie muß

sich inhaltlich ganz konkret im Kampf und im Minnedienst darstellen" (671). For the opposite point of view, see Blake Lee Spahr, "Gahmuret's Erection: Rising to Adventure," *Monatshefte für Deutschen Unterricht, Deutsche Sprache und Literatur* 83 (1991 Winter): 403–13. Spahr's claim that no one offers objective praise of Gahmuret overlooks Gahmuret's epitaph.

36. The principal objection to this universalist interpretation lies in the joking fashion in which Feirefiz's conversion and marriage to Repanse de Schoye are depicted. This is problematical by any measure, and neither Ortmann nor Hoffmann offers a compelling explanation. If one is allowed a moment of speculation, one could perhaps see Wolfram unable to compose the ending he truly wanted, which would have allowed Feirefiz to join the Grail Society and remain a heathen. But that is a topic for another day.
37. Perhaps the most useful place to begin surveying the voluminous secondary literature on the *Nibelungenlied* is the annotated bibliography by Otfrid Ehrismann, *Nibelungenlied: Epoche—Werk—Wirkung*, Arbeitsbücher zur Literaturgeschichte (Munich: Beck, 1987). See also Werner Hofmann, *Das Nibelungenlied*, Sammlung Metzler 7 (Stuttgart: Metzler, 1982).
38. Bert Nagel, *Das Nibelungenlied. Stoff—Form—Ethos* (Frankfurt: Hirschgraben, 1970) and Werner Hoffmann, *Das Nibelungenlied*, Interpretationen zum Deutschunterricht (Munich: Oldenburg, 1974), originally used the competing value systems as a tool of critical analysis. I follow here the general views of Walter Haug, which he summarizes in his article "Montage und Individualität im Nibelungenlied," *Strukturen als Schlüssel zur Welt: Kleine Schriften zur Erzählliteratur des Mittelalters* (Tübingen: Niemeyer, 1989), 326–338.
39. See Otfrid Ehrismann, 51.
40. Kurt Ruh, *Höfische Epik des deutschen Mittelalters*, Grundlagen der Germanistik 7, 2nd ed. (Berlin: Schmidt, 1977), here 13–23, defines these ideals, as they are presented in Hartmann's *Iwein*.
41. Edward R. Haymes, "Heroic, Chivalric, and Aristocratic Ethos in the *Nibelungenlied*, "*A Companion to the Nibelungenlied*, ed. Winder McConnell, Studies in German Literature, Linguistics, and Culture (Columbia, S.C.: Camden House, 1998), 94–104; here 101.
42. Ehrismann, 241.
43. See Hatto, *The Nibelungenlied*, 371.
44. Ehrismann, 241.
45. Norbert Voorwinden puts it succinctly: "Hilft er den Burgunden, die seit der Verlobung seiner Tochter mit Giselher seine Verwandten sind, so bricht er nicht nur seinen Vasalleneid Etzel gegenüber, sondern auch den Eid, den er einst in Worms Kriemhild geschworen hatte. Läßt er aber die Burgunden im Stich, so übertritt er ebenfalls zwei Verbote, nämlich das Verbot, gegen Verwandte zu kämpfen, und die Verpflichtung, diejenigen zu schützen, denen er das Geleit gegeben hat." See Norbert Voorwinden, "Zur Herkunft der Rüdiger-Gestalt im *Nibelungenlied*," *Amsterdamer Beiträge zur älteren Germanistik* 29 (1989): 259–270; here 267.

46. Hans Naumann, "Höfische Symbolik I. Rüedegers Tod," *Deutsche Vierteljahresschrift für Literatur und Geistesgeschichte* 10 (1932): 387–403; here 388, writes "Zwei *triuwen* ziehen an ihm, die er normalerweise unmöglich zugleich mehr erfüllen kann, wie die Dinge jetzt liegen: die *triuwe* des Lehnsträgers und Gefolgsmanns bindet ihn an Etzel, die *triuwe* der Freundschaft zieht sein Herz zu den Burgunden, die er hergeleitet und geherbergt hat."
47. Naumann reads this scene, extant in no other source, as the final confirmation of Rüdiger's virtue: *milte* which transcends any courtly, feudal, or clan obligation. Peter Wapnewski argues that the function of the shield-gift is to demonstrate the heroic *triuwe* of Hagen, who through his offer "die Freundestreue über die Gefolgsschaftstreue stellen . . . will." See Peter Wapnewski, "Rüdigers Schild," *Nibelungenlied und Kudrun*, ed. Heinz Rupp (Darmstadt: Wissenschaftliche Buchgellschaft, 1976), 134–178; here 162.
48. Jochen Splett's close reading of the Rüdiger-episodes is still quite valuable in its careful evaluation of the arguments and counterarguments. See Jochen Splett, *Rüdiger von Bechelaren: Studien zum zweiten Teil des Nibelungenliedes*, Germanische Bibliothek, Dritte Reihe (Heidelberg: Winter, 1968). See also Ian R. Campbell, "Hagen's Shield Request—*Das Nibelungenlied,* 37th *Aventiure*," *Germanic Review* 71(1996): 23–34.
49. This intersection of heroic fates, which brings Dietrich and Rüdiger together as exiles at the court of Etzel, is treated both in the "Ältere Not" and in the no longer extant variant of a Dietrich-epic which Andersson reconstructs from the Germanic and historical Dietrich traditions. See Theodore Andersson, *A Preface to the Nibelungenlied* (Stanford: Stanford University Press, 1987), 110–112. See also Ehrismann, 192–94, and Edward R. Haymes, "Dietrich von Bern im Nibelungenlied," *Zeitschrift für deutsches Altertum und deutsche Literatur* 114 (1985): 159–165.
50. The joy of all exiled fighting men (278).
51. Lexer I, 539.
52. See, for example, Splett, 74–75, who postulates an "ihm ad hoc zugewiesene Rolle." If we accept Rüdiger's exile status, this action is no longer incongruous, but rather essential, which explains the matter-of-fact tone Rüdiger adopts when justifying his deed to Etzel.
53. Ich wil ûf minen füezen in daz ellende gân (2157) / On my own feet I will go into exile (267).
54. Splett notes, "Ihm als Vertriebenem, der von Etzels Wohlwollen abhängig ist, komme die Ehre nicht zu, daß ein König um die Hand seiner Tochter anhält" (63).
55. Splett, 63.
56. See Roswitha Wisniewski, *Mittelalterliche Dietrichdichtung*, Sammlung Metzler 205 (Stuttgart: Metzler, 1986), 134–145.
57. Among many useful studies, see Werner Hoffmann, "Das Hildebrandslied und die indogermanischen Vater-Sohn-Kampf-Dichtungen," *Beiträge zur Geschichte der deutschen Sprache und Literatur* (Tübingen) 93 (1971): 138–150; Werner Schröder, "Hadubrands tragische Blindheit und der Schluß des Hildesbrandsliedes," *Deutsche Vierteljahresschrift für Literatur und*

Geistesgeschichte 37 (1963): 481–497; and Roswitha Wisniewski, "Hadubrands Rache," *Amsterdamer Beiträge zur älteren Germanistik* 9 (1975): 1–12, who explores the question whether Hadubrand's blindness is calculated.

58. The Nibelungenpoet uses the fate of the outsider to motivate better Dietrich's long-delayed intervention. This, as much as the impetuousness of Wolfhart, explains the Hero of Verona's sudden willingness to fight. Their deaths lead to Dietrich's intervention and eventual transformation from reluctant hero to superhero. Many commentators have cited the line "Dô gewan er widere rechten heldes muot (2325)," as evidence of Dietrich's traditional role as the reluctant hero, but few have identified the justification that is offered to the audience of the *Nibelungenlied*: the bond of hopelessness that exiles hold in common.

5

Visitors from Another Space:

The Medieval Revenant as Foreigner

ALINE G. HORNADAY

In his introduction to this collection, Albrecht Classen notes that the self can understand itself only when it has achieved a clear demarcation from the 'other.'[1] The other may be conceptualized here as any one of the many selves and ethnicities that function in the community and known world external to a self, the supposed denizens of regions beyond or invisibly beside the community and the known world, or indeed the external known world considered as a whole. The demarcation of the self takes definite shape when an other enters the community in which the self resides, as a stranger who in the ensuing dialogue enables the self to situate more precisely its boundaries of personality and self-understanding. During the Middle Ages, a period haunted by astounding numbers of revenants, these spectral beings functioned as a special sort of other, furthering the self's ongoing external and constructive dialogue both by appearing within the self's community, and by bringing into their dialogue a third, invisible, party that was equally foreign to the unregenerate self.

That sometimes unwelcome and intrusive third was an ideal self which both the living percipient and the "undead" ghost needed to internalize in order to enter the heavenly world, the "celestial fatherland" as Gregory the Great calls it.[2] But to idealize itself, as it were, the revenant required help from its interlocutor (which usually was the reason for its appearance when vengeance was not an issue). In turn, the living percipient of the revenant benefited by the latter's advice and information as the percipient worked to construct an ideal self. Thus, in a kind of triangulation, the revenant's requests for help and warnings provided either a model to guide the living self to the ideal, or a horrible example of how *not* to proceed as the earthly self constructed itself. Reports of conversations with medieval revenants, both ordinary people and saints, suggest that they were often believed to recognize a need to guide their interlocutors in this way. Their perceived existence and functions became a useful tool in the Church's effort to save the souls under its care.

From the modern point of view, the existence of this ideal self poses a serious problem. Today, with the aid of psychology we wish to liberate the self from all constrictions that hamper its development so that it can finish its work by achieving a completely integrated consciousness and the highest possible degree of self-realization. In our view, achieving this aim will produce a happy, well-adjusted, socially responsible individual. On the contrary, one who succeeded in constructing an ideal self in the medieval fashion no longer presented any individuality at all, since after having purged human failings, quirks, and sins, he or she partook of the ideal self which is everywhere one and the same. Medieval people considered that complete achievement of this aim qualified the soul for sainthood on earth and entrance into the heavenly kingdom. Clearly, the medieval goal of ideal selfhood is quite different from that aimed at in the construction of the self in modern times, even though in both periods the human self necessarily must begin to demarcate its appropriate limits and spiritual condition by reference to an other.

One can view the medieval demarcation as a two-step process, in which the self realizes itself by setting appropriate boundaries as approved by Christian teaching, and then must dissolve those boundaries to merge as far as possible into the ideal self. While saints achieve this condition while still living on earth, for the rest of unregenerate humanity the task will hardly be completed until after death. But the undead who had not yet earned citizenship in the celestial fatherland by achieving ideal selves, and who indeed continued to manifest or confess to definite, often undesirable, personality traits when they appeared, became important others in the work of bringing one's self closer to the ideal and earning entrance into Heaven. Still, the intrusion of the ideal self created an additional tension in human relations with undead revenants that contributed to the perception of the latter as foreign to humanity, for by implication revenants asked their interlocutors to change at the same time that they asked for help in changing themselves.

Yet by participating in the process of self-construction, ghosts helped the living eventually to transfer their citizenship to the heavenly fatherland that hovered so close to earth in the Middle Ages. We moderns live in a post-Copernican universe on a tiny planet, surrounded by vast reaches of interstellar space that we suppose may be populated by aliens from a multiplicity of worlds. In contrast, medieval people lived on a unique and enormous world enclosed by nearby, invisible spheres in the skies, by postmortem realms somehow coexistent with earth and densely populated by the dead, and by border regions on the frontiers of the afterworld where the undead wandered. These other worlds stood very close to earth, and the possibility of communication with them was well recognized. Indeed, popular imagination often equated the undead in their liminal, borderland situation to earthbound spirits like dwarves or fairies. The latters' existence was an article of faith for most ordinary people, who feared their magical powers and exploitation of humans.

But earthly spirits could have nothing to do with the returning dead any more than modern aliens do. Like modern aliens, and unlike revenants, spirits could abuse humans sexually or mate with them fruitfully (as did the fairy Mélusine, ancestress of the de Lusignan family).[3] Spirits also lived in visible regions on or under earth's known surface, even when they themselves could not be seen. Revenants, on the other hand, returned from invisible borderlands on the frontiers of Heaven or Hell, which after the last years of the twelfth century were officially absorbed into the antechamber to Heaven known as Purgatory.[4] The locations of Purgatory and the invisible borderlands were variously thought to exist upon, inside, or beyond the known earth. In the fourteenth century Dante conclusively mapped this extraterrestrial world's contours with consummate genius, forever enlarging the flat supernatural landscape of earlier reports into a three-dimensional scene. At all times, the medieval Church strictly controlled passports to the unearthly afterworld through rites of passage, exorcisms, and very severe punishments for trespassing upon Church prerogatives by disseminating heretical views about postmortem regions and their inhabitants. Although a considerable amount of literature has always continued to report visions of the world beyond death, since the apparitions reported in this literature function outside of earth they cannot be the same as the revenants whose alien quality terrified the humans they confronted on earth.

As a rule, medieval people reacted to individual revenants differently than they did to dead people as a body of ancestors, with whom they shared an ongoing communion within their own earthly community, and for whom they instituted memorial cults.[5] Revenants who appeared alone or accompanied by a few companions existed outside all communities or cults, neither alive nor truly dead. There was really no way that medieval people could conceptualize them except as foreign visitors from another space, no matter how familiar they might have been in life. As a result, a consistent alienation from perceived undead individuals shows itself again and again in stories from different times and places throughout the European Middle Ages. It is not any supposed reality of ghosts that matters here, but humanity's persistent response to the imagined undead, a quality of perceived otherness and foreignness that remained constant and menacing during the whole medieval period, whenever revenants and humans were supposed to meet.

William A. Christian's criterion for evaluating visions applies to meetings between humans and the undead: they are 'real' when "there is a substantial probability that the vision took place . . . [that is,] people present thought or said so."[6] This is the only possible standard by which to evaluate whatever 'reality' revenant stories possess; even obviously invented *exempla* take advantage of it by attributing the story to one or more people who were present when the revenant appeared. It scarcely needs to be pointed out that this "eyewitness standard" does not meet the requirements of scientific proof. It is doubtful whether applying Christian's standard to the available material for the study of revenants meets the requirements of legal proof either, since (with the exception of Inquisition records) almost all medieval ghost stories are recounted at second or third hand and plainly inadmissible in a court of law. We can only accept the criterion as the best one available to judge a mass of medieval literary, historical, and "pop theology" material.

The medieval literature that purports to describe the reality of revenants comprises written records of oral tales and folklore, together with stories that occur in chronicles, collections of correspondence, sermons and sermon collections, imaginative literary works, and the glosses to all of these. Medieval authors, reporting ghosts in Latin, used terms such as *anima, mania* or *maniaticus, larva, monstrum, umbra, phantasia, necromantia, praestigia, lemures, manifestatio,* and *spiritus*.[7] Some of these words carry connotations of evil, trickery, and black magic, hence they are not true synonyms, but rather reflect authorial views on the reality of ghosts and the causes of apparitions. Nor do these medieval words offer the exact correspondence of the words ghost and foreigner found in modern Chinese, in which the word used for foreigner, *gueilo*, literally means ghost (though the French term *revenant* implies a ghostly return). It appears that the notoriously xenophobic Chinese share the medieval European sense that ghosts are a kind of foreigners, and that in Chinese cultures the reverse is also true.[8] In modern times, English authors and translators of medieval works have used the words ghost, phantasm, phantom, spirit, specter, revenant (a French loanword), vampire, apparition, vision, and dream, gradually evolving into the modern usage in which the terms function as interchangeable synonyms.[9]

Since it tacitly equates revenants to visionary apparitions, this modern usage conforms to Augustine's fifth-century doctrine (elaborated from Tertullian) that undead revenants could only appear in dreams or visions sent by angels on their behalf without their knowledge—a doctrine that would be restated in somewhat different terms by Thomas Aquinas in the thirteenth century.[10] But by the sixth century, in practice Gregory the Great distinguished several ghosts in his *Dialogues* from visions, dreams, and apparitions, as did chroniclers and religious writers throughout the Middle Ages.[11] Following Gregory's practice, and in order to focus closely on earthly colloquies with the undead, we may define visions and dreams as insubstantial apparitions seen by people who are experiencing altered states of consciousness (whether awake or asleep), and which often pertain to extraterrestrial locales or spirits—nowadays angels, aliens, leprechauns, and so on—or may concern dead people. We may then define revenants or ghosts as dead people seen in earthly settings by people in normal waking consciousness, who may not realize that they are in fact seeing dead people. The revenants who are the subjects of this paper are no mere filmy phantoms or immaterial, ectoplasmic forms.

Gregory the Great reports at secondhand a story from a percipient who at first had no idea he was meeting a revenant.[12] The elderly priest of the church in Civitavecchia told Bishop Felix of Porto that he often visited the hot springs at Aquae Tauri for the health benefits of their steam. One day a new attendant waited on him with extreme courtesy, and thereafter continued to pay special attention to the priest whenever the latter went to the baths. The priest did not want to seem stingy or mean, so as a special gift he brought the respectful servant two consecrated wafers. But the man, sighing, refused them because he was unworthy to touch the holy bread. In life the lord of the place, he had been sent to tend the baths after his death because of his sins. He asked the priest to offer them in his name to the Lord. If the priest's intercession succeeded, the ghost said that he would vanish. After the astonished priest had offered mass for a week, when he returned to the baths the attendant was gone. So, says Gregory, we see how beneficial to souls is the mass and offering of the sacred host, for which the dead long.

In another of Gregory's stories, it is not quite clear whether or not the percipient knew at first that he was meeting a ghost. When Bishop Germanus of Capua went to the baths at Città San Angelo, to his great surprise he found the well-known Deacon Pascarius there, stoking the furnace for the hot bath.[13] Pascarius explained that before he died he had mistakenly supported the anti-pope Laurentius, and begged Germanus to pray for his release from servitude. If the bishop did not find him on his next visit, he would know his prayers had been answered favorably. Bishop Germanus prayed for Pascarius. Sure enough, when he next visited the baths, Pascarius was gone. According to Gregory, the deacon had sinned through ignorance, not error, and so his fault could be purged after death.

Gregory presents two *exempla* here that feature bathhouse steam rooms, which in Gregory's day were not yet considered haunts of vice best avoided by the clergy.[14] Here undead men underwent a postmortem punishment reminiscent of the fires of hell, but not so irrevocable. In the sixth century Gregory still believed that if their faults were not too grave, souls might be sent back to earth for correction, and appear there as normal human beings. Presumably Gregory and his informants believed that the percipients in these stories were permitted to encounter ghosts undergoing correction because as clergymen they were entitled to mediate between heaven and earth, and thus were empowered to release the revenants from their chastisement even before the Day of Judgment. The revenants that Gregory describes belong to the category of undead souls who need further correction both to repent their sins efficaciously and to understand and construct an ideal soul for themselves. At the same time, they furnish important morals for Gregory's readers which will enable the latter to benefit too, from knowledge of what they should and should not do in the future. Their setting in the baths shows that old Roman customs of cleanliness and health care persisted into the early Middle Ages, before the desirability of self-mortification and modesty became truisms in Christian doctrine.

The ghostly priest and former lord undergoing punishment in these two stories were certainly members of the contemporary upper class. In medieval ghost stories, many revenants in need of correction have come from the ruling élite, which may reveal a considerable amount of envy and resentment toward their masters among the lower orders, and even perhaps within the priesthood. Gregory, at any rate, is quite clear that noble birth is no guarantee of right conduct and may even be a hindrance to it. But in general, two major classes of revenants divide along moral rather than economic or political lines: saints, who though they sometimes frightened percipients proved to be helpful to mankind; and the undead, who seemed to be living people, but when they were identified as revenants appeared to lay percipients as terrifying strangers from a space between the worlds. Medieval theologians held that the whole living presence of saints permeated each of their relics. This simultaneous presence in heavenly and terrestrial communities privileged saints to continue to appear on earth as emissaries from Heaven, empowered to act on its behalf. Not so revenants. Though the Church finally decided that revenants must be demons masquerading in corpses, in popular fancy they retained undead status as former human beings whether they were vampires prolonging life on a notably foreign diet of human blood, persons who died untimely and haunted their "places of memory" until their normal life span would have ended, or souls tethered to earth by vital tasks or vengeance left undone, venial sins, or ritual impurities not yet expiated.

It is not surprising that the undead were perceived as threateningly foreign when they appeared as vampires risen from their graves to suck human blood. This type of revenant swarms in central and eastern Europe; similar beings in Celtic Scotland and Ireland (the Baobhan Sith) are fairies or even living human beings, not the undead. The Scots, for instance, recognize evil spirits like the vampirish kelpies, who emerge from streams as beautiful horses in order to attract unwary mortals, who mount them only to be carried into a loch and consumed, and Redcaps, hobgoblins who drink the blood of travelers who shelter in the small, square peel towers that defend Lowland dwellers from border raids.[15] Irish tradition reports that the woman mourner, the "bean chaointe," sometimes sucks the blood of corpses. But spirits and human mourners are not comparable to undead vampires. The literature on true vampires gives the impression that while vampires pullulate in east European folklore, which certainly has its roots in very early times, written reports of them first become numerous in the sixteenth century, and are overwhelmingly a phenomenon of central and eastern Europe.[16] Admittedly, an *argumentum e silentio* cannot prove that vampires were rare in medieval western Europe, but revenants cited as vampires by western authors on closer reading do often turn out to be less parasitical ghosts, who do not suck blood in spite of their malevolence toward humanity. This essay concerns the abundant lore of west European revenants, and therefore does not take vampires into account even though they are decidedly foreign to humanity in their eternal life, earthly wanderings and peculiar nutrition (an obvious objectification of the life force).

Three important general surveys of medieval European revenant lore have been published since 1950. In the first, written over twenty-five years ago, Ronald C. Finucane examined reports of European ghosts from their appearances in classic times until the twentieth century.[17] Finucane did not attempt to distinguish revenants and ghosts from other apparitions, since he found invented stories, visions, and *exempla* to be "as revealing of social assumptions as so-called authentic accounts." He preferred to investigate ghost stories as indicators of social values because he considered that the state of the evidence, the imitation of stories and continuity of expectation across millennia, in addition to problems of distortion and literary narration, nullified the value of ghost stories as accounts of "real" visitations. Finucane argued that "changes in social assumptions, particularly . . . theological opinions and scientific accomplishments, affected the ways that the living envisaged their dead. . . . Each epoch has perceived its spectres according to specific sets of expectations; as these change so too do the spectres . . . [who] represent not beings of [an]other world, but of this."[18]

In 1981, the French historian Jean-Claude Schmitt zoomed in to focus more closely on the specific field of western medieval ghost stories after the year 1000.[19] Schmitt too took these stories as evidence of *mentalités,* and like Finucane found a chronology of social innovation rather than authentic accounts. Schmitt argued that an "invasion of ghosts at the turn of the millennium articulated a new "solidarity of lineal kinship beyond death," though stories of hostile ghosts reflected "conflictual relationships at the heart of feudal society" as the Church struggled with fighting nobles over social violence and the Peace of God. After the twelfth century, the growing numbers of mendicant orders needed "massive and stereotypical narrative collections of *exempla*" for use in sermons. According to Schmitt, their extensive collections "transformed and saved the ghost story" as an "instrument of acculturation."[20] Also like Finucane, Schmitt held that changes in the ghost story's form and content expressed successive social norms in a historical morphology of the *genre.*

In 1986, in a general survey of revenant literature in central Europe and Scandinavia centered on the Middle Ages, Claude Lecouteux linked the dissolution of the solidly physical revenants known to classic Rome into the almost invisible, filmy shades of today to the gradual weakening over centuries of ancient communal ties of tribe, clan, and family.[21] He thus associated European developments in the concept of revenants to an evolving notion of foreigners as relational ties loosened. Lecouteux showed how the terrifying quality of these beings outside community, yet still tied to it, began to diminish little by little after the Middle Ages ended. He ingeniously traced this slow evaporation of ghosts through successive changes in the vocabulary employed to describe revenants century after century.[22] As a specialist in the lore of monsters and supernatural beings, Lecouteux also adumbrated a classification of some motifs from tales of revenants. This enormous task of classification will have to be completed before we can fully understand the forms, origins, and evolution of ghost stories in the various European regions.

By treating their materials as historical markers, Finucane and Schmitt gained a valuable analytical tool. Nevertheless, the historical developments they discovered in the ghost story did not affect a constant element within it during the entire Middle Ages: a frightening and hostile alienation that ordinary living people ascribed to revenants once they had identified them as ghosts. This alien foreignness holds good whether the ghost story is presented as an *exemplum* in sermon collections and chronicles, as an apparition in vision literature, as an account of an actual event, or as a ghostly interpretation of unquestionable facts or happenings. It comes across clearly in almost all of the tales presented by Lecouteux.

The after-death vicissitudes of a twelfth-century royal couple typify Finucane and Schmitt's chronological morphology of social assumptions, the foreignness in medieval perception of ghosts and ghost-related events, and the helpfulness of the comparative material presented by Lecouteux in elucidating real life occurrences. Their vivid personalities and troubled marital history may have caused contemporaries to cast King Philip II of France, and perhaps his first queen Isabelle of Hainaut, as revenants. From the time of his birth, contemporary clerics had promoted a supernatural atmosphere around Philip II, a late-born son greeted as a miraculous child by the French people. This supernatural aura intensified when the profoundly shaken fourteen-year-old prince postponed his first coronation, a year before his marriage to Isabelle, after a huge boar led him away from the hunt only to vanish deep in the forest of Compiègne like a malicious spirit in animal disguise. Philip wandered lost through the night, terrified by the medieval forest that Roger Bartra depicts as a haunt of demonic figures, mythical wild men, fugitives from justice, and threatening animals. Just so Dante wandered lost through a wood whose "very memory gives a shape to fear," in whose dark depths beings wandered that a prince or poet astray might well fear to meet, where fierce, terrifying beasts confronted him, so that he could only escape by taking the path through Hell.[23] The young prince Philip emerged from his own forest experience in emotional disarray, sick in bed for three days and too upset to hold the coronation ceremony for many weeks (originally set for the Assumption of the Virgin on August 15, it was postponed to All Saints' Day).

Thomas of Cantimpré presents a relevant, rather later *exemplum* set in the gloomy, pathless depths of an Alpine forest.[24] Like Philip having lost his way while hunting, a knight from Lausanne strayed in a silent forest as dusk fell and his two dogs barked far away. He followed the sound to a mountain meadow, where to his horror he saw the dogs darting repeatedly at a tall, elegant man covered with bloody wounds, who lay face down between two iron bludgeons. The man explained that he had gone with the Brabançons to fight in Poitou for Richard Lionheart against Philip II. There he abandoned himself to murder and lust, sparing neither sex, until he was carried off by a fever. But at the moment of death he wept for his sins with strong interior contrition. Then two demons snatched him away to torture him until Judgment Day with iron bludgeons. With savage blows, they chased his miserable soul across deep ravines and high mountains to the meadow where they had just left him. Through interminable tortures, the ghost had been sustained only by the hope of eventual pardon for his sins. As soon as the revenant finished his explanation, he and the bludgeons vanished "like a puff of smoke."[25] In the light of Thomas de Cantimpré's story, it is no wonder that the young prince Philip's night in a terrifying forest seemed supernatural to his contemporaries and probably to himself.

In keeping with this supernatural aura, after Philip died in 1223 an ailing cardinal in Italy saw a band of angels rescue his soul from demons carrying it off to Hell. One of the angels announced that Philip's public support of Mother Church had saved him from the consequences of his far from saintly private life.[26] Since this anecdote parallels a desire for escape from Hell expressed by many medieval revenants, it seems to present Philip as a ghost. But while revenants encounter humans on earth, in this case Philip appeared in a moralistic vision in an extraterrestrial setting, whose analogues date back to an extensive Carolingian vision literature.[27] Not all royals who appeared in this literature were as lucky as he. Some well-known visions claimed that only intercessionary prayers could deliver the great Charlemagne himself from eternal punishment. First impressions can be deceiving; this condensed anecdote belongs to the genre of carefully composed vision literature that Schmitt found to be growing in popularity in Philip's time.

Over thirty years before, Philip's nineteen-year-old queen Isabelle of Hainaut had died in childbirth in mid-March, 1190. A death like hers greatly intensified the already acute popular fear of haunting by persons who died untimely, for the mother had not undergone the prescribed rites of postpartum purification. Many canonists even prohibited church funerals for women who died during their confinements, fearing that blood might pollute the church.[28] Perhaps for this reason, Isabelle was not entombed "with great pomp" in the choir of the cathedral of Notre-Dame in Paris until May 22, 1190, two months after she died. She did not rest there undisturbed. Her little grandson's coffin was placed in her tomb in 1218, while Philip still lived, and church officials reexamined the tomb in 1699 during renovations to the high altar and choir. It is not known if Isabelle's coffin was opened before her entombment or on either of these occasions. In any case, when Viollet-le-Duc opened her coffin during further alterations to the choir in 1858, Isabelle's skull had disappeared.[29]

The otherworldly atmosphere that had hung about Philip and Isabelle's reign, the queen's early death in childbirth, Philip's erratic and capricious personality, and his "inhuman" treatment of her early in their married life, all lend credence to the possibility that the king felt guilty and fearful about her.[30] The speculation that he might have had Isabelle's body beheaded to keep her from haunting him gains some plausibility from a cure for haunting prescribed in a tale from Walter Map, set in the decade after her death. Map reported that night after night a Welsh corpse brayed out one of his former neighbors' names in a caricature of saints coming to conduct the dying to heaven, thus killing off each neighbor one by one. A brave soldier reported the problem to Bishop Gilbert Foliot of Herefordshire, who diagnosed a case of demoniac possession. The bishop cast out the demon by having the soldier cut off the corpse's head.[31] Similar stories occur in all ages and places in Europe. For example, centuries before, in Merovingian France, the Salian Franks customarily decapitated their dead enemies to prevent their vengeance on the living.[32] Foliot's cure for hauntings surely was known in late twelfth-century France, and possibly was practiced on Queen Isabelle.

These intriguing royal Capetian phenomena conform to an ambivalence toward the deceased that is present in medieval ghost stories, and still endures today. A similar conflicted human response to death is so well accepted by modern psychology that it appears in a vast professional literature as well as in advice columns of popular magazines, newspapers, and in self-help books. Alienation from the dead as it has existed at least since classic times often takes the form of an unacknowledged anger at the dead person for having left his or her survivors behind. This element of anger at an emotionally perceived abandonment by a departed loved one, which today continues to furnish a subtext to mourning the dead, appeared in the Middle Ages as a hostile foreignness that medieval survivors projected onto the departed souls whom they had once held dear. Nancy Caciola has collected medieval accounts of revenants' attacks on living people, particularly in Icelandic saga, which reveal how easily survivors projected their own anger upon the undead.[33]

Since departed souls were perceived as having left their earthly communities on the way to various postmortem communities in Purgatory (after the twelfth century), Heaven, or Hell, those among them who wandered on the edges of their ultimate destinations before achieving their post-mortem goals had become foreign to living humanity. As revenants they had entered the category of strangers, against whose strangeness the community now identified itself. People perceived them as "potentially menacing" others, who had become "sojourners" on earth, that is, "people who will remain in contact with societies and cultures physically at a distance from the districts of residence in which they temporarily reside."[34] So when they reappeared on earth, as sojourners they would now have "their own community and culture, . . . [and] come into a new environment."[35] But however alienated they might be from the earthly environment and their former communities, however much they were sojourners where once they had been residents, medieval revenants did not yet fully belong to extraterrestrial communities either. They needed their survivors' help if they were to escape the rigors of Hell and make a final transition into the celestial fatherland. In their liminal position on the thresholds of angelic or demonic regions, revenants were also vulnerable to earthly witches who could bring back the undead for the purposes of black magic, and to demons who could take over their bodies as a necessary, no less terrifying and more deceptive mask for earthly appearances. Because of these activities pursued by sorcerers and demons, and because still influential pagan concepts of the dead had hardly differed from pagan notions of gods and mythic spirits, popular folklore often equated ghosts to malignant spirits, which did nothing to lessen the terror they so often inspired.[36]

Although revenants known to their interlocutors or victims could scarcely appear as unknown earthly foreigners, they had become so alien that living people's ambiguous, wary, and fearful reactions to ghosts mirrored their reactions to persons known to be foreign strangers. Bishop Thietmar of Merseburg reported local priests' horrified response to great companies of eleventh-century ghosts who rose by night from churchyard cemeteries in Waldsleben, Magdeburg, Deventer, and Rotmersleben, often to the accompaniment of loud grunting sounds.[37] Mysteriously burning lamps shone in the churches in whose churchyards these cemeteries were located, while revenant priests conducted religious rites at the altars and their ghostly congregations sang psalms. Thietmar wrote that he believed truthful and reputable witnesses to these nocturnal rites, who told him that the dead priests who officiated at these ceremonies dealt summarily with living clergymen who boldly tried to interrupt and halt their unauthorized activities. One of Thietmar's sources explained that night was reserved for ghosts, day for the living, who intruded on ghosts at their peril ("ut dies vivis, sic nox est concessa defunctis").[38] This important distinction had apparently become a tenet of the European belief system since Gregory the Great's day, and often served to help identify ghosts.

William of Newburgh reported the revulsion met by some more convivial ghosts in the 1190s. A recently dead man was poorly received when he paid nightly visits to his terrified wife and brothers in a Buckinghamshire village. As a result, ghosts materialized and terrorized the villagers by holding their wild Bacchanalian revels in and around people's homes. When Bishop Hugh of Lincoln had his written absolution laid on the corpse's chest, the dead man and his companions vanished, never to return.[39] The modern literature calls these ghosts "vampires," though there is nothing in William's report to justify the word, unless the adjective "Bacchanalian" implies the savagery of Dionysian maenads who tear their victims limb from limb and eat their flesh. Yet vampirism and cannibalism are two different abnormalities. In any case, here again the terrifying revenants appear by night in the approved manner for ghosts.

Much later and far away, on February 2 and 26, 1320, in the diocese of Pamiers in southern France, the suspected heretic and "messenger of souls" Arnaud Gelis told inquisitors that when he saw his first specter one night he was terrified and implored it to go away without touching him.[40] The revenant who so frightened Gelis was his former employer, Canon Hugues de Durfort of Pamiers, who had died five days before. In Gelis's account, at its first appearance de Durfort's ghost conformed to the nocturnal custom for revenant appearances, but soon took control of the encounter and appointed a daytime rendezvous with Gelis in the cloister of the church at Mas-Saint-Antonin where he and his servant lived. When the canon duly reappeared, he requested Gelis to ask de Durfort's sister to have masses celebrated for his soul. After this first daytime meeting, Gelis talked by day to a number of high-ranking clerics in the same cloister and church (including several canons and the deceased Bishop Bernard of Pamiers), all of whom gave him valuable information about the hereafter and messages for their relations. Like Thietmar's ghosts, the revenants with whom Gelis associated used local churches for nightly rites; the ghosts in Pamiers left the churches at dawn to wander invisibly among the living, seen only by messengers of souls like Gelis.

Gelis continued meeting ghosts of all kinds and conditions by day and interpreting them to their survivors. As a messenger of souls, he bridged two communities in the manner of modern spiritualist mediums. Perhaps he could do so because he had been accredited to the postmortem world by churchmen who performed the rites that controlled it, and therefore was able to accept his ability to perceive by day the ghosts that swarmed everywhere around living people (whom he advised to move carefully in order to avoid jostling or stepping on the thronging but invisible revenants). It will be remembered that Gregory the Great's clergymen who met ghosts in the baths were also able to converse with them by day. Gelis testified that revenants knew they were estranged from the living, and that they wished that "all living men and women were dead," that is, that the living survivors and their dead could still feel themselves to participate in one community. Relations between ghosts and living people remained as strained as they had been three centuries ago in Thietmar's time, in spite of the existence of percipients like Gelis who acted as semi-professional mediums.[41]

In addition to creating the emotional barrier to which it testifies, the estrangement ascribed to revenants may also have affected other aspects of their perception by living people. Ronald Finucane, Jean-Claude Schmitt, and Nancy Caciola have all discussed the relative rarity of female ghosts in their material. This rarity is another sort of foreignness than the hostility and unease that has been described previously. It would seem to imply a perception among the living of a strange population mix in the postmortem community, unless it is an effect of transmission in the sources. Finucane found that in his overall sampling of medieval ghost stories "more than three-quarters of the ghosts and over three-quarters of the percipients were men. In two-thirds of the cases male ghosts were seen by men; women, both as apparitions and percipients, played a minority role."[42] Schmitt merely remarked that individual "female ghosts are rare."[43] Caciola, too, observed that "female revenants . . . [were] rare among the individual, hostile variety of the undead," but that even though individual women revenants were rare, "[women] seem to have been common as dancers" among the masses of ghosts often seen frolicking among the graves in churchyard cemeteries.[44]

In the record of Arnaud Gelis's first interrogation, the Bishop of Pamiers's notary Guillaume Peyre Barthe transcribed Gelis's accounts of eighteen individual male and five female ghosts. In the record of his second interrogation, either Gelis or the notary lumped together almost all of the female revenants Gelis discussed in the phrase "many of the dead women." Out of a multitude of visions in Gregory the Great's *Dialogues,* he distinguishes three revenant stories; following the same pattern, two concern men as both ghost and percipient, while in the other both ghosts and their percipient are female. Even in this tiny sample, two-thirds of the personnel are male.

The text of Gregory's story about feminine ghosts may reflect some disdain for women's perceived obstinate silliness, for he depicts two noble female revenants as foolish and hostile personalities. They had lived as religious in their own house near Saint Benedict's monastery, with an elderly male servant to serve their daily needs for food and household help.[45] Their bad language so upset their pious old servitor that he told Benedict about it. Benedict then informed the religious that he would excommunicate them if they did not improve their behavior. But they did not change; and when they died a few days later they were entombed in the local church. At their funeral mass, their old nurse saw them rise from their tombs and go out of the church when the deacon "*ex more*" asked anyone who did not wish to take communion to leave. Knowing that they had often done the same thing in their lifetime, she remembered that Benedict had warned them that he would deprive them of communion if they did not mend their ways and their language. Benedict then made an offering on their behalf which permitted them to rest in their tombs and presumably rescued them from the consequences of their foolishness. Gregory primly remarks that nobility of lineage all too often produces vulgarity of soul: these ladies failed to bridle their tongues as religious should do. In this *exemplum,* Gregory evidently intended to show the dangers of assuming that one's noble birth entitled one to Heaven, and the need to avoid bad language as well as to take communion regularly in order to achieve salvation.

Whereas Gregory's two foolish female ghosts rose out of their tombs to differentiate themselves haughtily from a living congregation of the faithful, Thietmar of Merseburg's revenants, who must have included women, remained a vague, shapeless mass except for the necessarily male priests who led their ceremonies. The perception of these undifferentiated throngs of ghosts and the statistical findings by Finucane and Schmitt, as well as Caciola's remarks on the presence of women's ghosts in large crowds of revenants, might be taken to imply an odd shyness or invisibility of individual female ghosts, rather than the strange population mix that at first sight they appeared to suggest. The evidence is contradictory. In any case, some sort of shyness or invisibility restricted to female ghosts seems quite unlikely, given that the sources make no reference to any such condition among revenants.

The record of Arnaud Gelis's interrogations suggests an explanation, perhaps supported by Gregory the Great's tale about the foolish religious. Either Gelis or the notary Guillaume Peyre Barthe who prepared the record may have grown progressively more bored with female ghosts, to the point where they began omitting the content of ghostly conversations when women chattered about matters that medieval men might consider trivial: the reuse of their silk sleeves by their survivors, the state of dead infants' souls, their grandchildren's welfare, and so on.[46] Male chroniclers, court reporters, notaries, and other scribes who drew up documents also probably soon grew tired of this sort of subject. Such an attitude would have been reinforced by the way in which war and its codes permeated medieval society: its warlike character, combined with the clerical misogyny revealed in anecdotes like Gregory's, may account for the comparative rarity of accounts of individual female revenants (who had little to say about knightly preoccupations). If this interpretation based on Gelis's testimony is correct, their rarity would have resulted from bias in the records rather than from the actual experience of medieval percipients of revenants. But to be sure on this point, a thorough statistical survey of the entire literature would be desirable.[47]

Whatever their sex, ordinary medieval ghosts usually asked their interlocutors for help through prayers, completion of tasks they had left undone, and feeding the poor in their names. By contrast, some extraordinary militant saints appeared on earth wherever the forces of righteousness needed help, in order to engage in physical combat for their cause. In the hagiographical presentation of revenants, the ever-present saints appear by day as a matter of course, unlike undead revenants who are segregated temporally by night. Already citizens of the "celestial fatherland," yet still alive and present on earth, saints are by definition holy and helpful. Therefore, male saints went to war with gusto in the cause of right. Santiago de Compostela—Saint James the Greater—is perhaps the most famous among these forceful revenants. An early medieval army of Spanish Christian soldiers supposedly saw him at the battle of Clavijo, riding a huge white charger knee to knee with them in the mélée, slaying Moors to right and left.[48] A century or two earlier in 627, as a rather unexpected feminine militant, the Virgin Mary appeared "as a battle queen, inciting her followers to victory" among defenders on the walls of the besieged city of Byzantium.[49] However, in this case the Virgin did not participate in the actual fighting.

According to our beliefs, we may explain these fighting saints as collective hallucinations under the stress of battle, or as realities easier to see in the heat of combat. Malcolm Bowie interprets them in terms of Wilhelm von Kaulbach's modern mural, in which he depicts "dead warriors . . . [who] fight on in the sky above the battlefield . . . [and appear] in Freud's *The Ego and the Id* as the very emblem of the stratified or compartmentalized human mind."[50] Kaulbach's "dramatic scene of self-division and mental contention" explains why militant saints can appear on battlefields as soldiers experience just such dissociations. Even as late as 1918, at the crucial battlefield of Mons in Belgium, an army of British soldiers saw protective beings hovering in the sky above them, whom the men interpreted as angels. It would be surprising indeed if similar apparitions had not occurred in the Middle Ages, given the period's constant warfare. It is even more surprising to find solidly physical revenants in the earthly scrummage of medieval battles.

Unlike militant saints on battlefields, the warrior chief Hellequin or Herlechin and his wild riders are undead revenants who cross benighted travelers' paths in a midnight cavalcade, accompanied by terrifying spirits.[51] This procession's personnel is even more frightening than a troop of human knights riding by at night, surely no rare event in the Middle Ages. Indeed in the forest of Maine on the night of January 1, 1091, when the young priest Walchelin heard the beat of the cavalcade's hooves coming up behind him as he walked home from visiting a sick parishioner, he thought at first that he was hearing the baron Robert de Bellême's cavalry on its way to besiege the castle of Courcy.[52] As happened in Walchelin's case, knights riding with

Hellequin deliver messages for their living survivors to the belated wayfarers who chance to meet the wild riders. For Hellequin's troop obeys Thietmar's division of time: day for the living, night for the dead.

When Walchelin attempted to cut out and mount a riderless charger from Hellequin's procession, to prove his veracity when he would recount what he had seen, in the process he narrowly escaped being killed by the accompanying spirits for trying to steal one of Hellequin's steeds. It hurt him severely even to touch the horse, which indicates its status as a spirit. Then too, Gervase of Tilbury recounts a story of a ghostly warrior rider who disappeared from the saddle when he was bested in combat, leaving behind a fierce black spirit horse who vanished at cockcrow.[53] Perhaps Santiago's charger and Hellequin's mounts are spirits, not ghosts, and the knights and their steeds do not necessarily belong together, but revenants are beyond normal earthly logic; in many tales ghosts and spirits are not clearly differentiated. Hellequin's dead knights and their horses probably originate in archaic pre-Christian beliefs, in keeping with which the warhorses of prehistoric Eurasian chiefs were sacrificed and buried beside them to carry them through the afterlife. After emerging from the military camps of half-Christianized Normans, the wild horsemen melded with ancient traditions of the armies of the dead as well as with medieval notions of the procession of the dead.[54] The association of medieval warrior revenants with horses or chargers probably also gained credibility from a vague association with the four horsemen of the Apocalypse. These latter harbingers of war and pestilence might also explain why Arnaud Gelis saw two dead horsemen with terrible wounds several times at a distance, riding "very thin nags."

Saints who had already made themselves known to the faithful might engage in daytime warfare to assure victory for the right, but saints in the making earned merit toward sanctification by other kinds of helpful miracles. Two holy women in early medieval Hainaut participated in such events, one as percipient and the other as miracle-worker after death. When the seventh-century Frankish aristocrat Waldetrude of Mons feared that she was neglecting her family by devoting too much of her time to prayer and good works, she asked God for guidance. Immediately the dead Bishop Géry of Cambrai walked into the church where she knelt in prayer and told her that she was doing just as she should.[55] This apparition (which may have been a vision, rather than a true ghost) was among the miracles that sanctified Géry, and Waldetrude herself would eventually earn sainthood and become the patron of Hainaut. Some time later, her niece Aye gave Waldetrude's convent in Mons large properties when she became its abbess. After Aye died, her heirs contested this donation. While their suit was being heard in the abbey church, Aye suddenly spoke from her tomb to insist that her gift was permanent, an unusual, purely aural appearance which helped to make her a local saint. Aye never seems to have had sainthood officially conferred upon her, even in the unstructured early medieval fashion in which an appropriate local bishop raised the dead person's relics before the altar and declared him or her a saint, but she was nevertheless invoked in Mons from the eighth century on and performed miracles there and elsewhere in Belgium.[56]

These two protective miracles were important steps in the process of creating sainthood for Géry and Aye early in eighth-century Francia. Another protective miracle may have been put forward with a similar aim in the case of Sancho I, king of León and Galicia, who died about 929. According to this story, after his death Sancho I often visited his queen Goto to give her advice. The second time Goto saw him, he asked her to give a fur he was wearing to a poor priest. The priest in turn placed it as a relic in the church of San Estéban at Ribas de Sil, where it remained as a proof of Sancho's visits; but in tenth-century Galicia this story was apparently not enough to sanctify the king, who remained a rather obscure regional Spanish monarch.[57]

Clearly, unedited first-hand medieval tales of revenants reported in literature (if any such exist) can scarcely be distinguished from the enormous numbers of extant *exempla* and an extensive vision literature, both of which aimed at teaching lessons essential to salvation by means of carefully chosen components and moral applications. Some stories recounted in this paper are obvious *exempla,* such as Gregory the Great's haughty women religious, Thomas de Cantimpré's bloody knight, Géry's comfort for Waldetrude, and so on. The great difficulty is to discern how far the people who told these stories or wrote them down believed that they were true, and to what degree the people who wrote them down, then found appropriate morals for them or expanded them to fit the authors' preconceptions. For example, Thietmar's "truthful and reputable" witnesses, if indeed he did not invent them, seem to have found him a receptive audience for their tales of ghostly nocturnal rites. To these accounts, Thietmar added morals of his own composition that bore out his desire to prove the existence of souls to his rude pagan congregations, though to us they do not seem completely appropriate for his purpose. In addition to the other grave problems inherent in the transmission of originally oral material through one or more written documents, most artificially composed *exempla* have likewise often been distorted by being passed through successive versions as sermon writers and chroniclers told and retold them in a society that valued tradition, and expanded them from earlier sources.

Such serious problems of transmission and adjustment make Arnaud Gelis's testimony to his inquisitor a precious source because it is first-hand, extensive, and reports conversations with ghosts that sometimes seem completely pointless and thus may be less artificial than the tales related by clergymen. The later inquisitorial proceeding against Joan of Arc also provides an extremely valuable first-hand account of aural appearances by saintly and angelic visitors from the afterworld. Inquisition records unfortunately only begin to be available too late for use in general surveys of medieval revenants in the style of Finucane, Schmitt, and Lecouteux. But they allow us invaluable glimpses of ancient belief systems that still continued throughout the Middle Ages to coexist uneasily with official Christian theology.

Because their problematic nature makes it impossible to take medieval ghost stories at face value, historians tend to evaluate ghost stories according to whether they use them to explicate historical trends, interpret them through the lens of modern psychology, see them as contrived *exempla,* or illustrate other aspects of medieval life. Jean-Claude Schmitt treats Orderic Vitalis's version of Hellequin's ride in terms of its expression of changing secular political attitudes as the story evolved through many texts and settings, while Brian Stock interprets it psychologically as "[an attempt] . . . through the most powerful of evocations—the deceased—to transcend living human bonds and to re-express them in spiritual terms" that contrast Hellequin's menacing band with Walchelin's religious brotherhood. Carlo Ginzburg studies the story as a strand in the "history of a nucleus of popular beliefs, which little by little . . . became assimilated to witchcraft," and Jeffrey Burton Russell calls it "a fairly typical *exemplum.*"[58] Indeed, these historians did not need to discuss whether or not Orderic or his source repeated a story in which either believed, and for which Orderic found a suitable moral. From their point of view any attempt at such an analysis would be pointless, since their material chiefly functions and has value for them as a source of historical markers for medieval social conditions, changing attitudes, and beliefs. This procedure has produced highly useful historical and interpretative results, since people who see ghosts will quite unconsciously fit a contemporary agenda and understanding to what they have seen or imagined; the marker they provide is all the more valuable for being inserted unconsciously into the text.

But whatever their percipients' and recorders' agendas, and whatever social innovation they marked, ordinary medieval revenants remained chillingly foreign. That aspect of the psychology inherent in these stories did not change over time, but remained constant through many cultural changes. Thietmar wanted his readers to understand God's mercy and the resurrection to come, yet his ulterior motive did not affect his reports of ghostly estrangement. Somewhat later, Orderic Vitalis reports the terror that Hellequin's wild riders instilled in a wayfarer upon whom they came by night. The Cathar suspect Arnaud Gelis could hardly state his agenda openly, but surely tried to ingratiate himself with inquisitors by describing the most edifying ghosts possible. Even so, the report of his interrogation begins with the usual medieval shrinking from revenants' foreignness, and goes on to note the irrevocable estrangement between the living and the undead, and the latters' nighttime activities. Clearly, ghost stories projected an anger that their tellers felt toward the dead onto the revenants themselves, whom theologians literally demonized (as in Walter Map's tale of a devil's summons to the hapless neighbors of a recently dead man). Ghosts, irrevocably other, became the ultimate foreigners.

As tales of others, the values of revenant stories for medieval clergymen lay in their use for creating self-understanding, clarifying and demonstrating the prescribed rules of moral behavior, and acting as tools for their hearers and readers to employ in constructing a viable self delimited from the revenant other. Thus they instructed living people how to create an ideal self that would win them entrance into the blessed realms of heaven. An almost universal, ageless tendency to feel anger and a sense of abandonment toward the dead might have subverted medieval selves by its emotional undesirability from a Christian point of view. Modern psychologists seek to bring this anger to consciousness and transcend it in the process of mourning. Medieval clergymen instead found it to be a positive value in the process of self-discovery and self-construction whenever people exteriorized their anger and projected it onto the undead person who had provoked it, as a threatening foreignness perceived as characteristic of the other. Although stories of revenants performed this positive work, they also had the negative effect of confirming popular belief in prehistoric, nonhuman, none too friendly, spirits. Some of these spirits later turned up as central figures in ghost stories after their communities had converted to Christianity, but baptizing ancient spirits only served to strengthen their hold on people's imaginations.

Thus, an examination of medieval ghost stories and *exempla* reveals a complex weave of strands from ancient myths about gods and spirits, popular beliefs about the undead, and elements of Christian teachings. Their complexities had begun to accumulate long before Christianity baptized and explicated ancient pre-Christian beliefs and attitudes toward the dead that coexisted with an instinctive mistrust of outsiders to the community. The resultant tangle of motifs in these tales is great enough to ensure that the modern historians quoted above, as well as many others who have written about these texts, can all have been correct in their somewhat different approaches to what they have found. The foreignness of revenants that this essay has traced from early medieval times until the late Middle Ages also existed as a basic element in *exempla* and ghost stories alongside many other motifs that occurred in them. This foreignness of revenants corresponded to a very ancient human reaction which consistently occurred over centuries and from region to region, the xenophobia that still plagues humanity today. In this respect, medieval specters not only held importance for the age-old necessity of constructing boundaries to separate one's self from the other, they took on new value as well for transcending these boundaries in order to construct an ideal self, newly defined according to Christian principles.

Notes

1. Thanks to Albrecht Classen's acceptance of an early version of this paper for his session on the concept of foreignness in the Middle Ages, presented in May, 2000 at the Medieval Congress in Kalamazoo, I have been able to develop my ideas on medieval ghosts here. I am very grateful to Professor Classen for this opportunity.
2. Grégoire le grand, *Dialogues,* ed. Adelbert de Vogüe and trans. from the Latin by Paul Antin, Sources chrétiennes 265, 3 vols. (Paris: Les Éditions du Cerf, 1979), 2:47, 3:19, "caelistis patriae."
3. Katharine Briggs, *An Encyclopedia of Fairies: Hobgoblins, Brownies, Bogies, and Other Supernatural Creatures* (1976: rpt New York, 1977), 285–287; Jean d'Arras, *Chroniques de Mélusine,* first collected ancient folk traditions about Mélusine in the 14th century. Briggs notes that the story "may be called the French romance version of the classical Lamia."
4. Jacques Le Goff, *La Naissance de Purgatoire,* Bibliothèque des Histoires (Paris: Gallimard, 1981) 240–246, for the timing of the birth of Purgatory. Prior to the development of a purgatorial theology, undead spirits wandered in desolate regions of earth, in which folk tradition continued to place them in spite of official doctrine.
5. Three insightful studies of these sentiments, as distinguished from attitudes to individual revenants, are Otto Gerhard Oexle, "Die Gegenwart der Toten," in *Death in the Middle Ages,* ed. Herman Braet and Werner Verbeke, Mediaevalia Lovaniensia Series I / Studia IX (Leuven: Leuven University Press, 1983), 19–77; Patrick Geary, *Phantoms of Remembrance: Memory and Oblivion at the End of the First Millennium* (Princeton: Princeton University Press, 1994); and Michel Lauwers, *La Mémoire des ancêtres, le souci des morts. Morts, rites et société au moyen âge (Diocèse de Liège, XI–XIIIe siècles)* (Paris: Beauchesne, 1996). Michelle L. Roper, "Uniting the Community of the Living with the Dead: The Use of Other-world Visions in the Early Middle Ages," in *Authority & Community in the Middle Ages*, ed. Donald Mowbray, Rhiannon Purdie and Ian P. Wei (Trowbridge, UK: Sutton Publishing Ltd., 1999), 19–41, recently studied the use of visions to create communal links between monasteries and their dead monks.
6. William A. Christian, Jr., *Apparitions in Late Medieval and Renaissance Spain* (Princeton, NJ: Princeton University Press, 1981), 7.
7. *Oxford Latin Dictionary,* ed. P. G. W. Clarke (Oxford: Clarendon Press, 1983); *Mediae Latinitatis Lexicon Minus,* ed. J. F. Niermeyer (Leiden: E. J. Brill, 1984). Authors use these words translated from their vernaculars according to their knowledge of classical Latin or its medieval equivalents, and their opinions about ghost stories.
8. Interview with Howard Holley, General manager, Xerox (China) Ltd., *The New York Times* (September 20, 2000) "Business Day" Section, p. C8: ". . . somebody used the term "gueilo" when referring to me. That's a Cantonese word for foreigner that literally means 'ghost' . . ." On checking with the Reference Desk at the Geisel Library, University of California, San Diego, I was informed by a Mandarin-speaking librarian that the Mandarin

words *yang guizi* that we translate as "foreign devil" in fact literally mean "sea ghost."

9. *Webster's Third International Dictionary* (Springfield, MA: G. & C. Merriam Co., 1966), uses these words to define each other and as synonyms. The *New Shorter Oxford English Dictionary,* 2 vols. (Oxford: Clarendon Press, 1993), defines a vision as a "person or thing perceived otherwise than by ordinary sight; specter or phantom as "apparition or ghost"; spirit as a "disembodied soul surviving after death"; apparition as a "ghost or phantom"; dream as a vision while awake or "images, thoughts, feelings or sensations when asleep." *Roget's International Thesaurus*, 3rd Ed. (New York: Thomas Y. Crowell Co., 1962), equates all the above words as synonyms.
10. Augustine,"De cura pro mortuis gerenda ad Paulinum episcopum," ed. J. Zycha, *CSEL* 41 (Vienna: F. Tempsky, 1890) Sect. V/3, XIII: 639–652. Thomas Aquinas, *Summa Theologica*, trans. from the Latin by Fathers of the English Dominican Province, 3 vols. (New York: Benziger Brothers, Inc., 1948), 3:2831–2832, Suppl. Q. 69 Art. 3, citing Augustine.
11. Grégoire le grand, 2:207–209, 3:153, 187–189.
12. Ibid., 3:153.
13. Ibid., 3:187–189.
14. *Exemplum* (pl. *exempla*) may be defined as a story or fable designed to edify its hearer or reader and teach the dangers of un-Christian behavior. Although these stories were designed primarily for use in sermons, they are also found in many chronicles and literary works, presented as straightforward ghost stories.
15. K. M. Briggs, *The Fairies in Tradition and Literature* (London: Routledge and Kegan Paul, 1967), 57–58.
16. See for instance Paul Barber, *Vampires, Burial and Death: Folklore and Reality* (New Haven: Yale University Press, 1988). *Shorter O. E. D.*, 2:3543, shows that the word and its cognates all originate in eastern Europe. Icelandic saga and the Danish chronicle of Saxo Grammaticus report a few cannibalistic corpses, however, in decidedly pagan settings. Jacqueline Simpson and Steve Roud, *A Dictionary of English Folklore* (Oxford: Oxford University Press, 2000), s.v. vampires (n.p.), note William of Newburgh's story of a revenant in 1196 whose body was found to be swollen, "turgid and suffused with blood . . . [so that] it might have been taken for a leech filled with the blood of many people." The authors decline to call the corpse a vampire, however, since William only states that it roamed the streets of Alnwick and caused plague to break out by corrupting the air by its "pestiferous breath."
17. R. C. Finucane, *Ghosts: Appearances of the Dead & Cultural Transformation* (New York: Prometheus Books, 1966).
18. Finucane, 2–3, 223.
19. Jean-Claude Schmitt, *Ghosts in the Middle Ages: The Living and the Dead in Medieval Society,* trans. from the French by Teresa Lavendar Fagan (Chicago: University of Chicago Press, 1998). Allen J. Frantzen, *American Historical Review* 105 (2000): 598–599, questions the value of Schmitt's conclusions, given his self-imposed narrow time frame and limitation of sources to Latin.
20. Schmitt, 223.

21. Claude Lecouteux, *Fantômes et revenants au moyen âge (Postface de Régis Boyer)* (Paris: Éditions Imago, 1986).
22. Ibid., 8–10.
23. Roger Bartra, *Wild Men in the Looking Glass: The Mythic Origins of European Otherness,* trans. from the Spanish by Carl T. Berrisford (Ann Arbor: University of Michigan Press, 1994), 80–83. The reference from Dante's *Inferno* is to Canto I, line 6.
24. Thomas de Cantimpré, *Thomas de Cantimpré: Les exemples du "Livre des Abeilles," une vision médiévale,* ed. and trans. from the Latin by Henri Platelle, Collection Miroir du Moyen Âge 4 (Turnhout: Brepols, 1997), 217–219. Thomas tells the story on the authority of Boniface, bishop of Lausanne (who supposedly heard the story from a nobleman of his diocese).
25. By Boccaccio's time, the elements of this story had rearranged themselves into a cautionary tale for girls who tortured their would-be lovers with coy refusals: deep in the pine woods near Ravenna, a rejected lover saw a man who killed himself for love of a cruel lady pursuing her naked ghost with fierce mastiffs; having ridden her down, he tore out her heart and threw it to the dogs, then the whole ghostly pursuit began again as she rose and raced away into the forest. Boccaccio also adds the detail that the pursuit took place in the same glades of the forest every Friday. *Decameron,* 5th Day, Chapter 8.
26. Philip's sister-in-law Sybille of Hainaut, Lady of Beaujeu, told this story to Bishop Étienne de Bourbon, an avid collector and preserver of historical anecdotes and *exempla*. Étienne de Bourbon, *Anecdotes historiques,* ed. A. Lecoy de la Marche (Paris: Renouard/Loones, 1877), 271–272. Philip II's panegyricist, Guillaume le Breton, *Philippidos,* ed. H. F. Delaborde (Paris: Renouard, 1885), 377, places the vision during Pope Honorius III's stay at Segni.
27. Paul Edward Dutton, *The Politics of Dreaming in the Carolingian Empire* (Lincoln and London: University of Nebraska Press, 1994). See also *Visions of Heaven and Hell Before Dante,* ed. and trans. from the Latin (or based on early translations) by Eileen Gardiner (New York: Italica Press, 1989), Introduction; and Alison Morgan, *Dante and the Medieval Other World,* Cambridge Studies in Medieval Literature 8 (Cambridge and New York: Cambridge University Press, 1990), for the context of medieval vision literature in general.
28. *Johannis Beleth summa de ecclesiasticis officiis*, ed. Herbert Donteil, CCCM 41–41A, 2 vols. (Turnhout: Brepols, 1976), 2:315–316, and Honorius Augustodunensis, *Gemma animae,* PL 172, coll. 583, 589, make this prohibition explicit. However the canonist Guillaume Durand de Mende disagreed, noting that if great care is taken to avoid soiling the church with blood, the dead woman's funeral may be held in church. *Gullielmi Duranti rationale diuinorum officiorum,* ed. Anselme Davril and Timothy M. Thibodeau, CCCM 140, 2 vols. (Turnhout: Brepols, 1995), 1:62.
29. *Cartulaire de l'Église Notre-Dame de Paris,* ed. Benjamin Guérard, 4 vols. (Paris: Crapelet, 1850), 4:29–30; M. Dubu, *Histoire, description et annales de la basilique de Notre-Dame de Paris* (Paris: Ambroise Bray, 1854), 155;

P. Battifol, "Les fouilles de chevet de Notre-Dame de Paris en 1858 d'après les registres du chanoine Ravinet," *Mémoires de la Société des Antiquaires de France,* 75 (1918): 248–260, here, 256–257; R. Johnes, "The seal matrix of Queen Isabel of Hainault and some contemporary seals," *Antiquaries Journal,* 40 (1960):73–76; and Alain Erlande-Brandenburg, *Le Roi Est Mort: étude sur les funérailles, les sépultures et les tombeaux des rois de France jusqu'à la fin du XIIIe siècle* (Geneva: Droz, 1975), 90.

30. Ernest Lavisse, *Histoire de France depuis les origines jusqu'à la revolution,* 9 vols. (Paris: Hachette, 1900–1911), 3:283: "[Philippe Auguste] s'est conduit inhumainement avec . . . Élisabeth et Ingeburge."
31. *Gualteri Mapes: De nugis curialium,* ed. Thomas Wright (1850; rpt. New York and London: AMS Press, 1968), 103–105. Though its editor indexed this case under the rubric "Vampires," and it is cited as such in the literature, an examination of the printed text found no reference to vampiric bloodsucking.
32. Lecouteux, 28–30.
33. Nancy Caciola, "Wraiths, Revenants and Ritual in Medieval Culture," *Past and Present,* 152 (1996): 3–45; here, 15–18. See also Lecouteux, *passim.*
34. William Chester Jordan, "Home Again: The Jews in the Kingdom of France, 1315–1322," in *The Stranger in Medieval Society,* ed. F. R. P. Akehurst and Stephanie Cain Van D'Elden, Medieval Cultures 12 (Minneapolis: University of Minnesota Press, 1997):27–45; here 30, and Derek Pearsall,"Strangers in Late-Fourteenth-Century London," Ibid.:46–62; here 46.
35. *Ibid.*, Preface: vii.
36. Valerie I. J. Flint, *The Rise of Magic in Early Medieval Europe* (Princeton, NJ: Princeton University Press, 1991), 213–216; and Jeffrey Burton Russell, *Witchcraft in the Middle Ages* (Ithaca: Cornell University Press, 1972), 50–52, 187.
37. "Thietmari Chronicon," ed. C. J. M. Lappenberg, *MGH, Scriptores,* 33 vols. (1826–1955; rpt. New York: Kraus Reprint Corp., 1963–1964), 3/2:723–871; here, 738; re-ed. R. Holtzmann, *MGH, Scriptores* Nova Series 13 vols. (Berlin: Weidemann, 1955–1980) 9/1:11–14; here 11–12. See Lauwers, 155, and Caciola, "Wraiths," for the "peuple des morts" who act as one, as in Thietmar's stories.
38. The source for this information was Thietmar's aunt, niece, or cousin (neptis meae) Brigid, Abbess of St. Lawrence, "Chronicon," ed. Holtzmann, 12.
39. William of Newburgh, *Historia Rerum Anglicarum,* ed. Richard Howlett, Rerum Brittanicarum Medii Aevi Scriptores (Rolls Series) 82, 2 vols. (1885; rpt. New York: Kraus Reprint Corp., 1964), 2:474–482 (Newburgh's Book V, ch. 22–24).
40. *Le Registre d'Inquisition de Jacques Fournier, evêque de Pamiers (1318–1325),* ed. Jean Duvernoy, Bibliothèque Méridionale (2 ser.) 41, 3 vols. (Toulouse: E Privat, 1965) 1:128–143, 533–552; "Confession of Arnaud Gelis, also called Botheler 'The Drunkard' of Mas-Saint-Antonin," trans. from the Latin by Nancy P. Stork (www.sjsu.edu/depts/english/Fournier/agelis.htm, 1996); and Emmanuel Le Roy Ladurie, *Montaillou: the Promised Land of Error*, trans. from the French by Barbara Bray (New York: Vintage Books,

1979), 345–351; here 347, which calls Gelis "the Bottler." Occitan *botheler* is akin to French *bouteiller*, the butler, who samples the wines he opens; Gelis's nickname "Botheler" could have resulted from his service with Canon Hugues de Durfort, or even for claiming to perform the butler's traditional task of opening bottles for the ghosts with whom he said he drank. Stork's epithet "Drunkard" implies that Gelis hallucinated ghosts while drunk; his testimony indicates a rather more complex state of affairs. The Latin text calls him Arnaldus Egidii, transliterated by Duvernoy, Stork and Barbara Bray as Arnaud Gélis with acute accent. Michel Vovelle, *La Mort et l'occident de 1300 à nos jours* (Paris: Gallimard, 1983), 51, however transliterates his name as Gelis. These authors do not explain the reason for their transliteration. In English, the accentless version seems preferable.

41. Carlo Ginzburg, *The Night Battles: Witchcraft & Agrarian Cults in the Sixteenth & Seventeenth Centuries*, trans. from the Italian by John and Anne Tedeschi, (New York and London: Penguin Books, 1985), 33–39, discusses the Inquisition record of a sixteenth-century Italian woman medium who functioned like Gelis.
42. Finucane, 84.
43. Schmitt, 63.
44. Caciola, 39.
45. Grégoire le grand, *Dialogues,* 2:206–209.
46. Male ghosts who spoke with Gelis made predictions or offered vital information to their survivors, and gave specific details of actions they wished people to perform. Female ghosts apologized for unfortunate actions, asked their heirs to stop wearing their silk sleeves, came to see their grandchildren, and explained the status of infants who had died. Both sexes asked for prayers and masses from the living, and requested their survivors to feed the poor.
47. John Coakley, "Friars as Confidants of Holy Women in Medieval Dominican Hagiography," in *Images of Sainthood in Medieval Europe,* ed. Renate Blumenfeld-Kosinski and Timea Szell (Ithaca: Cornell University Press, 1991), 222–246; here 223 and notes 7–9, comments that "mystical and paramystical experiences were attributed to women much more often to men . . . among mendicant saints . . . intellectual and mystical activity seems to have formed distinct masculine and feminine preserves, respectively." Similarly, medieval writers, and indeed medieval people in general, may have considered palpable revenants and earthy ghosts appropriate to male percipients and visions appropriate to female percipients. If so, such a bias might help to account for the rarity of female percipients and revenants.
48. Santiago's battlefield apparition was supposedly preceded by a predictive vision vouchsafed to Ramiro I, King of León, the night before the battle. R. A. Fletcher, *Saint James' Catapult: the Life and Times of Diego Gelmirez of Santiago De Compostela* (Oxford: Clarendon Press, 1984), 66–77, evenhandedly discusses this hagiography, with which historical dates of kings and battles in early medieval Spain cannot be completely reconciled.
49. Quoted from Henrietta Leyser, *Medieval Women: A Social History of Women in England 450–1500* (London: Weidenfeld & Nicolson, 1995), 62.

50. Malcolm Bowie, "Unceasingly blessed. Surging into the future, remembering the past: Liszt's loves and transformations," *The Times Literary Supplement* (November 19, 1999), 4.
51. Schmitt, 93–121; Brian Stock, *The Implications of Literacy: Written Language and Models of Interpretation in the Eleventh and Twelfth Centuries* (Princeton, NJ: Princeton University Press, 1983), 495–499; Bartra, 121; Ginzburg, 47–50; and Claude Lecouteux, *Mondes parallèles: l'univers des croyances du Moyen Âge,* Collection Essais (Paris: Honoré Champion, 1994), 47–51.
52. Orderic Vitalis, *Orderici Vitalis Historia Aecclesiastica: The Ecclesiastical History of Orderic Vitalis,* ed. and trans. from the Latin by Marjorie Chibnall, Oxford Medieval Texts, 6 vols. (Oxford: Oxford University Press, 1969–1980), 4:236–50; Orderic took the story as reported by Walchelin from a verbal account. His pages furnish the *locus classicus* of the tale of Hellequin.
53. Finucane, 300–301, citing Gesta Romanorum. The latter in turn depends on Gervase of Tilbury, *Otia imperialia* (Vatican Library Regina Lat. Ms. 407), originally written in the 1190s. See also Lecouteux, *Fantômes,* 102–106.
54. Christian, *Apparitions,* 53, notes the "processions of souls of the dead said to be seen until recent times in Galicia."
55. "De sancta Waldetrude, fundatrice parthenonis canonissarum, Montibus Hanoniae in Belgio," *AA SS,* April, 1:829–842; here 838. Anne-Marie Helvétius, *Abbayes, évêques et laïques: une politique du pouvoir en Hainaut au Moyen Âge (VIIe–XIe siècle),* Collections Histoire 92 (Brussels: Crédit Communal, 1994), 320–322.
56. Godfried Henskens, "De S. Aya Comitissa Montibus Hannoniae in Belgio," *AA SS,* April, 2:579–582. Helvétius, 48, 58–59.
57. Schmitt, 64, citing M. C. Diaz y Diaz, *Visiones de mas alla en Galicia durante la alta Edad Media* (Santiago de Compostela: publisher not cited, 1985) 63–81, which I have not been able to see.
58. Schmitt, 120–121; Stock, 498–499; Ginzburg, Introduction, xvii; Russell, 96–97.

6

The Foreigner Within:

The Subject of Abjection in *Sir Gowther*

MICHAEL UEBEL

The late fourteenth-century Middle English metrical romance *Sir Gowther* has largely been taken to be a kind of Christian exemplum, a salutary narrative whose protagonist presents a model of moral rehabilitation.[1] The thematic of transformation dominates critical responses to this poem, becoming then a matter of how one designates the trajectory of Gowther's dramatic change: sadistic sinner to healing saint, animal to man,[2] or "unholy wildman" to social being.[3] Implicit in these readings of the poem is the view that Gowther functions as an Everyman figure, a universal reminder of the good of self-purgation. George Kane's treatment of Gowther, though overly impressionistic, is perfectly consistent with these interpretations:

> Gowther attracts our attention, and even admiration, from the moment he comes into the world with a load of ill-fate upon him such as even the Greek tragic poets seldom devised. . . . With no hesitation or repining he turns from the enormities of his past life and the hideous inheritance of his paternity, and sets out simply and honestly to purify himself of the diabolic. . . . If a man is to be the son of a demon, and if he is to purify himself, this is how we would have him behave.[4]

By extension, this is presumably how we would have Christians, born with the mark of original sin, behave. Thus the poem's moral, according to Margaret Robson: "God only helps those who help themselves."[5] In this essay, I will resist the tendency to see the poem as one about Gowther's hygienic transformation, arguing instead that Gowther remains resolutely (and tragically) abject over the course of his career as royal son, knight, penitent, Christian soldier, lord, and finally miracle-working saint. Gowther's life story, I will show, is a deeply perverse one, involving finely imbricated psychopathologies such as sadism, masochism, and fetishism, and it is this web of perversity which indelibly marks Gowther from the moment of his demonic inception. Despite his multiple father-figures and what Jeffrey Cohen sees as his "triumphant," that is to say normalizing, Oedipalization,[6] Gowther remains fully the son of a demon, a perpetual foreigner, and inassimilable outsider to the changing social contexts through which he moves with limited agency.

One of the two extant manuscripts of the poem begins with an apotropaic prayer, to "Schilde us from the fowle fende / That is about mannys sowle to shende / All tymes of the yere" (4–6; protect us from the foul fiend [the devil] who brings mankind's soul to ruin all the time).[7] The poet then spends the next fifteen lines specifying what he in the end will refuse, on account of shame (21), to explain fully: namely, the "selcowgh" (13; strange) situation in which "A fende to nyeght wemen nere, / And makyd hom with chyld, / Tho kynde of men wher thei hit tane / For of homselfe had thei never nan" (14–17; a fiend lay with women so near, and impregnating them, they [the fiends] then took the form of men there for they themselves had no form). These demons, whose powers include the ability to assume the appearance of a woman's husband (7–9), "wrought ladies so mikil wo / That ferly it is to here" (11–12; caused ladies such great pain that it is wondrous to hear). The poet's narrow attention to the sexual or reproductive threat that demons pose to women as a group suggests, not surprisingly, that the women are to a degree complicit in propagating wickedness in the human world. From the outset of the poem women are marked as the site of evil and shame; it is through female sexuality that malevolence enters the world of men.

Gowther's conception and monstrous infancy dramatize the sexual disorder that reproduces ever more chaos and destruction. Gowther comes into existence because of his mother's hasty oath: "Scho preyd to God and Mare mylde / Schuld gyffe hur grace to have a chyld, / On what maner scho ne roghth" (61–63; she prayed to God and to gracious Mary that they should give her grace to have a child, she did not care how). One day, in her orchard, the lady meets a man, who appears "as lyke her lorde as he myght be" (67), and who, after laying her down under a tree, "with hur is wyll he wroghtth" (69; he had his way with her). The orchard setting is an obvious clue to the sexual peril that eventuates because of the Lady's misdirected wish. An enchanted landscape in which the beauty of nature is enhanced by human artifice, the orchard is especially suited for the uncontrolled production of fantasy since it is here that every element is designed to appeal sensually.[8] The Lady's fantasy immediately turns nightmarish: "When he had is wylle all don, / A feltured fende he start up son, / And stode and hur beheld. / He seyd, 'Y have geyton a chylde on the / That in is yothe full wylde schall bee' " (70–74; when he had taken his pleasure, he leapt up quickly, as a shaggy fiend, and stood up and looked upon her. He said, 'I have impregnated you with a child that in his youth will be very wild').[9]

This scene in a sense fulfills the prophecy contained in the opening prayer where the urgency of protecting women from this kind of monstrous violation is clear. Jeffrey Cohen's fine analysis of the poem (to which we will recur) identifies this hairy "fende" with the incubus, a creature with "a complex medieval genealogy."[10] The incubus was thought to be a demon, in some accounts a fallen angel, whose powers of shape-shifting and bewitchment allowed it to possess mortal women sexually.[11] A no less authoritative figure than Thomas Aquinas argued that because the devil himself lacks the capacity to reproduce he must steal his victim's seed (*semina*) in the fantasmal form of a succubus or incubus. According to Aquinas, "because the first corruption of sin through which humankind became a servant of the Devil comes to us by means of the generative act, the power of bewitchment is therefore granted by God to the Devil in this act more than in any other."[12] It would seem, at least according to the Thomist view, that the Lady is the unwitting victim of black magic, yet further elaboration of the incubus's intricate genealogy reveals that an unusual intersection of violations at work here—adultery and bestiality—not only points to the Lady's culpability but elucidates more completely Gowther's abject position beyond the limits of social and subjective identity.

Resolving the question whether or not the Lady was aware of the deception, that is, if she *intended* to transgress, is unnecessary,[13] given the transgressive nature of the sexual union that took place in the orchard, about which the poem is unequivocal: "To deyle with hom [fendes] was wothe" (99; to have intercourse with them was sinful). The *fende*'s animal appearance, its hairiness in particular, is a descriptive detail linking unnatural or sinful sexuality and demonic intervention. The "feltured fende," I suggest, would have been understood within a very specific demonological context, one that overlaps with zoological and medical discourses on cross-species sex. For example, William of Auvergne, in his chapter in *De universo* concerning incubi and succubi, discusses the sexual behavior of the bear, an animal to which medieval bestiaries and encyclopedias ascribe sexual behaviors very close to those of humans.[14] William identifies the bear as the ideal intermediary between the supernatural world and the mundane because the bear alone produces semen compatible with human modes of reproduction. Thus when incubi choose to fertilize a mortal, the bear is the form most readily assumed. The fiend in this poem has, in a sense, a double form as intermediary between the supernatural and the natural realms: he first appears as a man (in the form of the Duke's *Doppelgänger*) who, after inseminating the lady, assumes, or reverts back to, another intermediary form, a bear-like creature.

Such a union of animal and human can only produce monstrous forms, social and biological, according to the medieval canonists and encyclopedists.[15] The Saxon legend in which a knight's wife spends a long period of cohabitation with a bear is produced by William of Auvergne as evidence of the monstrous offspring resulting from interspecies sex: several children were born with human-like forms except for their bear faces.[16] Gowther's paternity ensures that he will become a monster, one whose lack of a hideous form makes his savage crimes against both individuals and social forms particularly unsettling.[17] The prevailing medieval assumption that a male child assumes the qualities of his father informs the charge leveled against Gowther by an old earl, who is imprisoned for expressing communal opinion on the boy's monstrosity:[18]

> Syr, why dose thou soo?
> We howpe thou come never of Crysten stryn,
> Bot art sum fendys son, we weyn,
> That werkus hus this woo;
> Thou dose never gud, bot ey tho ylle:
> We hope thou be full syb tho deyll.
> (204–209)

> [Sir, why do you behave so?
> We suspect that a Christian did not beget you,
> But that you are some fiend's son, we think,
> Whose acts cause us this grief;
>
> You never do good, but always the bad:
> We think that you must be close kin to the devil.]

Gowther's evil deeds, despite their utter monstrosity (e. g., raping nuns, setting widows on fire, and driving friars over cliffs), become intelligible within the terms of medieval assumptions about paternity that link virtue with the process of generation. These assumptions are well summarized by the elderly captain of Crathor in Jean de Bueil's *Jouvencel*: "I shall never believe that nobles who dishonor their arms were descended from the valiant fathers whose names they bear: one must suppose that their mothers had lechers in their mind when they engendered them. Maybe indeed they were actually in bed with them."[19] Dishonorable knights are the product of displacing the father, either by mental images or real bodies. At the relay point between fantasy and carnal presence resides the incubus, an irretrievably corruptive force.

Though only implied in the poem, the Lady's culpability, about which the captain of Crathor would have little doubt, is indicated by scientific texts offering explanations of how the mere possession of perverse thoughts at the moment of pregnancy could result in monstrous offspring. Vitelo, a thirteenth-century Polish scholar, is representative.[20] His theory concerning the forms demons such as incubi and succubi assume in order to work their evil upon women includes the traditional view (that incubi assume animal form) as well as what can be termed a psychological view. According to Vitelo's psychology, incubi, always invisible to the human eye, must be perceived by *phantasia* (imagination), the faculty located in the front of the brain that gathers and retains images. Thus it is the imagination, itself situated on the boundary between mind and matter, that permits demons to couple with mortals.[21] In the case of adultery, according to a thirteenth-century English manuscript of the prose Salernitan questions, the image of the husband remembered—materialized, in our poem, as the simulacral image of the husband—makes the child resemble the absent man rather than the (un)natural father.[22] As late as the seventeenth century, the power of the imagination was identified as causing conception.[23]

Vitelo, not deeply concerned with the actual process of reproduction given his focus on the role of *phantasia*, nevertheless cites a case of impregnation by an incubus directly relevant to *Sir Gowther*: the origin of the enchanter Merlin.[24] Merlin is offered as an example of a misbegotten creature, one whose identity is a confusion of the demonic and the human. Gowther, we learn, is Merlin's half-brother: the same incubus fathered both (94–96).[25] This familial association not only marks Gowther as part of legendary British history but also accentuates his hybridity. Gowther, like Merlin, embodies a volatile mixture of good and evil,[26] monstrous because he escapes the necessary order, and exists as a foreigner in a world where continuity and propriety rule. In late medieval demonology, Merlin is figured as the Antichrist of the Book of Revelation prophecy, and thus Gowther's fraternal relation to Merlin, as a recent editor of the poem put it, "would most certainly presage disaster for a medieval audience."[27] The birth of Gowther portends malevolence: his mother "was delyverid at tho last / Of won that coth do skathe" (101–02; at last gave birth to one who could do evil). And so, after his christening, Gowther became "breme and brathe" (105; fierce and unruly) or, as the Advocates manuscript has it even more suggestively, given the nature of the transgression against nature that engendered him, "breme as barre" (fierce as a wild boar [ME *bere*=bear]).[28] Gowther's career of evil begins immediately. As a nursling, he kills nine wet nurses by vampirically draining them:

> He sowkyd hom so thei lost ther lyvys,
> Sone had he sleyn three.
> The duke gard prycke aftur sex;
> Tho chyld was yong and fast he wex—
> Hende, harkons yee.
> Be twelfe monethys was gon
> Nyne norsus had he slon
> Of ladys feyr and fre.
>
> [He sucked them to death,
> and soon had killed three.
> The duke had six more found hastily;
> The child was young and growing fast
> Pay heed, gentle audience:

Before twelve months were past
He had slain nine wet nurses,
Ladies fair and free.]

(110–17)

More troubling at the level of the social, than the actual slaying of nine wet nurses, is the implication that his father, the duke, appears complicit in the killings. The slain women come from the higher ranks of society; they are "tho best in that cuntre, / That was full gud knyghttys wyffys" (108–09; the best in that land, who were the wives of very good knights). The duke's decision to sacrifice six more nurses, after the murder of the first three is a sign not only of helpless and destructive paternal indulgence but also of the violent kernel at the center of feudal society. "The tragedy of nobility," as Georges Bataille labeled it in his excursus on Gilles de Rais, a figure to whom Gowther can be usefully compared, is the close linkage between aggression and privilege that has the effect of turning death into "a game."[29] The knights who finally gather together to put an end to this serial killing, confront their ruler, informing him, through a rather droll use of litotes, that "hit was no gamun / To lose hor wyffus soo (119–20; it was no joke [game] to lose their wives in such a manner). The poet seems to be defusing, through humor, the threat Gowther's voracity and the duke's failed governance pose to the *socius*, before shifting our attention back to the scene of the familial (the maternal) where violence and disorder have no greater chance of being contained. Indeed, Gowther, given back to his mother, tears the nipple from her breast, causing the distraught woman to send for a priest and to flee to safety in her chamber (125–29).

Considered together, Gowther's preoedipal crimes represent a sadistic rebellion against the maternal, the earliest indication of his urge toward annihilation. Gowther makes a preternaturally early break from his mother (and her substitutes), attacking them at the very site of their life-sustaining power. The maternal breast becomes the object of oral violence, and it is plausible, as recent editors of the poem have suggested, that Gowther's infantile violence suggests the early presence of teeth.[30] Premature dentition, often associated with canine qualities (as in Shakespeare's *Richard III* and *King Henry VI*, Part 3),[31] had folkloric significance as a sign of vampirism, lycanthropy, or the intervention of sorcery.[32] The early use of teeth as a weapon is well attested in the extensive psychoanalytic literature on biting and oral sadism, where infantile teething and sadistic biting of others are activities through which inner tension, or displeasure, is temporarily discharged and aggressivity is directed outward.[33] The sadism of the mouth has, moreover, a particular logic: it aims at the alchemical transmutation of the world into what Janine Chasseguet-Smirgel has rather colorfully termed an "anal universe," an ambiguous world where intolerable differences are dissolved or wished away.[34] "The vampire," William Burroughs once said, "converts quality, live blood, youth, talent into quantity food and time for himself. He perpetrates the most basic betrayal of the spirit, reducing all human dreams to his shit."[35] The world and its multiplicitous others are chewed up, and swallowed, ultimately converted into homogenous waste matter. Gowther's rage against difference issues directly from his very constitution as a being whose split subjectivity (demon/man) threatens his existence from within. For Gowther to resolve his inner difference, he must begin mastering the otherness, the foreigner within who threatens to destroy the self. This inner demon represents sadism in its purest form, a destructive drive that, if not deflected outward, will finally tear the subject apart. Gowther's destructive behavior is thus compulsive: "He wold wyrke is fadur wyll / Wher he stod or sete" (173–74; he would do his father's [the demon's] will, wherever he happened to be).

Gowther's urge to annihilate the world, to level differences, and to install himself in the position of God's rival is perfectly consistent with the strategy of the perverse subject.[36] Gowther's rampage through his father's kingdom, a crime spree that includes deflowering virgins to spoil their marriages, raping wives and slaying their husbands, driving friars over cliffs, hanging parsons on hooks, killing priests and burning hermits, even burning "a powre widow" (200), can be seen as a desperate attempt to reverse the threat of annihilation from within by gaining omnipotent mastery of the object, or outside, world. His violence, directed at the institutions of the Church and knighthood, is a sweeping repudiation of both the idea and practice of reproduction—ultimately, of sex itself. The spiritual propagation of God's word and the cultural reproduction of chivalric values are stifled by Gowther's attacks. He erases and pollutes familial bloodlines while destroying the secular and religious institutions supporting and promoting them. The fact that one of his hunts (an ideal chivalric activity) culminates in horrific acts of sexual violence against an entire priory of nuns underlines just how deep his desire to eradicate the possibility of reproduction runs. After raping the nuns, Gowther locks them in their "kyrke," and burns it to the ground, thereby preventing the possibility of any progeny. Gowther effectively negates the sexual scene, his cruelty producing only words, in the form of an evil reputation: "Then went his name full wyde" (189).

Gowther's destructiveness, while constituting him socially as an abominable "duke of greyt renown" (166), also performs the complex private work of self-possession and agency-recuperation.[37] In the desperate, yet finally doomed, attempt to save himself, Gowther plunges into the presymbolic realm of the imaginary, a space where Lacan and Granoff locate the fetishist, a subject for whom relationships lack "the mediation of a third person which provides the transcendent element through which one's relation to an object can be sustained at a given distance."[38] Abolishing transcendent and mediating institutions such as the Church and chivalry, Gowther substitutes in their place an intense imaginary attachment to his weapon, the sword that he had made for himself when he turned age fifteen (136–39; 256–58; 286–91; etc.). This "fachon bothe of styll and yron" (139; falchion made of steel and iron) assumes from the beginning a strong fetishistic value. Gowther, the only man who can lift the sword (138), retains possession of the weapon from this point on, refusing to surrender it even when the pope—one of his rotating surrogate fathers—later demands that he do so. The blade itself is foreign; curved like a sickle, it symbolizes the brutality of the Saracen other, whose very identity, as Norman Daniel has shown, was imagined throughout the Middle Ages to inhere in the double threat of violence and sexuality.[39] Gowther has in effect become Saracen, his sadism and his fetishism interanimating to the point of a pure will to power.

This will to power is symptomatic of an impoverished self trapped, as Gregorio Kohon phrases it, in a "tyrannical predicament of hate."[40] As an internally divided subject, Gowther appears to know himself only through masochistically identifying with his victims' submission, for what is essential for him in fact only happens to and is experienced by others. From Gowther's point of view, the hostile external world must be unmade through pain because his inner aggressivity is felt as persecuting him from the outside.[41] This subtle form of masochism, at the heart of which is sadism, prefigures the more overt masochism of Gowther's later triumphs and sacrifices on the battlefield in service of the Emperor. The momentary suppression of violence is, however, not inconsistent with Gowther's masochistic strategy, for when the old earl confronts him with the truth of his genetic identity—that he cannot be Christian, that he must be born "other"—Gowther, keen to know his true identity almost as if to justify his paranoic anguish, responds with remarkably restrained aggression. Rather than slaying the earl outright, he imprisons him, and then sets off to the castle where his mother is immured and confronts her, setting "his fachon to hur hart" (220). After learning the truth of his conception from his mother's description of the primal scene (227–30), he prays to God and to the Virgin Mary "to save hym fro is fadur tho fynde" (238; to save him from his father the fiend). Here Gowther's masochism is sublimated in the form of religious humility. Furthermore, this pious encounter with his mother, as Jeffrey Cohen has perceptively argued, opens up more questions than it purportedly answers, confronting Gowther "suddenly with the elemental nonsensicality of his coming into being."[42] Yet while Cohen sees Gowther's "pornographic" glimpse of the primal scene as an incitement to symbolization, whereby the unnatural encounter is to be "fit into a meaning-system not reducible to 'mere' sex," I would suggest that such a meaning-system, one Cohen equates with "transcendence," is crippled by his intractable perversity. For Gowther, a private meaning-system, though non-symbolic, has been operating continually in the shape of his fetish-sword, which has the precise function of relieving the anxiety generated by his own destructive impulses.[43] Gowther's sword cuts, as it were, two ways: it is the instrument of his will to power and it is the thing that saves him from paranoiac-masochistic immobility. The sword's very permanence as an object capable of remaining intact and always accessible outside the body means that any sadism directed at it would remain without response:[44]

His fachon con he with hym take,
He laft hit not for weyle ne wrake,
Hyt hong ei be his syde.

[He did take his falchion with him,
He would leave it [behind] neither for joy nor pain,[45]
It hung always by his side.]
(256–58)

A crucial facet of his identity, the sword weathers the vicissitudes of "weyle" (joy) and "wrake" (pain), furnishing a sense of stability in a projected world that Gowther perceives as perpetually threatening.[46] This experience of stability, however perverse, means that Gowther will never take the risk of abandoning his sword.[47] Simultaneously an externalization of his vulnerability and of his sadism, the falchion is a permanent marker of his abjection, confirming his status as someone for whom culture has yet no proper meaning. Indeed, the sword becomes increasingly important in the ensuing text, always undermining the authenticity of Gowther's purported salvation.

Gowther becomes further entrenched in perversity when he meets the pope to confess and learn the penance he must perform. Notably, Gowther confesses to no crimes, in part at least because news of the enormity of his violations against the Church have already reached Rome (280), but he does confess his fiendish origins by rehearsing his familial history (271–73). Gowther presents himself as victim rather than sinner, even responding to the pope's outrage that "thou hast holy kyrke dystryed" (280; you have destroyed holy churches) with the rather audacious remark, "Nay, holy fadur, be thou noght agrevyd" (281; No, don't be angry, holy father). The pope then issues a two-fold penitential commandment: he must lay down his sword (286) and he must eat only the food that he can snatch from the mouths of dogs, all the while remaining speechless (292–95). Gowther rejects the first command, insisting " 'This bous me nedus with mee beyr: / My frendys ar full thyn' " (290–91; This sword I must carry with me; my friends are very few). Sensing perhaps that Gowther's perversity is intractable, the pope makes no further commands regarding the sword, and instead relies on his second order to do the work of correcting him.

The pope charges Gowther with a penance that puts socializing activities such as eating and speaking at the basic level of instinctual drives. Gowther's sadistic urge, his will to destroy the object world, must be diverted, focused back on the self, through a primal process of abjection, a kind of masochism involving the intense self-surveillance necessary, for instance, to refuse the sociality of his fellow human beings. Forced to descend into the foundations of the social and the symbolic, to take up a position at the dawn of the speaking subject, Gowther is immersed more profoundly in the very state he had never been able to move out of, the abject. The pope, in short, sentences Gowther to more time in the realm of what Julia Kristeva calls abjection. Not simply a condition of animality or defilement as anthropologists such as Edmund Leach and Mary Douglas have defined it, abjection describes the dialectical process by which, prior to symbolization and acculturation, subject and object confront and collapse into one another: the hybridity of man and animal, for example. The subject is locked in a cycle of suicide and self-transcendence, for abjection "wavers between the *fading away* of all meaning and all humanity . . . and the *ecstasy* of an ego that, having lost its Other and its objects, reaches, at the precise moment of this suicide, the height of harmony with the promised land."[48] Pulling Gowther toward negativity and ideality simultaneously, abjection, itself a kind of foreigner within, disrupts subjective coherence and development, forestalling it indefinitely. Gowther, haunted by his abject origins, remains suspended between oblivion and sublimity.

This abject position at the intersection of humiliation and transcendence corresponds neatly with the dynamics of masochistic perversion, whereby, as classical psychoanalysis theorizes it, the masochist is suspended between the desire to annihilate an anxiety-producing reality and the wish to protect, at any cost, a cherished fantasy.[49] What results for the masochist is a kind of "living death," for he can only, according to the Freudian logic of melancholia, live secure in one (important) part of his identity by proving the futility of another part.[50] Remarkably, the pope attempts to turn the sadistic Gowther into a masochistic knight by compelling him to focus his identity on one part of body, his mouth, transforming the site of his original sins (the oral attacks on his nurses and mother)[51] into a sign of penance. Gowther is forced to regulate both what enters and leaves his mouth, but in order to do so he must paradoxically return to an archaic state of utter dependency and humility—that of the *infans* (in Latin: [one] unable to speak). The pope conceives of Gowther's penance as a lesson in the value of passivity, that is, how to accept reality (and its symbolic Others: sociality, morality, spirituality) without desiring to replace or destroy it. Appropriately, the mouth becomes the key organ, for prior both to its speech function and its sadistic function (biting) it serves as the child's primary reality-tester, wherein, as Otto Fenichel puts it, "the first reality is what one can swallow." "Recognizing reality," Fenichel writes, "originally means to judge whether something helps to gain satisfaction or whether it raises tensions, whether one should swallow it or spit it out." Incorporation, a way of submitting to rather than rejecting the other, is thus "the basis for all perception" and the founding moment of ethical (ego) judgment.[52] Gowther is, in effect, sent back to this archaic ego state, a beginning point for the rebuilding of his reality-sense and the recreation of his ethical judgment.

Learning not to reject or "bite" reality, reducing it to undifferentiated waste, is Gowther's penitential mission, one, however, that does not alter Gowther dramatically. After Gowther leaves the pope, he finds himself in "anodur far cuntre" (305; another country far away), where, while resting at the foot of a hill for three days, a greyhound brings him a loaf of white bread each day before nightfall. It is remarkable that the greyhound itself is a kind of foreigner, an oriental dog introduced by Egypt to the European breeds,[53] possessing, in other words, an origin in alterity like Gowther's own.[54] Behind this miraculous feeding are, of course, hagiographic traditions in which holy or righteous men are helped by faithful dogs (e.g., St Roch and Tobias)[55] or in which a greyhound and a cynocephalic giant become saints (St Guignefort and St Christopher, respectively).[56] Yet these traditions, if anything, highlight just how far from saintliness Gowther is. The visiting greyhound, which leaves after making three deliveries, ostensibly defeats the point of Gowther's penance, for what was to be a difficult task—wrestling with a dog for its bone—has become effortless, as easy as receiving the bread of the Eucharist during mass. Passivity, however, may be the real point: Gowther is compelled to base his interactions with this gentle other—beast, oriental—upon restraint and receptivity. Nonetheless, Gowther's trained desire appears without any traces of self-torment usually associated with asceticism.

If we take seriously here the allusion to the Eucharist, then it becomes clearer what this scene with the miraculous greyhound represents. The dog/god's bread does not signify Gowther's sacramental conversion; instead it is the vehicle by which he is returned to an early state of non-aggressivity.[57] Franz Borkenau, in his exceptional discussion of the self-contradictions inherent in the dogma of the Eucharist, notes that, given the strict medieval injunctions against touching the Host with the teeth, it

> has to be swallowed, not eaten, has to be consumed like a liquid, not like a compact body. In other words, the psychological attitude requested from the faithful is that of the suckling before the biting stage, of the infant at the mother's breast, receiving satisfaction without the interference of any aggression. The infant at the mother's breast is the embodiment, the quintessence of love without aggression.[58]

But, as Borkenau stresses, this sacramental restoration of a "stage of primal purity" is doomed to fail, primarily because it can appear only as part of a contradiction, a tension between underlying and lasting aggression—the desire to bite the Eucharist[59]—and the dream of some satisfying union. The image of a dog transporting bread in its mouth, careful to keep it intact, condenses this tension perfectly: an animal is imagined to be defeating its own instincts. Aggression, however, always contaminates what would otherwise be an exemplary model of restraint and *caritas*. We should recall that Nietzsche found ascetic existence contradictory precisely because self-torment, which he equates with guilt before God, inevitably gives way to "*ressentiment* without equal, that of an insatiable instinct and power-will that wants to become master."[60] Nietzsche's man of *ressentiment* thus bears striking resemblances to the masochist of Freudian psychoanalysis: both intensely feel and loudly proclaim their guilt, yet their feelings of culpability issue in violence rather than humiliation. If crime, at least in part, necessitates self-punishment, the masochist, man of *ressentiment* that he is, will survive it, convinced then that he is more powerful (hence more transgressive and so more guilty) than he previously imagined. Within just such a cycle, guilt contributes to immobilizing Gowther, owing to the intrusion of perverse elements blocking the genuine humility and repose required as antidotes to criminal guilt.

With the greyhound having failed to appear on the fourth day, Gowther sets off and immediately discovers an emperor's castle, where he is admitted and takes up residence, much to the bepuzzlement of the steward who attempts to chase away Gowther with a stick for having taken up a seat under the head table (334–36). The emperor suspects from the outset that this strange man, who will not speak and is now fed under the table, may be performing a penance (343–47). Gowther refuses all delicacies offered him, eating only "what so he from tho howndus wan, / If it wer gnaffyd or mard" (359–60; what he took from the hounds, even if it were chewed or spoiled). "Hob hor fole" (Hob their fool), as Gowther is named by the court, is thus fed "among tho howndys" (367), and even sleeps in a tiny chamber, a kind of doghouse, hidden by a curtain (368–69). It would seem that Gowther is carrying out, not without passion, the prescribed penance by physically mimicking a dog's life. Yet Gowther's "becoming-dog" is, of course, purely demonstrative; he cannot, unlike a conventional lycanthrope,[61] actually, that is to say physically let alone mentally, become canine. His goal, assume modern commentators on the poem, is quite different anyway: he is to become a fully Christian man. Gowther's canine orientation, however, fails to work as a sign of his conversion and penitence precisely because it involves what Jean-Clet Martin has called an "unclean betrayal": "The relation between church and barbarians, and the reterritorialization that results from it . . . mark the spot of an unclean betrayal. . . . Becoming Christian is the index of an incorporeal transformation, attributable to things and bodies without belonging to them."[62] By corporealizing his transformation, while submitting to the Church's "order-words,"[63] Gowther only turns himself into a damned soul, becoming, in effect, another version of the "hethon hownde" (392; heathen hound) he will eventually fight in the emperor's name.

Gowther contaminates his soul—for he cannot do otherwise—by abjecting himself as a dog. This hybrid dog-man was, throughout the Middle Ages, seen as an image of the punishment that submission to sin brings down upon mortals. Even the religious debates, begun by Augustine in *The City of God*, contending whether *cynocephali* were men with the souls of animals or men so degraded that they had forfeited the possibility of grace leave no doubt as to the status of the dog-men as images of punished desire and radical alterity.[64] In both eastern and western traditions of anti-Muslim polemic, Saracens and *cynocephali* were often associated, the former depicted as a race of dogs, often confronting crusaders in innumerable hordes.[65] Gowther's identification with the dog-enemies of Christendom is metonymically reaffirmed when he massacres, with his oriental falchion "full styffe of stele" (487), the "heathen hounds" whom he resembles at the level of the imaginary. In the service of the emperor, Gowther, having prayed for and miraculously received three sets of armor, weapons, and horses (in color order: black, red, white), single-handedly wreaks havoc on the heathen army, led by a Sultan whose sole motivation for war is the lust he has for the emperor's daughter. The poet's graphic descriptions of slaughter (421–29, 466–74, 586–600) caused by Gowther's "fachon large and long" (613), as well as Gowther's ritualistic attention to his own wounds and what they signify (526–34), remind us that the battlefield, described by Cohen as a preeminently "self-effacing space," is the proper scene of Gowther's masochism, his physical suffering and sacrifice for a cause greater than himself (Christendom, the emperor, his maiden daughter).

Gowther, Cohen points out, "is most strongly himself when he learns the power of masochism: in self-denial is his self-assertion."[66] This masochistic self is, however, a rather peculiar one: it is excessive rather than ascetic, aggressive rather than passive or defensive, mobile rather than fixed or fixated (e.g., Gowther's multiple identities in colored armor), and restorative rather than dissipating. Gowther is indeed most firmly himself as masochist, yet this abject subject position responds to the demands of penance (humility and charity) without ever forfeiting its sadistic prerogatives. Here Theodor Reik's crucial insight into the dynamics of self-denial is relevant: masochism does not neutralize aggression by turning it against the self, but rather detours it by way of apparent submission, before *aggression returns to claim fulfillment*. Gowther's "triumph" in the last third of the poem is that, through his self-sacrifice, he never has to renounce power. This "ruse of power," to borrow Judith Butler's formulation of masochism's key strategy,[67] leaves in place an intractable perversity based on pain and submission. It is as if Gowther can only demonstrate how much power he possesses by how much of it he is able to sacrifice, to spend, to "trash."

Having referred to Gowther's abjection as an oscillation between disappearance and sublimity, I would now like to push a bit further by suggesting that Gowther's story is one of the pursuit of this contradiction, to the point where death and sublimity merge. After Gowther successfully defends the emperor against the Sultan, is absolved by the pope, and marries the emperor's daughter, he performs various charitable deeds, marries his mother to the old earl, to whom he also gives all his land, and endows an abbey. After many years of wise rule (715–17), Gowther dies and is buried at the same abbey that he endowed—a return to origins in more ways than one, if we recall that Gowther destroyed an abbey in his youth. Gowther is remembered by "Cryston pepull" as "a varré corsent parfett" (721; a truly pious person) who "suffurd for Goddus sake" (726). Gowther becomes a miracle-working saint, dramatizing the collapsing point of death and transcendence: restoring eyesight to the blind, voice to the mute, posture to "tho crokyd," sanity to the mad, and "mony odur meracullus" (733–37; many other miracles). The poem comes to an end with a double reminder of and return to Gowther's origins: it is mentioned once more that he was "geyton with a felteryd feynd" (742), while the fully cyclical nature of his development is stressed: "Thus syr Gowther coverys is care, / That fyrst was ryche and sython bare, / And effte was ryche ageyn" (739–41; thus Sir Gowther recovers his estate, who was first rich and then poor and afterward was rich again).

The final passages of the poem dramatize the inertia of abjection that I have been arguing entraps Gowther, whose status as a miracle-working saint solidifies his identity as a kind of obsessional object of the kind that his fetish-falchion had represented for him all along. Gowther's hagiography is, then, the story of his completion as sublime fetish, that object that, rather than satisfies desire, instead *causes* it. St. Gowther's existence means that the desire of the "Cryston pepull" to be healed will never cease. Yet Gowther is not simply a catalyst for salvific desire, since "a saint's business," Lacan remarks, "is not *caritas*. Rather he acts as trash [déchet]; his business being *trashitas* [il décharite]. So as to embody what the structure entails, namely allowing the subject of the unconscious to take him as the cause of the subject's own desire."[68] Lacan calls the saint "the refuse of jouissance,"[69] for, from his inert position, he fails to satisfy, eliciting ever more desire. However, the desire the saint elicits is not heterogeneous; it coincides perfectly with the saint's single will. There is, to paraphrase Slavoj Zizek, something extremely unsettling, even obscene, in this experience of desire as already the desire of the other.[70] What seems here another arcane proposition of Lacanian theory is actually fundamental to the general theory of perversion. Perversion arises when the subject's own desire is (taken to be) at the same time the other person's desire. Gowther thus continues to have a contaminative effect, outlasting his death, on the people around him. There is, in other words, a perversity inhabiting what the poet sees as evidence of God's grace (738).

If there is a lesson in *Sir Gowther*, it may be that subjectivity is less malleable the more the other is included within its larger parameters. The poem offers, then, a rather unique medieval experiment with power and identity, where the subject finds its destination in a structure whereby maximizing its power coincides with annihilating that very power. An economics of identity is at work here: the demon within Gowther furnishes him with raw force, a sadistic energy wrapped in masochism, the extinguishing of which stops him cold, such that he will forever be equated with his burial place. Contrary to the ideal penitential process, eradicating the demon, the foreigner within Gowther, fails ultimately to bring him to a state of transcendence. His salvation, his saintliness, is merely the culmination of a perverse process whereby Gowther ossifies, entombed "in schryne of gold" (725).

Notes

1. See, for example, E. M. Bradstock, "The Penitential Pattern in Sir Gowther," *Parergon: Bulletin of the Australian and New Zealand Association for Medieval and Renaissance Studies* 20 (April 1978): 3–10.
2. Gowther "is an animal who needs to become a man" (151), writes Margaret Robson in her "Animal Magic: Moral Regeneration in Sir Gowther," *The Yearbook of English Studies* 22 (1992): 140–53.
3. Eve Salisbury, "Sir Gowther: Introduction," in *The Middle English Breton Lays*, ed. Anne Laskaya and Eve Salisbury, Middle English Texts (Kalamazoo, MI: Medieval Institute Publications, 1995), 263–72. The term "unholy wildman" is Penelope B. R. Doob's; see her *Nebuchadnezzar's Children: Conventions of Madness in Middle English Literature* (New Haven: Yale University Press, 1974).
4. George Kane, *Middle English Literature: A Critical Study of the Romances, the Religious Lyrics, Piers Plowman* (London: Methuen & Co. Ltd., 1951), 32.
5. Robson, "Animal Magic," 153.
6. See Jeffrey Jerome Cohen, "The Body Hybrid: Giants, Dog-Men, and Becoming Inhuman," in his *Of Giants: Sex, Monsters, and the Middle Ages*, Medieval Cultures 17 (Minneapolis: University of Minnesota Press, 1999), 119–41; on Gowther's multiple fathers, see Cohen, and Robson, "Animal Magic," 146. Robson counts five fathers (the fiend, the Duke, the Earl who eventually marries his mother, the pope, and the emperor), to which we could even add a sixth, God.
7. Sir Gowther is found in two late fifteenth-century MSS (British Library Royal 17.B.43 and National Library of Scotland MS Advocates 19.3.1), both of which derive from the Northeast Midlands. The Royal MS (from which the opening prayer is usually supplied in modern editions) was probably intended for a more refined audience, since it lacks the graphic details of Gowther's rape and destruction of a convent. The edition quoted is *Six Middle English Romances*, ed. Maldwyn Mills (London: J. M. Dent & Sons, 1973).

8. In this way, "the medieval orchard promised endless pleasure" (322); see Danielle Régnier-Bohler, "Imagining the Self," in *Revelations of the Medieval World*, ed. Georges Duby, trans. Arthur Goldhammer, vol. 2 of *A History of Private Life* (Cambridge: Belknap Press of Harvard University Press, 1988), 322–23. For a reading of the orchard scene as derivative of apocryphal legend, see M. B. Ogle, "The Orchard Scene in *Tydorel* and *Sir Gowther*," *Romanic Review* 13 (1922): 37–43; cf. Laura A. Hibbard [Loomis], *Medieval Romance in England* (London: Oxford University Press, 1924), 49–57, esp. 54, where she objects to Ogle's interpretation.
9. There is a veiled association here of Gowther and Ishmael, in whose fate both Muhammad and Islam are, according to anti-Muslim polemic, foreshadowed. Genesis 16:12 is the key point of reference: Ishmael "shall be a wild man [*ferus homo*]. His hand will be against all men, and all men's hands against him: and he shall pitch his tents against all his brethren." See, for example, the account of Muhammad's origins and rise to power in ch. 2 of William of Tripoli's *Tractatus de statu Saracenorum et de Mahomete pseudopropheta et eorum lege et fide*, in Hans Prutz, *Kulturgeschichte der Kreuzzüge* (Hildesheim: Georg Olms, 1964), 575–98, esp. 576.
10. Cohen, "The Body Hybrid," 123.
11. The deceptive nature of shape-shifting demons is expressed in an exchange between the summoner and the friar of Chaucer's Friar's Tale; see *The Riverside Chaucer*, ed. Larry D. Benson, 3rd ed. (Boston: Houghton Mifflin, 1987) III (D), 125, ll. 1457–68.
12. Thomas Aquinas, *Commentarium in quator libros sententiarum*, IV, dist. 34, art. 3; also, *Summa theologiae*, 1, q. 51, art. 3, in his Opera omnia, ed. A. Borgnet, 38 vols. (Paris: Louis Vivès, 1890–99). Cf. q. 25, art. 7, *De veritate*, in his *Quaestiones disputatae*, 5 vols. (Turin: Marietti, 1953).
13. Robson is convinced that the Lady was fully aware that the man was not her husband; see her "Animal Magic," 141. While it is highly debatable whether, as Robson maintains, the Lady *entered* the orchard ready and willing to copulate with man or fiend, it is certainly true, as Cohen points out, the Lady had no qualms about turning her terrible situation to advantage after *leaving* the orchard. The Lady, in a parody of the Annunciation, tells her credulous husband that an angel declared to her that that night they will conceive a child; see Cohen, "The Body Hybrid," 122.
14. William of Auvergne, *De universo*, bk. 3, ch. 25, in *Opera Omnia* (Venice: D. Nicolinum, 1591), 1009. Vincent of Beauvais (*Speculum naturale*, bk. 19, ch. 118) emphasizes the association of bears and humans in matters of sexuality: "Bears do not make love like the other quadrupeds, but can embrace each other mutually, like human beings." William of Auvergne notes in addition that the bear has a face resembling that of a man (*De universo*, 1009).
15. Bestiality was commonly seen as part of the triad of "unnatural" sexualities, along with homosexuality and masturbation. Alexander of Hales, whose *Summa theologica*, Roger Bacon griped, was heavier than a horse, characterized bestiality as the most grievous kind of sexual crime against nature; see his *Summa theologica . . . cura PP. Collegii S. Bonaventurae*, 4 vols.

(Quaracchi: Ex typographia Collegii S. Bonaventurae, 1924–48), 2–2.3.5.2.1.8.1.

16. William, *De universo*, 1009; cf. Vincent, *Speculum naturale*, bk. 22, ch. 41, where he modifies Aristotelian theory (in *De generatione animalium*) on the subject of coitus between different species, arguing not only that sexual relations are possible (contra Aristotle), but that they produce monsters. Interspecies sex portends disaster in the story of Melusine and her sons: in Thüring von Ringoltingen's (1456) version, Melusine, a half-human and half-snake being, united with a mortal man, gives birth to sons whose demonic qualities are not detectable, except in one case, her son Horribel. Melusine warns her husband Reymund that, unless Horribel is killed, great wars will ensue and they will be ruined. The story of Melusine resembles *Sir Gowther* in other ways as well and bears further investigation. A good discussion of the Melusine myth is in Albrecht Classen, *The German Volksbuch: A Critical History of a Late-Medieval Genre*, Studies in German Language and Literature 15 (Lewiston, NY: Edwin Mellen Press, 1995), 141–62.
17. Indeed, we learn later in the poem that Gowther is peerlessly handsome (336–38). Gowther is a fully liminal creature, situated between superlative humanity and beastliness. His abjectness inheres in this in-between condition.
18. For Diego de Valera, the Castilian knight who wrote a significant treatise on nobility (*Espejo de Verdadera Nobleza*, in *Prosistas Castellanos del Siglo XV*, ed. Mario Penna [Madrid: Ediciones Atlas, 1959]) which circulated widely in French translation, this notion of paternity is a "chose veritable"; see Bibliothèque Nationale MS Fr 1280, f. 39. A later French translation, based on a different MS (Bibliothèque Royale, Brussels, MS 10979), is provided in Arie Johan Vanderjagt, *Qui sa vertu anoblist: The Concepts of Noblesse and chose publicque in Burgundian Political Thought* (Groningen: J. Mielot, 1981), 258.
19. Jean de Bueil, *Le Jouvencel*, ed. Leon Lecestre (Paris: Renouard, H. Laurens, successeur, 1887–89) 2: 82.
20. See Vitelo, *De causa primaria paenitentiae in hominibus et de natura daemonum*, in Jerzy Burchardt, *List Witelona do Ludwika we Lwówku Slaskim : problematyka teoriopoznawcza, kosmologiczna i medyczna*, Studia Copernicana XIX (Wroclaw: Zaklad Narodowy im. Ossolinskich, 1979), 161–99. On Vitelo's demonology, see Eugenia Paschetto, *Demoni e prodigi: note su alcuni scritti di Witelo e di Oresme* (Torino: G. Giappichelli, 1978).
21. The incubus was long considered to be a fantasy that occurs during sleep, one that produces somatic effects such as feelings of suffocation or oppressive weight. Macrobius links the *visum* (or *phantasma*) to the imagining of incubi, which "according to popular belief" press sleepers with weight; see his *Commentary on the Dream of Scipio*, trans. William Harris Stahl, Records of Civilization: Sources and Studies 48 (New York: Columbia University Press, 1952), I.iii.7. Pascalus Romanus offers a strictly medical explanation that involves a condition of the circulatory system during sleep; see bk. 1, ch. 10 of his *Liber thesauri occulti* in Simone Collin-Roset, "Le *Liber thesauri occulti* de Pascalis Romanus (un traité d'interpretation des songes du XIIe

siècle)," *Archives d'histoire doctrinale et littéraire du Moyen Age* 30 (1963): 111–98; here 158. Along these lines, see also Bernard of Gordon, *Lilio de medicina: un manual basico de medicina medieval*, ed. John Cull y Brian Dutton, Medieval Spanish Medical Texts Series 31 (Madison: Hispanic Seminary of Medieval Studies, 1991), II, ch. 24.

22. Shame brings to mind the image of the deceived man; see *The Prose Salernitan Questions*, ed. Brian Lawn, Auctores Britannici Medii Aevi 5 (London: Oxford University Press for the British Academy, 1979), B 46, 22–23.
23. In 1637, a woman whose husband had been gone for four years was thought to have conceived a child through the force of imagination; see Pierre Darmon, *Le mythe de la procréation à l'âge baroque* (Paris: J.-J. Pauvert, 1977), 107.
24. Vitelo, *De causa primaria paenitentiae*, 177. He also cites a case from Padua that occurred in 1265: a woman confessed to have lain with a horned goat, an animal whose demonic nature was attested by the fact of disappearance after the act.
25. In Geoffrey of Monmouth's *Historia regum Britanniae*, Merlin is the son of the King of Demetia's daughter, who, as a nun, was visited by an incubus, who sometimes assumed the shape of a handsome youth and other times remained invisible (see *The History of the Kings of Britain*, trans. Lewis Thorpe [New York: Penguin, 1966], 167–68). In Robert de Boron's twelfth-century *Merlin* and in the later Middle English prose *Merlin*, the magician is begotten as a result of a plan by the fiends of Hell to revenge Christ's Harrowing of Hell, an event in which the Old Testament patriarchs were freed from Satan's bondage. Their plan is to create their own demonic agent—a sort of Antichrist—who will do their bidding in the cosmic struggle between good and evil. Such a being is soon fathered upon a virtuous woman by a demon that impregnates the pious daughter of a wealthy man while she is sleeping. The lady's confession, however, saves her son, who, though born with a hirsute body and astonishing prophetic powers, escapes the evil influence of his demonic father. Gowther, unlike Merlin, does not escape his father's will to power, even if he avoids his sadism in later life.
26. Recall that in Layamon's *Brut*, Merlin's mother describes the father ambiguously as "The fairest thing that ever was born, as it were a tall knight arrayed in gold; oft it kissed and oft it me embraced. I know not whether it were an evil thing or on God's behalf dight" (quoted. in J. A. MacCulloch, *Medieval Faith and Fable* [London: Harrap, 1932], 54).
27. Eve Salisbury, "Sir Gowther: Introduction," 266. Salisbury cites J. A. MacCulloch, *Medieval Faith*.
28. A suggestion of hirsuteness is heard in Celtic *barr* ("bushy top").
29. Georges Bataille, "The Tragedy of Gilles de Rais," in *The Trial of Gilles de Rais*, trans. from the French by Richard Robinson (Los Angeles: Amok, 1991), 37–43.
30. *The Middle English Breton Lays*, 299–300, n. 130.
31. See *Richard III*, Act IV, scene iv, ll. 49–50; *King Henry VI, Part 3*, Act V, scene vi, ll. 74–76.
32. See Paul Barber, *Vampires, Burial, and Death: Folklore and Reality* (New Haven: Yale University Press. 1988), 30.

33. See, for example, Karl Abraham, "A Short Study of the Development of the Libido, Viewed in the Light of Mental Disorders" (1924), in *Selected Papers of Karl Abraham*, trans. Douglas Bryan and Alix Strachey (New York: Basic Books, 1953), 418–501; and Leonard Shengold, "More about Rats and Rat People," *International Journal of Psychoanalysis* 52 (1971): 277–88.
34. See Janine Chasseguet-Smirgel, "Perversion and the Universal Law," *International Review of Psycho-Analysis* 10 (1983): 293–301.
35. William S. Burroughs, "Immortality," in ibid., *The Adding Machine: Selected Essays* (New York: Seaver Books, 1985), 131.
36. An overlooked insight of Freud's, expressed in a letter to Wilhelm Fliess (January 24, 1897) where perversion is described in terms of a devil religion: "I am beginning to grasp an idea: it is as though in the perversions, of which hysteria is the negative, we have before us a remnant of a primeval sexual cult, which once was—perhaps still is—a religion . . . Perverse actions, moreover, are always the same—meaningful and fashioned according to some pattern that someday will be understood. I dream therefore of a primeval devil religion with rites that are carried on secretly, and understand the harsh therapy of the witches' judges" (*The Complete Letters of Sigmund Freud to Wilhelm Fliess, 1887–1904*, trans. and ed. Jeffrey Moussaieff Masson [Cambridge, Mass.: Belknap Press of Harvard University Press, 1985], 227).
37. Sadism and fetishism both constitute attempts to resolve problems of identity and alterity; see Joyce McDougall, *Plea for a Measure of Abnormality* (New York: International Universities Press, 1980).
38. Jacques Lacan and Wladimir Granoff, "Fetishism: The Symbolic, the Imaginary and the Real," in *Perversions: Psychodynamics and Therapy*, ed. Sandor Lorand and Michael Balint (London: Ortolan, 1965), 274.
39. See Norman A. Daniel, *Islam and the West: The Making of an Image* (Edinburgh: Edinburgh University Press, 1960).
40. Gregorio Kohon, "Fetishism Revisited," *International Journal of Psycho-Analysis* 68 (1987): 213–28; here, 226.
41. It was Melanie Klein who focused on the primitive defense mechanisms of splitting and projective identification as intrinsic to the object relations of the "paranoid-schizoid" position; see her "Notes on Some Schizoid Mechanisms," *International Journal of Psycho-Analysis* 27 (1946): 99–110.
42. Cohen, "The Body Hybrid," 127.
43. A point stressed by several authors: S. M. Payne, "Some Observations on the Ego Development of the Fetishist, *International Journal of Psycho-Analysis* 20 (1939): 161–70; W. H. Gillespie, "A Contribution to the Study of Fetishism," *International Journal of Psycho-Analysis* 21 (1940): 401–15; and Phyllis Greenacre, "Certain Relationships between Fetishism and Faulty Development of the Body Image," *The Psychoanalytic Study of the Child* 8 (1953): 79–98.
44. Greenacre also suggests that the fetish's stability serves to stabilize the sense of a body that is in flux; see Greenacre, "Certain Relationships," 94. This seems particularly suggestive in the case of Gowther, whose growth is

markedly rapid and defamiliarizing, leading Cohen to elaborate the association with giantness (see "The Body Hybrid," 123).

45. Or, alternatively, "He lifted it neither for joy nor pain": a reading that suggests the very presence of the sword (hanging forever by his side) is a stay against further violence.
46. Robson, while diagnosing Gowther as a psychotic child, points to the defensive function of his falchion, "his magic talisman" (149) against social pressures; see Robson, "Animal Magic," 148–49.
47. It is noteworthy that in the French *Robert le Diable*, upon which the Middle English story of Gowther is based, Robert, in all versions but one (which never mentions his sword), abandons his sword before setting out to meet the pope.
48. Julia Kristeva, *The Powers of Horror: An Essay on Abjection*, trans. Leon S. Roudiez (New York: Columbia University Press, 1982), 18.
49. See Theodor Reik, *Masochism in Modern Man*, trans. from the German by Margaret H. Beigel and Gertrud M. Kurth (New York and Toronto: Farrar and Rinehart, 1941).
50. See Fritz Wittels, "The Mystery of Masochism: The Masochist Punishes the Undesirable Person within Himself," *The Psychoanalytic Review* 24 (1937): 139–49; and Gustav Bychowski, "Some Aspects of Masochistic Involvement," *Journal of the American Psychoanalytic Association* 7 (1959): 248–73.
51. The maternal breast is in reality the first object for the infant, and is therefore charged with special significance as that which initiates the split between what is satisfying (good) and what is frustrating (bad). The breast and mouth constitute the first ground upon which an ethical system can develop; see R. E. Money-Kyrle, *Psychoanalysis and Politics: A Contribution to the Psychology of Politics and Morals* (London: Gerald Duckworth and Co., 1951).
52. Otto M. Fenichel, *The Psychoanalytic Theory of Neurosis* (New York: W. W. Norton, 1945), 37.
53. Saara Lilja, *Dogs in Ancient Greek Poetry*, Commentationes Humanarum Literatum 56 (Helsinki: Societas Scientiarum Fennica, 1976), 11.
54. Ancient authors attest that the Egyptians revered the dog—probably the greyhound: Herodotus, *Historia* 2. 65–67; Strabo, *Geographica* 17.1.40; and Aelianus, *De natura animalium* 10.45. We should note, too, that in the tradition of north African Islam the greyhound is the only dog that is possessed of *baraka*.
55. St. Roch (or Rock), a healing saint of the fourteenth century, is represented in medieval art as accompanied by a dog with a loaf of bread in its mouth (e. g., screen painting in Devon and Norfolk). Though he is still invoked against disease today in France and Italy, he seems to have been particularly famous in England, as evidenced by the preservation of his name in the Sussex place name St. Rokeshill. See Donald Attwater, *The Penguin Dictionary of Saints*, 2nd ed. revised by Catherine Rachel John (London: Penguin, 1983), 289. The apocryphal story of Tobias, probably known to the Gowther-poet, tells how Tobias's dog accompanied him on a difficult journey to restore the eyesight of

his master's father. The biblical point of reference for both is the story of Elijah being fed by ravens in the wilderness (1 Kings 17:5).

56. See Jean-Claude Schmitt, *The Holy Greyhound: Guinefort, Healer of Children Since the Thirteenth Century*, trans. from the French by Martin Thom (Cambridge: Cambridge University Press, 1983). St. Christopher's earliest western hagiography is found in an eighth-century manuscript (Würzburg University Library Mp. Th. F28; cited in Walter Loeschcke, "Darstellung des kynokephalen hl. Christophorus," *Forschungen zur osteuropäischen Geschichte* 5 [1957]: 38–58; here 39). Ratramus of Corbie's ninth-century *Epistola de Cynocephalis* (PL 121: 1153–56) provides a scholastic treatment of the saint. Walter of Speyer's tenth-century *Passio Christophori* (in *Poetae Latini Aevi Carolini*, ed. Karl Strecker. Monumenta Germaniae Historica IV, II (1914; Munich: Monumenta Germaniae Historica, 1978], 807–840) is the greatest of the Western hagiographies. Its popularity as a hagiographic tale is attested by two early Irish sources: Oengus the Culde's eighth-century *Felire* and the *Passio Sancti Christophori* (text in M. J. Frazer, "The Passion of Saint Christopher," *Revue Celtique* 34 [1913]: 307–25). The second codex of Cotton Vitellius A. xv., the Nowell Codex, contains, along with *Beowulf* and three other articles, a *Life of St. Christopher*, the beginning of which is lost. Because of its apotropaic function, the image of this dog-headed saint was placed on bridges, church doors, and city gates; see *Histoire des saints et de la sainteté chrétienne*, 11 vols. (Paris: Hachette, 1986–88) 2: 104–07, s. v. "Christophe."
57. This is a psychological, as opposed to spiritual, state.
58. Franz Borkenau, "Stages on the Road to Western Civilization," in his *End and Beginning: On the Generations of Cultures and the Origins of the West*, ed. Richard Lowenthal (New York: Columbia University Press, 1981), 411.
59. Injunctions against biting the Eucharist attempt to prohibit "the essence of the totemic orgy—the tearing to pieces of the god" (Borkenau, "Stages," 410–11), as well as to assuage the guilt generated by such an orgy, real or imaginary, actual or desired.
60. Friedrich Nietzsche, "What is the Meaning of Ascetic Ideals?," in his *On the Genealogy of Morals*, trans. from the German by Walter Kaufman and R. J. Hollingdale (New York: Vintage, 1967), 117.
61. Here Cohen's comparison of Gowther to Marie de France's werewolf-protagonist Bisclavret (Cohen, "The Body Hybrid," 129–30) is helpful to the extent that it reminds us that becoming animal is a change in accident, not substance, to put it in terms of one of the elementary preoccupations of twelfth-century logicians. Bisclavret remains a wronged husband, thinks and eventually, when given the opportunity, acts as a wronged husband, despite his wolf's body.
62. Jean-Clet Martin, "Cartography of the Year 1000: Variations on *A Thousand Plateaus*," in *Gilles Deleuze and the Theater of Philosophy*, ed. Constantin V. Boundas and Dorothea Olkowski (New York: Routledge, 1994), 280.
63. For Deleuze, the "order-word" is the imperative function of language, with the "order" being understood in both senses, as the statement that commands and the injunction that establishes a hierarchy. "Every order-word . . . carries

a little death sentence," according to Deleuze, because it carries with it the implicit presupposition of absolute, or what Brian Massumi calls somewhere, "funereal" normality (Gilles Deleuze and Félix Guattari, *A Thousand Plateaus: Capitalism and Schizophrenia*, trans. from the French by Brian Massumi [Minneapolis: University of Minnesota Press, 1987], 76).

64. See St. Augustine, *Concerning the City of God against the Pagans*, trans. Henry Bettenson (New York: Viking Penguin, 1972), 662. The Bodleian Library's Douce bestiary (MS Douce 88 II, fol. 69v) moralizes the dog-men thus: "Cenocephali qui canina capita habent, detractores et discorded designant . . . qui labeo subteriore se contegunt eos figurant de quibus dicitur labor labiorum operiet eos." The bestiary at Westminster Abbey (MS 22, fol. 1v) likewise figures the dog-men as dissenting persons. The imensely popular *Gesta Romanorum* (ed. Hermann Oesterly [Hildesheim: Georg Olms, 1980]), under chapter 175 entitled "De diversitate et mirabilibus mundi cum expositione inclusa," discusses the dog-men first among the Plinian races as a figure for preachers who should wear animal skins as a sign of penance and as proper example to the laity (574).
65. The identification of cynocephalics with Muslim "Turks" extends beyond the medieval polemical tradition. Such an identification often gained its polemical force from popular folktales and romances. David Gordon White, in his outstanding book on the mythology of the dog-men, mentions the Slavic folk identification of Turks with dog-headed man-eaters; see his *The Myths of the Dog-Man* (Chicago: University of Chicago Press, 1991), 61–62. The conflation of Saracens and dogs occurs in the French *chansons de geste*, where Muslims are frequently portrayed as barking dogs when they rush into battle; see C. Meredith Jones, "The Conventional Saracen of the Songs of Geste," *Speculum* 17 (1942): 201–25; here, 205.
66. Cohen, "The Body Hybrid," 136.
67. Liz Kotz, "The Body You Want: Liz Kotz Interviews Judith Butler," *Artforum* (November 1992), 88.
68. Jacques Lacan, "Television," trans. from the French by Denis Hollier, Rosalind Krauss, and Annette Michelson, in *Television/A Challenge to the Psychoanalytic Establishment*, ed. Joan Copjec (New York: W. W. Norton, 1990), 15.
69. Lacan, "Television," 16.
70. Slavoj Žižek, *Looking Awry: An Introduction to Jacques Lacan through Popular Culture* (Cambridge: MIT Press, 1991), 108.

7
Sir Gowther: Imagining Race in Late Medieval England

JESUS MONTAÑO

In late 1291 the news slowly filtered to the West that Acre, the last and largest Christian stronghold, had been captured by the Mamluk sultanate of Egypt. The remainder of the Holy Land fell easily into Mamluk hands. The news of the loss of the Holy Land was met with consternation, if not horror. Western Europe's crusading spirit, which had slumbered through most of the thirteenth century, now awakened to the stark realities of Europe's precarious position.[1] Later developments throughout the century added to the widespread concern in the Christian West.[2] However, no recovery missions were immediately organized. Instead, the crusades in the fourteenth century were waged in literary works urging military unity, political alliances, and strategic religious conversions. The increased consciousness of the political and ideological necessity of the Crusades generated a bewildering assortment of carefully prepared cultural propaganda by numerous thinkers and pious travelers. Whereas political reality could not keep up with historical events, the rise of Crusade literature was a response to a desire to play out the crusading impulse in imaginative literature.[3]

Sir Gowther[4] fits within the literary history of crusade literature, constituting an example of both propaganda regarding the Muslim East and a vision of Christendom overcoming its non-Christian neighbors. At the heart of these narratives is a search for accommodations to—and the meanings of—the perplexities of intercultural life. Because of their agenda, these narratives provide a definitive blueprint of the ways in which one group of people construct another group. However, for too long we have focused on the product of that narrative representation. We thus have found static notions of race, usually based on visual or overt signifiers. Instead of focusing on the product, I wish to analyze the process of racial construction. This means that the study changes from what race is to how race is made in the medieval period. It is one thing to say that the Other possesses different skin tone or hair; it is quite another to place those signifiers in a field where they are hierarchically valued and given meaning. In other words, why is it that one group has certain features and, more important, how are those features to be interpreted?

Narratives such as *Sir Gowther*, I argue, allow us to see the processes by which race is constructed. What they show us is that racial construction was indeed an exhaustive process of associations, using a wide variety of ideas in order to construct the Other. Medieval ideas of race were based on an invented set of signifiers. As in our own world, these racial signifiers were fluid and malleable, dependent on a wide range of associated ideas and performances. Languages could be learned and cultural practices adapted. Furthermore, as *Sir Gowther* illustrates, medieval writers understood that imagining the Other meant ascribing to them stories and images that would be generally read by a wide audience.

Sir Gowther is a metrical romance that imagines what the blending of races—those of the East and those of the West—might mean for a Western Christian community. While most critics to date have read the text as participating in the tradition of secular hagiography, I argue for a reading that addresses questions of race in the text.[5] The focal point of this strategy is to examine the portrayal of Sir Gowther as a Saracen. In doing so I will map the biological and cultural constructions of race and ethnicity and thus expose the narrative quality of ethnic identification and the processes for racial conversion and integration. Given the historical and geographical circumstances of the romance, I will explore the various ways in which Gowther's racial identity is circumscribed, how it is made evident to the hero, and how the hero must reject that identity. Further, the process that the story lays out for the redemption of the hero will be examined. While on the surface the narrative is playing out a religious conversion, the description and attributes of the conversion can be read as cultural change. In this case, the hero can convert only by casting off the very things that determine his difference. The goal is to examine the mechanisms used in late medieval England for drawing racial boundaries and the ways in which those boundaries were crossed.

Devilish Beginnings

Sir Gowther is set in Austria, where the Duke and his wife are without children after more than ten years of marriage. Because of the lack of an heir the Duke approaches the Duchess and tells her that because she is barren, they must part: "Y tro thu be sum baryn, / Hit is gud that we twyn; / Y do bot wast my tyme on the" (53–55) [I know you are barren, / It is good that we twin (part); / I do but waste my time on you]. Devastated, the lady runs out and prays to God and Mary for a child "On what maner scho ne roghth" (63) [In whatever manner she did not care]. She is then visited in an orchard by a figure that at first resembles her husband, but after having sex with her, turns out to be an incubus. Frightened, the lady runs to her husband and tells him that an angel visited her with the good news that they should expect a child. Without waiting the two dash off to have sex.

The child born soon grows fierce, violent, and ravenous, so much that he sucks his wetnurses to death and tears the nipple off his mother. At the age of fifteen the young Gowther makes a falchion of steel and iron that only he can wield: "made a wepon that he schuld weld / (No nodur mon myght hit beyr): / a fachon bothe of styll and yron" (137–39) [made a weapon that he should wield, / No other man might it bear; / a falchion both of steel and iron]. In an effort to indoctrinate, and perhaps calm, his rebellious son, the Duke knights him with a long broad sword. However, unable to curb Gowther's escapades, the Duke dies of grief. The Duchess, unable to bear the guilt of her secret, flees to a nearby castle. Gowther continues his evil practices by attacking churches and terrorizing the religious and women.

Gowther's evil actions continue until one day an old earl accuses him of not being of Christian strain. Perturbed, Gowther forces his mother at sword's point to tell him the secret of his conception. Upon hearing the truth, the horrified Gowther goes to Rome and confesses his sins to the pope, who tells him to remain totally silent and to eat no meat except from the mouths of dogs: "Thou eyt no meyt bot that thou revus of howndus mothe, / Cum thy body within; / Ne no worde speke for evyll ne gud" (293–95) [You eat no meat but that you take from hounds' mouth / To come inside your body; / Nor any word speak for evil or good]. Further, the pope tells Gowther to leave his sword behind; Gowther refuses. He then goes to the court of the German emperor, where he is known as Hob the Fool.

Blood and Belonging

Sir Gowther begins with a genealogical question set in the outermost frontiers of the Christian world. This narrative setting in a geographical and in an imaginative sense is important because the frontier is the interaction zone of cultures and societies.[6] To the medieval mind geographical space denoted who or what occupied that space. Many of the places, cities, and people were not exactly real; instead, they were the "alien . . . cultures existing beyond the boundaries of the European known world."[7] Therefore, when the *Gowther* poet sets the narrative in Austria, for an English audience he in fact places his narrative in the borderlands of cultural and racial exchange, the boundary between the known and the unknown.[8]

Along with the borderlands setting, Gowther's birth and childhood have much in common with representations of Saracen and Christian marriages in the popular crusade literature of the period. The theme of the monstrous child born to racially different parents is found in the *King of Tars*, where a self-sacrificing Christian princess marries the Sultan as a way of bringing peace. When the offspring is born, it is a formless lump of flesh. The mother then requests that the child be baptized, and the child immediately changes into a beautiful boy. Induced by the miracle, the Sultan accepts the Christian faith and changes from black to white in the baptismal waters.[9] This theme of colors representing racial miscegenation is also present in Wolfram von Eschenbach's Middle High German *Parzival* (ca. 1205), where Feirefiz, Parzival's half-brother, looks like a magpie, signifying both his bicultural and religious identity. Interestingly, although his courtly and knightly abilities are without question, Feirefiz is allowed in the Grail community only after his baptism and subsequent marriage.[10] Another story is found in several chronicles where a child born of a Muslim-Christian union is a shaggy masculine creature.[11] Once the child is baptized, the child loses all his hair and becomes smooth-skinned and beautiful.[12] The early fourteenth-century Anglo-Latin text, *Flores Historiarum*, for example, relates that the daughter of the king of Armenia married Cassanus, King of the Tartars.[13] The child born to the couple was hairy and disfigured. The father ordered the child to be burned, but the mother interceded. After the child was immersed three times in the baptismal font, it changed into a beautiful boy. The miracle converted the whole community. A letter written to Jaime II of Aragon tells that the King of the Tartars married a Christian princess.[14] In this case, a child was produced after a miraculous conception resulting from a prayer to the Virgin Mary. The child born was half human and half animal. After the child was baptized, however, it became totally human. In another story, a Christian woman married to the king of the Tartars bears a child that is half black and half white. Once baptized, however, the blackness disappears.[15] The overtly visual monstrosity of the child is the direct result of the racial miscegenation. Although Gowther's putative father is the Devil, the poet relies heavily on racial miscegenation concepts and ideas found in popular crusade literature such as the *King of Tars* romances, related analogues of which can be found in England, France, Germany, Italy, and Spain.[16]

These genealogical problems recall that the story begins with a very reckless wish by Gowther's mother. While his nominal father is the Duke of Austria, the audience is told that Gowther's real ancestry is satanic. For this reason, critics have read *Sir Gowther* based on religious and hagiographical models.[17] However, the reckless wish and the satanic conception have much in common with intermarriages and children born out of Christian and Muslim unions. The *Gowther* poet purposefully creates a dialogue centered on the questionable results found in crusade romances. The key to understanding the process of racial construction in *Sir Gowther*, therefore, is examining how religion and miscegenation ideas are intertwined. The tale explicitly relates that Gowther does not belong religiously to the community, and he is therefore Othered along conventional ideas of racial difference.

Saracen Portrait

These comparisons between Christian and Saracen unions and Gowther's ancestry provide clues for understanding how Gowther's racialized identity is circumscribed. For example, the Saracens and Gowther are alike in that both are outside the Christian community because of something occurring somewhere in their genealogy. They both have inherited their exclusion. In the case of the Saracens, they were from the line of Ishmael, the disinherited son of Abraham, while Gowther was conceived in an illicit union.[18]

It is important to note that genealogy and inheritance are interpreted from a religious paradigm. Therefore, the main racial signifier of difference and Otherness is illustrated in religious terms. In the eyes of medieval Christian writers, especially those of popular *chansons de geste*, the Saracens are the offsprings of the devil. The Saracens because of their ancestry are conventionally portrayed as an "evil people; they spent their lives in hating and mocking Christ and in destroying His churches. They are the children of the author of all evil, the Devil."[19] Further, the Saracens are frequently presented as "physical monstrosities; many of them are giants, whole tribes have horns on their heads, others are black as devils. They rush into battle making weird noises comparable to the barking of dogs."[20]

Seen from this religiously inflected viewpoint, Gowther and the Saracens are very similar. They are born from the devil. Significantly, these physical and inner monstrosities that are religiously interpreted manifest themselves into racial signifiers. Physical, visual, and even language differences are given meaning and value. Whatever real physical bearings, cultural practices, or language the Saracens may possess, Christian Europe already sees them under the worst of lights. In this field of knowledge, Saracens are imagined as the complete Others of Christian Europe.

And yet, the similarities between Gowther and the Saracens do not end with their satanic births. Gowther's inner rapacious disposition suggests that he has much more in common with the monstrous Saracen race. Thus, Gowther's racial identity requires a fuller analysis, especially an examination of the symbolic value of Gowther's sword. Being of the aristocracy, Gowther's identity should be shaped by the item that represents his role in society: a warrior. Since the twelfth century the social identity of the knight had changed from solely one of providing leadership and protection of society to one in which the tenets of chivalry were religiously organized and the primary duty was the protection of the Christian faith. For example, the dubbing of the knight, while originally performed by a knight on a novice or squire, became increasingly religious and ritualized to the point where a religious figure performed the dubbing.[21] Hence the intent of Gowther's father may have been to force Gowther into a social role in which the major function was the preservation of the cultural pillars: the Christian faith and feudal society. Because he does not change his ways once he is a knight, however, his actions, while seemingly demonic, can also be read as unknightly. Gowther's sins then can be read as a failure to follow the codes of his class. What this leaves us with is that we can interpret Gowther's actions simultaneously as both being demonic (a religious problem) and unknightly (a social problem).

Gowther does not carry an ordinary broadsword. In fact when his nominal father gives him a broadsword at the dubbing, he spurns it for his curved hand-crafted falchion, a representative weapon and symbol of Saracens.[22] Critics have struggled with what to do with the falchion. Maldwyn Mills states that the falchion is "the outward and visible symbol of both his unbridled violence in his unregenerate days, and his militancy in his later career."[23] To Mills, the sword is a significant symbol and talisman. Only E. M. Bradstock acknowledges that the sword is of Oriental origin and a weapon that a Saracen would carry.[24]

Bradstock does not follow the metaphorical association any further. And yet, because the sword is an Arabic falchion and because he is so attached to it, I suggest that the falchion provides an intrinsic key to Gowther's racial identity. At the age of fifteen Gowther fashioned the weapon out of steel and iron. Because of his young age and lack of metallurgical skill, the creation of the sword means that the proclivity toward a falchion and the ability to use it by the young Gowther could only come from an innate and natural force. Without instruction or perhaps even knowledge of the symbolic value of what he had created, Gowther makes a weapon that was the very image that Christian Europe held of Islam and Saracens.

Gowther's actions for the first part of the text could thus be read as a mixture of beliefs regarding Saracens. His racial identity is constructed out of pseudo-genetic origins and visual signifiers. The negative impulses are shown to be innate and uncontrollable urges. Gowther is essentially evil because he comes from a "strain" of beings that are themselves evil. The falchion functions as the outward and visible symbol of these inner qualities. Gowther's racial identity is constructed out of popularly held stories, signs, and ideas about Saracens.

Up to this point, Gowther fits into the theory that figures race as being natural and traits of the individual and his community being innate as well. Those traits are in the blood, so to speak.[25] Part of the problem of deciphering race relations in a medieval sense is that these biological markers are taken as the sole determiners of how race is understood. But as noted, Gowther's racial identity is constructed out of various narratives. Among these narratives is an invented origin for Saracens that defines their Otherness to the Christian community. Then there are the various symbols and images that outwardly signify racial difference. Thus, natural racial traits, which are supposedly biological and innate, are constructed out of narratives, visual signs, and historical and cultural contact. In a sense, blood is invented and imagined.

In addition, Robert Bartlett notes that "other criteria—custom, language, and law—emerge as the primary badges of ethnicity. In contrast to descent, they share a common characteristic: all three are malleable. They can, indeed, with varying degrees of effect, be transformed not only from one generation to the next, but even within an individual lifetime. New languages can be mastered, new legal regimes adopted, new customs learned."[26]

In order to understand medieval race relations, it is necessary to acknowledge the symbolic meanings of the biological markers and, more important, to analyze how those markers are continually being imagined and invented. It is this practical side of race relations that needs to be analyzed in *Sir Gowther*. While most crusade romances represent racial difference by marking the body either black or white, the *Gowther* poet concentrates on inward racial signifiers that are displayed visually and outwardly by the falchion. The hero's descent and his biological categories in the first part of the narrative foreground the transformational process of cultural conversion in the second half. In doing so, the text examines the ways in which individuals are brought into the community.

Heathen Hound

Beginning his life of repentance, Gowther goes to the court of the Emperor of Germany where, in the public space of the dining hall, he will eat only food brought to him by dogs. Shortly thereafter, the Sultan demands as a marriage partner the Emperor's daughter, who is mute. The Emperor refuses by stating "And Y wyll not, be Cryst wonde, / Gyffe hor to no hethon hownde" (388–89) [And I will not, by Christ's wounds, / Give her to no heathen hound]. It is interesting that the same word "hownde" is used in a span of less than a hundred lines to refer to two very different things: Gowther being fed by hounds and the Emperor thinking of the Saracens as hounds. As in many romances, the *Gowther* poet uses images of race that his audience would have easily understood. As a result of more than three centuries of crusades, the connection between the race of dogs and the Saracens became a widespread belief. As John Block Friedman points out, "the epithet 'dog' was used of the Moslems literally as well as figuratively. [Moreover] there was a fairly widespread connection of Saracens and Cynocephali [dog-head people] in the Middle Ages, in both East and West, as the Moslems were often described by Christians as a race of dogs."[27] One reason for these associations was the Christian belief that Mohamet was a disgruntled Christian heretic, a Roman cardinal who was not elected pope and later denied the divinity of Christ. As followers of Mohamet, the Saracens themselves denied the logic of the Word and thus lost their humanity.[28]

Along with the religious associations between Saracens and dogs, these images of race were of standard use in medieval crusade literature. Medieval romances often portrayed the Saracens rushing into battle "making weird noises comparable to the barking of dogs."[29] The *Gowther* poet's use of the phrase, "heathen hound," would appear to be a kind of alliterative shorthand that accurately draws racial symbolic connotations. For example, in the *King of Tars* the princess marries the Sultan in order to save her father's kingdom. Similar to *Sir Gowther*, when the Sultan of Damascus sends an envoy to ask for the princess's hand in marriage, he is rebuked by the "heathen hound" phrase. According to the ambassador, "þe king of Tars / Of wicked wordes is nou$_3$t scars; / Heþeh hounde he gan þe calle" (91–93) [the King of Tars / Of wicked words is not scared; / Heathen hound he called you]. Evidently, the Saracens are aware of the implied meaning of the words. Also, in a short battle before the princess acquiesces, the narrator describes the action as thus: "þer hewe houndes on Cristen men / & feld hem doun bi ni$_3$en & ten. / So wilde þai were & wode" (169–71) [there, colored hounds on Christian men / and felled them down by nine and ten. / So wild they were and crazy]. In this scene, the wild and crazed Saracen hounds defeat the human Christians. Lastly, in one of the more arresting moments of the narrative, the princess, on her marriage bed, dreams:

An hundred houndes blake,
& bark on hir, lasse & more.
& on þer was þat wald hir take;
& she no durst him nou$_3$t smite
For drede þat he wald hir bite,
Swiche maistri he gan to make.
& as sche wald fram hem fle,
Sche seye þer stond develen þre,
& ich brent as a drake . . .
& afterward þer com an hounde
Wiþ browes brod and hore;
Almost he hadde hir drawen adoun,
Ac þurth Jhesus Cristes passioun
Sche was ysaved.

(423–44)

[A hundred black hounds, / And bark on her, less and more. / And one was there that would take her; / And she did not dare smite him / For dread that he would bite her, / Such mastery he began to make. / And as she would flee

> from him, / She saw there standing three devils, / And each burned as a dragon . . . / And afterwards there came a hound / With broad and hoary brows; / He almost had her drawn down, / But through Jesus Christ's passion / She was saved.]

The princess's dream is a representation of her predicament. The hundred hounds are the Sultan's people, and the single hound is her husband. The constant barking paralyzes her with terror, and the princess fears that hounds will bite her. In the passage, all the racial signifiers are present. We note how the Saracen language is compared to barking, and they threaten her by snapping at her. Visually, the Saracens are portrayed as black and hairy. As this passage illustrates, the phrase, heathen hound, was used to racially represent the Saracens.

This drawing together of a literal event and a metaphorical employment of the same concept forces the comparison between Gowther's identity and the Saracens even closer. In a sense, Gowther's life has been fueled by his currish impulses. The convergence of the figural animal impulses and the literal eating from dogs highlights the depravity of Gowther's previous life and, more important, provides a look at the dynamics for his transformation. The fact that Gowther has to humiliate himself by eating from actual dogs is part of the process of conversion. It publicly demonstrates Gowther's private connection to the Saracens. Because the whole process is framed by a Christian sense of repentance, Gowther's conversion shows the complex ways in which religion and culture interact. The Christian mechanisms of repentance, contrition, and absolution are here working analogically to help along Gowther's cultural conversion.

Culture and Conversion

The Sultan attacks on three consecutive days. On the first day, Gowther prays for help and is given black armor and a steed of solid black. He joins the fight but is unrecognized by all except the Emperor's daughter. On the second day of the battle, Gowther prays and is given red armor and a red steed. On both days, he wins the field and repels the invaders. It should be noted that he uses his falchion, that he has carried with him all this time, in the battles. In fact, the narrative paints several images of Gowther's flashing sword cutting off heads and striking torsos. On the third day, Gowther receives white armor and a white horse. Again, he routs the Saracens. Near the end of the battle, however, a Saracen spears Gowther through the shoulder. Seeing this, the Emperor's daughter swoons and falls from the tower supposedly to her death. Miraculously she revives a couple of days later and is then able to speak. She tells the court that their savior is none other than Gowther. The pope, seeing this as a sign from heaven, absolves Gowther. In the end, Gowther marries the Emperor's daughter and later rules Germany. When he dies, Gowther is made a saint.

Through these events at the end of the narrative Gowther is brought into the community. He is part of the Christian community in that he has recognized his sins, repented, and has been absolved. The fact that he was given armor by God in order to fight the enemies of Christianity is taken as a sign from heaven that Gowther has performed his good works. We also notice that Gowther's penitence has been predominantly visual and public. From the first time he confessed to the pope, to his eating from the dogs, and finally to the fight against the Saracens in the end, Gowther casts away his sins on the public stage.

Symbolically, Gowther's overtly visual and inner monstrosity, which is caused by his devilish origins, is replaced directly after the battles. The armor color changes from black to red and then to white to illustrate his acceptance into the Christian community. Importantly, for most medieval writers, color polarities were a way of depicting morality or immorality, whiteness usually meaning salvation and blackness immorality.[30] This visual metamorphosis theme finds its way into popular literature such as the King of Tars romances. In the *King of Tars* the child born undergoes a metamorphosis and changes into a beautiful boy. Likewise, the Sultan, upon accepting the Christian faith, changes from black to white in the baptismal waters.[31] The blackness and the monstrous appearance denote Otherness to the community. Once the person is accepted into the community, racial difference seems to disappear.

The color symbolism in *Sir Gowther*, however, is more complex in its ideas about cultural conversion. Gowther's parents go through the usual antidotes to right their son: baptism and knighting. Gowther should lose his inner blackness at either the baptism or the knighting. However, it is not until he has gone through his public humiliation of eating with dogs that he is allowed to begin the color change. By fighting in black armor on the first day of the tournament, Gowther shows his relationship with the Saracens, on a religious and cultural level. Fighting in red armor on the second day relates to an important religious idea, the blood of Christ baptizing the new convert. The white armor is the last because it represents the final stage of conversion. Gowther is now part of the moral community; he has been cleansed. The wound he receives on the last day proves that he belongs, that he is willing to make a blood sacrifice. The shedding symbolically shows that all Christians are in effect held together by the blood of Christ.

In these ways, the *Gowther* poet shows the multiple relations between hagiography and race studies. Gowther is brought into the Christian community through the performance of religiously guided good works. Because the main signifier of racial difference between Christians and Muslims is religion, religious conversion necessitates a cultural conversion as well. While the first part of the romance created the illusion of race as stable, the cultural conversion and acceptance into the community of Gowther shows the invented and constructed nature of race.

As in most romances, Sir Gowther is rewarded by marriage. The full importance of this marriage cannot be overstated. Fourteenth-century Europe stood in a precarious position after centuries of slumber and ineptitude on the crusading front. Medieval writers urged not only military unity but strategic religious conversions and political alliances. The dream of oriental romances throughout this period was the matrimonial and political union of Christian and Saracen.[32] Stable and static notions of race had no place in such endeavors. Indeed, the future of Europe rested on the conversion and inclusion of the Other. In these facets, *Sir Gowther* clearly illustrates the processes necessary for inclusion into the community.

Race and Inclusion

The *Gowther* poet, following tradition, carefully demonstrates the political and religious necessity of the Crusades. In the crusading strategies of the fourteenth century, however, a great deal of attention is paid to issues surrounding race and cultural conversion. The pretext for war is that the Sultan had demanded to marry the Emperor's daughter, and the Emperor had refused to give his daughter to a heathen hound. In a sense, the battles take place not because of a religious war but because the Emperor did not want his daughter to marry into a different racial community. Questions that arise from "unusual" unions trouble the text throughout. The narrative begins with a child being produced between a devil and a woman and almost ends with a marriage between a Saracen and a Christian. The first union produced a terror to the community. Because this first union had much in common with Saracen and Christian marriages found in other Crusade fiction of the period, it would seem probable that a union in the second part of the text would result in the same kind of devil-like progeny. The *Gowther* poet, however, while he plays with the idea for a prolonged time, squashes the possible marriage between the Sultan and the Emperor's daughter. Significantly, Gowther plays the lead role in combating the Sultan's forces, and thus foils the dangerous marriage. Clearly this is not the Gowther of the first part of the narrative; instead, this is a person who has been accepted because he adheres to the laws, customs, and religion of his new community.

In addition, Gowther succeeds by keeping and quite adeptly using his falchion. The outward and visible symbol of Saracen identity is the primary instrument that he uses to reject his previous identity and be allowed in the community. Gowther does not totally lose his prior identity, but he turns to new allegiances. The text shows that although Gowther is now a complex combination of Christian and Saracen elements, he is firmly identified with a single cultural community, a Christian one. This important theme demonstrates that race in the medieval mind was imagined as composed of various malleable and fluid signifiers. Gowther marries the Emperor's daughter because his racial identity is less determined by biological criteria and defined more according to custom, law, and religion.

Sir Gowther illustrates the ways in which racial boundaries were constructed out of narratives, symbols, and cultural contact. The story is directly about Christian and Saracen relations and the boundaries between the two. The romance demonstrates that these boundaries were malleable, fluid, and continually redrawn. Gowther, in crossing these racial boundaries, shows that medieval people were searching for accommodations to the meanings and perplexities of intercultural life, but giving certain preference to the Christian paradigm.

Notes

1. Norman Housley, *The Later Crusades, 1274–1580* (Oxford: Oxford University Press, 1992), 15–22.
2. Western European concerns include the loss of Acre in 1291, the ensuing stranglehold of trade routes, and the rise of Ottoman forces. The propaganda efforts were helped immeasurably by cultural memory of another event in the late thirteenth century. On December 22, 1299, Ghazan, ruler of the Il-khanid Mongols of Iran, inflicted a crushing defeat on the Mamluk sultan. In a still depressed Europe, news of Ghazan's victory was, perhaps naturally, overoptimistic. As Denis Sinor states, "news was abroad to the effect that Ghazan had conquered the whole of the Holy Land and even Cairo, that he had given back their former holdings to the Templars and the Hospitallers and was to entrust the Dominicans with the guard of the Holy Sepulcher." Ghazan seems to be implicated in this public relations move, for he immediately sent several embassies to the pope, to Philip IV, and Edward I. Ghazan's letters urged the Western European powers to assist him in the overthrow of the Egyptian sultanate. Although the letters do not detail the parceling out of land in the Mongol/European venture, European leaders such as Pope Clement V and James II of Aragon believed that the Mongols would bequeath them Outremer. Not long afterward, "recovery treatises" began to appear with the Mongol assistance theme. Of the more noteworthy, William Adam in 1317 submitted his *De modo Sarracenos extirpandi* to cardinal Raymond William of Farges, the nephew of Pope Clement V. In the carefully detailed memorandum, Adam assigned the Muslims a considerable part in the operation. Also of note, Raymond Étienne in 1332 sent his *Directorium ad passagium faciendum* to Philip VI of France. In the treatise Étienne advocated an assault on Egypt with the help of the Mongols. He concludes with several reasons why the Mongols hate the Mamluks and why the Mongols would ally themselves with the Christians. After the 1330s, however, the Mongol Empire of Persia collapsed into civil war. The possibility of aid from the Mongols also collapsed. The dream was to "continue to haunt the imagination of western potentates even after the decline of the crusades." See Aziz S. Atiya, "The Crusade in the Fourteenth Century," in *A History of the Crusades*, ed. Harry W. Hazard, vol. III (Madison: University

of Wisconsin Press, 1975), 3–26, and Denis Sinor, "The Mongols and Western Europe," in *A History of the Crusades*, ed. Harry W. Hazard, vol. III (Madison: University of Wisconsin Press, 1975), 513–44.

3. Unlike their predecessors, who were usually viewed as eccentric and radical enthusiasts, crusade propagandists of the fourteenth century wrote extremely well thought-out and refined treatises that combined scholarly and literary modes of expression. The propagandists themselves were well-connected advisors to the princes of Europe. In addition, most of the propagandists had spent considerable time studying the enemy, by traveling throughout the regions as merchants, missionaries, or pilgrims, or by being thoroughly versed in the Muslim ways of life, mastering the Arabic tongue, and reading the Koran. As an example, one of the great writers and missionaries of the fourteenth century, Raymond Lull, spearheaded the effort to promote the Crusades. Lull advocated the idea of converting Muslims to Christianity. Like many of his contemporaries, especially those associated with the cloth, Lull saw little benefit in killing the body and the soul therewith. This is not to say that his treatises advocated only pacifist missionary activity; instead, the treatises seemed to promote varied approaches dealing with economic trade embargoes, military activity for control, and missionary programs for conversion. In other examples of writing for the Crusades, Peter DuBois's treatise entitled *De Recuperatione Terre Sancte*, which he wrote at the court of Philip IV and dedicated to Edward I, systematically deals with the legal and administrative problems of organizing a Crusade and governing the newly conquered territory. He further adds that missionary efforts should begin immediately, starting with the teaching of Oriental languages to prospective missionaries. Once the territory is in Christian possession, the old Templar and Hospitaller priories should be utilized for teaching. See Atiya, "The Crusade in the Fourteenth Century," 3–26 and Sinor, "The Mongols and Western Europe," 513–44.
4. *Sir Gowther*, in Maldwyn Mills, ed., *Six Middle English Romances* (London and J. M. Dent and Rutland, VT: Charles E. Tuttle, 1973), 148–68.
5. Criticism on *Sir Gowther* has largely concerned itself with hagiography or the genre and origins of the story. See E. M. Bradstock, "*Sir Gowther*: Secular Hagiography or Hagiographical Romance or Neither?" *AUMLA: Journal of Autralasian Universities Language and Literature Association* 59 (1983): 26–47, and Shirley Marchalonis, "*Sir Gowther*: The Process of Romance," *Chaucer Review* 6 (1981–82): 14–29. For an overview of the criticism and textual sources, see Anne Laskaya and Eve Salisbury, "Introduction to *Sir Gowther*," *The Middle English Breton Lays* (Kalamazoo, MI: Medieval Institute Publications, 1995), 263–72.
6. See Robert I. Burns, "The Significance of the Frontier in the Middle Ages," in *Medieval Frontier Societies*, ed. Robert Bartlett and Angus McKay (Oxford: Clarendon Press, 1989), 307–30.
7. John Block Friedman, *The Monstrous Races in Medieval Art and Thought* (Cambridge: Harvard University Press, 1981), 1.
8. Dorothee Metlitzki notes that "whenever we find it in medieval romance, the marriage of Christian and Saracen as a literary theme seems to be Arabo-Byzantine in origin, and relates in particular to events in Asia Minor, the loca-

tion of Christian provinces nearest to the Muslims." See Dorothee Metlitzki, *The Matter of Araby in Medieval England* (New Haven: Yale University Press, 1977), 137.

9. Ibid., 137.
10. Wolfram von Eschenbach, *Parzival*, trans. Helen M. Mustard and Charles E. Passage (New York: Vintage Books, 1961). For further information on interpreting Feirefiz in terms of courtly and religious character development, see David Blamires, *Characterization and Individuality in Wolfram's Parzival* (Cambridge: Cambridge University Press, 1965), 438–64; see also Albrecht Classen's introduction and David Tinsley's contribution to his volume.
11. Judith Perryman, ed., *The King of Tars, ed. from the Auchinleck MS, Advocates 19.2.1,* Middle English Texts, no. 12 (Heidelberg: Carl Winter, 1980), 42–9.
12. Metlitzki, *The Matter of Araby*, 137–8.
13. Perryman, *The King of Tars*, 42–3.
14. Ibid., 43.
15. Metlitzki, *The Matter of Araby,* 138.
16. Ibid., 137. A surprisingly similar case can also be found in the chapbook *Melusine*, such as in the German version by Thüring von Ringoltingen (1456); see Albrecht Classen, *The German Volksbuch: A Critical History of a Late-Medieval Genre*. Studies in German Language and Literature, 15 (Lewiston, Queenston, and Lampeter: The Edwin Mellen Press, 1995), 141–62.
17. See note 5.
18. See Gloria Allaire, "Portrayal of Muslims in Andrea da Barberino's *Guerrino il Meschino*," in *Medieval Christian Perceptions of Islam*, ed. John Victor Tolan, Garland Medieval Casebooks 10 (New York: Garland, 1996), 243–70.
19. Meredith Jones, "The Conventional Saracen in the Songs of Geste," *Speculum* 17.2 (1942): 201–25.
20. Ibid., 205.
21. For further information see, Marc Bloch, *Feudal Society*, trans. L. A. Manyon (Chicago: University of Chicago Press, 1961), and Joachim Bumke, *Courtly Society: Literature and Society in the High Middle Ages*, trans. Thomas Dunlap (Berkeley: University of California Press, 1991).
22. In much iconography of the period, Saracens are represented as wielding a curved falchion. For two examples, see the mappamundi, Borgia XVI, or the Catalan Map. See J. B. Harley and David Woodward, eds. *The History of Cartography*, vol. 1 (Chicago: University of Chicago Press, 1987).
23. Maldwyn Mills, "*Sir Gowther,*" 215.
24. Bradstock states that the falchion is "an apt weapon for a ferocious persecutor of Christians. Further, like its Saracen creators who had 'their dark origins in the race of Cain' but were always reclaimable through baptism, and like Gowther himself who was born of a devil, this falchion has the potential for good or evil." Bradstock 7, quotation found in Laskaya 300.
25. Robert Bartlett, *The Making of Europe: Conquest, Colonization, and Cultural Change 950–1350* (Princeton: Princeton University Press, 1993), 197.
26. Bartlett, *The Making of Europe*, 197.

27. Friedman, *The Monstrous Races*, 67.
28. Ibid., 67–68.
29. Jones, "The Conventional Saracen," 205.
30. Friedman, *The Monstrous Races*, 65. Also, for a particularly useful discussion on medieval aesthetics concerning color and color symbolism, see Umberto Eco, *Art and Beauty in the Middle Ages*, trans. Hugh Bredin (New Haven: Yale University Press, 1986).
31. Metlitzki, *The Matter of Araby*, 137.
32. Metlitzki notes that both Christians and Muslims saw the importance of inter-religious and binational marriages. The child born of such unions is, as she states, "he who will bring about the harmonious union of two warring peoples." Ibid., 140.

8

Margins in Middle English Romance:

Culture and Characterization in *The Awntyrs off Arthure at the Terne Wathelyne* and *The Wedding of Sir Gawain and Dame Ragnell*

JEAN E. JOST

Marginalization, placing a person in a position of secondary importance, influence, or power because of age, gender, race, social class or status, occupation, or any other criterion, well may be a psychological fact of human existence, but its morality has often been challenged. Even when most fully instantiated, its principles of division, separation, and opposition are seen as suspect, dangerous, illegitimate. Historic factors—war, struggle for survival, economic insecurity, personal or national intimidation—may account for this alienating of those outside one's peer group; unfortunately, the phenomenon of distancing is so widespread as to affect society, inspiring those who record it in literature, psychology, or chronicle to detail its occurrence and ramifications. Within the war-ridden English Middle Ages, militant, even violent history has been the context for its literature. Beleaguered writers finding a hundred years of battle and bloodshed at their very doorstep invariably record conflict and contention, particularly within the romance genre. Here, love and war, unity and division, and the personal and the public battle for primacy coexist in an uneasy truce. Here, marginalization of the "Other," the opposition or the enemy, in a society determining its own identity becomes the focus of the story, the myth of heroes and monsters.

Both *The Awntyrs off Arthure at the Terne Wathelyne* and *The Wedding of Sir Gawain and Dame Ragnell* present the early Arthurian society struggling for identity and authority, contending more consciously with the external threat to coherence than the internal divisions which developed later and festered more slowly over time. Both offer the double focus of personal and political contention between individuals and kingdoms. The first depicts a supernatural ghost and a natural knight (in each of its respective parts) who is the center of the action, the meaning and message of the romance. The second includes a virtuous but supernaturally enchanted hag, her unscrupulous brother partially rehabilitated into chivalric society, a morally ambiguous, unheroic Arthur, and a generous savior in the person of Gawain, himself atypical and extraordinary. Ironically, the romance genre exists to recount insiders' adventures with these Others, who thus take on an inordinately significant role, despite, or even because of their marginalized status.

The Awntyrs off Arthure at the Terne Wathelyne[1] presents several categories of marginalized characters in an exotic romance of coming and going, of residents and visitors, of life and death, of fear and rejoicing. Not all of them are ultimately integrated into society. The romance polarities encompass a wide spectrum of behavior, an effective use of gender, and a fresh presentation of alterity from multiple perspectives. Two arresting women embodying elde and youth, death and life, chastity and peace, lust and discontent are particularly far from the social center. Despite external differences, they offer remarkably consonant admonitions against the prevalent hegemonic aristocratic code; both are unsuccessful in their missives from the margins—they modify no behavior, avert no tragedies, attenuate no immorality, perhaps because of their marginal status.

Arthur's hunt, traditional induction into fairyland, begins in a greenly vegetative world, lush and opulent in color, texture, and sound where "[the] falle of femailes in forest [were] frydde" (7).[2] This forest enclosure sets up artificial boundaries between realities: the castle and the woods, the real and the magic, the natural and the supernatural; these dichotomies prepare for the supernatural realm of blizzard whiteness and tarn blackness, both starkly contrasting the vibrant, natural May morn. As present time surrenders to ghostly time, the rich castle disappears in the wake of forboding "depe delles" (6) and "dymme skuwes" (groves) (53); courtly dukes and dussiperes give way to an unseemly unclad inhuman female form; the "wlonkest in wedes"(9) are replaced by charred remains "[i]n the lyknes of Lucyfere, layetheste in helle" (84)—the hegemonic world has become a topsy-turvy inversion.

Under Gawain's protection, the glittering be-ribboned earthly resident Gaynor "Gaili she glides" (26) on her white mule, a grimly ironic foreshadowing of the supernatural visitor's eerie gliding under her own power. The very presence of Gaynor's mother, a deathly skeletal image of her former glory, admonishes her against lustful tendencies—what Gaynor herself could become. Protected by her blue hood "Of pillour, of palwerke, of perre to pay" (Of fur, rich cloth, of jewels) (19) and "a short cloke þat þe rayne shedes" (20), the well-garbed Gaynor epitomizes the center, the courtly establishment. As Robert J. Gates suggests, "A large part of the effect of the moral warning of this episode in *The Awntyrs* is due to the contrast between the beautiful and richly clad queen and her black and naked mother, disfigured through lust."[3] She is as starkly different from the courtly inhabitants in their gloriously green world as conceptually possible. Her message is as alien as her presence.

The complacent, aristocratic Gaynor begins her journey safely ensconced upon her mule, carefully shrouded from the more dangerous and marginal mystical forest. Here by the green well, "Arthur withe his erles ernestly rides" (33), leading the hunt to its station, and foreshadowing the more significant earnest injunctions of the two immanent outsiders. When the hunting party, "pruddest in palle" (66), pursues the deer, Gawain and Gaynor encounter a magic marvel by the laurel, traditional transformative tree. Gone the fair May morn; "The day wex als dirke / As hit were mydni$_3$t myrke" (75–76). Fighting the "sneterand snawe" (82), they saw a fearful "lau oute of a loghe . . . (flame / light out of a lake) / In the lyknes of Lucyfere, layetheste (most loathsome) in helle" (83–84)—no proud hunter, but a suffering soul reconstituted as a blackened skeleton!

Most spectacularly embodying the figure from the margins is this specter of Gaynor's mother, whose charred bones and snake-haired face preclude identification.

> Bare was þe body and blake to þe bone,
> Al bi-clagged in clay, vncomly cladde . . .
> On þe chef (top) of þe [cholle] (jowl)
> A pade (toad) pikes (pokes) one [hir] polle (head),
> Withe eighen holked (sunk) ful holle,
> That gloed as þe gledes (embers).
>
> (105–06, 114–18)

Round the ember-eyed head circled frightful serpents. Unnatural sights and sounds overwhelm the misplaced courtly pair, clearly out of their domain. As Ralph Hanna points out, "The toads and snakes provide a final macabre touch designed to remind Guenevere and Gawain of the dreadful fate which they are unwittingly preparing for themselves."[4] The weeping, wailing phantom, "$_3$auland and $_3$omerand (howling and lamenting) with many [a lowd $_3$elle]" (yell) (86), neither human nor other, she emerges from the black bog, no verdant green life but a peripheral space of nebulous origin. The ghost's fearsome hollering temporarily evokes a responsive terror and crying in the once-proud, self-satisfied queen who humbly asks Gawain's interpretation of the supernatural events: "[W]hat is þi good rede?" (93). The obtuse Gawain can only offer a natural explanation—an eclipse—a totally unfounded interpretation of the darkness. Their blindness here symbolizes their ongoing moral blindness and inability to understand or heed the supernatural prophecy of "þe grisselist goost þat euer herd I grede" (99).

This ghostly foreigner of nebulous essence and purpose emanates from a mysterious smokey haze in a cacophony of ambiguous wailing. Her demeanor is incomprehensible, undefinable, and alien to the community she seeks. However, the message of her sermon is as clear as a bell:

Mekenesse and mercy, þes arne þe moost,
[Haue] pite one þe poer, þat pleses heuen king;
. . . charite is chef, and þene is chaste.
(250–52)

Her purpose to offer moral instruction, concretely reveal the results of sin, provide appropriate tangible correction, and prophesy future disaster if behavior is not remedied, is as marginal to the court as her non-human appearance. Her prophetic foreboding and ominous message cannot be incorporated into the fabric of the sunny afternoon, the luxuriant lifestyle of her visitors, or the carefree attitude they so blythely embrace. Thus she remains distinctly outside the communal environment, an alien presence the courtly couple would soon forget.

Despite her previously beautiful shape, rosy complexion, and soft skin, now the ghost is "lyk to Lucefere" (165), and though her audience be king or emperor, if their souls are as polluted, "Thus shul ye be" (169). Cursing her body, she yells "I gloppen and I grete!" (I fear and I cry) (91). Her words indicate she was once part of this community, a Christian with face and figure fair and kings in her bloodline. In fact, she was once queen, even "Gretter þene Dame Gaynour" (147), ruling over palaces, parks, ponds, and plows, part of the hegemonic construct. But in her death, something has removed her from its protection, and brought her to this pitiful state outside the human community of her youth. It is sin.

The phantom's purpose is to intrude upon the peaceful complacency of her daughter and her knight-protector Sir Gawain, revealing that sin and its consequent alienation are equally unpalatable, antisocial, extra-communal, and death to the soul. This spiritual marginalization, excommunication from the community of the sanctified, is doubly painful, effecting physical marginalization as well. The phantom specifically warns Gawain of pride and Gaynor of lust, the sins to which each is most vulnerable. Gawain should heed her advice:

. . . hertly take hede while þou are here,
Whanne þou art richest araied and ridest in þi route;
Haue pite one þe poer [whil] þou art of powere,
(171–73)

for once you are dead, it will be too late. He cannot hear the message. When Gawain asks how the army will fare which

. . . defoulene þe folke one fele kinges londes;
And riches ouer reymes with-outene eny righte—
Wynnene worshippe in werre þorghe wightnesse (bravery) of hondes,
(262–64)

the ghost bluntly replies “Your king is to couetous, I warne þe sir kni$_3$te” (265); remember, Fortune’s Wheel will not favor Arthur forever.

Addressing the Queen, the visitor from hell admits “I brake a solempne a-vowe” (205) in conceiving Gaynor, and hence reveals to her: “Þat is luf paramour, listes, and delites, / Þat has me li$_3$te and [lenge] lo$_3$ in a lake” (213–14). Punishment is severe:

> Þer folo me a ferde of fendes of helle,
> Þey hurle me vnhendely, þei harme me in hi$_3$te;
> In bras and in brymstone I brene as a belle.
>
> (186–88)

Retribution is clear; the remedy for those still on earth is equally plain:

> Fonde (Try) to mende thi mys,
> Thou art warned y-wys,
> Beware be my wo!”
>
> (193–95)

The apparition advises: a message from the margins. It remains unheeded. Rather than thoughtfully evaluating her experience, acknowledging unchecked lust as her weakness, and recoiling from it in the future, Gaynor reduces her adventure to its lowest common denominator: she dismissively orders masses for her mother’s soul. Although Gaynor pays for the requested masses, she quickly ignores the import of her mother’s message, the prophetic warnings against lustful behavior. Too easily she forgets this Outsider, her own flesh and blood, as she carries on her courtly life. Hanna may be right in claiming that “Gawain and Guenevere are forced to recognise that life must be lived in the consciousness of the Last Things and that imitation of divine charity and mercy is an imperative even in the aristocratic world of love and war.”[5] But their awareness is short lived, and seems not to have penetrated to the level of conscience. Never do either of them display the least hint of guilt or discomfort. With the grand gesture of ordering masses to be said by others—a denial of personal responsibility—Gaynor is no longer under the sway of the vision, or its injunction against pride and vow-breaking. At odds with the hedonistic court temperament, the prideful mood of the day, the indulgent message of the moment, the luxuriant ethos of the community, and the playful behavior of this refined aristocracy, the phantom arrives and departs—the outsider from hell, unwelcomed, unaccepted, and unheeded.

Heralded by Arthur’s bugle and a breaking of the clouds into glorious sunshine, Part II, however, is no more successful in ensuring moral reformation than its predecessor; in the person of the lovely young citole player announcing Sir Galeron’s arrival, it ushers in as beautiful and charming a form as the ghostly apparition was horrific. This "setoler (citole or cittern player) with a symballe / A lady lufsom" (343–44) provides pleasingly musical sounds, unlike the harsh screaming and screeching of the ghost. If the previous ghostly visitor emerged from the strange black bog, a setting alien to the court, this human visitor arrives during the dinner ritual and within the very court setting familiar to its inhabitants. This fleshly maid, "A lady, lufsom of lote, ledand a kni$_3$te" (344) physically as much a part of the courtly milieu as the ghost was distinct from it nevertheless brings with her a hostile message from another land. If the ghost's country was supernatural, hers is much too real, for as Galeron's representative, she reminds the court that her country has been usurped by the very Arthur who foolishly sits in front of her gazing in star-struck admiration.

Unlike her predecessor who eerily glided into view accompanied by screeching moans, she nobly "rydes vp to þe heghe desse bifor þe rialle, / And halsed Sir Arthur hendly one hi$_3$te" (345–46). Neither her voice nor her visage evokes the distress of the phantom. Rather than shocking sensation or emotion, she would call upon "resone and ri$_3$te" (350) for her champion. She stirs no fear in the heart of her listeners, but inspires Arthur to gush "Welcome, worþely wight . . . whe[þ]ene is þe comli kni$_3$te, / If hit be þi wille?" (361, 363–64). His deference and admiration hospitably welcome the outsider. Just as the narrator carefully articulated the ghastly appearance of the phantom ghost in Part I, so does he precisely describe that of the lovely young maid here:

> Here gide (gown) was glorious and gay, of a gresse grene;
> Here belle (cloak) was of blunket (wool) with birdes ful bolde
> [Botonede with besantes] and bokeled ful bene;
> Here fax (hair) in fyne perre (jewelry) was fretted in folde,
> Contrefelet (ribbons) and kelle (headdress), coloured fulle clene.
> (366–70)

This visage exemplifies everything the phantom was not. The brightness of the court scene contrasts the black and white of the tarn—each domain being dominated by a woman representing its brand of otherworldliness. The maid of Part II, however, is not alone, introducing her cohort the knight to whom she cedes authority; he is as brightly clad as she—his glowing gloves and quilted jackets recall the embers of the ghost's eyes. Conversely, the fair fabrics and ruby-studded accoutrements, personal and military, are as plentiful as the phantom's were scarce. Her naked vulnerability is matched by his well-armored protection. Just as Gawain asked the ghost its mission, so Arthur asks the knight:

> What woldes þou, wee (man), if hit be thi wille?
> Tel me what þou seches and wheþer þou shalle,
> And why þou, sturne one þi stede, stondes so stille.
> (405–07)

Her meek beseeching—relegated to the spiritual domain—is supplanted now by his aggressive demanding—concomitantly fulfilled by militarily rewinning his physical lands.

In Part I, the apparition has arrived to: (1) seek masses for her own soul; (2) stop Gaynor from repeating her mother's adultery and gruesome punishment; (3) dissuade the court from its prideful, extravagant lifestyle; and (4) stop Arthur's acquisitive military forces from usurping other's lands. Hers is an all-encompassing admonition from the spiritual beyond, delivered with shockingly vivid detail in a supernatural setting. The Knight in Part II, on the other hand, arrives from another earthly kindgom, for purely pragmatic reasons, consonant with their shared courtly existence. He boldly remarks:

> Wheþer þou be cayser or king, here I þe be-calle
> Fore to finde me a freke to fight with my fille;
> Fighting to fraist I fonded fro home.
>
> (410–12)

The phantom's purposes were prayerful, moral, and religious, while the emissary and her knight's are military: as a man of action, Sir Galeron wastes no words seeking an adversary. After accusing Arthur of winning his lands "in werre with a wrange [wile](trick) / And geuen hem to Sir Gawayne" (421–22), Galeron demands a rematch, a less gruesome prospect than the ghost's for Gaynor and company. Like her predecessor, the elderly and decrepit ghost, the young maiden's knight reprimands Arthur and his refined court for their immoral conduct—here the illegitimate conquest of his land. While the apparition is an otherworldly Outsider, with an unpalatable message delivered in a fantastic milieu, the visiting couple are this-worldly Outsiders from another royal court delivering an unsought, but ultimately acceptable challenge in terms comprehensible to Gawain and Gaynor.

The military challenge, paralleling the apparition's spiritual one, is direct and clear: Galeron of Galloway and his lady came to find a contender and to win back his lands. Sir Galeron lists the usurped lands, accusing Arthur of unjust military practices: "Þou has wonen hem in werre with a wrange [wile] / And geuen hem to Sir Gawayne—þat my hert grylles" (421–22). The now silent maid is the foil to Gaynor's gregarious mother: (1) in her inverse embodiment incarnate in her beauty and attire; (2) in her extension in the natural world of warfare; and (3) as a parallel moral agent seeking their recalcitrance and repentance. Her cohort, equally an Outsider, reiterates the ghost's warnings on his own terms, similarly chastising Arthur's offensive or illegitimate military ventures. Galeron threatens that Gawain

. . . shal wring his honde[s] and warry þe wyle (curse the trick)
Er he weld (possess) hem, y-wis, [at] myn (v)nwylles.
Bi al þe welth of þe worlde, he shal hem neuer welde,
While I þe hede may bere,
But he wyne hem in were,
Withe a shelde and a spere,
On a faire felde.

(423–29)

The concrete battle Galeron initiates parallels the spiritual one the ghostly phantom offered to Gaynor and Gawain; in both cases, the letter of the law will be fulfilled, but not the spirit. In neither case do the recipients accept the criticism laid against them—pride, adultery, unbridled aggression—and alter their behavior. Both guilty parties superficially resolve the immediate crisis by having masses said or winning the battle, but ignore the larger, far more serious warning. That they do so at this early stage of the Round Table's inception, blithely ignoring their clearly demarcated character flaws, will ultimately threaten its survival. They choose the path of least resistance, ignoring these Outsiders with the inside information necessary to their welfare.

The earthly challenger Sir Galeron is offered courtly accoutrements—embroidered bedcovers and bright tapestries—provisions for his horse, and a dainty feast, while the ghost from hell weeps without comfort in the tarn. In contrast is the situation of

. . . Þat kni$_3$te
And his worþely wi$_3$t,
With riche dayntes di$_3$te,
In siluer so shene.

(452–55)

The only thing shining in the tarn are the phantom's glowing eyes! Since the court well understands Galeron's challenge, however much they dislike it, they concede to his request, which Gawain accepts. Neither Gaynor, Gawain, nor the court are quite so understanding or accepting of the phantom's spiritual challenge to their moral code. Too easily is her warning dismissed, for instead of pondering their experience, "The wise [on swilke wondirs] for-wondred þey were" (334).[6]

At the beginning of the spectacular, far-witnessed battle over Galeron's sovereignty (unlike the frightful, solitary battle over the court's souls in Part I), the knight places his worthy companion in Gaynor's company, a fit pair to judge the contest. The contestants' armor and garb, their steeds "Al in gleterand golde—gay was here gere" (496), Gawain bedecked "withe tranes (devices) and true-loves bitwene" (510) are matter for prideful display, a flaw against which the mournful phantom has but recently warned. Equally unheeded is the court's militarism, ironically highlighted by the narrator's description of the knights' battle: "So jiolile þes gentil iusted one were" (502). As the violent battle continues, the scapegoat appears to be Gawain's horse Grissell, an innocent fatality of the knights' conflict. The fierce fray, with bloodshed on both sides, is pierced by Galeron's companion who "sk(ril)les and sk(ri)kes (shrieks and screams)" (536). Onlookers mourn and "Gaynor gret (cries) for her sake" (597). With both contestants in dire condition, Galeron's lemman

> . . . gretes one Gaynour with gronyng grylle:
> "Lady makeles of mighte,
> Haf mercy one yondre kni$_3$te,
> That is so delfulle di$_3$te (sorrowfully treated)."
>
> (620–23)

So, prompted by this Outsider, Gaynor beseeches Arthur on her knees to stop this bloodbath, to "Make þese knightes accorde" (635). With neither knight conquering, heroism is impossible; if this mutual slaughter continues, the dual deaths of two noble knights are inevitable. A reprieve, inspired by the women's agency, is legitimate for both. After, Arthur commands peace, "Þei held vp here hondes" (663) in submission. Gawain goes further in offering reparation for previous Round Table offenses, but only after he has been soundly trounced in battle: "And to þe rounde table to make repaire— / I shall refeff him in felde in forestes so faire" (684–85). Awareness of the evil of future aggressive attacks totally eludes the man. His is an action in the concrete here-and-now, motivated by specific current advancement, not a theoretical military or moral strategy. Just as the first Outsider's admonition to feed the poor, be humble, faithful, and peaceful was ignored, her demands being met at the most superficial level of trental-saying, so the second Outsider's admonition is satisfied only at the most superficial level of reconciliation: yes, the knights will cease tearing their mutual bodies apart; no, the court will not acknowledge its illegitimate usurpation of all its lands across the empire, but simply surrender the Scottish lands currently at issue with this local defeat. In fact, so insistent upon saving face at all costs, the court coopts Sir Galeron into joining their fair band, thereby swallowing the margin into the center to neutralize its power. As a Knight of the Round Table, Galeron is restricted, preempted from countering the aggressive actions it once condemned. This gives the illusion that Outsiders are only relegated to the margins because they have not been invited to be part of the center.

The romance title appears doubly imprecise: the tarn setting is primarily a feature of the first part, the courtly feast and contest of the second, occurring some distance from the bog; and the adventure is more properly Gaynor's, Gawain's, and Galeron's than Arthur's as the title suggests. That the romance derives its title from Part I may suggest its supernatural tone and didactic message is privileged by the author; Part II's military aggression gaining in moral stature by association.

The function of both Outsiders, the fear-inspiring ghost from another realm of existence and the lovely maid from another courtly realm, is to point out Round Table deficiencies and inspire, through the ugly or the beautiful, a renewed moral conscience. The inside information both Outsiders share is the necessity and the means to alter this prideful, militaristic court's destructive direction. Perhaps those firmly entrenched in its system of self-centered ritual display and aggressive warfare—Gaynor, Gawain, Arthur—lack the distanced vision to perceive the precarious moral precipice on which they teeter. Only dispassionate, uninvolved Outsiders who know, but do not participate in its lavish rites and ceremonies, its acquisitive military posture, possess the perspicuity and wisdom to evaluate the court's moral stance with clarity and objectivity. Only Insiders with humility and readiness to hear might profit from the revelation.

The Awntyrs-author has crafted a concrete world, centered on and accommodating to the privileged court. To it he has sent two marginalized women, unequally received visitors, who present an alternative vision of reality—both of which Arthur and his coterie have long and steadfastly ignored. Ironically, the role of these Outsiders is salvation of the Insiders—if and when the court perceives and follows their admonitions. The real power thus lies in the marginalized region of truth which must be apprehended by the central elite. Unfortunately both natural and supernatural foreigners fail in their mission to instruct and convert, just as—to their peril—the court, in its prideful power, ignores the warning of danger. Rather, Gaynor, Arthur, and the knights blithely and inexorably pursue their quest for lust and luxury, a course calculated to bring doom tumbling down upon the entire Round Table civilization.

The Wedding of Sir Gawain and Dame Ragnell[7] (c. 1450)[8] likewise utilizes supernatural plot elements and characters to create an otherworldly environment and a sense of foreignness. Its female protagonist, the most ostensibly "Other" judging by appearances, is wickedly enchanted, thus dehumanized in appearance; but unlike Gaynor's ghostly mother, she does not return from the afterlife, screech her warning in hideous howls, or threaten her interlocutors with her ghastly specter of death personified. Gromer Somer Jour, on the other hand, remains morally Other, and is less redeemed than his virtuous sister. While Sir Galeron, in *The Awntrys off Arthure at the Terne Wathelyne,* is quite fully reintegrated into Round Table society, Gromer here is partially accepted into its folds, despite his remaining warts. Arthur, representing the expected norm, is shown to be flawed, with Gawain—Other by his virtue—supplanting the head of the realm with his devotion and generosity.

This most famous of two major *Wife of Bath's Tale*[9] analogues marries characters of varying worthiness and respectability: those centrally located within the social and cultural milieu are united to those teetering on the margins. Three of these, alien to the social norms of the poem and the time, represent a type of alterity, highlighting and contrasting the center, the courteous Sir Gawain. This elusive character, whose Celtic manifestation waxes and wanes with the sun, wears an ambiguous reputation through Arthurian lore. His reputation, similarly waxing and waning with the romancer's whim, encompasses both positive and negative traits: polite *chivalrie* as in *Gawain and the Green Knight* and successful military and amatory prowess as in Malory and other Middle English romances on the one hand, and lascivious roguery, as in Sir Bredbettle and hostile aggression as in Malory on the other. The anonymous author of this poem, however, sets Gawain spinning in the dead-center of this universe, the unambiguous lodestar and focal point for the rotating Others.

More intriguing, perhaps, are the unique characters orbiting this "sun-figure," gravitationally and narratively held in some relation to him, but simultaneously carving their own eccentric paths. Surprisingly, those exemplifying the marginal Other are not directly pitted against Gawain, epitome of the traditional hegemonic code; rather, they gain in their alterity—become more distinctly Other—by contrast to the centralized, idealized position of their sun-figure. Together, the path at the Gauvanian center and those paths hovering at the margin intersect in Venn-diagram fashion to establish a total, unique galaxy.

Velma Bourgeois Richmond details a more specific definition of what comprises the "center" within Middle English romance:

> The characteristic knightly hero is a man whose attitudes and ideas are well defined and constant. Whatever the circumstances, he behaves in accordance with a set of values which is both clearly established at the onset and continually reiterated and refined through many trials and adventures. Typically his point of view is not that of the world in which he must live; most frequently it comes from a heightened perception, a sense of value that gives the human beings a dignity and significance which are denied or rejected by the world which challenges him.[10]

That Gawain fits this description and that the Others fail to do so explains their relative positions as center and outsiders.

Most obviously Other, and most fascinating, is "Gromer Somer Joure," a hodgepodge of a man with a hodgepodge of a name having multiple linguistic origins. Donald B. Sands glosses his name this way: "An odd name, suggesting otherworldliness, *gromer* perhaps being from ME *grom* > man = (the Old Norse form is *gromr*), *somer* perhaps being ME *sumer* > summer =

and *jour* suggesting Old French *jour* > day = or > time=."[11] In speaking of Old French romance heroes, William MacBain interestingly points out that "The newcomer to court is in the vast majority of cases perceived by the audience, if not by the 'insiders,' as a superior being. He is generally more handsome, more accomplished, more courtly, and more competent in tourneys and in single combat situations."[12] Sir Gromer seems to defy this stereotype. Perhaps a foreigner in Arthur's kingdom, this "quaint grome"[13] (50) first appears to Arthur alone, not the court, eschewing the comradeship of the whole. He has the effrontery to challenge the mighty king himself, thereby setting himself outside the confraternity of the courteous. Further, initially this armed warrior seeks out the unarmed Arthur, not requesting an encounter, but simply threatening death, defying all courtly or cultural combat rules. Arthur quips, "Shame thou shalt have to slee me in venere / Thou armid and I clothid but in grene, perde" (82–83). Gromer's unrefined speech, bellowing "King" at Arthur, and his uncouth behavior, rudely demanding his royal victim discover "whate wemen love best in feld and town" (91), reinforce this alienation. Although Arthur warns "If thou slee me nowe in this case, / Alle knightes wolle refuse thee in every place" (67–68), the threat of alienation intimidates not this angry man. Perhaps Arthur's unauthoritative demeanor invites such unseemly ridicule, for what king would tolerate a subject ordering him around? Gromer stands apart from the moral, and perhaps natural "human" norm, and Arthur's placating words will not ameliorate his harsh stance.

Even his sister Dame Ragnell thinks ill of him, betraying him by surrendering the secret to his detriment. Learning of his betrayer, he responds characteristically cruelly:

> And she that told thee nowe, Sir Arthoure,
> I pray to God, I maye see her bren on a fire,
> For that was my suster, Dame Ragnelle.
> That old scott [trollop], God geve her shame,
> Elles had I made thee full tame . . .
> Alas, that I evere see this day!
>
> (473–77, 481)

Although the source of Ragnell's deforming enchantment is never revealed, Gromer is certainly not helping to extricate her, or wishing to reverse her enchantment. These sibling-Outsiders remain estranged even from each other, falling on opposite sides of the moral center in helping or loving humanity. Furthermore, always outside the circle, the vindictive, antisocial Gromer never mellows, is converted, surrenders, or reconciles himself to the center, exiting with his curse against Arthur on his lips: despite, or because of Arthur's victory, he sputters ". . . mine enime thou wolt be" (482).

While the author sets Gromer up as the primary Outsider, this stranger nevertheless seems to have a legitimate grievance against Arthur, thus putting the king himself in some moral jeopardy. The poet thereby knocks Arthur off the center which he is expected to inhabit, into the margins of the poem. Although the tale begins in the time of the renowned King Arthur, "curteis and royalle. / Of alle kinges Arture berithe the flowir" (6–7), the king selfishly and arrogantly demands preference at the hunt when a hart is spotted.

Hold you stille, every man,
And I wolle go myself, if I can
With crafte of stalking.
(28–30)

He stalks the animal alone, "half a mile, / And no man withe him went" (38–39), contravening the spirit of camaraderie marking the Round Table confraternity. His attempts are rewarded when "doun the dere tumbled so deron" (43), but still "the king was withe the dere alone" (49)—until Gromer Somer Joure intrudes. Even this stranger notices the aberration, for after threatening Arthur for his acquisitive behavior, he highlights his alienation, inquiring "What sayest thou, king alone?" (60).

Further, Sir Gromer claims Arthur has "me done wrong many a yere . . . Thou hast gevin my landes in certain / With great wrong unto Sir Gawen" (55, 58–59), both military aggression and a severe, ongoing violation of the cultural norms of their bond. Similarly, Galeron of Galloway levels the same claim against Arthur in *The Awntyrs off Arthure at the Terne Wathelyne*, thus uniting the two otherwise dissimilar Outsiders in their criticism of Arthur's land usurpation. In fulfilling his task to discover what women want most, the king finds himself again on questionable moral ground. First, Arthur breaks his oath to tell no living creature of their arrangement by admitting to Gawain "This othe [returning in one year to answer his question] I made unto that knighte, / And that I shold never telle it to no wighte" (173–74). Not only does he break his promise, but he also consciously recounts the fact of his foreswearing, proving his disdain for that oath.

Second, Arthur rehearses his adventure to Gawain in cowardly fashion, seeking comfort and begging for assistance. Rather than bravely accepting his encounter—which in fact is already over—and quietly returning home to fulfill his obligation, he weakly, dependently complains: "Alle this is my drede and fere" (181). His thinly veiled request for assistance is transparent. Third, as Sands points out, "the King is selfish enough to foist his personal onus off on his nephew and best friend,"[14] thus defying his own chivalric code. The responsibility is his, not Gawain's. When Arthur first hears Dame Ragnell's demand, he is shocked, but almost immediately agrees to coerce Gawain in order to save his own life:

"Mary," said the king,"I maye not graunt thee
To make warraunt Sir Gawen to wed thee;
Alle lyethe in him alon.
But and it be so, I wolle do my labour
In saving of my life to make it secour."
(291–95)

Arthur clearly privileges his own bodily salvation over Gawain's happiness, willfully acceding to anything to save his own neck. His courage and autonomy in solving his own problem are sorely lacking. Upon meeting his nephew, Arthur manipulatively evokes his pity by threatening suicide: "Alas, I am in point myself to spille, / For nedely I most be ded" (330–31).

Third, Arthur defies all courtly and tactical protocol in his rude treatment of this powerful woman who can save his life, commenting "So foulle a lady as ye ar nowe one / Sawe I nevere in my life on ground gone" (306–07). A courtly gentleman, much less a king, should display more decorum and politeness, regardless of circumstances or the state of the lady. No role model he. Although Arthur wins the contest to saves his life through Ragnell's aid, he is so appearance-conscious that "The king of her had great shame" (515). Neither gratitude nor gentility modify his embarrassment, reinforcing his moral marginality. Fourth, his blatant betrayal of Gromer and disloyalty to Gawain in disregarding his nephew's life place Arthur outside the accepted scope of socially courteous behavior, and are in fact reiterated in Arthur's childish behavior elsewhere. His unnatural social isolation is magnified in Sir Gromer's specific injunction that he must seek the truth *alone.*

In contrast to Arthur's moral alienation from the norm, Dame Ragnell initially represents physical alterity of the "loathly lady" variety, at first being aesthetically unattractive, officious, and rude at table. Her appearance is frightful because her features appear to be unnatural:

Her face was red, her nose snotid withalle,
Her mouithe wide, her teethe yallow overe alle,
Withe blerid eyen gretter then a balle;
Her mouithe was not to lak;
Her teethe hing overe her lippes;
Her cheekis side as wemens hippes;
A lute she bare upon her back.
Her neck long and therto great;
Her here cloterid on an hepe;
In the sholders she was a yard brode;
Hanging pappis to be an hors lode;
And like a barelle she was made;
And to reherse the foulnesse of that lady,
Ther is no tung may telle, securly;
Of lothinesse y-noughe she had.
(231–45)

She is an Outsider because her countenance and behavior are contrary to those of a human being, to say nothing of a beautiful, demure courtly lady. As Susan Crane notes, the ugly manifestation of her body "instantiate(s) a repulsive aggressive womanhood that supplements the desirable femininity"[15] of which she will later be capable. Here, every feature is as it should not be—face red instead of white, mouth wide instead of narrow, teeth yellow instead of pearly white, eyes bleary instead of clear; her teeth are buck, her cheeks wide, her neck too long, her hair clumped up, her shoulders manly, her shape like a barrel. Her palfrey is incongruous—"an unsemely sighte" (248), for it is inexplicably gay, and beset with beauteous precious stones. As if the audience were yet unconvinced, the narrator continues to expound upon her unlikely visage:

She had two teethe on every side
As boris tuskes, I wolle not hide,
Of lengthe a large handfulle;
The one tusk went up and the other doun;
A mouthe fulle wide and foulle y-grown.
With grey heris many on,
Her lippes laye lumprid (lumped) on her chin;
Neck forsothe on her was none y-seen—
She was a lothly on!

(548–56)

This masterful depiction of the unexpected, and the nearly animal-like appearance, what Crane calls "a 'forshapen' body that is repulsively animal,"[16] replete with three-inch-long fingernails of claw-like dimension, place the lady on the aesthetic and hence social margins. At her marriage, the narrator makes it even more specific: "So foulle a sowe saw nevere man" (597). Continuing her social non-conformity with a bit more aggressive rebellion, she refuses a quiet little marriage, "To be married in the morning erly . . . 'As privaly as we may' " (570–71), demanding

I woll be weddid alle openly . . .
I wolle not to churche tille highe masse time
And in the open halle I wolle dine,
In middis of all the route.

(575, 578–80)

Accentuating her appalling appearance, she dons the most elaborate wedding attire possible "worthe three thousand mark" (592).

At her own wedding, Ragnell lacks manners and good breeding, displaying behavior "not curteis" (602), for after taking the most prominent place on the high dias,

She ete as moche as six that ther wore . . .
Her nailes were long inchis three;
Therwithe she breke her mete ungoodly [indelicately]
Therfore she ete alone.
She ette three capons and also curlues three
And great bake metes she ete up, perde . . .
Ther was no mete cam her before,
But she ete it up lesse and more,
That pratty (completely) foulle dameselle.
(605, 607–11, 613–15)

Her abnormally voracious appetite in inhaling vast quantities of food, her personal hygiene and unappetizing manner of ingestion find her an unnatural outcast, eating alone. As Crane suggests, "Ragnell's demand for a public wedding and her gross display of gluttony at the wedding feast are presumably her own flourishes on the stepmother's transformation of her shape, flourishes that make her grotesque body memorable and meaningful even after her return to beauty."[17] Her alterity thus transcends the moment, permanently subsisting after the abatement of her spell, perhaps because the nature and degree of her deformity so shocks the audience.

Further, she is an Outsider in that she boasts a unique double physical manifestation, both ugly and beautiful, shared by no one else, and a double moral manifestation, initially intransigent but ultimately morally exemplary, or at least socially accommodating. According to Crane, "Dame Ragnell describes the spell she was under as a bodily deformation ('thus was I disformyd') and the narration concurs that breaking the spell restores the lost truth of her body."[18] The audience, surprised by her physical and emotional transformations, can never quite forget her deformed manifestation, however. Because her grotesque body resists erasure, Ragnell can never eradicate her status of "Outsider."

Finally, unlike all the others, she has the answer! This gives her power, authority, and moral stature, for "If I help thee not, thou art but dead" (266); but this power places her beyond, and apart from, the others. Her evaluation of parity and match-making is likewise different: less superficial and externally based than that of the court, who would match two equally attractive young people of the same social class. Her reasoning places her outside the norm: "Forsothe . . . I am no qued (evil person; derived from O.E. cwed, *dung*). / Thou must graunt me a knight to wed" (279–80). Her demand suggests that: "My physical appearance and social class are irrelevant, so since I am such a good person as to save your valuable life, I deserve a goodly knight, in fact the best." Few in the court would have willingly concurred, but Arthur has no choice: "it must be so, or thou art but ded; / Chose nowe, for thou maiste sone lose thine hed" (288–89), she threatens.

Thus Dame Ragnell, of the ugly countenance and name, of the beautiful body and soul, and of the moral conscience and intellect is alienated because she falls on both sides of the norm, but not within it. Not a woman of compromise, she both is, and perceives things as extremes, as bi-polar alternatives, as black and white, cruel and kind, ugly and beautiful. She fails to recognize her fallacy of bifurcation. Compounding her strange beastliness, disposition to excess, and bi-polar view of reality, her mysterious supernatural transformation, from hag to heavenly, ensures her place as Outsider. Even her new visage cannot redeem her status as alien.

The hero of the poem is not the titular head of the realm, but the knight who extricates the king from his dilemma. In fact, even Gawain can be called Other insofar as he is the greatest knight, and here most generous, dissimilar to his peers. Unlike his analogue in the *Wife of Bath's Tale*, in *The Wedding of Sir Gawain and Dame Ragnell* he commits no crime from which to be exonerated. The difference is that his alterity is to be desired, sought, emulated, and conforms to Round Table courtesy. He is the exemplar, and hence the center of moral authority, embodying the courtesy for which the court is so well known. His goodness and excellence exonerate him from the state of alienation, for his is the desired norm. Other characters, in and out of Arthur's court, lack in generosity, kindness, civility, and conformity to prescribed rules for gentility.

Gawain is their very essence, for several reasons. First, he hears Arthur out, not condemning him for breaking his oath of silence to Gromer. Second, in agreeing to share voluntarily Arthur's fate of seeking what women seek most—"I shalle also ride anoder waye"(187)—he accepts responsibility and contributes his time and effort to Arthur's cause. Third, he offers untold reassurances to Arthur, to alleviate his cowardly fear:

> Whatsoevere ye do I hold me paid;
> Hit is good to be spyrring (enquiring);
> Doute you not, lord, ye shalle welle spede;
> Sume of your sawes shalle helpe at nede.
> (220–23)

Fourth, having compiled a book of answers, he rides into court offering his advice and services to Arthur. Furthermore, and most significantly, he readily agrees to marry the foulest lady alive: "I shalle wed her and wed her again, / Thoughe she were a fend, / Thoughe she were as foulle as Belsabub" (343–45). His devotion to his uncle is unconditional. Despite Gawain's personal feelings toward the lady, he immediately and unreservedly complies, for "To save your life, lorde, it were my parte, / Or were I false and a great coward" (351–52). Not only that, but he wishes Arthur not to worry about this traumatic event: "I wolle wed her at whate time ye wolle set; / I pray you make no care" (367–68). Fifth, when Arthur rides off to complete the transaction alone, Gawain would accompany him if possible, saying "My lord, God spede you on your jorney, / I wold I shold nowe ride your way, / For to depart I am right wo"(387–89). He offers his king unconditional devotion, to facilitate anything Arthur needs, saying "Sir, I am redy of that I you highte" (534) just to save Arthur. Even the obstreperous Dame acknowledges Gawain's virtue before her transformation, claiming "For thy sake I wold I were a faire woman, / For thou art of so good wille" (537–38). Gaynor and her ladies wept in pity for the plight of this "true knighte" (540), acknowledging his munificence. Sixth, Gawain's boudoir demeanor is exemplary. When the loathly bride asks "Yet of Arthours sake kisse me at the leste; / I pray you do this at my request" (635–36), Gawain discounts his revulsion and politely replies "I wolle do more / Then for to kisse" (638–39). It is hard to imagine his comrades doing the same.

Gawain's shocked reaction to Ragnell's transformation elicits "A Jhesu! . . . whate are ye?" (644), the lady finds "unkinde"(646). His courteous apology is sincere: "A, lady, I am to blame; / I cry you mercy, my faire madame— / It was not in my mind" (647–49). Seventh, this fair knight freely surrenders his decision, "when will she be fair and when foul?" to his bride:

> But do as ye list nowe, my lady gaye.
> The choise I put in your fist.
> Evin as ye wolle, I put it in your hand,
> Lose me when ye list, for I am bond.
> I put the choise in you.
> Bothe body and goodes, hart, and every dele,
> Is alle your own, for to by and selle.
>
> (677–83)

Ragnell well appreciates that "corteis knighte," exclaiming "Of alle erthly knightes blissid mot thou be / For now am I worshippid" (686–87). Inadvertently, this hero has freed the enchanted maid from her necromantic spell: "She was recovered of that that she was defoilid" (710), for which Ragnell gratefully retorts: "God thank him of his curtesie" (778). In a world less than morally perfect, Gawain's alterity is the ideal, the sought-for mode of action, the moral center.

Ultimately, are these Others in *The Wedding of Sir Gawain and Dame Ragnell* successfully reintegrated into the social orbit from which they spun, or the moral orbit from which they may not have spun? Have they achieved what William MacBain calls "reconciliation with society?"[19] Perhaps the truest answer is a qualified "somewhat." Most significantly, the authorial stance, in finally acknowledging the claims of Gromer Somer Joure, changes from resistance to adulation. Although he remains gruffly mannered and physically alienated, he is somewhat exonerated by the claims of justice and Arthur's aggression. On the other hand, the loathly lady is externally and obviously transformed: her beauty surpasses even Gaynor's. Further, her goodness ultimately overcomes the stigma of ugliness, quite dissipating it, not merely because of her good deeds, but because of others' perception of her. Memory is all that remains. Arthur himself is reintegrated by his generous act of embracing Sir Gromer into his society as much as by discovering the answer to what women want. His potential militarism, however, remains. Ironically, only Gawain, "the center," the core of chivalry remains Other—in that he steadfastly continues as the paragon, the ideal knight of merit and virtue. This strange type of inversion adds yet another dimension to a rich and satisfying poem of persistent amalgamation: the integration of the margins and the center of hegemonic power, authority, and most of all, virtue.

Middle English romance, basing its plot on chivalric *aventure*, inevitably confronts the Other from the outside, and sometimes from the inside. The degrees and types of alienation, physical, moral, or even emotional, present the basis for conflict, as the plot also presents the means for (re)integration. The ghostly phantasm of Gaynor's mother in *The Awntyrs off Arthure at the Terne Wathelyne*, by her nature, cannot be integrated into living society; but her message of warning might have been better heeded. Had Gaynor admitted her sexual vulnerability and its ramifications, so potently embodied by her skeletal mother, perhaps she might have averted tragedy. Had Gawain admitted the Arthurian tendency to military aggression, perhaps the court might have averted internal and external war, and the demise of a once-great society. Had Arthur admitted Galeron's claim to his own lands, perhaps he might have stopped seizing other lands, and heeded his own house more carefully. In *The Wedding of Sir Gawain and Dame Ragnell*, Sir Gromer's message is not fully discounted, although his alien presence never quite reaches the status of "courtly." He may have achieved integration into society with his Round Table admittance, but he fails to rekindle sibling loyalty with his sister Ragnell. On the other hand, the nature and cause of her alienation, enchantment by another, allows efficient reintegration with its dissipation; only a lingering memory of her physical deformities remain, for her virtue displaces its alterity. Gawain alone remains the Other, but in this case, a desirable one, for only he represents the moral and physical ideal toward which the entire court strives. At this inception of the Round Table society, he represents the challenge to virtue; had he become the norm, the center, and not the atypical hero, chivalry might have overcome aggression. The "Death of Arthur" might then have been replaced by "The Birth of a Nation." In the tragedy that ensues, the initial conception of the Other, and the failure to reintegrate that Other into chivalric society, are at the heart of the saga, precipitating its birth, its growth, and its death.

Notes

1. An early version of this segment on *The Awntyrs off Arthure at the Terne Wathelyn* was delivered at the Thirty-Fourth International Conference on Medieval and Renaissance Studies at Kalamazoo, May 1999.
2. Robert J. Gates, ed. *The Awntyrs off Arthure at the Terne Wathelyne: A Critical Edition* (Philadelphia: University of Pennsylvania Press, 1969). Subsequent quotations are taken from this edition. Difficult words are glossed in parentheses; square brackets are the editor's additions.
3. Gates, 25.
4. Ralph Hanna III, ed. *The Awntyrs off Arthure at the Terne Wathelyn* (Manchester: Manchester University Press, 1974), 31.
5. Hanna, 28.
6. Hanna's edition based on the Bodleian Douce 324 reads this line somewhat differently: "The wise of we wedres (weather), forwondred wey were" (p. 79, l. 334); this emphasizes the marvels of the weather rather than the marvels of the phantom emerging from the bog with screeching voice and horrifying vision.
7. An early version of this segment on *The Wedding of Gawain and Dame Ragnell* was delivered at the South Eastern Medieval Association Meeting in Knoxville on October 15, 1999; for the critical edition, see Sands, note 10.
8. The author remains anonymous despite P. J. C. Field's hypothesis (in *Romance and Chronicle: A Study of Malory's Prose Style* [London, 1971]) that the author might be Thomas Malory. I thank Felicia Ackerman for pointing out Field's hypothesis.
9. The other analogue is John Gower's "A Tale of Florent," in the *Confessio Amantis,* ed. Russell A. Peck (New York: Holt, Rinehart and Winston), 1968.
10. Velma Bourgeois Richmond, *The Popularity of the Middle English Romance* (Bowling Green: Bowling Green University Popular Press, 1975), 17. 11. Donald B. Sands, ed. *Middle English Verse Romances* (New York: Holt, Rinehart and Winston, Inc., 1966, rpt. 1988. 1991, 1993, 1997), 327. 12. William A, MacBain, "The Outsider at Court, Or What is So Strange About the Stranger?" *The Court and Cultural Diversity*, ed. Evelyn Mullally and John Thompson (Cambridge: D.S. Brewer, 1997), 364.
13. This and subsequent quotations are taken from the edition by Donald B. Sands.
14. Sands, 324.
15. Susan Crane, *Gender and Romance in Chaucer's Canterbury Tales* (Princeton, NJ: Princeton University Press, 1994), 88.
16. Crane, 151.
17. Crane, 89.
18. Crane, 87.
19. MacBain, 365.

9

Cannibal Diplomacy:

Otherness in the Middle English Text *Richard Coer de Lion*

LEONA F. CORDERY

The text of *Richard Coer de Lion* (*RCL*)[1] falls into the genre of English crusading literature and is an anti-Saracen text of "forced conversion or kill." It soon becomes apparent to both audience and reader, however, that this text contains an element not included in other texts of the same genre:[2] that of cannibalism. Acts perpetrated upon "others" considered to be so inferior that they can be eaten without qualms, like animals. It is my aim to show how cannibalism in *RCL* is presented and justified through two very vivid descriptions of the preparation and eating of Saracens, and that this motif, in the way it is presented in this text, epitomizes intolerance and contempt toward the Saracens as the temporal and spiritual "other."

The text of *RCL* was written at the beginning of the fourteenth century by a French author and was later translated into English. Brunner points out that there are no existing French manuscripts with which to compare this English version, so that no examination of the source material is possible. The French source would probably have included descriptions of cannibalism gleaned either from chronicles or word-of-mouth information as elucidated below.

There is, however, a reference to cannibalism in French chronicles which, I feel, has a direct impact upon this text. The *RCL* text repeatedly refers to the disagreements between and the clear dislike for one another felt by Philip of France and Richard I, the two main Christian protagonists in *RCL*; indeed Philip finally deserts the crusading cause to return to France for what are termed political reasons. Richard clearly has political problems with regard to his French lands at home and his liegelord Philip. So much so, that Richard builds mighty fortresses to defend his lands in France against Philip. One of these fortresses is Chateau Gaillard which lies on the Seine between Rouen and Paris. Its modern construction, design, and defense weaponry made it, in the eyes of contemporary twelfth century experts, invincible.

After Richard's death this fortress became the focal point of Philip II's political objective of taking the rich Duchy of Normandy. Indeed, McGlynn states that this fortress was the "key to Normandy." The English under the rule of King John tried to hold on to this strategically vital fortress. The events of horrific cannibalism during the ensuing siege[3] were recorded in the "Philippidos," a Latin poem by William the Breton who was chaplain to Philip II. Modern descriptions of this historically vital siege are practically limited to the study by Kate Norgate.[4] A clear indication that the topic of cannibalism was considered taboo for later Christian scholars.

The English army defended Gaillard against Philip's army. The castle, in keeping with feudal rules, gave shelter to the surrounding community, which meant that provisions were greatly stretched threatening its effective defense, and ultimately the commander of the fortress, Roger de Lacy, Constable of Chester, was forced to throw out the noncombatants, the "useless mouths." These people were now trapped between the fortress and the French army who, in turn, refused to let them pass. They sought protection under the crags of the castle and had to live off the few animals, grass, herbs, and finally, in an act of desperation, had to resort to cannibalism. As McGlynn points out keeping too many noncombatant mouths to feed inside a garrison had fatal results: lack of food could lead to food riots, a reason why, for example, the Greeks did not permit the Franks to enter their cities during the Second Crusade. This is also the military reason why Richard did in fact have almost three thousand Saracens killed at Acre because he did not have the food to feed them, nor did he have the military manpower to guard them.

The dilemma confronting a garrison commander is highlighted in the example of the sieges of Gaillard and with reference to the *RCL* text, Acre. From a military strategy point of view Richard was seen by the medieval audience to have the legitimate right, indeed it was his military duty, to kill his Saracen prisoners in order to save his own men and uphold the siege. Richard's predicament is clear: he either had to guard his Saracen prisoners or kill them, releasing them would have been akin to suicide. This point is adopted by the author of the text *RCL* but is taken one step further in that the Saracen prisoners at Acre are seen to be a possible source of food. The incorporation of descriptions of cannibal acts perpetrated on the Saracens are clearly thought by both the French and English authors to pander to the tastes of a sensationalist and probably intolerant audience. The material for such tales were gleaned and freely taken and adapted from numerous sources.[5]

The *RCL* text was written about one hundred years after Richard's death, by which time he was already considered an English hero. Richard was in reality hardly able to speak any English, being of French origin, and staying in England only rarely to collect taxes for his military adventures. Indeed, Richard even stated once that if he could sell London he would do so.[6] However, he became the epitome of English chivalry and knighthood, and in literature ranked with such legendary greats as Alexander, Charlemagne, and King Arthur. The Richard legend is furthermore underpinned by the tales of Robin Hood, who showed undying loyalty to this outstanding king.

Whereas crusading texts have what might be called a "happy end" for the Christians, that is the annihilation or conversion of the Saracens, the *RCL* text attempts, at least in part, to present a realistic true historical picture, where Richard is not automatically, as a Christian king, victorious over the enemies of Christendom, but is forced to reach a compromise with Saladin. This indicates that the author is intent on presenting authentic material and not the totally bogus, fantastic descriptions found in numerous other texts of this genre. What is more, the hero, Richard, is seen to be let down by his fellow protagonists: Philip II of France and Leopold of Austria. Whereas Philip is described as being moody, unreliable, and inconsiderate to his army, Richard has true chivalric traits, is generous, and has diplomatic aplomb and kingly virtues.[7] Moreover, Philip, Richard's liege lord in France, informs Richard that when they take Jerusalem it will belong to him and not Richard (*RCL* ll 5898–5899). Richard refuses to accept this and Philip almost throws a childish tantrum with rage, from which he apparently later falls ill and is forced to return home to France.[8] This English translation of a French source functions almost throughout as positive propaganda for the English king Richard.

Indeed, Richard's predicament in the text is similar to that of the classical hero Odysseus or the female character Emaré from the eponymous romance.[9] They have faith in their cause which is marred by those around them; they have to fight alone and have only their faith and inner will to sustain them. Ultimately they have to wait for the intervention of God or the gods, but this dogged perseverance and faith is the stuff of heroes; shining moral examples for the audience.

The English author bases his story, in part, on reliable sources: combining both factual cannibal acts perpetrated by the Franks in the First Crusade, and the predicament of a garrison commander, in this case King Richard, in dealing with the hungry, but from a military point of view "useless" and potentially dangerous noncombatant Saracen prisoners of war. The author is clearly acquainted with the conditions, problems, and military demands faced by a Christian army fighting in the Holy Land, in particular those of the threat of starvation and the need for effective military strategy. Thus there are numerous references by the author to the importance of food for the crusading armies and the fear that food sources could be depleted. The supply lines to the West were often in reality harried by the Arabs, and living off the land proved to be impossible for the large Christian army in agriculturally inhospitable regions. Even the greatest Christian fervor for regaining the Holy Land could only too easily be thwarted by lack of supplies. The importance of food is reflected by the author giving whole food lists (*RCL* ll 1755–1764;

ll 6050–6054) and how food and feasts are important (*RCL* ll 1783–1788) even after battles *(RCL* ll 4634–4652). The author knows of recipes describing how to prepare and cook horses for the Christians dying of hunger at Acre (*RCL* ll 2837–2876). McGlynn points out in his article that finally "hunger conquers all."[10] Thus, the difference between victory and defeat for a crusading army often lay in possessing sufficient provisions.

This permanent food worry facing crusading forces is also supported by the Arab chronicler Ibn al-Athur, who describes the disastrous situation of the Frankish army during the First Crusade: "After conquering Antioch, the Franj (Franks) went without food for twelve days. The nobles devoured their mounts, the poor ate carrion and leaves. . . . Desertions were running at an alarming rate."[11] There are records of the French eating Arabs during the First Crusade after they had taken Ma'arra under the leadership of Bohemund, the chronicler Radulph of Caen reports: "In Ma'arra our troops boiled pagan adults in cooking pots; they impaled children on spits and devoured them grilled."[12] As a result, and probably feeling somewhat guilty, the Frankish commanders tried to explain their actions to the Pope in a letter: "A terrible famine racked the army in Ma'arra, and placed the cruel necessity of feeding itself upon the bodies of the Saracens."[13] The inhabitants of the Ma'arra region saw "fanatical Franj, the Tafurs, roam through the countryside openly proclaiming that they would chew the flesh of Saracens and gathering around their nocturnal camp-fires to devour their prey."[14] Yaghi-Siyan, the emir of Antioch, sends spies into the Frankish camp where they witness how a man is roasted on a spit and eaten, with the threat that a similar fate will befall anyone else caught spying.[15] Indeed, in Turkish epic literature, the Franks are invariably described as "anthropophagi."[16] The Christian chronicler, Albert of Aix states: "Not only did our troops not shrink from eating dead Turks and Saracens; they also ate dogs!"[17] From these reports it becomes clear that cannibalism was considered a feasible and obviously justifiable solution to the food problem.[18] In *RCL* hunger is Richard's justification for eating Saracen. Thus, cannibalism in the *RCL* text has a realistic background.[19] The question, however, of its reception and acceptability by a courtly audience remains.[20]

The author of *RCL* lays great store by giving thorough descriptions of crusading warfare. He goes to great lengths to describe how Richard's army is equipped (*RCL* ll 1648–1665; 2891–2920; 4382– 4412), and also Saladin's army (*RCL* ll 2957–3004) is clearly experienced in battle and siege strategies, and fully aware of the violent and gruesome aspects of battle:

> Manye a kny$_3$te þere loste his armes,
> And manye a stede drow$_3$ his harmes;
> *(RCL* ll 3023–24)

[Many a knight lost his arms in battle, and many a horse its entrails.]

Many an hors hys guttes drow$_3$.
(*RCL* l 5120)

[Many a horse dragged its entrails along.]

or referring to Richard:

Men my$_3$ten see hym wiþ my$_3$te and mayn
Schede þe Sarezynys blood and brayne.
(*RCL* ll 7051–7052)

[One should see him spreading the blood and brains of the Saracens around with all his might and main.]

Most crusading texts contain these types of gory details, but in this particular text the author describes very realistic injuries caused in arm-to-arm combat situations, and emphasizes the fact that the crusades were certainly not courtly tournament affairs, but bloody and gory arenas of slaughter and intolerance[21] consisting of, in part, unreliable and ill-prepared armies.[22] Richard, like his men had great problems coming to terms with the hardships of military life in the Holy Land; a factor that leads to the first instance of cannibalism in the tale. Even Richard, with his privileged position as military leader, is unable to deal with the conditions and falls ill at Acre through the adverse climate and bad food:

Why Kyng Richard so syke lay,
þe resoun j $_3$wo telle may;
Efor þe trauaylle off þe see.
And strong eyr off þat cuntree,
And vnkynde cold and hete,
And mete and drynk þat is nou$_3$t sete
To hys body, þat he þere ffonde,
As he ded here in Yngelonde.
(*RCL* ll 3041–3048)

[I will tell you the reason why King Richard lay there so ill; because of the long sea voyage, the strong air in that country, the cruel cold and heat and the meat and drink there that did not agree with him like in England.]

It is the responsibility of his English retinue, in keeping with feudal rules, that it ensures that he, as their king, must at all costs be restored to health; after all, their lives depend on him: their liege lord. During his illness Richard craves for pork, but there is none to be had (*RCL* ll 3072–3076).[23] Using an old faithful knight of Richard's as a mouthpiece, the author seems to be informed that Saracens taste of pork (*RCL* l 3088 ff.). What is more, the knight, that is, the author, gives a detailed recipe as to how to cook "a Sarezyn $_3$onge and ffat;" (*RCL* l 3088; a Saracen, young and plump):

Jn haste þat þe þeff be slayn,
Openyd, and hys hyde off fflayn,
And soden fful hastyly,
Wiþ powdyr, and wiþ spysory,
And wiþ saffron off good colour.
(*RCL* ll 3089–3093)

[Kill the swine quickly, remove his insides and flay him, then boil him quickly adding flour, spices and saffron to give him a good color.]

The spices of the East are an important ingredient, even for the English taste. What is more, in true good housekeeping manner and for humorous effect, nothing of the Saracen is wasted:

And soupyd off þe broweys a sope,
(*RCL* l 3099)

[And drink a soup made of his head,]

The Saracen here is not treated like a human at all, but like a piece of meat; like a piece of common pork for boiling. He has not been killed in a battle situation, but slaughtered as food. How is this to be interpreted, and is it justifiable? William the Breton in his Siege of Chateau Gaillard chronicle regrets the acts of cannibalism that force people to eat other humans to simply exist.[24] How does the English courtly audience feel toward eating Saracen? As a courtly audience it would be aware that no stone must be left unturned to save the life of the king in his role as feudal lord and temporal leader. Deliberately killing a Christian, and the emphasis here must be on deliberate, means spilling the blood of Christ,[25] and is therefore unacceptable. A Saracen, however, is a nonbeliever, an "other-believer," who cannot go to heaven anyway, cannot be redeemed and has no soul, therefore, justifiably ranks with the animals: thus killing a Saracen deliberately as food to save the life of a Christian king is considered permissible and wholly justifiable.

It is essential for the story line and as information for the audience that Richard finds out that he has eaten Saracen and not pork, because his reaction is all important for an audience aware of the authority he possesses as king and legend who fought for the Christian cause: does he condone or condemn this act? Thus Richard asks the cook whether he can see the head of the pig, an unusual request for a king to a cook. The cook, clearly fearing repercussions, is frightened and says that he no longer has the head to show him.

Richard, however, insists and the cook presents the corpus delicti with perhaps unexpected results, at least for a modern audience:

Hys swarte vys whenne þe kyng seeþ,
Hys blacke berd, and hys whyte teeþ,
Hou hys lyppys grennyd wyde:
"What deuyl is þis?" þe kyng cryde,
And gan to alu$_3$e as he were wood.
(*RCL* ll 3211–3215)

[When King Richard saw his dark face, his black beard and his white teeth and his lips were in a wide grin, he cried out: "What devil is this?" And he began to laugh out loud.]

Richard's reaction tells all; his laughter shows that he finds eating Saracen amusing and thus acceptable, he has no qualms that this act is in any way problematic: neither Richard, nor the old knight seem to have the slightest reservation in eating Saracen. Only the cook is portrayed as being unsure whether this is right and could be seen as functioning like a conscience, questioning the fact that eating Saracen is the same as eating ordinary meat. He plays the role of the devil's advocate; can eating Saracen be acceptable? The conscience of the audience is assuaged by the reactions of Richard and the old knight both of whom are seen to represent the epitome of Christian chivalry.

To a medieval Christian, English audience the gruesome description of the Saracen head reflects the intrinsic "otherness" of the Saracens. However, the blackness of the beard, the awesome appearance of a grinning dead head, is not off-putting to the hardened warrior Richard, who says that Saracen tastes very good, and now that he knows the recipe for preparing Saracens he can feed them to his soldiers in future (*RCL* ll 3216–3225): he will not be faced with the dilemma of so many garrison commanders of not having enough provisions for his army. The author clearly revels in his gruesome description of how Richard enjoys every bit of his Saracen:

Beffore Kyng Rychard karf a kny$_3$te,
He eete ffastere þan he karne my$_3$te.
þe kyng eet þe fflesch, and gnew þe bones,
And drank wel afftyr, for þe nones:
(*RCL* ll 3109–3112)

[A knight did the carving for King Richard, who ate faster than the other could cut. The king ate the meat and gnawed on the bones and afterwards drank well.]

This is a very casual description with a tone of gruesome amusement. Neither is this the only incident of eating Saracen in the text: indeed, the second description is even more detailed and barbaric than the first. In the second instance, Saracens are actually served up to fellow Saracens. The fact that the author presents a second occasion of eating Saracen is a clear indication that he has not been confronted by criticism from the audience after the first incident, which would logically have resulted in his not mentioning the topic again. On the contrary, the anti-Saracen propaganda has probably found favor with the audience, encouraging the author to use the theme once again. This would, of course, be a reflection of the general low esteem and contempt in which the Saracens are held. The author and audience continue to wallow in this attitude when Richard asks his military leaders to describe in lurid detail how they have brutally annihilated the Saracen enemy (*RCL* ll 4655–4705).

Saladin has cut Richard's supply line into Acre. However, Richard holds a trump card: 60,000 Saracen prisoners. (In reality the number was about 3,000 which shows that this crusading text has also succumbed to exaggeration like all other texts of its genre). Richard stipulates clear conditions for their release: one being the return of the Holy Cross. Saladin in turn tries to strike an agreement with Richard by sending old, seasoned emissaries accompanied by animals packed with treasure. Richard says he is not interested, that his riches overshadow those Saladin has offered and he does not need them. However, Richard with the diplomatic manner expected from someone of his rank, invites Saladin's emissaries to stay for dinner. The dish he serves them is noble Saracens. The audience is given a detailed recipe of this dish as personally laid down by Richard:

Kyng Rychard callyd hys marchall stylle,
And in counsayl took hym alone:
"I schal þe telle what þou schalt don.
Priuely goo to þe prisoun,
þe Sarezynes off most renoun,
þat be comen off þe ryhcheste kynne,
Priuely slee hem therin;
And ar þe hedes be of smyten,
Looke euery name be wryten
Vpon a scrowe off parchemyn;
And bere þe hedes to þe kechyn,
And in a cawdroun þou hem caste,
And bydde þe cook spe hem ffaste;
And loke þat he þe her off stryppe,
Off hed, off berd, and eke off lyppe.
Whenne we schol sytte and eete,
Loke þat ȝe nouȝt fforgete

To serue hem herewiþ in þis manere:
Lay euery hed on a platere,
Bryng it hoot forþ al in þyn hand,
Vpward hys vys, þe teeþ grennand;
And loke þey be nothynge rowe!
Hys name faste aboue hys browe,
What he hy$_3$te, and off what kyn born(e).
An hoot hed brynge me beforn;
As j were weel apayde wiþal,
Ete þeroff ry$_3$t faste j schal,
As is were a tendyr chyke,
To se hou þe oþere wyl lyke."

(*RCL* ll 3410–3438)

[King Richard called his marshal secretly and when they were alone gave him instructions: "I will tell you what to do. Go secretly to the prison, kill the most renowned Saracens from the richest families and make sure that before you cut off their heads that their names are written down on a roll of parchment. Then take the heads to the kitchen and throw them into the cauldron. Tell the cook to cook them fast and make sure he removes the hair from their head, beard, and lips. When we sit down and eat don't forget to serve us in the following way: lay every head on a platter, carrying this in your hand, serve it up hot and whole with the faces upwards, with grinning teeth and make sure that they are not raw! Attach every name around the right forehead, give both name and family. Place one of the piping hot heads in front of me, from which I will then eat with satisfaction as if it were a tender chicken, and I will see how the others (the emissaries) like it.]

It is clear in this instance that Richard is very aware of what he is doing, not like the first incident where he is only informed later that he has eaten Saracen. He also treats what must be Saracen knights of noble birth in a most unchivalrous manner. In crusading texts the authors go to great lengths to show the audience that the Saracen knights and noble fighters are worthy adversaries to raise the deeds of prowess performed by the Christians. Here, however, Richard treats the Saracen aristocracy and knighthood with utter derision and contempt.

What is more, Richard is instrumental in the preparation of the Saracens on this occasion. It is very important to Richard that the Saracens served up can be clearly identified by marking them with their names. These are not simply a nameless, faceless enemy, but individuals, Saracen individuals, who should be the valiant adversaries of Christian knights, and who are degraded to becoming merely a meal like any other piece of meat.

Whyl that we may wenden to ffy$_3$t,
And slee þe Sarezynes dounry$_3$t,

Wassche þe fflesch, and roste þe hede;
Wiþ oo Sarezyn j may wel ffede
Wel a nyne, or a ten
Off my goode Crystene-men.
Kyng R. sayd, j you waraunt,
þer is no fflesch so norysschaunt
Vnto an Ynglyssche Cristen-man,
Partryck, plouer, heroun, ne swan,
Cow ne oxe, scheep ne swyn,
As is þe flessche of a Sarezyn:
þere he is ffat, and þerto tendre, . . .
And euery day we scholde eete
Al so manye as we may gete.
Into Yngelonde wol we nou$_3$t gon,
Tyl þay be eeten euerylkon.

(*RCL* ll 3541–3562)

[As long as we continue to fight and kill Saracens, wash the meat and roast the head, I can feed at least 9 or 10 of my good Christian men with one Saracen." King Richard continued: "I assure you no meat is so nourishing for an English Christian man, not partridge, plover, heron or swan, not cow or ox, sheep or pig is as good as the meat of a Saracen who is plump and tender . . . and every day we should eat as much as we can get. We don't want to return to England until we have eaten every one.]

Therefore, according to Richard there is no better food than Saracen for good Christian English soldiers. Saracens are in ample supply and what is more, they are a superior foodstuff when compared to meat or poultry. Indeed, Richard informs Saladin's emissaries that Saracen could easily become the staple diet of his army, and that he is in no rush to return home to England as there are sufficient Saracens to keep the English army supplied for a long period of time.

When Saracens are cooked for the emissaries, Richard wants their heads cut off. This is the punishment of a criminal, not the death of a nobleman in battle. The Saracens are treated like common criminals, this means that they fall outside the chivalric code of values and honor. Once the heads have been cut off they are then to be cooked like pigs' heads: boiled. Reference to them being presented on a platter certainly has no connotations of John the Baptist, with whom the audience would sympathize, but from this description one would rather tend to think of a dressed hog's head at a medieval banquet. The faces of the Saracens have to be shaved. The beard was considered by the Arabs to be a sign of virility.[26] Thus the demand to shave the heads would infer that the Saracens are also robbed of their masculinity, denying them their knightly identity as courtly lovers. The removal of the facial hair could be seen as a necessity before boiling, but black hair is also a reminder to the audience of the association with the devil and the sign of Cain. Their blackness highlights their "otherness" to the Western Christian audience, being a reflection of their interior "blackness."[27]

Richard has a Saracen head served to himself and also to the Saracen emissaries, who quite understandably do not really know what to make of all this. They are aware that they must behave diplomatically correctly toward Richard, however, they also fear for their own lives: perhaps their own fate is looking up at them from a platter. They begin to weep when they see that members of their own families are served up to them. Richard's steward then begins to cut up Richard's Saracen head for him and Richard begins to eat quickly and heartily (RCL l. 3481); naturally the Saracen emissaries think that Richard is mad and the devil's brother.

When the emissaries do not eat, Richard becomes angry and tries to intimidate them into eating the macabre meal. What is more, Richard points out that eating Saracen is frequently on his personal menu plan as an hors d'œuvre:

> Ffrendes, beþ nou$_3$t squoymous,
> þis is þe maner off myn hous,
> To be seruyed ferst, God it woot,
> Wiþ Sarezynes hedes al hoot:
> But $_3$oure maner j ne knewe!
>
> (*RCL* ll 3509–3513)

[Friends, don't be so squeamish, this is a custom in my house, God knows, to be served up a hot Saracen head first. But I don't know your customs!]

However, Richard does not really suppose that Saladin's emissaries will eat their own kin, because after a while he has other "normal" food served to them. This has really been a diplomatic ruse so that the emissaries will return to Saladin and tell him how ferocious and unpredictable he is and relate his savage attitude to Saracens: a tactical move on Richard's part to instill fear into his adversary. Nevertheless, this banquet is an extreme act and demonstrates the utter contempt Richard has for the Saracens, it is highly unlikely that he would have had fellow Christians deliberately killed and prepared in the same way to intimidate a fellow Christian enemy: these are only acceptable tactics for nonbelievers. Richard tells the emissaries that he will send them back safely to Saladin because:

> For j ne wolde, ffor no thyng,
> þat wurd off me in þe world scholde spryng
> I were so euyl off maneres
> For to mysdoo messangeres.
>
> (*RCL* ll 3517–3520)

[Because I would not like, under any circumstances, that the world should say of me that I would have such bad manners as to harm emissaries.]

Although he has killed and eaten Saracen, Richard is clearly aware that he must also be seen to behave in a noble, chivalric manner as a true diplomat: an example to all rulers. This is all very tongue-in-cheek on the part of the author: on the one hand Richard eats Saracen noblemen, but on the other is seen to be a stickler for diplomatic behavior. The emissaries return to Saladin and tell him:

Kyng R was a no(ble)man,
(*RCL* l 3566)

One would expect them to be horrified or angry, instead they obviously consider themselves to be inferior and do not seem surprised that Saracens have been reduced to the level of animals.[28] It is clearly important to the author to point out to his audience that the Saracens do not even really take themselves seriously, that Richard is a noble king, and that such a small detail of eating Saracen and serving it up to Saracen emissaries is but a minor quibble. In the text the Saracens seem to accept themselves as being inferior, doubting their own value: they have very low self-esteem. What is more, to add insult to injury and to highlight the gruesome details for the audience once again, the author has the emissaries retell the gory details to Saladin: an encore for the Christian audience.

The author, aware that this is a crusading text reminds the audience of the looks and aims of a true crusading knight epitomized in Richard. The author does this by describing Richard as donning several different disguises at the beginning of the text to test his knights and followers. One of these is crusading garb to draw the attention of the audience to the aims of crusading against the nonbelievers:

Vpon his shulder a crosse rede,
That betokeneth Goddes dede
With hys ennemyes for to fyght,
To wynne the cross yf that he myght.
Vpon his heed a doue whyte –
Sygnyfycacyoun of the holy spryte –
To be bold to wynne the pryse.
And dystroye Goddes enemyes.
(*RCL* ll 389–396)

[On his shoulder was a red cross, the meaning of this being that he should fight the enemies of Christ, in order to win back the cross, if he could. On his head was a white dove, the sign of the Holy Spirit, to help him be brave and win the prize and destroy God's enemies.]

The aims are clear: to either convert or kill all Saracens. What is more, this aim is blessed by the Holy Spirit. Richard's armor is the sign that he must fight against the Saracens as a temporal leader,[29] the dove as the sign of the Spirit, is a sign that he is also fighting in the name of the spiritual Christian leader, the pope. Thus Richard has been given both temporal and spiritual powers. The dove is certainly not to be interpreted as a sign of peace, it is a sign that this war against the Saracen nonbelievers is the wish of God, and that the crusaders are guided by the Spirit of God. The Holy Places must once more be in the possession of the Christians (*RCL* ll, 1269–1234), and Richard will rescue the faith from the infidels.

Saladin and Richard are seen to vie for the military upper hand (*RCL* ll 3699–3778). However, Saladin has extensive lands and possessions and is, therefore, in a position to offer Richard titles, even the lands of India as far as those of Preester John.[30] Richard, as a good Christian, refuses the offer[31] saying:

J wolde nought lese my lordes loue
For alle the londes vnder heuene aboue.
(*RCL* ll 3727–3728)

[I would not lose the love of my lord, not for all the lands under heaven.]

thus underlining the fact that his belief in God is more important than lands or titles. (This comment is a definite stab at both the Saracens whose faith is often seen to be weak in crusading texts, but also once again at Philip, who is depicted as being easily bribable, and Richard's brother John who is repeatedly trying to rob Richard of his crown back home in England). Richard immediately counters Saladin's offer:

And but j have þe croys to morwe,
His men schole dye wiþ mekyl sorwe.
(*RCL* ll 3729–3730)

[And if I don't have the cross tomorrow, his men will die with great sorrow.]

Saladin does not comply with Richard's demands. When this becomes clear Richard has the 60,000 Saracen prisoners in Acre (he leaves 20 for ransom purposes) taken out of the city with their hands tied behind their backs like criminals and has them beheaded.[32] This bloody scene is then followed by:

Merye is in þe tyme of May
Whenne foules synge in here lay
(*RCL* ll 3759–3771)

[Merry is the time of May, when birds sing their songs.]

This description possibly marks a major pause in the text. However, after such a bloody scene to simply go back to the life of the courtly idyll would, of course, serve as a further highlighting of the contempt held for the Saracens: the point would not be lost on the audience that the killing of 60,000 Saracens is of no real import.

The author underpins the prejudices and intolerance toward the Saracens in the text with divine intervention. Whatever happens to the Saracens is the wish of God. An example is provided when Saladin challenges Richard to a tournament saying that he will procure the horses. Saladin has the horses put under a black magic spell so that Richard can never win. The aim being that in this way Richard's legendary chivalric prowess will be questioned and Saladin will be the victor. However, Saracen magic is not effective against the Christian God: an angel warns Richard who ultimately turns out to be the victor (*RCL* ll 5481–5602).

The merciless destruction of the Saracens is seen to be the wish of God when an angel from heaven tells Richard what to do with the prisoners at Acre:

> Seynyours, tuez, tuese,
> Spares hem nou₃t, behediþ þese!"
> Kyng Richard herde þe angelys voys,
> And þankyd God and þe holy croys.
> þey were behedyd hastelyke,
> And caste into a ffoul dyke.
>
> (*RCL* ll 3749–3754)

> ["Sirs, kill, kill them, don't spare them, behead them!" King Richard heard the voice of the angel and thanked God and the Holy Cross. They were quickly beheaded and cast into a foul ditch.]

The Saracens are not even worthy of a burial, they are once again treated with utter contempt. And this with the God's blessing.

According to William of Malmesbury, it was accepted in the Middle Ages that the world was divided into two: the Christian empire and the empire of the "others." The comparably small empire of the Christians was confronted with the formidable empire of the nonbelievers, who posed both a permanent spiritual and temporal threat to Christendom. In crusading texts these nonbelievers worshipped the heathen gods Termagaunt, Apolyn, and Mahount (or a variety thereof), and when nonbelievers died their souls went straight to Satan (*RCL* l 7054). The soul as the Christians' most valuable asset had to be saved from these pagans, thus these "Goddes wytherwynes" (*RCL* l 6062; Enemies of God) had to be converted to the Christian faith or killed. As Richard himself puts it when advising Philip of France, for strategic reasons, to get himself a strong military foothold in a Saracen town or city:

Spares non þat is þerjinne.
Sles hem alle, and takes here good,
But ₃yff þey graunte wiþ nylde mood
To be baptyzed in ffount-ston:
Elles on lyue loke ₃e lete non!
(*RCL* ll 3966–3970)

[Spare none in the city. Kill them all and take their goods if they are not prepared to be baptized through kindly methods. Don't leave any of them alive.]

Later he chastises Philip for not having killed all the heathen Saracens saying that by not having done away with them he has done God a great falsehood (*RCL* ll 4693–94), after all they are "dogges off fals ffay" (*RCL* l 4338; dogs of false faith), which is why Thomas Multon "slou₃ euery modyrsone" (*RCL* l 4308 and the same attitude *RCL* ll 4597–4600; slew every mother's son). Fulk Doyly, for instance, brags to Philip what he has done at the city of Ebedy:

What scholde dogges doo but dye?
Al þe fflok hoppyd hedeless;
In þis manere j made pes,
Destroyyd alle þe heþene blood.
(*RCL* ll 4672– 4675)

[What should dogs do but die? The entire people ran around headless; in this way I made peace: I destroyed all the heathen hounds.]

Once again after this battle the Saracens are not buried, they are not worth the effort, the Christian army has "better things to do": "No man wolde þo dogges berye; Crystene-men resten, and maden hem Mer(ye) (*RCL* ll 4585–4586; no man wanted to bury the dogs. The Christians rested and enjoyed themselves) or what Sir John Doyly says over a dead Saracen knight: "Dogge þer þou ly; And reste þe þere tyl domysday" (*RCL* ll 4546–4547; Lie there, you dog, and stay there till domesday). Indeed, Richard considers it an actual bonus for his men when they are all able to take the head of a Saracen as a trophy (*RCL* ll 5649–5651). Richard says that all this has been made possible by his own temporal help and God's spiritual support (*RCL* l 5652). From this one can assume that God and Richard are fighting as a team.

Before leaving England Richard has a special axe made to kill Saracens: "To breke therwith Sarasyns bones" (*RCL* l 2212; to break the Saracen bones with). An axe would not really be considered a courtly weapon to be used in chivalric combat. An axe would be used to kill animals or behead criminals; it is not a weapon with which to kill knights. Indeed, the object of using the axe is to "schede þe Sarezynys blood and brayn" (*RCL* l 7052; to shed Saracen blood and brains).[33] Thus, in this text one does not bother to fight the Saracens in a chivalric way that is, using a sword, the Saracens are only worthy of being hacked down by axes.

In crusading literature it is the aim of the Christian knights to behave in a courtly fashion, using courtly weapons. Thus the Richard text does not fit into this framework. In other crusading texts it is the chivalrously dubious Saracen giants who resort to using brute force and axes to kill their enemies, not the courtly Christian knights. In this text Richard goes "Saracen bashing," to achieve the annihilation of the nonbelievers. He does not consider the Saracens to be on an equal chivalric footing which means that fighting them does not even bring Christian knights honor. They are so inferior that they can even be used as food: their inferiority is based on the fact that they are different physically and spiritually.[34] The Saracens are shown to be frightened of Richard in his wild and irrational behavior and think he is a demon from hell:

þe Sarezynes, as j ȝou telle,
Sayden he was a deuyl off helle;
And onyr þe bord loþen he,
And drownyd hemself in þe see.
(*RCL* ll 2579–2582)

[The Saracens, I tell you, said he was the devil from hell, and they jumped overboard and drowned themselves in the sea.]

It is in fact historically recorded that when Pope Honorius III appealed to Henry III to participate in a crusade, he stressed the memory of Richard I, expressing the belief that his very name still struck terror in the minds of the Saracens.[35] However, although Richard treats the Saracen enemy with contempt, the author makes sure that he also maintains the diplomatic behavior essential for a good king in the eyes of the audience. As mentioned above, the author is repeatedly walking a tightrope showing Richard as an exemplary diplomat but also as someone who eats his enemy. This explains why it is not really that surprising when Richard goes around hacking Saracens to death and eating them. Nevertheless, at the same time he refuses to take up the offer of a Saracen traitor to kill Saracens while they are asleep:

I am no traytor, tak þou kepe,
To sloo men whyl þey slepe.
(*RCL* ll 6449–6450)

[I am no traitor, mark you, who kills people while they are asleep.]

Richard's chivalric and diplomatic behavior is compared to the negative behavior of his fellow Christian rulers (*RCL* ll 1504–1546; 2115–2162; 2365–2388; 3813 ff). This implies that Richard is seen as a hero in the eyes of the audience: a king of great noblesse and character, thus what he does is right.

Richard's diplomatic aplomb comes to the fore at the end of the text, where he has been deserted by his allies, who have put temporal gains above spiritual ones and he is unable to take Jerusalem alone. He has to swallow his pride, meet with the Saracen Saladin, and despite his weak military position, is able to secure free access to the Holy Places where the Christians can worship in peace and without fear (*RCL* ll 6890–7202). It would seem surprising that Saladin, with his military advantage, is prepared to make peace at all with someone who has killed and eaten his fellow countrymen. We, as the audience, here possibly once again see that the Saracens are portrayed as suffering from low esteem: they themselves feel inferior which is why they are prepared to compromise. However, this could also be a reference to Saladin's wisdom and beneficence which was also legendary in the West.[36]

The cannibal passages in the *Richard Coer de Lion* text encapsulate the most negative Saracen propaganda in any crusading poem. The text does not only describe the slaughter of the infidels but portrays them in their "otherness" as being so contemptible and inferior that they are no more than soulless animals fit to be served as food. This text clearly supports and encourages the audience in its xenophobic opinion of the Saracen "other."

Notes

1. Karl Brunner, *Der mittelenglische Versroman Über Richard Löwenherz,* (Vienna and Leipzig: Wilhelm Braumüller, 1913).
2. Information taken from a text corpus of thirty-six Middle English crusading texts which are in the process of publication. Leona F. Cordery, *The Picture of the Saracens in Middle English Literature.*
3. My sincere thanks go to John Peltier for pointing out this information.
4. Sean MyGlynn, "Useless Mouths," *History Today*, June 1988, taken from Kate Norgate, *England Under the Angevin Kings*, vol II. Burt Franklin Research & Source Works Series 351. Selected Essays in History, Economics, and Social Science 76 (1887; New York: B. Franklin, 1965).
5. As there was no problem with copyright in the Middle Ages, the free use of sources as authority was not only possible, but actively encouraged. See Carl Lofmark in *The Authority of the Source in Middle High German Narrative Poetry*. Bithell Series of Dissertations (London: Institute of Germanic Studies, University of London, 1981).
6. "I would sell London if I could find a buyer rich enough to buy it." Taken from John Gillingham, *The Life and Times of Richard I* (London: Weidenfeld and Nicolson and Book Club Associates, 1973), 56.

7. Richard is repeatedly chastising Philip in the text for not treating his men correctly.
8. It is clear, however, that there are also political overtones here, that Philip simply wishes to take advantage of Richard's absence in Europe, in the same way as Richard's brother John tries to do in England.
9. *The Romance of Emaré*, ed. Edith Rickert. Early English Text Society, ES 99 (Oxford: Oxford University Press, 1908 for 1958).
10. Sean McGlynn, "Useless Mouths," June 1998.
11. Amin Maalouf, The Crusades Through Arab Eyes, trans. Jon Rothschild (New York: Al Saqi Books, 1984), 34.
12. Ibid., 39.
13. Ibid., 39.
14. Ibid., 39.
15. Ibid., 29.
16. Ibid., 93.
17. Ibid., 39.
18. A similar modern dilemma has confronted plane crash victims where it is questionable whether cannibalism is justifiable.
19. In her article "The Romance of England: *Richard Coer de Lyon*, Saracens, Jews, and the Politics of Race and Nation," in *The Postcolonial Middle Ages*, ed. Jeffrey Jerome Cohen. The New Middle Ages (New York: St Martin's Press, 2000), Geraldine Heng highlights the amusing joke elements of the *RCL* text, referring to Richard's laughter on finding out he has eaten Saracen, and the general lightheartedness with which the text deals with this subject. However, these cannibalistic descriptions reflect the view held by numerous Eastern Christians who were disgusted by the vulgar, brutish, and uncivilized behavior of the Western European rabble.
20. Maalouf mentions the fact that the cannibalism that took place during the First Crusade was mentioned in European histories up to the nineteenth century when for reasons of missionary ideas this information was omitted. Maalouf, *The Crusades Through Arab Eyes*, 270.
21. The bloody pogroms exercised on the Jews en route to the Holy Land as a "warm up" for the real thing also spring to mind here.
22. In many cases the poor, who were not able to survive at home, decided out of sheer need to join the crusading forces. Adriaan H. Bredero, *Christendom and Christianity in the Middle Ages, The Relations between Religion, Church and Society*, trans. Reinder Bruinsma, (Grand Rapids, MI: W.B. Eerdmans, 1994) 80–86; 105–107. The ill-preparation was the reason why so many waves of crusaders were unsuccessful.
23. As neither Muslims nor Jews eat pork there would not be many pigs kept for purposes of consumption. This, however, also gives us an insight into the eating habits of the English at that time. It is also interesting to note that one of the tests employed by the Spanish Inquisition in the hunt for heretics was whether they ate pork or not, if they did not, they were doomed.
24. Sean McGlynn, "Useless Mouths," June 1998.
25. Bredero, *Christendom and Christianity in the Middle Ages*, 107.

26. Orientals were often amused and sometimes even scandalized by the clean-shaven faces of most of the Frankish knights. Maalouf, *The Crusades Through Arab Eyes*, 274.
27. As the King Horn text puts it: "Sarezyns lope and blake" (King Horn l. 1414), *King Horn*, ed. George H. Knight, Early English Text Society, OS 14 (Oxford: Oxford University Press, 1962).
28. One frequently finds in crusading texts that the Saracens quickly lose faith in the efficacy of their gods; this is a sign of the alleged superiority of the Christian faith.
29. The further motive must also be the rescue and strengthening of the economically desirable Kingdom of Jerusalem.
30. At this time the lands of the East were thought to go as far as China, Seres, where the people were so near to the edge of the world that they could touch the morning star, "þwerldes ende" (Alis. l. 36) in *Kyng Alisaunder*, ed. G.V. Smithers, Early English Text Society, OS 227, vol. I (Oxford: Oxford University Press, 1952 for 1961).
31. The text gives one the definite impression that Philip of France would not have refused the offer.
32. This conjures up memories of the First Crusade when the Christian forces entered Jerusalem and slaughtered all Muslims and Jews in the city. The chronicles tell us that the Christian army stood ankle-deep in blood.
33. In *Sir Ferumbras*, for example, the Saracen giant Alagalofre uses an axe in battle (S.F. ll. 4431–36) in *Sir Ferumbras*, ed. Sidney J. Herrtage, Early English Text Society, ES 34 (1879; Oxford: Oxford University Press, 1966).
34. As mentioned before, in most crusading texts Saracen knights are portrayed as being equal in prowess, otherwise battle would not bring the Christian knight honor. Some Saracen knights are even described as being as handsome as Christian knights so that in the event of their conversion to Christianity their appearance is in keeping with that of an ideal Christian knight. In this way integration into the Christian courtly circle is readily given. *The Lyf of the Noble and Crysten Prynce, Charles the Grete*, ed. Sidney J.H. Herrtage, Early English Text Society, ES 36, 37 (1881; Oxford: Oxford University Press 1967).
35. Simon Lloyd, *English Society and the Crusades 1216–1307*, Oxford Historical Monographs (Oxford: Clarendon Press, 1988), 33.
36. Mustafa Maher, "Saladin. Salaheddin," *Herrscher, Helden, Heilige*, ed. Ulrich Müller, Werner Wunderlich, with the assistance of Lotte Gaebel. Mittelalter-Mythen 1 (St. Gallen: UVK, 1996), 157–72.

10

Anselm Turmeda:

The Visionary Humanism of a Muslim Convert and Catalan Prophet

LOURDES MARÍA ALVAREZ

Medieval religious polemic often made use of the confessional discourse of converts to lend factual credibility and emotional weight to the doctrinal arguments being made against the convert's former religion. Petrus Alfonsi, a twelfth-century Jewish convert to Christianity, styled his *Dialogi contra Iudaeos* as a disputation between Moses, his erstwhile Jewish self, and the new Christian Petrus.[1] Nicholas Donin, a former Jew, argued for the Christian side in the Paris Disputation of 1240. Pablo Christiani, another *converso*, debated Nahmanides in the Barcelona Disputation of 1263.[2] The former Joshua Halorqui, baptized Jerónimo de Santa Fe, took on his former coreligionists in the Tortosa Disputations of 1413–14, and authored the anti-Jewish tract *Hebraeomastix*.[3] In the case of these and other *conversos* who participated in anti-Jewish polemic, the disputant's command of Hebrew and knowledge of Talmud—and often his familiarity with Arabic culture and science—were the crucial rhetorical underpinnings for attacks on Judaism and Islam. The persuasive power of the theological argument was bolstered not only by the convert's "insider" knowledge of his former religion, but also the personal account of conversion, the confession of his earlier sin and error.

On a discursive level these texts wed the penitential aspect of public confession and renunciation of sin with claims of missionizing zeal. They were addressed to the potential convert, and in accordance with polemical tradition dating back to early Christianity, took as their premise articles of faith, scripture, or natural science accepted by those "still in darkness." Yet, as we see in Alfonsi's (Latin-language) text, addressing potential proselytes was in some cases little more than a superficial rhetorical conceit. The knowledge of the convert functions as a confirmation of the truth of the adopted religion—for those who are already believers—and highlights the willfulness of those *infidels* who chose to persist in their ignorance, thus reinforcing the boundaries between Self and Other, and ultimately contributing to the logic that drove the expulsions of "foreign" religious elements.

At the same time, the sincerity of the convert is always subject to suspicion and interrogation. This was especially true in the context of the medieval competition between the three monotheistic faiths; a change in religious affiliation was far more than a private matter of belief. Almost universally, there were substantial material incentives for embracing the creed of the ruling elite. Tax policies are but one example. Islamic polities levied a poll-tax (*jizya*) on non-Muslims; as conversions increased, the amount assessed on the remaining taxpayers increased, hastening the pace of conversion.[4] In al-Andalus, the numbers of Christians adopting Islam prompted concern among the authorities about the weakening of the tax base, and further inflamed resentment toward the *muwallads*, the descendants of recent converts to Islam.[5] Political and religious authorities commonly offered myriad inducements for the conversion of prominent figures in minority religious groups; incentives included important political or religious posts and sometimes marriage into powerful families. Public figures—whose conversions might easily be attributed to opportunism—undoubtedly felt the greatest pressure to justify their actions before the community they adopted and the one that they spurned. Under the shadow of suspicion, converts such as Alfonsi, Donin, Cristiani, and others redoubled their attacks on their former religion trying to separate themselves in a definitive way from their past beliefs.

Yet not all converts succumbed easily to the cycle of recrimination and blame (directed at their former coreligionists) demanded of them in the climate of the ever-hardening line separating religious communities in the late Middle Ages. Those who flirted with the boundaries, or even subverted and destabilized them would become the focus of competing claims, accusations, and propagandistic efforts aimed at either completely discrediting them or resolutely placing them on one side or another of the border.

Because first-person accounts of medieval Christian-Muslim conversions are relatively rare, the writings of the fourteenth-century Majorcan Muslim convert Anselm Turmeda provide a valuable counterpoint to the more numerous histories of *conversos,* or new Christians of Jewish background. His interest to students of the medieval period is compounded by the fact that in addition to his Arabic-language autobiography and anti-Christian polemic, he also wrote extensively for a Christian audience in his native Catalan language, earning a place of honor in the annals of Catalonian literary history. These two bodies of texts—those directed to Muslims and those for Christians—offer the reader a fascinating glimpse of life on the border between cultures, languages, and religions. Whether the different vantage points in the texts are seen as inherently contradictory—and perhaps duplicitous—or as products of a dynamic intercultural textuality, they provide fertile ground for exploring the symbolic import of the liminal figure of the apostate/convert in the context of inter-religious competition in the medieval and early modern periods, and the regional and linguistic rivalries dividing the Iberian Peninsula. Moreover, the discrepant modern readings of this controversial figure have reflected the larger contest in Spain between Castilian centralism and "particularisms" or regional nationalist movements, as well as the inner dynamics of a modern Catalan nationalist discourse strongly rooted in myths about the medieval past and foundational literary figures such as Turmeda.

No one is quite sure why sometime late in the fourteenth century, Anselm Turmeda, a Franciscan friar born in Majorca, apparently a confessor to the Aragonese royal family, traveled to Tunis, renounced his holy orders and Christian faith, and converted to Islam.[7] The explanations for his flight range from a desire to escape dangerous political entanglements to his resentment of the discipline—or the hypocrisy—of his religious order. Several modern commentators have speculated that he experienced a personal crisis of faith provoked by the Averroistic doctrines then in vogue in the universities of Paris and Bologna.[8] A Tunisian scholar—who, unlike his Western counterparts sees no reason to doubt Turmeda's sincerity—suggests that he might have been a descendant of conquered Muslims, and thus his conversion constituted simply the recuperation of his ancestral faith.[9] No matter the initial reason or reasons for his move—which no doubt for Turmeda himself were subject to the revision of memory's backward glances—his new life in Tunis presents even more unanswered questions. Known there as ᶜAbd Allah al-Tarjumān al-Mayurqī,[10] he was a prominent figure in the court of the sultan Abū al-ᶜAbbâs Aḥmad and later in that of his son, Abū Fāris ᶜAbd al-ᶜAzzīz. Yet despite his new political and religious allegiances, he remained involved in events in Europe, corresponding with monarchs and popes, apparently requesting—and later rejecting—several safe-conducts for his return. He wrote several works in Catalan which earned him enduring fame: the *Llibre de bons amonestaments* [*Book of Good Precepts*] (1396),[11] a widely circulated collection of aphorisms; the *Cobles del regne de Mallorques* [*Verses on the Kingdom of Majorca*], which was, among other things, an exile's lament for the island of his birth; a series of esoteric political prophecies;[12] and his masterwork, a wide-ranging allegorical disputation between man and animal, *La disputa de l'Ase* [*The Debate of the Ass*] (1417–18).[13]

Long after his death, his biography would be embellished with tales of Christian martyrdom. According to the account published by Baltasar Sayol (1694),[14] a dream led him to repent his grievous error; he proceeded to publicly repudiate Islam and died at the hands of an angry mob. Jaime Coll, in his 1738 "Vida y martirio de el muy reverendo Padre Fray Turmeda" ["Life and martyrdom of the most reverend Father Friar Turmeda"],[15] asserted that the Majorcan was held captive in Tunis against his will. The human drama is accentuated in that version, for after saving Turmeda from the mob, it was the king himself who executed his former protégé when the latter rejected the sumptuous gifts he was offered to reconsider his turnabout. The myths surrounding the reverend friar unraveled late in the nineteenth century when J. Spiro published a French translation of *Tuḥfat al-adīb fī radd ᶜalā ahl al-ṣalīb* [*The Gift of the Writer to Refute the Partisans of the Cross*] (1420),[16] an autobiographical account of the conversion to Islam of ᶜAbd Allah ibn ᶜAbd Allah el Dragoman followed by an anti-Christian polemic. Although Spiro was unaware that the Majorcan-born ᶜAbd Allah was Turmeda, it was not long before Rubió i Lluch and Menéndez Pelayo made the association.[17]

The attribution of this Arabic-language, anti-Christian polemic to the ex-Franciscan foregrounded the issue of his personal integrity, provoking questions about his sincerity, and condemnations and defenses of his apparent duplicity. The controversy increased when the Spanish Arabist Asín Palacios' accused Turmeda of plagiarizing an Arabic source in composing the *Disputa de l'Ase*.[18] For many critics the plagiarism charge only added further confirmation of his deviousness. Yet, Turmeda's writing seems to have always been read through a moralizing lens; the defenders of his saintliness were all too ready to overlook some of his more heterodox pronouncements or his cynical jibes at the Church. It might be said that Turmeda invites such scrutiny by making himself a central—if not *the* central—character in his own works, by so consistently referring to his life story and relying on it as a source of authority.

Turmeda's liminality and ambiguous confessional status give his Catalan-language works the oracular power of a voice that is at once distant and clear, a voice inspired by a vision that transcends distance. This is perhaps most obvious in the series of esoteric prophetic texts he wrote treating matters political and ecclesiastical both in Majorca and more broadly throughout Europe. If, as Turmeda himself observes, no man is a prophet in his own land, Anselm Turmeda becomes a prophet in his native land—and his adopted country—by becoming a foreigner.

The *Cobles del Regne de Mallorques* [*Verses on the Kingdom of Majorca*] is the least cryptic of Turmeda's prophetic texts; its hendecasyllabic verses are at times quite lyrical. Written at the behest of "alguns honrats mercaders de Mallorques" [some well-regarded Majorcan merchants], this long poem eludes facile categorization. It begins with a plaintive evocation of place rendered distant, an exile's poignant enumeration of birds, flowers, fish, and the variety of fruits grown there. The central event of the text is the poet's lengthy exchange with a resplendent, yet weeping, island queen. The queen celebrates Majorca's past accomplishments, her intrepid merchants, the valor of her seamen, the erudition and saintliness of her scholars, yet those earlier heights make her fall from glory all the more bitter, and she laments the divisions which bring her dishonor.[19] Anselm agrees with her, but recasts the issue in a crucial way: "Senyora, son avantatge/ cascun d'ells cerca per si;/ va dient a son vesí:/ "Jo no són de ton llinatge" [Lady, his own advantage/ each one seeks for himself;/ telling his neighbor: / "I am not of your lineage"] (26). That is to say, the problem lies not in the *existence* of difference, but in using difference, be it in lineage or religion, as an instrument for personal gain.

The acuteness of Fra Anselm's insight springs not only from the distance that gives him a (presumably neutral) vantage point outside of those conflicts, but also from the fact that he transcends the linguistic boundaries between opposing parties: "O de les tres lletres mestre!/ Lo morisc vos és tot clar/ e en l'hebraic sóts molt destre" [Ye, learned in the three languages/ Arabic is crystal clear for you / and in Hebrew you are quite skillful] (27). The insistence on Turmeda's mastery of multiple languages, on a kind of multiculturalism *avant la lettre,* is more than a claim to rhetorical (and prophetic) authority. It is rather, I would argue, integral to his message of reconciliation and unity.

The fictional Anselm reminds the queen that before the rule of the Christians, the people of the island shared such love and concord that they banded together against the king for the common good. The king used magic and astrology to divide his subjects and bolster his personal power, and this brought ruin, for the count of Barcelona easily defeated the newly factious kingdom (27–31). The analogy with the current situation leads Anselm to offer a solution with a decidedly mystical quality:

> Devem creure fermamente
> que Déus creà la natura,
> e sota son manament
> jau cascuna creatura.
> E vostre poble, que factura
> és [de] Déu omnipotent,
> vulla'l pregar humilment
> llur divís torn amor pura.
> (32–3)

> [You must believe firmly
> that God created nature
> and beneath his emanation
> lies every single creature.
> And your people are divided
> by almighty God,
> pray humbly to him that their division
> turn to pure love.]

Turmeda's invocation of a neo-Platonic concept of divine emanation as well as his association of the present crisis with the motion of the stars, "per elles és pobretat,/ riquea e senyoria,/ malaltia e sanitat" [through them there is poverty/ riches and lordship,/ illness and health] (32) is not developed enough here to link it definitively with the cosmology and the cyclical notions of time of the *Ikhwān al-Ṣafā'* (Brethren of Purity), whose work played a large role in his later *Disputa de l'Ase*.[20] However, the assertion of the need to recognize the fundamental worth and dignity of every creature, a kind of ontological reconciliation—certainly the central message here—is also a cornerstone of the thought of the *Ikhwān*. Turmeda repeatedly refers to himself in the *Cobles* as *missatger* (messenger) and his mission (the text itself) as *missatgeria*. His value to the island of his birth is located precisely in standing outside, and bringing—in Catalan—an other-worldly enlightenment. His book is the foreigner returned home, a pilgrim's dream of return.

In making the historical analogy with Islamic Majorca, Turmeda seems to suggest that his more tolerant world view has also been rendered foreign by the sectarian strife plaguing the island. The violent pogroms that shook the whole of Spain in 1391 were the most definitive of signs that earlier harmony between religious communities had been shattered: in Barcelona alone, four hundred Jews were murdered. Waves of baptisms followed.[21] Although Fra Anselm is noncommittal about the reasons for his own flight; it may be related to persecution of Judaizers—Judaizing New Christians—or possibly persecution of heterodox elements within the Franciscan order, telling us: "viu mon companyó cremar" [I saw my companion burn] (38). The call for mutual respect and reconciliation had a clearly personal dimension, as the text makes a rather transparent request for a safe-conduct or writ for the author through the fictional Anselm's own request for such a guarantee as a reward for his message. So then, why did Turmeda reject the safe-conduct that he was subsequently offered? Could the request itself have been a rhetorical ploy, a gesture to demonstrate a sustained emotional allegiance to the island, a wish to return, but to a Majorca that lived only in Turmeda's memory and imagination? Does his conduct reflect a deep-seated ambivalence or simply a pragmatic desire to keep his options open?

Turmeda also wrote darker, more cryptic prophecies; of these, only four are extant: "Les prometences" (1405), "O Babilònia, tu Barcelona" (date uncertain), "Ne crec pas" (1406?) and another prophecy (in the mouth of the Ass) at the conclusion of the *Disputa de l'Ase*, "En nom de la essencia." Visionary texts were in vogue throughout Europe; Catalan authors were especially prolific in this regard.[22] Apocalyptic fervor had been rising throughout Europe since the time of Joachim de Fiore (1130/5–1201/2),[23] and the Great Western Schism (1378–1417) only heightened speculation about the end of days. Surely, most contemporary observers believed, one of the two popes was the Antichrist. However, unlike those of his compatriots Arnauld de Villanova (1240–1311),[24] John of Roquetaillade (de Rupescissa) (d. 1362), and Vincent Ferrer (1350–1419),[25] Turmeda's prophecies are not rooted in Biblical exegesis but in his insistent (yet unverifiable) claims to deep knowledge of astrology.

The persistent themes of the *Profecies* follow those already described in the *Cobles*. The poem "Les prometences" dwells on the contest between Europe divided and weakened by the Great Schism, and "la gent pagana," that is, the non-Christian world. From the safe distance of Tunis, he denounced the corruption of the Church: "sots pell d'ovella / lo món enganen / . . . / la clerecia / per sa malia / lo món desfaça." [in sheep's clothing / they deceive everyone / . . . / the clergy / in its evil / destroys the world] (90). Crisis is manifest in a persistent unreadability of signs; it is the mission of the *profecia* to reveal that which "l'escriptura / sota figura / havia closes" [scripture had hidden beneath allegory] (90), to expose hypocrisy and falsehood, as well as to read the future in the stars. While the *Profecies* invoke many of the common elements of apocalyptic discourse—cataclysmic wars, the stench of rotting corpses, pestilence and famine, sons turning against their fathers, and the vision of an era of peace and unity following the "tempesta"—the texts lack any mention of the Antichrist or of the beasts and iconography typically associated with Christian apocalypse. Indeed, Turmeda's vision might be called transreligious; he condemns all perturbations in the order of things. The forced conversions of the Muslims—"[el] gran ultraje / fet al morisma" [the great outrage / done to the Moors]—are no less of a problem than the Schism and other forms of strife and dissension wracking Europe.

While the popularity of Turmeda's *Profecies* waned as time robbed the predictions of their interest, the appeal of his *Llibre de bons amonstaments* [*Book of Good Precepts*], composed in 1396, was much more enduring, forming a part of the Catalonian primary school curriculum until the nineteenth century. These moralizing verses, despite heavy dependence on a thirteenth-century Italian source, *La dottrina dello schiavo di Bari*,[26] reflect the author's pragmatic approach to moral issues. To be sure, the text abounds with perfectly noncontroversial maxims, similar to those found in the wisdom literature or *hikma* common to the three religious traditions:

> Temps de repòs, temps de obrar . . .
> Can hauvràs temps no el lleixs anar;
> hom pereós mai avançar
>
> (56)
>
> [Time to rest, time to work . . .
> When you have time, don't let it run;
> A lazy man never gets ahead]
>
> Si vols que diguen bé de tu,
> no parles mal de negú
>
> (57)

[If you want good said about you,
speak badly of no one.]

However, in a series of verses perhaps rendered all the more subversive because they have been inserted (in sheep's clothing) in a context of self-evident aphorisms, Turmeda takes on issues of truth and falsehood, power and the corrupting influence of money:

Vulles tostemps dir veritat
de ço que seràs demanat;
mas en cas de necessitat
pots dir falsia.
Vulles prendre un bos castic:
no faces brega ab hom ric
si tu es pobre e menic;
lo plet perdries.
Diners de tort fan veritat,
e de jutgt fan avocat;
(62)

[Desire always to speak the truth
in that which you are asked;
but in case of need
you can speak falsely.
Take a good piece of advice:
don't litigate against a rich man
if you are poor and weak;
you will lose the case.
Money turns harm into truth,
and makes the judge an advocate.]

Is Turmeda saying that an untruth, spoken in case of need, is a kind of legitimate self-defense of the weak and poor in a world corrupted by money? Given Turmeda's reiterated expressions of concern with forced conversions (and perhaps his own apparently ambivalent situation), is this a tacit endorsement of *taqiyya* (dissimulation), the doctrine that made it licit for Muslims in time of persecution to adopt the exterior practice of another religion as long as in one's heart one remained faithful to the teachings of Islam?

The question of the truthfulness of Fra Anselm "en altra manera apellat Abdal·là" [also called Abdallah] and the apparent incongruity of an apostate writing what was understood to be a Christian didactic work is addressed in the prose incipit. The short introduction—in all likelihood a later addition—explains that even though Anselm had not followed his own *amonestaments*, he did well to disseminate them, especially if his readers prayed for his soul. In the end it remains unclear if the *falsia* (falsehood) here consists in courting a Christian readership by insinuating that he is not a sincere Muslim (when in fact he is), or in concealing his true Christian faith from his Muslim patrons. Another possibility also merits consideration, especially given the importance of Averroism in the universities that Turmeda attended. The great commentator of Aristotle, Ibn Rushd (d. 1198)—known in Europe as Averroes—had defended the independence of philosophy in the face of theological attacks. Denying the existence of any contradiction between revealed religion and philosophy, he asserted that both are legitimate methods of apprehending the divine. It was this doctrine which led to accusations against Averroes' European adherents of promulgating an incoherent "double truth." [27] As the detractors of Averroism pointed out, the logic that explains away the fundamental contradictions between peripatetic philosophy and revealed religion is a short step from a rationalist relativism that would deny the importance of the differences separating creeds. Whether or not Turmeda had encountered Averroism in Europe, he could have certainly found radical anti-sectarianism in the writings of the *Ikhwān al-Ṣafā'*, who holds that "religions, doctrines, sects are only different paths of approach, different means and avenues, but the Goal we seek is one. From whatever quarter we seek to encounter Him, God is there."[28] Certainly, from this vantage point, Turmeda's didactic writings for a Christian audience do not so much engage in deception, as simply participate in the rhetorical conventions of Christian texts in order to facilitate the reception of his deeper, more transcendental, message.

Turmeda's cultural intertextuality, his attraction to universalist and esoteric currents within Islamic intellectual circles, his self-deprecating irony and humor, and his bitter condemnations of the hypocrisy of the Church are most prominent in his lengthy prose work the *Disputa de l'Ase*. The plot of the work revolves around an allegorical debate between Man, represented by Fra Anselm, and Beast, represented by the "Ase Ronyós de la Cua Tallada" [the Mangy Ass with the lopped-off tail]. The debate begins when the animals charge Anselm with a verbal crime: "que vós dieu públicament, i sosteniu, prediqueu i afirmeu que vosaltres, fills d'Adam, sou més nobles i de major dignitat que no som entre nosaltres, animals" [that you have said publicly, and defended, preached and affirmed that you, sons of Adam, are more noble and of greater dignity than are we animals] (34–35).

Indeed, as Asín Palacios demonstrated, Turmeda had borrowed the general idea of a verbal contest between man and animal and some details of the debate itself from a section of the *Rasā'il* ("Epistles") of the *Ikhwān al-Ṣafā'*, "The Case of the Animals versus Man Before the King of the Jinn." However the accusation of plagiarism (and vulgarization) over simplifies the relationship between the two texts and precludes any serious consideration of Turmeda's relationship to Islamic philosophy, both as he would have encountered it in Tunis and, before his conversion, in Europe. Although a comparative study of the two works is beyond the scope of the present article,[29] even a brief examination will reveal the complexity of the relationship between the cosmology and religious and political thought of the Brethren of Purity and Turmeda's own idiosyncratic views, thus disproving Giraldo's assertion that "Turmeda (along with the majority of his contemporaries) was naïve" (27) and "not an original thinker" (105). Turmeda could—especially when addressing his European audience—approach the tenth-century text with the irreverence of a foreigner, unconstrained by the weight of normative and often ahistorical interpretations of *turāth*, Islamic tradition.

As in the Arabic "Case of the Animals," Turmeda's interspecies debate—which Anselm attends under the protection of a "safe-conduct and guarantee"—frames pointed observations about human arrogance, measured out with a good dose of humor and self-deprecation. Anselm's claim that the human form is the most balanced and that animals are misproportioned is easily rebutted by the Ass, who rebukes Anselm for defaming the Creator by insulting his creation. The camel's long neck allows him to reach the grasses he eats (and scratch his rear end with his teeth). Clearly, the Ass claims (while winking at the audience), each animal is proportioned in accordance with its needs. Each successive "proof" of human superiority advanced by Anselm is easily demolished by the Ass, whose comic banter is punctuated with erudite references to the Bible and classical sources such as Cato.

Even in those sections where Turmeda follows the general scheme of the earlier Arabic text, he cannot resist the urge to poke fun at it—and himself. If the *Ikhwān al-Ṣafā'* presented each animal as an idealized, undifferentiated representative of its species, and each man of his nation or tribe, Turmeda presents each character steeped in his own uniqueness and idiosyncrasy. The format of the disputation, as well as the content of the text itself is constantly destabilized by self-conscious nods to the reader. Anselm's own interior monologue sometimes intrudes, usually to ironic effect. His baseness is revealed, for example, in his cowardly thoughts before the large gathering of animals and in his disdain for the animals' rather scruffy choice of representative (for the character Anselm, unlike his audience, is not privy to the literary convention of the eloquent ass):

> Per la cual cose, girant-me, vegí a mon costat un dolent i malaurat ase, tot escorxat, mocós, ronyós i sense cua; el cual, segons jo crec, no hauria valgut deu diners a la fira de Tarragona; i em vaig tenir per escarnit, coneixent clarament que ells es burlaven de mi. Emperò, més per por que per vergonya, em calgué contentar-me i pacientment suportar.
>
> (38)

> [Therefore, turning around, I saw at my side an ill and emaciated ass, all scurvy, runny-nosed, mangy and tail-less; which, it seemed to me, wouldn't

have fetched two dinars at the fair in Tarragona; and I felt ridiculed, recognizing clearly that they were mocking me. However, more out of fear than shame, I decided to cheer up and bear it patiently.]

For his part, the Ass loses no opportunity to make cutting, sarcastic remarks to Anselm: "Pensar abans de parlar es saviesa, i vós feu el contrari: que parleu abans de pensar; i això és gran i alta follia, mesclada amb major bogeria" [Thinking before speaking is wisdom, and you do the opposite: for you speak before thinking; and that is a great folly, combined with an even greater lunacy] (51). "Frare Anselm, em sembla que vós sou un poc dolç de sal i lleuger de pes. . . ." [Friar Anselm, it seems to me that you are short of lights [literally: lacking in salt and lightweight] (70). Some of these insults form part of an intertextual joke rendered doubly comic because they spring from aphorisms Turmeda collected in the *Llibre des bons amonestaments*. Even Anselm's growing respect for the Ass—who has not only proved a nimble debater but, as Anselm recalls, served as the mount of Jesus when he entered Jerusalem—is ironic, for his sudden humility comes after the insects join in the fray, irritatingly pointing out how defenseless humans are from the pestering and indignities provoked by lice, bedbugs, flies, mosquitoes, and the like.

The Ass interrupts the debate to tell bawdy *exempla* of the seven sins—as perpetrated by clerics—remarking "I us faig saber per tal que no estigueu enganyat, que jo sé tant d'afers dels religiosos, que us semblarà que jo hagi estat conventual o religiós en cadascuna de les dites ordres" ["Let it be known, so that you will not be under false impressions, that I know so much about the *affairs* of the clergy, that it seems as if I had been a *conventual* or monk in each order mentioned"] (119–120). These stories are a sardonic condemnation of how the clergy manipulates the ignorant and abuses its power and privilege. Most notable among them is the story of Fray Juliot, who uses the sacramental power of confession to convince a rather credulous young bride that tithing extends to sex; that is, she owes to God (in the person of his representative, Fray Juliot) the tenth part of the relations she has with her husband. The text so gleefully indulges in the details of the bride's exaggerated account of her husband's sexual demands (and Fray Juliot's eager calculation of services due), that the exemplary value of the story seems all but forgotten.

In each story the narrative revels in names, places, and even dates, betraying a naked delight in storytelling not unlike that of Boccaccio's *Decameron*. As in the Italian work, the emphasis on specificities and contingency signals a profound epistemological shift vis-à-vis earlier medieval exempla which are meant to be paradigmatic, reflecting unquestionable truths of ethics or conduct. Writing on the *Decameron*, Stierle notes: "Because there is an ambiguity between contingency and sense, the exemplary value of each story is, ironically, placed in question. Contingency overcomes exemplarity; however it never triumphs definitively."[30] It is this same gap that separates Turmeda's ideas of representation from those of the *Ikhwān al-Ṣafā'*, bringing the *Dispute* much closer to Cervantes's classic satire of picaresque fiction, the "exemplary novel" *El coloquio de los perros* [The Dogs' Colloquy].

The debate comes to its conclusion when the Ass, having first mocked Anselm for an error in an earlier prophecy, recites a prophetic poem similar in form and content to Turmeda's various *Profecies*. Intrigued by the mysterious verses, Anselm hastens to conclude the debate, for the Ass has promised that the explanation awaits the resolution of their dispute. It is only then that Anselm reveals his trump card, the definitive proof of man's superiority over beast: Jesus took human, not animal, form. The contest thus concluded in his favor, Anselm returns home content, and the prophecies remain a mystery that presumably can only be deciphered in the unfolding of time. Does the dispute function as an ironizing frame for a serious prophecy? Is Anselm mocking the credulous audience who listened to his earlier prophecies with such interest (not unlike the gullible young bride)?

In the case of the Brethren of Purity, one can easily understand their recourse to diverse textual strategies for dissimulating their political views (and the identities of the group's members). Their heterodox syncretism encompassed diverse Islamic and pre-Islamic intellectual currents (including Babylonian astrology with Indian and Iranian additions, Hellenistic sciences, neo-Platonic theories of divine emanation, Mu^ctazilite rationalism and Sufi mystic tendencies), and they were considered dangerously heterodox in their time. For the *Ikhwān*, beneath the surface (*ẓāhir*) meaning of religious texts—and their method allows them to read all of creation as a divine "text"—lies a more fundamental, and elusive inner (*bāṭin*) meaning. The (*ẓāhir*/*bāṭin* dichotomy is inscribed in their *Epistles* as well; even the interpolated stories are dense with symbolism meant to be intelligible only to initiates. By contrast, the ironies and inversions, contradictions and complexities of the *Disputa de l'Ase* make the text far more slippery. Turmeda explodes the very idea of a binary opposition between surface and deep meanings; all meanings are destabilized.

Turmeda's only extant Arabic work, the autobiographical polemic *Tuḥfat al-adīb firadd^calā ahl al-ṣalīb* [*The Gift of the Writer to Refute the Partisans of the Cross*] both clarifies and problematizes his Catalan-language works. His account—tailored for a Muslim audience—of how he came to embrace Islam is remarkable. A trusted teacher confided to him that the Paraclete foretold in the New Testament (John 14:16) was none other than Muḥammad.[31] However his teacher was too old (and cowardly) to renounce his life of privilege in Christian Europe and risk hardship and rejection by moving to an Islamic country to openly lead the life of a Muslim. This is a curiously inverted form of *taqiyya*, in which the dissimulation consists in the *failure* to publicly convert, the refusal to openly acknowledge the beliefs that he privately claims.

The account of Turmeda's own spiritual journey ends at the moment of conversion; in that sense, the autobiographical portion of the book is less a spiritual autobiography (à la Augustine) and more a social and political document which provides many fascinating details of commerce, trade, taxation, and public works in late medieval Tunis. Turmeda's description of the accomplishments of the sovereign makes a fascinating counterpoint to his earlier critiques of European society. The Sultan brought peace after years of civil war, eliminated many crushing taxes on foodstuffs and other commodities sold in the market, and ended the royal monopoly on the production of soap. The panegyric of the justness, generosity, and good government of the Sultan is certainly one of the most salient aspects of the book's political utility, not only to Turmeda personally, but also as a means of promoting specific social and economic policies which brought relief to ordinary citizens.

Although the *Tuḥfa* has been useful in reconstructing the details of Turmeda's life, it presents the reader with the challenge of reconciling the vehemently anti-Christian polemic with the universalist rhetoric of his earlier works, or even the ironic and irreverent pose of the *Disputa*. One cannot discard the idea that Turmeda's European contacts and his Catalan writings ultimately awakened local suspicions about his fidelity to Islam. Thus, his autobiography and polemic would have functioned—in a manner analogous to the discourse of the *converso*—as a badge of proof of his complete separation from the members of his former community, while at the same time furnishing the (Muslim) reader with additional confirmation of the illogic and distortions of the Christians. The grammatical errors and awkward phrasing pointed out by critics—Massignon called his style "franchement mauvais" [decidedly bad][32]—give the text a certain authenticity; the foreigner speaks Arabic with an accent.

However, Mikel de Epalza raises several points that cast serious doubt on the authorship of the polemic attached to the decidedly authentic autobiography.[33] The line of attack against Christianity follows the familiar arguments of Islamic anti-Christian treatises: the contradictions between the different books of the New Testament are evidence of falsification and error, Jesus was indeed a prophet but claims to divinity were a later fabrication, the dogma of the Trinity is incompatible with monotheism, and so on.[34] Yet in the case of the *Tuḥfa*, the lack of sophistication in the presentation of the arguments, as well as prominent factual errors about Christian teaching, seem at odds with Turmeda's long years of theological training. Epalza also notes the marked difference in tone between the autobiographical and polemic sections; the second part abounds with vitriol and contempt for Christian doctrine, and repeatedly describes the Gospels as "falsehoods, lies and untruth"("*bāṭil, kithb wa zūr*") (282). Perhaps most convincingly, there is no mention of the manuscript in Arabic sources until 1603, when it was translated into Turkish and presented—with a preface written by Tunisian notable Muḥammad Abū al-Ghayth al-Qashshāsh—to the Ottoman emperor Aḥmad I.[35] Epalza cautiously advances the theory that the anti-Christian polemic could have been added by a Morisco[36] closely associated with al-Qashshāsh, Aḥmad al-Ḥānafī, himself the author of anti-Christian writings in Spanish. The close coincidence between al-Ḥānafī's Spanish writings and many pages of the *Tuḥfa* add significant weight to this idea. If indeed this was the case, it is sadly ironic that a Morisco, a descendant of the forcibly converted Muslim population and a victim of the "outrage" denounced centuries earlier by Turmeda, would use the ex-Franciscan's life story as a foil for his own bitter anti-Christian diatribe.

In any case, regardless of the doubts about the authenticity of the polemic—and in the end Epalza himself withholds judgment—what should not be lost in the debate is that many aspects of Turmeda's life and work are paradigmatic of a time when the borders between nations and religions, and the conditions that created tolerance or intolerance were fluid and local. Any attempt to understand Turmeda must confront not only the vexing question of the multiplicity of perspectives invoked by and imposed upon the apostate/convert, the fugitive/exile, but the perhaps even thornier question of historical periodization. From the shores of Tunis, Turmeda had a clear view of a Europe devastated by religious division and endless wars, and gripped by the apocalyptic fear of the Antichrist. In hindsight we can see that he stood at the brink between medieval sensibilities and an early modern humanism. As Cervantes did almost two centuries later, he used an earthy humor and a dazzlingly complex irony as tools to reflect the philosophical disputes of his era.

One of the central tenets of modern Catalan nationalism is the collective memory of a brilliant and cosmopolitan medieval culture, a kind of universalism that is contrasted with what is often described as Castilian impulse to impose uniformity (always at the expense of Catalan language and culture). Catalonia's location on the Mediterranean, its mercantile economy and a certain political pragmatism are some of the factors that explain the often friendly interchanges with other cultures. The Catalans enjoyed almost four centuries of largely peaceful relations with the Muslim governments of al-Andalus, not joining in the *Reconquista* efforts of their Iberian neighbors until the twelfth century. They thus had access to Arabic science and technology much earlier than their counterparts in the remainder of Christian Iberia. Long before the great libraries of Toledo passed into Christian hands—setting the stage for the crucial translation movements of the twelfth century—the monastery of Santa Maria de Ripoll (near Barcelona) was stocked with books purchased from the Arabs. By 950 Ripoll was a hub of translation activity, disseminating treatises on the construction and use of the astrolabe—hitherto unknown in medieval Europe—as well as on arithmetic, geometry, and astrology. As Tavani asserts in his *Per una història de la cultura catalana medieval*: "Així, doncs, en definitiva, durant l'edat mitjana, els contactes entre catalans i musulmans van ser particularment intensos y mostraren, per ambdues parts, una obertura i una voluntat de diàleg poc corrents en aquella època, sobretot a la península ibèrica." [So thus, without doubt, the contacts between Catalans and Muslims would be particularly intense during the Middle Ages, and demonstrate, on the part of both sides, an openness and desire for dialogue uncommon in that time, especially on the Iberian Peninsula.][37]

The fluidness of the Catalan borders is manifest in the abundant cases of conversion, abjuration, apostasy, and other religious comings and goings at that time. For example, Berenguer, the viscount of Barcelona, known as *Revertarius,* was captured by Almoravid forces sometime before 1131 and became the leader of their Christian militias deployed in Morocco against the Almohads. As his epithet signals, The Reverter adopted Islam yet later retracted his conversion, continuing to serve the Almoravid leaders ᶜAlī ibn Yūsuf and his son Tāshfīn.[38] Now, in the context of the universalist shadings of the Catalanist movement, cases such as The Reverter's and Turmeda's are read—at least by some commentators—as testaments to cultural openness, free-thinking, and political pragmatism (as opposed to the ideological fanaticism ascribed to the Castilians). As Montoliu writes about Turmeda:

> És molt nostre, és molt català aquest original aventurer de l'acció i del pensament . . . amb el seu fàcil poder de transplantar-se i adaptar-se a diferents climes materials i espirituals . . . És molt nostre pel seu esperit transcendentalment errant, aventurer i cosmopolita que enllaça, tot i llurs contradicciones i discrepàncies, totes les grans figures del pensament català: Ramon Llull, Arnau de Vilanova, Lluís Vives."
>
> (92)

> [He is very much ours; this original adventurer in both action and thought is very Catalan . . . and his ease in transplanting himself, adapting to different material and spiritual conditions. He is very much ours for his transcendentally wandering, adventuresome and cosmopolitan spirit that embraces, in all of its contradictions and discrepancies, all of the great figures of Catalan thought: Ramon Llull, Arnau de Vilanova, Lluís Vives.]

Montoliu's insistence that Turmeda is "ours" is no doubt a reply to Asín Palacios and other detractors of the former Franciscan (further conditioned by the repression of Catalanist sentiment during Franco's regime). Yet it would be a mistake to cast Turmeda as a figure primarily of interest to *Catalan* literature and history, thus reinscribing the borders that much of his writing works against. The rich tapestry of the medieval period, its local differences, contradictions, and heterodoxies come into sharper focus with the broader study of the regional literatures of the time (Galician, Catalan, Occitan, etc.) which were marginalized, rendered foreign and obscure by the political domination of Castilian and French (and remain marginalized in the curriculums of most departments of Spanish or French literature). Certainly Turmeda should be read as emblematic of a place and time in which religious and cultural boundaries were more porous, and his works should challenge us to abandon the mindset of binary oppositions that casts him as either saint (whether it be Christian or Muslim) or duplicitous scoundrel and to come closer to understanding the complexities and contradictions of a life lived on the border between cultures and religions.

Notes

1. Alfonsi wrote his anti-Jewish tract shortly after his baptism in 1106. The text is available in a Latin-Spanish bilingual edition: *Dialogo contra los judíos*, ed. Klaus Peter Mieth (Latin text), Spanish trans. Esperanza Ducay, (Huesca [Spain]: Instituto de Estudios Altoaragoneses, 1996).
2. See Morris Braude, ed. *Conscience on Trial: Three Public Religious Disputations Between Christians and Jews in the Thirteenth and Fifteenth Centuries* (New York: Exposition Press, 1952) and Robert Chazan, *Barcelona and Beyond: the Disputation of 1263 and its Aftermath* (Berkeley: University of California Press, 1992). Anna Sapir Abulafia, *Christians and Jews in Dispute: Disputational Literature and the Rise of Anti-Judaism in the West (c. 1000–1150)* (Aldershot, Hampshire: Ashgate, 1998). The autobiography and anti-Jewish polemic of a twelfth-century Jewish convert to Islam, Samuel al-Maghribī affords an interesting comparison with the writings of the conversos; see Samaual ibn Yahya al-Maghribī, *Ifḥam al-yahū*. Silencing the Jews, ed. and trans. Moshe Perlmann. (New York: American Academy for Jewish Research, 1964). For a view on Jewish anti-Christian disputation during that time, see Daniel J. Lasker, *Jewish Philosophical Polemics against Christianity in the Middle Ages* (New York: Ktav, 1977). Zoroastrian converts to Islam were also active in pro-Islamic apologetics as is documented in Guy Monnot, *Islam et religions* (Paris: Maisonneuve et Larose, 1986).
3. There were several fifteenth-century converso writers who wrote against the Jews and Judaism. See Chapter 6 of Norman Roth, *Conversos, Inquisition, and the Expulsion of the Jews from Spain* (Madison: University of Wisconsin Press, 1995).
4. For a general bibliographical overview on conversion to Islam, see R. Stephen Humphreys, *Islamic History: A Framework for Inquiry* (Princeton: Princeton University Press, 1991), 273–283. For the *jizya*, see P. Hardy, "Djizya" *Encyclopedia of Islam*, 2nd ed., vol. 2 (Leiden: Brill), 559–567.
5. Hugh Kennedy, *Muslim Spain and Portugal: A Political History of al-Andalus* (London: Longman, 1996), 67–68.

6. The stakes for "judaizing" conversos could be extremely high, especially after the establishment of the Spanish Inquisition. Because Jews, as non-Christians, were exempt from the jurisdiction of the Inquisition, they could, as Kamen documents "pay off old scores" against their former coreligionists (who often had become their most fervent oppressors). See the excellent study by Henry Kamen, *The Spanish Inquisition: A Historical Revision* (New Haven: Yale University Press, 1998), 18; on the positions of power and prestige held by conversos in late medieval and early modern Spain, see 28–34.
7. The details of Turmeda's life are most thoroughly explored in Agustin Calvet, *Fray Anselmo Turmeda: Heterodoxo español* (Barcelona: Casa Editorial Estudio, 1914). See also J. Miret i Sans, "Vida de fray Anselmo Turmeda," *Revue Hispanique* 24 (1911): 261–296 and Mikel de Epalza, "Nuevas aportaciones a la biografía de fray Anselmo Turmeda (Abdallah al-Tarchuman)," *Analecta Sacra Tarraconesia* 38 (1965): 87–158.
8. Calvet is the most enthusiastic supporter of this idea, although it is also espoused by a good number of commentators, including Miret i Sans, who calls him "un racionalista más avanzado que la mayoría de sus contemporáneos." [a rationalist more advanced than the majority of his contemporaries], and Marfany, who calls his position typical of Renaissance humanism. See Joan Lluis Marfany, *Ideari d'Anselm Turmeda*, 2nd ed. (Barcelona: Edicions 62, 1980).
9. Muḥammad al-Buhlī al-Nayyāl, "Bayna qubba wa ṣafḥa kitāb," *al-Idhaa* [Tunis] 37 (1–10–1960) cited in Míkel de Epalza, *Fray Anselm Turmeda (Abdallah al-Taryuman) y su polémica islamo-cristiana* (Madrid: Hiperión, 1994), 12.
10. ᶜAbd Allah, "servant of God," was a common name among converts to Islam and is a common name among Arab Christians. See F. Codera, "Apodos o sobrenombres de Moros españoles," *Recueil de travaux d'érudition dédiés à la mémoire de Hartwig Derenbourg par ses amis et ses élèves* (Paris: E. Leroux, 1909), 323–324. Al-Tarjumân = "the Translator" al-Mayurqī = "the Majorcan."
11. Anselm Turmeda, *Llibre de bons amonestaments i altres obres*, ed. Mikel de Epalza (Palma de Mallorca: Editorial Moll, 1987). All citations refer to this edition.
12. Ibid. See also Ramón d'Alós, "Les profecies den Turmeda," *Revue Hispanique* 24 (1911): 480–496; Jordi Rubió, "Un text catalá de la Profecia de l'Ase de Fra Anselm Turmeda," *Estudis Universitaris Catalans* 6 (1913): 9–24; A. Raimondi, "Profecies de Anselm Turmeda," *Archivio Storico per la Sicilia Orientale* 11 (1914): 232–249; Pere Bohigas i Balaguer, "Profecies de fra Anselm Turmeda," *Estudis Universitaris Catalanas* 9 (1916): 173–181. Another text, the *Llibre de tres*, has occasionally been attributed to Turmeda. See Martín de Riquer, ed. *Llibre de tres* (Barcelona: Qc, 1997).
13. R. Foulché-Delbosc, "La disputation de l'Asne" *Revue Hispanique* 24 (1911): 358–479, provides the text of the first French edition (1544). See also Armand Llinarés, *Anselm Turmeda, Dispute de l'Ane* (Paris: J. Vrin, 1984), for another edition of the same text. The lost Catalan original has been reconstructed several times. See Lluis Deztany, ed., *Llibre de Disputació de l'ase*

contra frare Encelm Turmeda (Barcelona: [J. Horta], 1922); *Disputa de l'ase*, ed. Marçal Olivar (Barcelona: Editorial Barcino, 1993). For an English translation, see Zaida I. Giraldo, *Anselm Turmeda: An Intellectual Biography of a Medieval Apostate, including a Translation of the "Debate between the Friar and the Ass,"* (Ph.D., CUNY, 1975). Citations here refer to the Olivar edition.

14. See Calvet for a full account of the legends that grew up around Turmeda's alleged martyrdom in Tunis.
15. Jaime Coll, *Crónica seráfica de la Santa Provincia de Cathalunia* (1738) cited in Calvet. *Op. cit.*
16. J. Spiro, ed. and trans., *Le Présent de l'homme lettré pour réfuter les partisans de la croix* (Paris: E. Leroux, 1886). Míkel de Epalza, *Fray Anselm Turmeda (Abdallah al-Taryuman) y su polémica islamo-cristiana* (Madrid: Hiperión, 1994), provides an edition of the Arabic original with facing-page Spanish translation with an extensive introduction.
17. Manuel de Montoliu, *Eximenis, Turmeda i l'Inici de l'Humanisme at Catalunya*, Les grans personalitats de la literatura catalana, vol. 4 (Barcelona: Alpha, 1960), 70.
18. M. Asín Palacios, "El original árabe de la Disputa del asno contra fray Anselmo Turmeda," *Revista de filología espanola* (1914): 1–51. Everette E. Larson further explores the issue of plagiarism in "The Disputa of Anselmo: Translation, Plagiarism or Embellishment?" *Josep Maria Sola Sole: Homage, homenaje, homenatge: Miscelanea de estudios de amigos y discipulos*, ed. Antonio Torres Alcala, Victorio Aguera, and B. Smith Nathaniel (Barcelona: Puvill Libros, 1984), I: 285–296.
19. Estanislao Aguiló focuses on the poem's historical value as a record of the leading monastic figures of Majorca at that time. See "Anselmo Turmeda. Apéndice," *Museo Balear*. Segunda época. II (1885), 218–226, 256–264.
20. The most complete English language study of the cosmology of the *Ikhwān al-Safâ'* is Seyyed Hossein Nasr, *An Introduction to Islamic Cosmological Doctrines* (Boulder: Shambhala, 1978), 25–104; also useful are Ian Richard Netton, *Muslim Neoplatonists: An Introduction to the Thought of the Brethren of Purity* (Edinburgh: Edinburgh University Press, 1991); and Yves Marquet, *La Philosophie des Ihwan al-Safa* (Algiers: Société Nationale d'Edition et de Diffusion, 1975). There is no complete English translation of the writings of the group. Lenn Evan Goodman has edited and translated the section of the work which inspired Turmeda: *The Case of the Animals versus Man Before the King of the Jinn* (Boston: Twayne, 1978).
21. See Yitzhak Baer, *A History of the Jews in Christian Spain*, 2 vols. (Philadelphia: Jewish Publication Society, 1961–66), II: 95–134.
22. See Pere Bohigas i Balaguer, "Profecies catalanes dels segles XIV i XV. Assaig bibliogràfic," *Butlletí de la Biblioteca de Catalunya* VI (1923): 24–49; José María Pou y Marti O.F.M., *Visionarios, beguinos y fraticelos catalanes (siglos XIII–XV) [Reprint of 1930 edition]*, ed. and intro. J. M. Arcelus Ulibarrena (Madrid: Ed. Colegio "Cardenal Cisneros," 1991).
23. Joachim's calculations, based on his tripartite theory of history, in *Expositio in Apocalypsim*, led him to predict the end of the second era of man would take place in 1260. See Marjorie Reeves, *The Influence of Prophecy in the*

Later Middle Ages: A Study in Joachimism (Oxford: Clarendon Press, 1969). See also Richard K. Emmerson and Ronald B. Herzman, *The Apocalyptic Imagination in Medieval Literature* (Philadelphia: University of Pennsylvania Press, 1992).

24. See Clifford R. Backman, "The Reception of Arnau de Vilanova's Religious ideas," *Christendom and Its Discontents: Persecution, Exclusion, and Rebellion, 1000–1500*, ed. Scott L. Waugh and Peter D. Diehl (Cambridge: Cambridge University Press, 1995), 112–131.
25. See Pedro M. Cátedra, *Sermón, sociedad y literatura en la Edad Media: San Vicente Ferrer en Castilla (1411–1412): estudio bibliográfico, literario y edición de los textos inéditos*, Estudios de historia ([Valladolid]: Junta de Castilla y León, 1994).
26. See Francesco Babudri, *La figura del rimatore barese Schiavo nell'ambiente sociale e letterario duecentesco di Puglia e d'Italia* (Bari: Societa Editrice Tipografica, 1954), 167–80, for an edition of the *Dottrina*.
27. The classic study remains that of Ernest Renan, *Averroès et l'Averroïsme [1852]*, ed. Alain de Libera (Paris: Maisonneuve & Larose, 1997). For a more updated look at the question of Averroism and the campaign (with a lucid introduction on a difficult subject) against it, see Thomas Aquinas, *Contre Averroès*, ed. and trans. Alain de Libera (Paris: GF-Flammarion, 1997). Averroes's own position on the subject of the harmony between philosophy and religion is most succinctly and directly treated in *Discours décisif de Averroès*, ed. Marc Geoffroy (Paris: GF-Flammarion, 1996).
28. Goodman, ed. and trans. *The Case of the Animals*, 194.
29. See my "Beastly Colloquies: Rhetoric, Translation and the Quest for Justice in Two Medieval Disputations Between Animals and Men," forthcoming.
30. Karlheinze Stierle, "Three Moments in the Crisis of Exemplarity: Boccaccio—Petrarch, Montaigne, and Cervantes," *Journal of the History of Ideas* 59.4 (1998): 581–595; here 582.
31. Turmeda's argument that the coming of Muhammad was foretold in the New Testament was a familiar one in the Islamic world. He links the mention of Amad, (one of the names of Muammad, derived from the same root: ḥ-m-d) in *Qur'ān* LXI, 6 with the Paraclete. Traditional Christian exegesis has identified the Paraclete with the Holy Spirit. See Epalza, *Fray Anselm Turmeda*, 34–36, for a discussion of the question and further bibliography.
32. Louis Massignon, *Examen du "Présent de l'homme lettré" par Abdallah Ibn al-Torjoman* (Rome: Pontificio Istituto di Studi Arabi e d'Islamistica, 1992).
33. Epalza. *Fray Anselm Turmeda*, 166–168.
34. Ibid, 92–188, which also provides some bibliography on Islamic apologetics. Several prominent examples of anti-Christian polemic have been translated into European languages; see David Thomas, ed., *Anti-Christian Polemic in Early Islam : Abu 'Isa al-Warraq's "Against the Trinity"* (Cambridge: Cambridge University Press, 1992); Georges Tartar, ed., *Dialogue islamo-chrétien sous le calife Al-Mamun (813–834): les epitres d'Al-Hashimi et d'Al-Kindi* (Paris: Nouvelles editions latines, 1985); Miguel Asín Palacios, *Abenhazam de Cordoba y su historia crítica de las ideas religiosas* (Madrid: Turner,

1984) [Contains Spanish translations of selections from *Faṣl fī al-milal wa-al-ahwā wa-al-nihal*]; al-Ghazālī, *Refutation excellente de la divinité de Jesus-Christ d'après les Evangiles*, ed. Robert Chidiac. (Paris: Bibliothèque de l'École des Hautes Études, 1939). Arabic sources are numerous (and often voluminous); one starting point is ᶜAbd al-Majīd Sharafī, *al-Fikr al-Islāmīfīal-raddᶜalā al-Nasārā ilā nihāyat al-qarn al-rābiᶜ*. Kulliyat al-Adab wa-al-ᶜUlūm al- Insāniyah, 6,29 (Tunis: al-Dar al-Tunisiyah lil Nashr, 1986).

35. Epalza, *Op cit.*: 43–55. Al-Qashshāsh was a prominent and politically powerful Sufi mystic; a former student of his wrote a lengthy biography, which has recently been edited, al-Muntaṣir ibn al-Murābit ibn Abī Lihyah Qafsī, *Nūr al-armāsh fī manāqīb al-ᶜQashshāsh* (Tunis: al-Maktabah al-ᶜatīqah, 1998).

36. The term *Morisco* designates those Spanish Muslims who were forcibly converted to Christianity following the abrogation of the religious freedoms granted them by the 1492 Capitulations of Granada. Many, if not most, of the Moriscos continued some form of practice of Islam. The Moriscos were expelled from Spain in 1609, following a tumultuous century of suspicion, conflict and occasional uprisings. See especially Anwar G. Chejne, *Islam and the West: the Moriscos, a Cultural and Social History* (Albany: State University of New York Press, 1983); and Antonio Domínguez Ortiz, *Historia de los moriscos: vida y tragedia de una minoría* (Madrid: Alianza Editorial, 1985).

37. Giuseppe Tavani, *Per una història de la cultura catalana medieval* (Barcelona: Curial, 1996), 30.

38. Evariste Levi-Provençal, ed., *Documents inedits d'histoire almohade: fragments manuscrits du "legajo" 1919 du fonds arabe de l'Escurial* (Paris: P. Geuthner, 1928), 89–96; Henri Terrasse, *Histoire du Maroc des origines a l'établissement du Protectorat français*, 2 vols. (1950), I, 285–86.

11
Social Bodies and the Non-Christian 'Other' in the Twelfth Century:
John of Salisbury and Peter of Celle

CARY J. NEDERMAN

One of the most distinctive advances in European political thought during the twelfth century was the wide application of organic or holistic imagery in order to capture and express the complexities of social relations. Whereas in earlier times such simple models as the tripartite division of society into warriors, laborers, and priests had sufficed,[1] authors of the 1100s began to devise more sophisticated and realistic metaphors for communal order.[2] This development is consonant with the increasingly naturalistic character of twelfth-century theories of government and community,[3] as well as with the newly vital conceptions of *res publica* and *universitas* encountered in the Roman law materials that had once again begun to circulate.[4] In contrast to early medieval ideas of society, which had largely revolved around the dominant theme of hierarchical subordination and rule, the holistic approach tended to promote standards of reciprocity, cooperation, and inclusion among the members of the community.

One may still wonder, however, whether the tendencies toward the recognition of communal diversity and complexity evident in twelfth-century writings really amounted to any very significant change in the fundamental religious assumptions behind medieval social theory. In other words, did not such ideas remain bounded by an overarching premise of uniformity engendered by the Christian mania for doctrinal conformity? This is precisely the issue raised by Anna Sapir Abulafia in her important recent study, *Christians and Jews in the Twelfth-Century Renaissance*. Abulafia claims that the emerging "concept of Christian wholeness" associated with the rise of political naturalism and corporation theory had the effect of relegating unbelievers to "outsider" status. She observes, "Non-Christians like Jews did not fit easily into the theoretical paradigms . . . set up concerning the nature of society and its aims . . . It is impossible to imagine any part of this state not being

Christian."[5] While holistic ideas of social order may have served to encapsulate and integrate the various classes and strata of Christian society in a single unit, Abulafia maintains, it had the effect (albeit perhaps unintended) of excluding the non-Christian from a communal identity.

Here, I examine two examples of such holistic social thinking from the mid-twelfth century—John of Salisbury's *Policraticus* and Peter of Celle's *The School of the Cloister*. I argue that neither of these works is so exclusivistic in attitude toward the Christian nature of community as Abulafia suggests. Rather, I show that John's theory of the republic is constructed to offer universal standards of social order, applicable to non-Christian as well as Christian societies. Moreover, Peter explicitly constructs his holistic conception of the monastic community in part on values that he acknowledges to be extra-Christian in origin. As with certain other thinkers of the twelfth century—Peter Abelard comes especially to mind—John and Peter prove more tolerant toward otherness than one might expect.

John of Salisbury

Although the organic metaphor comparing the political community to a living creature was widely employed during the Middle Ages, there is no version of the analogy more innovative and influential than that presented by John of Salisbury in the fifth and sixth chapters of his major treatise, the *Policraticus* (completed in 1159). Of course, until recent years, it was generally assumed that the *Policraticus*'s conception of the body politic was not John's invention at all, but an adaptation of a now lost treatise of instruction addressed to the Emperor Trajan, mistakenly ascribed by John to Plutarch. Thanks to the meticulous (though for a time, controversial) scholarship of Hans Liebeschütz in the middle of the twentieth century, we know that John devised the *Institutio Traiani* as a cloak under which to cover his own originality.[6] This should hardly be considered a shocking maneuver on John's part; medieval authors regularly fabricated or severely distorted sources in order to establish textual authority for their own, innovative ideas.

What ought to attract our attention about John's forgery of an authoritative basis for his conception of the body politic, instead, is the alleged provenance of the source. Rather than selecting a Christian author as the originator of the organic metaphor, John attributes it to a relatively obscure (in the twelfth century) pagan writer and makes its addressee a pagan Roman Emperor famed for his superlative virtue. In other words, John consciously selects a (fraudulent) non-Christian source for framing the organic order of society. Indeed, he confronts this issue directly in the Prologue to Book Five of the *Policraticus*:

> We will heed what Plutarch proposes about this matter [the body of the republic]. Subtracting the superstitions of the gentiles, there is validity in the judgments, in the excellent words and the sacred morals of so great a ruler as can readily be perceived in the commands of Trajan. Yet if anyone disputes Trajan's faith or morals, these could be ascribed to the times rather than to the man. If Virgil was permitted to acquire the gold of wisdom from the clay of Ennius, in what way is it hateful to us to share in our own learning from what is written by the gentiles?[7]

John holds that the principles pertaining to a properly arranged social body are by no means inherently Christian in bearing. Rather, since the precepts of the well-ordered republic were identified by a pagan philosopher and transmitted to an exceedingly moral but unbelieving emperor, it is presumably the case that any community containing wise rulers and just subjects is capable of apprehending and applying them, regardless of religious convictions. That Plutarch and Trajan shared "superstitious" beliefs is a historical accident of no import. Reason, not revelation, plays the leading role in designing the body politic.

This becomes evident in John's depiction of the constitution of the political organism. He begins with the simple naturalistic observation that the commonwealth may be likened to a "body which is animated."[8] The differentiation of the offices of political society may thus be represented in a manner analogous to the distinction of the parts of the human anatomy. The body politic properly speaking is ruled by the prince, who "occupies the place of the head."[9] At the heart of the commonwealth lies the senate, composed of the counselors whose wisdom the ruler consults. The senses correspond to the royal judges and local agents such as sheriffs and bailiffs who exercise jurisdiction in the king's name. The financial officers constitute the stomach and intestines of the body, while the two hands are formed by the tax-collector and the soldier respectively. Finally, John compares the feet to the artisans and peasants "who erect, sustain and move forward the mass of the whole body."[10] Each of the parts of the organism, according to the *Policraticus*, has its own definite function which is fixed by its location within the overall scheme of the body. None of the members may be excluded or removed without serious damage to the whole. The security of the body politic, therefore, can only be maintained by means of a joint commitment to a public good which benefits every part without distinction, so that "each individual may be likened to a part of the others reciprocally and each believes what is to his own advantage to be determined by that which he recognizes to be most useful for others."[11] John's political body is one in which, beyond all social differentiation, there is "mutual charity reigning everywhere,"[12] because all segments are attuned to the same enduring common purpose which encompasses the valid interests of the whole.

How does religious faith and ritual fit into John's model of the well-ordered body politic? He acknowledges that, like all bodies, the commonwealth is guided by a soul; specifically, the place of the soul belongs to them "who institute and mold the practice of religion, and who transmit the worship of God (not the 'gods' of which Plutarch speaks)," namely, the priesthood.[13] There must, in John's view, be a religious component to the political organism. Even in "superstitious" societies such as pagan Rome, where "Augustus Caesar himself was constantly subject to the sacred pontiffs,"[14] religion plays a guiding role in public life. John clearly thinks that the priests of the Christian church, as representatives of the one true religion, ought to form the soul in the body politic of his own day. Yet, as for Abulafia, his point of departure is strictly neutral with regard to which religion directs the communal order.[15] Rather, he imagines that it is possible to substitute the worship of Plutarch's "gods" with the worship of the single Christian deity: Plutarch's "starting point is from reverence for the gods, whereas ours is from reverence of God."[16] John later tries to absolve "Plutarch" of the charge of sacrilege by offering an esoteric speculation: Plutarch simply adopted the commonplace point of view, fearing to doubt publicly what, as a philosopher, he questioned privately, namely, the conventional pagan teachings.[17] However ironic such a statement is meant to be (for, of course, John himself has created the pagan text ascribed to Plutarch), the *Policraticus* seems prepared to concede that Christianity is not, strictly speaking, a necessary condition for a political community oriented toward the common good as he conceives it. The only necessary requirement is that society embrace **some** form of religious faith. How different is this from another English John—John Locke—who over five hundred years later insisted that atheists must not be tolerated because they are destructive of social bonds?[18]

Could a well-ordered body politic be sustained, however, if there were to be internal dissention over the nature of the confession to be followed? Must it be one religion that guides the body, or might multiple religious perspectives coexist? There is reason to suppose that a unity of religion may not be strictly entailed by John's theory of organic wholeness. Let us keep in mind that his criteria for judging the welfare of the community remain primarily temporal ones. The presence of a cooperative spirit within diverse sections of the community stems from John's identification of the "health" of the body politic with the practice of justice by the organs and members. Indeed, his definition of the common good in terms of justice contains a recognition of a correlative obligation on the part of all members of the commonwealth: "Inasmuch as the duties (*officia*) of each individual are practiced so that provision is made for the corporate community, as long as justice is practiced, the ends of all are imbued with the sweetness of honey."[19] Every organ of the body must conduct itself according to the dictates of justice if the polity is to exist as a corporate whole. John's conception of justice in public affairs applies to the physical good or harm of the body's members. Following Cicero's formula in *De officiis*,[20] the *Policraticus* asserts, "Justice consists chiefly in this: do not do harm and prevent the doing of harm out of duty to humanity. When you do harm, you assent to injury. When you do not impede the doing of harm, you are a servant of injustice."[21] The essence of justice pertains to a responsibility toward the well-being of others; this responsibility entails not simply a negative obligation to refrain from the commission of injury, but a positive duty to protect others from harm as well. Since justice is the salient characteristic of the common good, it determines the manner in which each of the bodily members performs its functions. Hence, not only kings and magistrates, but even the lowliest of parts, are viewed by John as agents of public justice. This arises from the fact that the function of each segment of the organism is absolutely necessary for the welfare of all the others.

It would presumably be unjust, then, to injure a productive member of the community—or to turn one's back on such injury—even if one did not embrace that person's privately held religious sentiments. As long as the religious dissident performs his appropriate tasks in a manner conducive to the common good, justice demands toleration. John roughly captures this principle in a useful distinction between "vices" and "flagrant crimes." The commission of vice constitutes a minor offense, which can be "endured" by the government and community if the person who engages in the vice declines (noncoercive) correction. By contrast, flagrant crimes, which endanger the well-being of the body politic, must be strictly punished according to the laws of the society.[22] This distinction illuminates how a diversity of moral and theological standpoints within a single society may be tolerable, so long as the maintenance of overall communal health is not threatened. John asserts that it is a greater evil for a ruler to punish members of the community too zealously for their ostensive faults than to indulge them with too great a measure of mercy.[23]

John's willingness to forebear vices within the community instead of eliminating them coercively reflects, in large measure, one of the important features of the well-ordered community for John, namely, its promotion of liberty. Since I have addressed John's concept of liberty at considerable length elsewhere,[24] I will simply signal at present how this theme relates to the issue of diversity within the body politic. First, the health of the body depends crucially for John upon the freedom of all its members to judge and speak for themselves. It is functionally impossible for parts of the whole to collaborate efficiently if they do not share some measure of the "December liberty" that ancient Roman slaves enjoyed, namely, the ability to express grievances and criticisms to superiors without fear of retributive punishment. A purely hierarchical ordering of members is far too likely to produce the myriad forms of tyranny that the *Policraticus* identifies. Second, as a consequence of John's adherence to the epistemological views of the Ciceronian

New Academy, he maintains a moderately skeptical stance about the human capacity to grasp truth with absolute certainty. As a result, he insists that members of society possess a *ius*, a right, to inquire into and dispute about a broad range of questions, including fundamental issues of moral and political philosophy as well as theology. Only a few matters (such as the existence of a single God) are excluded from doubt, according to John; most problems are sufficiently unsettled that the uncertainty of their solution will be honestly admitted by a reasonable person. Thus, freedom to question and doubt must be defended and upheld unconditionally by church and state alike.

These factors suggest that John of Salisbury's arrangement of the body politic is open to embracing diversity within its unity. For John, indeed, the two principles of difference and identity are mutually reinforcing, rather than incommensurable. Could this acceptance of difference extend to Jews and other non-Christians? While John does not take up the issue as explicitly as, say, his teacher Peter Abelard,[25] his construction of the political organism on an extra-Christian foundation, in conjunction with his minimalistic requirements for religious doctrine as a condition of membership in the community, suggest that his theory can withstand a broadly inclusive interpretation.

Peter of Celle

A life-long friend and correspondent of John of Salisbury, Peter, Abbot of the monastery of Celle, is seldom ranked among the first tier of twelfth-century authors. Perhaps best known for his letters, Peter also composed a number of sermons and brief treatises touching on subjects important for his fellow monks. Late in his life, Peter turned to a topic with which he was intimately familiar: the organization of claustral discipline. *The School of the Cloister*, written in about 1179, is not an attempt to prescribe a given rule of monastic order but to present a general account and defense of claustral life. Peter's concern is to demonstrate how the discipline imposed by monastic confinement improves the condition of the soul and prepares it for divine judgment. The lesson that discipline has an edifying and purifying effect, he acknowledges, derives from an array of sources, including the Jews. The third chapter of *The School of the Cloister*, entitled "Comparison between Jewish Claustral Discipline and Ours," observes that "just as the commandments of the law written on the two tables contained the Jewish discipline, so every regular, whether canon or monk, must live between two inheritances, that is, the framework provided by the Rule and the good customs handed on by his elders."[26] For Peter, studying the conduct of the Jews can be a useful aid to establishing the terms of Christian discipline.

Turning to the arrangement of monastic life itself, Peter frames his conception of the cloister in recognizably holistic terms echoing the social discourse of the twelfth century. In language reminiscent of (and possibly derived from) John of Salisbury,[27] Peter states that "charity melts and unites all those spirits in the love of God and of each other. When they have been molded together in one spirit, they are as tightly bonded as if there were only a single spirit in the whole multitude."[28] In this sense, the monastery is reminiscent of a well-ordered city.

> How pious, good, safe, and pleasant it is for brothers to live together in the cloister. When brother helps brother, the city is fortified . . . The cloister is a city because there claustrals come together to live good lives; it is fortified because they live under the protection of the God of heaven. The discipline of the cloister is an iron gate which leads into the city.[29]

The analogy from monastery to city is an important one: it is not enough that religious live as individuals according to the will and law of God; their discipline is complete only when they share a communal life and reciprocally assist one another in achieving their mutual goal. In addition to cooperation, monks also learn through the experience of community to humble themselves by voluntary submission to their Rule and to their superiors.

The very program embodied in *The School of the Cloister* would consequently appear *prima facie* hostile to any religious perspective short of rigorous and ascetic Christian devotion. How could non-Christians or their values play a role in the formation of monastic community? Surprisingly, however, Peter observes that the ordering of the cloister must take cognizance of the divergent purposes which human beings seek to realize. According to Peter, the source of human diversity (religious as well as cultural) was the Fall—not in the sense that diversity is evil, but in the sense that it stems from humanity's active effort to maintain "a spark of the natural good" by means of discovering "many disciplines,"[30] including those of the philosopher and the Jew (the two usual interlocutors in twelfth-century Christian interreligious dialogues)[31]:

> Every nation under the sun and every region, according to its capacity, devised for itself a discipline of reason, which was to be the form of life both for the disorderliness of fools and the rightness of the prudent. The philosophers set up their discipline, the Jews received theirs, the Christians theirs, the Christians theirs, and finally the hermits and the claustrals theirs.[32]

Each of these ways of life has its own ends, and its own characteristic activities and methods, all of which arise from a partial attempt to restore what was lost in the human lapse from first creation. Thus, "the philosopher intends to acquire human glory and favor for himself" by scrutinizing "the secrets of the earth," abandoning "the obstacles of the flesh and the burdens of the world," sharpening his wit, disputing ideas and words, and teaching in the schools. Likewise, the goal of the Jew is acquisition of "the goods of the earth"; he "strives to purify the flesh through sacrifices and offering," living "in the letter of the flesh" according to the "husk of the law" in which he is instructed "in the synagogue." Peter stipulates in similar fashion the purposes and qualities of the Christian layperson and of the monk.[33]

The point of Peter's quite extensive comparison is not, as one might expect, to disparage the pursuits of the philosopher, the Jew, and (to a lesser extent) the ordinary Christian in contrast with the cloistered religious. In fact, however, Peter insists that the latter have much to learn from the other disciplines, and should incorporate into their community those principles that they all share.

> Let our discipline have in common with the philosopher a fruitful silence, with the Jew a continual sacrifice, with the Christian the shared solace of charity, and with its own profession a special submission to the divine will. Let our discipline, like the philosopher's, exclude concern with worldly preoccupations. Let it, with the Jew's, carry out worship of one God. Let it commend itself to grace with the Christian's . . . Let it fulfill the beginnings of its vows with the philosopher, the middle elements of them with the Jew, their farthest parts with Christians, and their ultimate reaches with a free will joined to grace. Let the claustral harvest what is green with the philosopher, what is fertile with the Jew, what is ripe with the Christian, and what is fruitful with his vow.[34]

The monastic life builds upon the other forms of existence that have naturally arisen in the aftermath of the Fall. The cloister affords a superior way of serving God, in Peter's view, but it, too, remains imperfect and must comprehend humanity's fallen state. Therefore, monasticism cannot reject out of hand the other ways and means of human living, but must learn from and appropriate what is true and useful in alternative modes of social organization. Nowhere in *The School of the Cloister* does Peter condemn outright the philosopher or the Jew, let alone the lay Christian. Their perspective may be limited in comparison with the monk, but their positive qualities are to be valorized, not reviled.

That Peter of Celle is able to integrate religious and intellectual otherness even into his conception of the Christian cloister may seem to be a remarkable feat. In fact, the observations made by Peter, and also by John of Salisbury, seem to me to be excellent examples of an approach that the philosopher Michael Sandel has recently labeled "judgmental toleration." By this phrase, Sandel appears to mean that tolerance is afforded to minority groups or practices for the sake of some other, greater social good.[35] John's functionalist conception of community certainly encourages this sort of "judgmental toleration": we forebear those who possess differing (perhaps repugnant) viewpoints because they make direct contributions to the common welfare which is the purpose of political affairs. In a similar vein, the lessons to be derived from noncloistered (even non-Christian) religious render valuable their presence and justify their social inclusion.

There is, then, nothing inherently or exclusively Christian about the holistic and organic accounts of society that came to be articulated during the twelfth century. Doubtless Abulafia is correct that some versions of communalism had the intended or inadvertent consequence of maneuvering Jews and other non-Christians (or unorthodox Christians) out of a public identity. But mainstream churchmen could with equal ease employ holistic language and metaphors to maintain a place for minorities within the dominant Christian paradigm. If this represented no great step forward in the recognition and inclusion of persons and groups outside the norm of medieval Christianity, then neither did it necessarily reflect a move away, toward a more repressive or exclusionary organization of society.

Notes

1. See Georges Duby, *The Three Orders: Feudal Society Imagined*, trans. A. Goldhammer (Chicago: University of Chicago Press, 1980); Paul Edward Dutton, "*Illustre civitatis et populi exemplum*: Plato's *Timaeus* and the Transmission from Calcidius to the End of the Twelfth Century of a Tripartite Scheme of Society," *Mediaeval Studies* 45 (1983): 79–119; and Giles Constable, "The Orders of Society," *Three Studies in Medieval Religious and Social Thought* (Cambridge: Cambridge University Press, 1995), 251–360.
2. Tilman Struve, *Die Entwicklung der organologischen Staatsauffassung im Mittelalter* (Stuttgart: Hiersemann, 1978); Jacques Le Goff, "Head or Heart? The Political Uses of Body Metaphors in the Middle Ages," Michel Feher, ed., *Fragments for a History of the Human Body*, Part Three (New York: Zone Books, 1989), 13–26.
3. Gaines Post, "The Naturalness of Society and the State," in *Studies in Medieval Legal Thought: Public Law and the State, 1100–1322* (Princeton: Princeton University Press, 1964), 494–561; Cary J. Nederman, "Natural, Sin and the Origins of Society: The Ciceronian Tradition in Medieval Political Thought," *Journal of the History of Ideas* 49 (1988): 3–26.
4. Pierre Michaud-Quantin, *Universitas: Expressions du mouvement communitaire dans le moyen age Latin* (Paris: J. Vrin, 1970).
5. Anna Sapir Abulafia, *Christians and Jews in the Twelfth-Century Renaissance* (London: Routledge, 1995), 54–55.
6. The original article by Liebeschütz was "John of Salisbury and Pseudo-Plutarch," *Journal of the Warburg and Courtauld Institutes* 6 (1943): 33–39. For an overview of the controversy engendered by the allegation of his fabrication, see Janet Martin, "John of Salisbury as Classical Scholar," and Max Kerner, "Randbemerkungen zur *Institutio Traiani*," in Michael Wilks, ed., *The World of John of Salisbury* (Oxford: Basil Blackwell, 1984), 179–201, 203–06.
7. John of Salisbury, *Policraticus*, 2 vols., ed. C.C.J. Webb (Oxford: Clarendon Press, 1909), I, 280–81 (selections trans. Cary J. Nederman [Cambridge: Cambridge University Press, 1990], 65).

8. Ibid., I, 282 (66).
9. Ibid., I, 298 (69).
10. Ibid., I, 282–283 (67).
11. Ibid., II, 59 (126).
12. Ibid., II, 86 (184).
13. Ibid., I, 282 (66).
14. Ibid., I, 282 (67).
15. Abulafia, *Christians and Jews in the Twelfth-Century Renaissance*, 54–55.
16. John of Salisbury, *Policraticus*, I, 184 (68).
17. Ibid., I, 294.
18. John Locke, *A Letter Concerning Toleration*, ed. James Tully (Indianapolis: Hackett, 1983).
19. John of Salisbury, *Policraticus*, II, 63 (131).
20. Cicero, *De officiis*, ed. Walter Miller (Cambridge, Mass.: Harvard University Press, 1913), 25.
21. John of Salisbury, *Policraticus*, I, 277 (62).
22. Ibid., II, 78–79 (140–141).
23. Ibid., I, 266–267 (53–54).
24. The following paragraph builds on Cary J. Nederman, "The Aristotelian Doctrine of the Mean and John of Salisbury's Concept of Liberty," *Vivarium* 24 (November 1986): 128–42; idem., "Freedom, Community, And Function: Communitarian Lessons of Medieval Political Theory," *American Political Science Review* 86 (December 1992): 977–986; and idem., "Toleration, Skepticism, and the 'Clash of Ideas': Principles of Liberty in the Writings of John of Salisbury," John Christian Laursen and Cary J. Nederman, eds., *Beyond the Persecuting Society: Religious Toleration before the Enlightenment* (Philadelphia: University of Pennsylvania Press, 1998), 53–70.
25. See Peter Abelard, *Dialogue of a Philosopher with a Jew and a Christian*, trans. Pierre Payer (Toronto: Pontifical Institute of Medieval Studies, 1974).
26. Peter of Celle, *The School of the Cloister*, in *Peter of Celle: Selected Works* Hugh Fleiss, ed. and trans., (Kalamazoo: Cistercian Publications, 1987), 73.
27. Cf. W.J. Millor, H.E. Butler and C.N.L. Brooke, eds., *The Letters of John of Salisbury*, vol. 1: *The Early Letters (1153–1161)* (London: Thomas Nelson and Sons, 1955), 181–182.
28. Peter of Celle, *The School of the Cloister*, 88.
29. Ibid., 84.
30. Ibid., 85.
31. On the genre of the interreligious dialogue, see Cary J. Nederman, *Worlds of Difference: European Discourses of Religious Toleration, c. 1100–c. 1550* (University Park: Pennsylvania State University Press, forthcoming 2000), chap. 2.
32. Peter of Celle, *The School of the Cloister*, 85.
33. Ibid., 85–86.
34. Ibid., 87.
35. Michael J. Sandel, "Judgemental Liberalism," in *Natural Law, Liberalism, and Morality*, ed. Robert P. George (Oxford: Clarendon Press, 1996), 107–112.

12
Religious Geography: Designating Jews and Muslims as Foreigners in Medieval England

DAVID B. LESHOCK

Francisco Stand, ho! Who is there?

Marcellus Friends to this ground.

—WILLIAM SHAKESPEARE, *HAMLET*[1]

Geographical proximity, being from the same ground, functions as an attribute of identity, one in which we distinguish the familiar from that which is foreign. In late medieval England, we see evidence that such a sense of identity based on geography was becoming increasingly important. The idea of "Europe" and even "England" became more central in many texts about identity. A look at two texts about the world at this time shows that the connections of geographic identity, in whose representations class and family differences are effaced, were not extended to Jews and Muslims, even though they both inhabited the same space as those who produced the texts.

The Hereford *mappamundi* and *The Book of John Mandeville*[2] share a common operation: they are important creative works of group identity. They do not project an established, *a priori* identity but rather are interventions into the construction of identity. We must see them as both descriptive and, perhaps more important, performative symbolic acts. While describing the world and the reader's place in that world, these texts construct that world for the reader, a representation that has powerful implications, if accepted, for that individual's sense of self and sense of place. As Nelson Goodman argues, "Identity or constancy in a world is identity with respect to what is within that world as organized."[3] In a Christian-centered world, identity is connected with religion, and these texts support such an identity. However, they also support another layer of identity, which is linked to geographic space. These two texts in particular show the ways that both geography and religion can influence the construction of identity, and thereby determine what is "foreign."

This identity, linked to lived geographic space, is not, of course, the only source of cultural or individual identity. It is one of a group of concentric spheres of often overlapping identity markers, including religion, family, and gender. Thorlac Turville-Petre avers that for the late medieval English people, there "were many overlapping identities, of occupation and class, of gender, of religion, of family, borough and shire."[4] The Hereford map and *The Book of John Mandeville* evince that identity is linked with spatial location, but during this time period it significantly overlaps with religion. The idea of a Christian empire and a connection between Christians is strong; nevertheless, in some portions of these texts, identity is situated with respect to factors other than religious affiliation. Within Europe, however, these texts show that the category of religion can trump geographic proximity in the distinction of those who belong and those who are foreign.

In their description of both England and Europe, these texts participate in the creation of "imagined communities" as defined by Benedict Anderson. They posit communities that are "a collectivity of people which, although its members may be widely divergent and will never meet the others in that group, nevertheless assumes a 'deep, horizontal comradeship.' "[5] For these texts, geographical proximity creates such a community. This conception does not imply necessarily that these constructions are negative, although Anderson's work often shows how they are. The important fact to acknowledge is that these are constructions, which require further, continuous constructing and reinforcing. These texts are elements in the construction of such communities, for good or bad. Anderson affirms that "all communities larger than primordial villages of face-to-face contact (and perhaps even these) are imagined. Communities are to be distinguished, not by their falsity/genuineness, but by the style in which they are imagined."[6] Thus, the construction of the world in these texts follows what Nelson Goodman calls "worldmaking": the construction of a world in which modes of organization "are not 'found in the world' but *built into a world*."[7] His construction highlights the fact that worldmaking is a narrative; it is a discursive construction of that world, one built by, not merely described by, story.

The constructed nature of communal identity does not weaken its power; social identity, in fact, has implications for action or behavior. These links of identity offer justification for certain types of behavior which allow destruction and killing, activities seemingly against other strictures of a community. The immediate background to the texts in question in this study is the crusading impulse which allowed Christians to act in ways very much different than those exemplified by the life of Jesus. The common metaphor of a "homeland" captures the essence of what nationalism or even general territoriality suggests. The metaphor of a "home" to describe a "land" implies ownership and exclusivity for "familial" types of relations, such as "brotherhood." The construction of a "homeland" lends tremendous weight to collective identity formation; our modern world consistently shows the power, again, for good and for evil, of such a metaphor.

The England that produced the Hereford map and *The Book of John Mandeville* was one that had immediate concerns about territoriality, nationhood, and identity. By 1282, Edward I had subjugated Wales and hoped to annex Scotland. He also had claims to land in France. Edward was very much interested in defining England and what that territory included. The Scots were a source of anguish for all three Edwards. The anxiety about separating the Scots from the English appears quite prominently on the Hereford *mappamundi*. On the map, the connection between Scotland and England is virtually nonexistent—just a tiny link in a color different from that of the rest of the land, which connects what might seem to be two completely separate entities.

This specifically English spatial identity corresponds to a historical Englishness cultivated by Edward I. Edward I was particularly interested in tracing a lineage back to King Arthur to legitimate his reign, and this connection to a British hero highlights the belief in an identity based on specifically English heroic values. The political worth that these connections held also proves the ideological power of the romance to influence markers of identity. Later, Edward III also connected his reign with the cult of Arthur, establishing the Order of the Garter. This preoccupation with what it means to be English was the climate of the original audience of these texts under study.

So, this concern for what was "English" is evidence of a nascent nationalism in this time period. Hastings Rashdall notes that Oxford University ceased to use the term "nations" in 1274, "a symbol of that complete national unity which England was the first of the European kingdoms to affirm."[8] Rashdall overemphasizes the unity of "nationalism" at this time, although he does provide important evidence of the emergence of a new aspect of an identity, tied to geographic space at this time. We must locate this new ideology within the existing constructs of European collectivity or Christendom for, as Raymond Williams maintains, "definitions of the emergent . . . can only be made in relation to a full sense of the dominant [culture]."[9] There is tension between an idea of Christendom or more specifically Europe and that of England as separate, sovereign, and different entities. *The Book of John Mandeville* demonstrates a strong pull to define Englishness at the same time it codifies and supports the notion of a European collectivity. We see an overlap between the two, yet the nationalism, more important at the time of the Hundred Years' War, is an emergent ideological construction for England. *The Book of John Mandeville* uses the collective pronoun "we" to describe both "European" and the more specific "English."

In 1290, Edward I expelled all Jews from England, perhaps the strongest evidence of a link of space and identity at this time. This act highlights the fact that many people felt that foreign people inhabited *their* land. The distinction of lived space and identity in the case of the Jews supported the idea that geographic space should be peopled by a homogeneous group, and the further idea that without the Jews it would be; England would be more "English." To be sure, these distinctions between living in the same space and sharing the same identity are the results of a vested interest, a condition of the time that Turville-Petre calls a "useful vagueness over what it meant to be English,"[10] yet they highlight the power of identifying a particular space with a particular group.

The expulsion of the Jews was intricately tied to the expression of what I will call "medieval nationalism,"[11] a nascent idea in the fourteenth century. Salo Baron avers that earlier in English history, shortly after the Norman conquest, the population had an existing Anglo-Saxon majority and a small but dominant Norman minority; the Jews at the time of expulsion, therefore, were "intrinsically no more foreign than the aristocracy."[12] The idea that Jews could not live in the same land is an indication that England had begun to define itself as a land with a homogeneous population, a single identity. Contemporary chronicler Pierre de Langtoft claims a unified support for such a measure, an implicit nod to a homogeneous collective, when he states "there is nobody who opposes it, / To expel the Jews."[13] Obviously, he does not count the opinion of the Jews and can therefore attest to the unanimous decision of the nation. The imagined community had expelled the "foreign" element in its homeland. A similar operation, a symbolic expulsion, appears textually on both the Hereford map and *The Book of John Mandeville*.

The Hereford *mappamundi* is one of the largest medieval *mappaemundi* to survive. This map of the world was produced ca. 1290 by a Richard of Holdingham (*haldingham*), according to an inscription on the map. This map loosely follows the basic model of the "T-O map," a tripartite schema which fit the three known continents into a circle in which Asia on top was separated by a "T" by the convergence of the Don, Nile, and Europe and Africa were split by the Mediterranean. According to P. D. A. Harvey, the purpose of a *mappamundi* was "philosophical and didactic: a schematic representation of the earth that in the more detailed examples was to give a great deal of information about its inhabitants and their relationship to the deity."[14] I would add that the placement of those inhabitants, including the viewers of the map, also provided significant information about the relationship of those peoples of the earth with one another. In essence, the map produces not only "religious" identity but also what modern critics may call a "secular" identity, although at the point in history from which we receive the map, a distinction between the two would be an overstatement. Nevertheless, although the map shows evidence of a secular identity, the Hereford map evinces the ability to suspend a secular identity based on geography for Muslims and Jews.

The Hereford map was a text of real, "scientific" value to its original audience, not just a work of art, despite how different that designation seems from our modern views of accuracy. To modern eyes, the map is laughable in its depiction of the lands of the earth. Scale appears to be a concept beyond the grasp of our cartographer, and any usefulness to anyone for travel or knowledge about boundaries appears restricted. Yet to assume that the curiosities of the map are due merely to gaps in scientific knowledge is to misunderstand the methods of medieval worldmaking. Proclamations against the horrific misrepresentations of the medieval *mappaemundi*[15] were virtually universal until John Kirtland Wright's landmark study, *The Geographical Lore of the Time of the Crusades: A History of Medieval Science and Tradition in Western Europe*. Wright insightfully argues that

> it is a mistake to regard accuracy as the goal of the medieval map maker. . . . The maps were more or less in the nature of diagrammatic sketches on which the features of the earth's surface were shown in a general way, and the draftsman understood perfectly well that all he could hope to give was a rough approximation to relative positions.[16]

Wright concludes that "most medieval maps—including wall maps—were nothing more than rough diagrams converted into works of art."[17] Wright, in my opinion, overemphasizes the purpose of the medieval map as merely art, yet he was the first to assert strongly that accuracy was not the chief concern of the medieval mapmaker.[18]

Many contemporary critics since Wright, who accept that the Hereford map is an active text of worldmaking, focus in large degree on the Christian elements of the map, yet the map cannot be constrained by merely a religious reading. This map is both "religious" and "secular." It would be impossible to extract one purpose from the other, because both are inextricably linked, as they were for most conceptions of life on earth for the Christian Middle Ages. To be sure, everyone did not agree on the religious meanings of earthly life, but a religious background may safely be assumed to pervade most cultural documents of the late European Middle Ages, either in the text specifically, or in the methodology of various interpretive communities. The iconography of Christ in judgment at the top of the map, and the emphasis on representing the spaces of Biblical events, are indeed crucially important elements of the map. However, the Hereford map emphasizes other important features of geographic space to a greater degree than it merely delineates Biblical stories. David Woodward maintains that the "primary purpose of these *mappaemundi*, as they are called, was to instruct the faithful about the significant events in Christian history rather than to record their precise location."[19] Yet this analysis begs the question as to why such information would be placed on a map structure; there were, after all, other types of paintings that could focus more space and emphasis on the Christian events.

Moreover, the connection between Christianity and geographic, earthly space has not always been a priority. As Woodward notes, in "early Judaism the importance of the location of events was emphasized, but early Christianity showed little interest in such things, with certain important exceptions such as the journeys of Saint Paul. The teachings of Christ emphasized the spiritual and not the physical world."[20] The change to an interest in physical location is therefore distinct from an organic necessity in Christianity. The Hereford map is indeed a religious document, yet its emphasis on the physical world is not simply an appendage to the Christian-based model. The Hereford map exhibits an extreme interest in what now would be called "secular" knowledge of the world.

The inclusion of beasts and peoples throughout the world is indicative of this strong interest in the physical attributes of the secular world. Moreover, many place names on the map do not exist in the Bible, nor do the monstrous peoples. One could well ask, for instance, what has the sciopod to do with Christ; the map must not be solely a religious document. Furthermore, Marcia Kupfer attests that the groupings of texts in library catalogs in numerous eleventh and twelfth-century examples "suggest that geography, an adjunct to history, belonged to a realm of secular knowledge made available through the study of the liberal arts."[21] A map was an educational tool, not simply art nor iconography, although it could also serve as a work of beauty or devotion. These maps are misread, however, if the only emphasis is on their "religious" role without consideration of the scientific purpose of many of the maps, the Hereford included.

Although the map has what modern viewers consider fantastical creatures, it was a "scientific" rather than primarily symbolic document for its audience. The Hereford map was a vehicle for the dissemination of serious knowledge. The map is not primarily symbolic, in the manner of fables of talking animals. Many of the features on the map may have elements of symbolism, yet the map parallels the information in the medieval encyclopedias, compendiums of knowledge.[22] Rudolf Wittkower notes that the monstrous races in the late medieval period often had allegorical meanings. He states that in one thirteenth-century bestiary "the pygmies stand for humility and the giant for pride, the cynocephali typify quarrelsome persons, and the people who cover themselves with the lower lip are the mischievous, according to the word of the psalm: 'Let the mischief of their own lips cover them.' "[23] Yet Wittkower also acknowledges that even though these creatures or peoples were invested with allegorical significance, they were considered real. These creatures on the Hereford map were not only symbols or personifications. They existed as part of the natural world, and their allegorical significance, when they were invested with such, was a means of explaining how these existing creatures fit into God's overall plan.

To look at the Hereford map as a true text of worldmaking is to suspend our modern mental representation, which is influenced by the Mercator projections and globes—our modern texts of worldmaking, which shape our own ideas about the world—to accept that the Hereford map did represent the world for its audience. Even if that view was just a schematic representation, without the assumption of actually scale and shape, the map reproduced the important features of the world for those who read it. The map highlights the connotations which become attached with certain geographic spaces. By looking at how the map represents the world, we learn how the mapmaker(s) constructed the idea of its audience, with a collective identity, and can speculate as to how its real audience would have interpreted its place in the world around them, a world whose borders were both geographic and religious.

Worldmaking in the Hereford *mappamundi* is more complex than a simple religious representation of the world. To be sure, the map highlights a distinction very prominently at the top of the map, between good Christians, who will ascend to Heaven, and all others, who will descend into Hell. Yet the map elucidates identity in more than just a simple dichotomy. The map delimits concentric and overlapping circles of identity, from Christian to European to English for its original audience. "European" is an important marker of identity on the map, which treats the continent in significantly different terms than the rest of the world. The other two continents are full of strange peoples (both threatening and not) and peculiar beasts. The monstrous races that dominate the visual field of the map are difficult to place into the binary system of Christian/non-Christian on the top of the map. Augustine himself had difficulty interpreting these peoples.[24] Yet all the beasts and peoples, whether they would be frightening or not for the original audience, provide the exotic appeal of the map, a link to someplace not "here." The map offers a portrait of a medieval worldview that sees the surrounding world outside the safe confines of Europe, and even on the edges, to be a world dominated by the strange and marvelous, and quite often threatening. By showing the exotic and foreign elements of Asia and Africa, the map posits the familiar Europe as the normal and natural. The threatening and strange are both visual and textual, so both literate and illiterate audiences would get a flavor of the hostile spaces outside Europe.

Some critics have noted the extreme placement of the monsters on the edges of the earth as a suggestion of their distance from God. John Friedman suggests that in medieval world maps "monstrous men are symbolically the farthest from Christ of anything in creation, and are represented in a narrow band at the edge of the world, as far as possible from Jerusalem, the center of Christianity."[25] This type of presentation certainly would emphasize the religious function of the map, and explain the meaning of the monstrous races neatly within the dichotomy of Christian and non-Christian. However, the monstrous races on the Hereford map appear in various locations throughout

Asia and Africa. More significantly, England itself is just as far from Jerusalem as southern Africa.[26] How the inhabitants of England would be different would have to be understood as some sort of *a priori* identification with Christianity. The map also exhibits the idea that some geographic spaces, and their legitimate inhabitants, are superior than others. "England" is obviously valued differently from southern Africa, even though both are equidistant from Jerusalem on the map.

The map also offers an indication of how non-Europeans could easily become suspect and associated with the monstrous and savage. Joyce Salisbury notes, "[a]s people began to define humanity by behavior, the possibility was opened for redefining people who had previously been accepted as human. Early Christian thinkers had categorically stated that all people were human. By the late Middle Ages, however, some groups of people seemed to be less human than others."[27] Salisbury specifically mentions that women and the poor were often equated with the animal. Using the map, we can see how the association of monstrous races with certain areas could expand these distinctions of class and gender into the realm of geography. Just as some authors could denigrate women or the poor into the realm of the animal, so could they devalue those peoples who lived in the areas of the monstrous.

In addition to the placement of the wild and foreign in far away places, the map erases groups from Europe that an English audience would consider foreign, that is, Jews and Muslims. Europe is free of these elements, since no mention is made of them in Europe, and they are instead specifically represented in Asia. The map effectively says that even though there may be Jews and Muslims in Europe, they are in fact not at "home" but are fugitives from their rightful place, far off in Asia. They become, in effect, as strange and foreign as the other residents of the fringes, the monstrous races.

Moreover, within the British Isles, distinctions between the regions and their identities further fracture the constructed audience of the map into smaller circles. This subgroup of identity, "English" within "European," is not as significantly bounded as European is from identity connected to the other continents. It is a vague notion on the map, yet it definitely exists and would carry weight on the local level for the original audience, who knew wars with Scotland and Wales as well as previous wars with France. Distinctions between groups of people into identifying groups need not be as severe as monstrous versus human. Modern residents of New York may feel distinct from residents of Los Angeles and identify themselves differently. Even that benign distinction is an example of how people identify themselves in relation to outsiders. The Hereford map does just that to varying degrees; it identifies outsiders in varying degrees of contrast to a constructed collective "us."[28]

This map was first and foremost a map; a visual representation of territory and peoples that the medieval English audience would have taken as true, if not an "accurate" diagram of that world by modern standards. Yet, in its methods of showing boundaries between spaces, it also shows boundaries between peoples, connecting space and identity. By situating the rest of the world, the map posits an "us," a narrative collective that is contrasted from the exotic and strange around the world. The difference of Europe from the other two continents creates a European collectivity that stands apart from the barbaric and monstrous characteristics of Asia and Africa. Yet, at the same time, the specific English audience is also delimited by geographic markers.

The map establishes that geographic proximity is vital to a sense of communal identity. However, the map's designation of Jews and Muslims betrays an uneasiness about using solely geography. The society that produced the map did not consider Jews and Muslims part of the European community for religious differences; therefore, they are expelled from the geographic space on the map. Thus, although the Hereford map can be read as a text which delineated identity of a secular nature, at the same time the treatment of Muslims and Jews is a retreat from such an emphasis on geographic identity. Jews and Muslims are residents of Europe at the time of the map's production, but on the map itself, they are erased.

Jews were an ubiquitous evil group in various medieval tracts, and they, of course, make an appearance on the Hereford map. Kathleen Biddick comments that medievalists have resisted using terminology like medieval "colonialism" as anachronistic, yet she argues that the "period of colonization and ethnography begins to look very different if one includes Jews."[29] She uses the work of Johannes Fabian, who shows how cultures often "detemporalize" other cultures, so that they do not have an autonomous existence, but rather exist as if they lived in the past of the interpreting culture. For much of modern ethnography until recently, technology and governing structures could be placed on a timeline of Western culture, to determine how "primitive" or "backward" another culture was. Hence, much modern ethnography has used the classification "primitive" to describe other cultures. For a discussion of the medieval period, the idea of detemporalization is somewhat useful for discussing the peoples on the map, but the concept of "primitive" is anachronistic.

In medieval ethnography, other cultures of the map are not considered "primitive," perhaps because that would provide a link with the culture that produced the map. For the medieval audience, existing in a time before Darwin, an intimate connection of these monstrous races to them would be both unthinkable and blasphemous. Medieval ethnography does deny coevalness, but it does not relegate the other peoples of the world to their own human past; it relegates them rather to "divine" time. The monstrous peoples of the Hereford map, unlike the primitive peoples of modern ethnography, are not, even in theory, ever going to attain the level of the contemporary medieval audience.[30] They can never become the "us," the collective that medieval ethnography assumes, no matter how much time passes. In sum, the idea of human "progress" as a society was relatively impossible. The sole criterion was Christianity; no one could "progress" past it. Human development existed only on the scale of God and Christian values; evolution was yet to be an overarching theory of cultural development.

In addition, Biddick's point about detemporalization of the Jews should be expanded to include all religions on the Hereford map. Biddick claims that to "rephrase Fabian, there is a 'persistent and systematic tendency' to place Jews in a time other than the present of Christendom."[31] Yet one must remember that the idea of a Christian "present" is for the most part an insignificant distinction. The geographic space of the map is also a history which sees Christ in Judgment overseeing the entire world. Earthly time is collapsed; one is either Christian or not. In this sense, a Jew or Muslim is a heretic of ahistorical significance. This operation parallels Fabian's conception of detemporalization, but the Hereford map uses the distinction of religion rather than that of progress. Therefore, whether another religion temporally pre-dates Christianity, as does Judaism, or post-dates it, as does Islam, the net effect is non-Christian, and temporal differences are insignificant for the Last Judgment.

Jews are represented in only one place on the map, where they are further detemporalized through a specific connection with Muslims. Near the Dead Sea, a group of men kneel before an idol. The men are labeled Jews ("Iudei"). The idol represents the golden calf, and the one on the map appears to be defecating, an activity upon which the eyes of the visible face of one of the Jews is focused. The calf bears the label "mahu*m*," associating Jews with Muslims, and in the process denying any autonomous religious practice to either. This detemporalizes both Muslims and Jews into generic heretics or idolaters.

Furthermore, in achieving this detemporalization, the map makes a distinction between Jews and the Israelites of the Old Testament. The representation of the Israelites shows up along a dotted line that follows their exodus as described in the Bible. The line begins in Egypt, where the text narrates, "Hic congregatus populus israel in ramisse · exiit de egipto altera die post pasca ·" [Here the whole of the people of Israel in Rameses left Egypt the day after Passover].[32] The line next leads to a passageway through the Red Sea, cut for the line to pass: "transit*us* filior*um* israel p*er* mare rubrum" [Passageway of the sons of Israel through the Red Sea]. After advancing past Mount Sinai, and Moses receiving the Ten Commandments, the line passes by the Jews ("Iudei") worshipping the golden calf, labeled Mohammed. Here, these particular Israelites are labeled "Jews" for the only time along the course, and this is the only specific, textual mention of "Jews" on the map. The course proceeds westward through a looping pattern and passes the Jews before the golden calf again. The line runs past Lot's wife and ends at Jericho, accompanied by the explanation, "Usq*ue* ad civitate*m* Ierico ducebat moyses pupolus israel ·" [Moses did lead the people of Israel right up to the city of Jericho].

The line of the exodus of the Israelites passes by the Jews who worship Mohammed on the map twice on its meandering course, clearly signifying that the "Israelites" are distinct from the "Jews." A split has therefore taken place between those who were Jews (the Israelites) who prefigured Christians, yet because of historical necessity could not be Christians, and the contemporary Jews, born after Christ, who have no excuse to remain Jews. The map uses the incident of the golden calf as the differentiation between the Jews and the Israelites. In this distinction, the Old Testament Jews are recuperated for a Christian history, while contemporary Jews are cast out with the Muslims as common heretics worshipping a defecating idol. The contemporary Jews, and of course Muslims, demonstrate by their actions that they will join the groups at Christ's left side in Judgment on the map, those consigned to Hell.

Muslims are erased from the Christian community of the map by their actions, and are deleted from the European community by their symbolic expulsion from the Iberian peninsula. In Spain on the map, the two political divisions noted on the country retain their Roman names: "Hispania Citerior" and "Hispania Inferior" (substituted for the "Hispania Ulterior" of the Romans). Although many places on the map keep their Roman names because of the sources and authorities of the map, the effect of this anachronism is particularly powerful in Spain. Roman Spain existed years before Islam existed, and the anachronism serves to expunge the Islamic presence of that country. Moreover, the one reference to Islam is the "mahu*m*" idol mentioned above, which sits in Asia, at a safe distance outside of the European community. The pictorial representation of Mohammed in Asia is the only mention of Islam; the map does not list any Muslims. Indeed, the ones worshipping Mohammed turn out to be Jews; Muslims themselves are completely erased from the entire map.

In addition, in the same picture as the "mahu*m*" idol, Jews are expelled visually from the space of Europe on the map, just as they were in body from England at, or just after, the time of the production of the Hereford map. Specifically represented in Asia, Jews are not only detemporalized but deterritorialized. If the "home" of the Jews lies in Asia, their presence in Europe is as a foreign people. The England that expelled all Jews in 1290, around the time of the map's production, believed that no matter how long they had lived there, the Jews had no right to call England home. Territory is thus given an identity, with which the people living there are identified or from which they are expelled.

The Book of John Mandeville appears less than one hundred years after the Hereford map and shows a similar sense of the importance of geography to identity. *The Book* describes the travels of a specifically English narrator throughout much of the known world. *The Book* was one of the most popular of medieval books and many manuscripts survive in numerous languages. The Middle English text from the late fourteenth century is a translation from a French language manuscript. Although some modern historians subscribe to the view that there was a John Mandeville who did write the text (even if he may not have traveled), the consensus in modern scholarship is that the identity is fabricated, and most commentators call the narrator the "Mandeville-author."[33] Debate also continues as to whether the text was initially released in Britain or the Continent. Yet my concern is not where it was originally produced, but rather how an English audience would read the book believed to be by an English knight. *The Book* would obviously speak directly to an English audience, and the text specifically refers to an English collective. The idea of a local author probably would make an English audience predisposed to concur with the various characterizations of the text. The text itself continually couches itself in terms familiar to its audience, constructing a characteristic English interpretation of the world.

The Book of John Mandeville has much in common with the visual narrative of the Hereford *mappamundi*. Indeed, Mandeville even claims that his book was the basis for a *mappamundi* which the pope approved:

> And our*e* holy fad*er* of his spec*i*al gr*a*ce remytted my boke to be*n* examyned & pr*e*ued be the Avys of his seyd conseill, Be the whiche my boke was preeued for trewe jn so moche þat þei schewed me a boke þ*at* my boke was examynde by, þ*at* comp*re*hended full moche more be an hundred p*ar*t, be whiche the Mappa Mundi was made aft*er*.[34]

Mandeville's claim—that his book was so true that it was the basis for the *mappamundi*—is evidence that these maps were assumed to be legitimate documents that represented what the world "looked like." Just as today our maps suggest that north is "up," Mandeville's perspective allows him to tell his audience that north is "the left syde of the world."[35]

The prologue to *The Book* sets up the important function of the text as a construction of a collective identity through its use of the first person plural. Early in the narrative, Mandeville emphasizes the importance of the Holy Land and exhorts all good Christian men "to conquer*e* oure right heritage."[36] This is the first place in the narrative in which "oure" is used in a context that may not be interpreted as all humankind. When Mandeville speaks of "oure lord" earlier in the prologue, the collective theoretically includes all people because in Christian theology Jesus is lord over all, whether people acknowledge it or not. But the "oure" in "conquer*e* oure right heritage" refers to Christians specifically.

The collective identity signified by "oure" also coincides with the geographical area of Europe. In evidence, Mandeville distinguishes between "oure lond" and the land of Prester John who is a Christian in the East. The collectivity privileged by the text is therefore not entirely a religious collectivity; *The Book* constructs a collectivity that is based in large part on geographic proximity. This understanding of culture is based upon an assumption of shared culture in a specific geographical space. Mandeville refers to a collective European identity: "wee duelle*n* in Europe"[37] and finishes his narrative by saying that he is the person who "dep*ar*ted fro*m* our*e* contrees."[38] Mandeville here explicitly refers to a common European identity, with a shared possessive adjective signifying a shared identity. The first person plural pronoun "oure" which Mandeville uses assumes a unified, collective European readership. Because of this assumed collectivity, the text need not describe the way through most of Europe. The author tells the reader at the beginning of the text "troweth not þ*a*t I wil tell ȝou all the townes & cytees & castelles þ*a*t me*n* schull go by for þan scholde I make to longe a tale."[39] It is true that it would of course make a longer narrative than the manuscript given, but a more logical explanation is that "we" don't need to be told the way around "oure countrees." The constructed European reader has no need for a travel narrative about his/her own territory in a general text about the world. In addition, the lack of a detailed description of Europe in *The Book* allows the reader to assume that all references to Muslims are to those people who should dwell outside of Europe, erasing their place in Spain as the Hereford map did before it.

Iain Higgins argues that the book's audience "is defined as a religious community."[40] However, people who are Christian occupy spaces in Asia and Eastern Europe, but are not included in the collective "us." Geographic space is therefore an important marker of identity for *The Book*. Although "Christian" is a necessary element of the community that the text constructs, it is not sufficient. The narrative defines the mythical Christian priest Prester John and other groups as Christians even if they follow slightly different forms of Christianity from the European version; Mandeville states that Prester John and "a gret p*ar*tie of his contree also" is Christian although they "haue not all the Articles of our*e* feyth as wee haue*n*."[41] Although they are Christian (and potential allies), "they" are not "we."

Moreover, the distinctions of the geographic space are value-laden. The idea, for instance, that the continents were peopled by the sons of Noah plays an important role in assigning a sense of shared identity to a particular space. Mandeville tells the reader that Asia is populated by the descendants of Cham (the son who saw his father naked), who "for his crueltee" took the greatest section, Asia.[42] And after the founding of Babylon, Mandeville states that at "þ*a*t tyme the fend*es* of helle came*n* many tymes & leyen w*ith* the wo*mm*e*n* of his gen*er*acioun & engendered on he*m* dyu*er*se folk as MONSTRES" (146). Moreover, he continues, "of þ*a*t gen*er*acioun of CHAM be*n* come*n* the PAYNEMES & dyu*er*se folk þ*a*t be*n* in yles of the see be all ynde."[43]

The text explicitly associates Asia, which is populated by the descendants of Cham, with Hell's demons and monsters, vilifying the heritage of the people(s) of Asia in contrast to the "right heritage" of Christian Europe.

Mandeville is fairly liberal with the category of "Christian."[44] He is also quite distinct from the Hereford map in his relatively sympathetic description of Islam. Far from the overwhelmingly negative portraits of Muslims and Islam on the map, and a vast array of texts in its time, *The Book* systematically explains Islam to his audience without overt invective. Donald Howard lauds Mandeville for the lack of condemnation: "His objectivity and tolerance, even to infidels, remain exemplary. Far from excoriating their errors, he seems altogether optimistic about their closeness to the truth."[45] Howard is overly rosy about Mandeville's tolerance, yet in the historical moment Mandeville's treatment of Islam is indeed a model of open-mindedness.[46]

Much of Mandeville's account of Islam is claimed as being from a first-hand experience with the Sultan of Egypt; indeed, Mandeville claims a close relationship with the Sultan: "I oughte right wel to knowen it for I duelled w*ith* hi*m* as soudyour in his werres a gret while, a$_3$en the Bedoynes."[47] Higgins avers that although this is probably fiction, many Christians did serve as mercenaries for the Sultan either with or without Church approval,[48] and so it is not entirely impossible. For the original audience, whose members were not collating the text with known sources, nothing suggests that Mandeville should be disbelieved. Mandeville further comments on the regard that the Sultan had for him: "he wolde have maryed me full highly to a gret Princes dought*er* $_3$if I wolde han forsaken my lawe & my beleue."[49] The original audience has no reason to suspect falsity, although this event occurs in a number of romances. Moreover, by relating this incident, Mandeville can discuss Islam from an informed and relatively fair viewpoint for his time, while reassuring his audience that he is a devout Christian.

Mandeville correctly disseminates information about Islam in some particulars, a welcome change from the misinformation in many medieval texts about Islam; Norman Daniel shows that often, despite reliable knowledge, Islam was willfully misrepresented.[50] In contrast, Mandeville mentions the holy book of Islam ("Alkaron"), and offers a summary of Muslim belief, providing some accurate information. Mandeville also claims to have read it himself: "as I haue often tyme seen & radd" is how he puts it.[51] He relates that the Saracens drink no wine nor eat swine's flesh,[52] for instance, actual prohibitions from the Qur'an. He also mentions the month of Ramadan: "þei fasten an hool moneth in the $_3$eer & ete*n* nought but be nyghte & þei kepe*n* he*m* fro*m* her*e* wyfes all þ*at* moneth."[53] This type of information portrays Islam as a religion of considerable devotion, a significant departure from most discussions of Islam at the time.

Mandeville also avoids a common medieval misconception, that Muhammed was a god for Muslims rather than a prophet. Daniel avers that a common misunderstanding of Islam is that Muhammed must be to Islam what Christ is to Christianity.[54] The origin of "Mohammedism" as a name for Islam stemmed from this misunderstanding. Mandeville, however, tells that "þei seyn also þ*at* Abraham was frend to god And þ*at* Moyses was familier spekere *with* god & Ih*es*u crist was the woord & the spirit of god & þ*at* Machomete was right messag*er* of god. And þei seyn þ*at* of theise .iiij. Ih*es*u was the most worthi & the most excellent & the most gret."[55] Mandeville, then, firmly places Muhammed in the ranks of prophet, and asserts even that the Saracens recognize the primary importance of Jesus, who is indeed a prophet appearing in the Qur'an. Mandeville's account is thus far from the polemic misunderstandings or misrepresentations of his time, and he goes to some length to assert the correspondence of Islam to Christianity.

Throughout his account of Islam, Mandeville does not set up a strawman portrait but gives the relevant connections to Christianity. Like Christians, Muslims believe that "the gode schull gon to p*ar*adys & the euele to helle."[56] In addition, Mandeville relates that they believe in the Virgin Mary: "þei beleeuen & speke*n* gladly of the virgine Marie & of the Incarnac*ioun*."[57] Most significantly, they believe that Jesus was a prophet and he "was sent fro*m* god all myghty for to be*n* myrou*r* & esample & tokne to alle me*n*."[58] Such information would make the Muslims much less alien to his audience.

But though they might appear less alien, Mandeville does not argue for leaving them alone. There are a few telling differences between the two religions, yet Mandeville argues that the many similarities of Islam to Christianity would facilitate conversion of Muslims. All they need is someone to tell them the right message: "be cause þ*at* þei gon so ny oure feyth þei ben lyghtly co*nuer*ted to cristene lawe wha*n* me*n* p*r*eche he*m* And schewe*n* he*m* distynctly the lawe of Ih*es*u crist & whan [men] tellen he*m* of the p*ro*phecyes."[59] Though still invasive, this is a different strategy from the crusade announced in the prologue of *The Book*, certainly. We see contradictions between the method of force promised in one section and that of preaching promulgated in another, though both methods are meant to achieve a fully Christian world. Mandeville's emphasis here on conversion does at least appear to create a possibility of community, albeit only when Muslims convert. The text thereby leans toward a tolerant attitude in religion, though it cannot completely escape the dominant rhetoric of crusade.

The tolerant stance to Islam explains an otherwise surprising association with a Muslim character, when *The Book* offers a satiric portrait of Western Christianity from the mouth of the Sultan of Egypt. Mandeville shares a private conversation with the Sultan, who asks him how Christians govern themselves in his country. Mandeville answers "right wel, thonked be god,"[60] but the Sultan replies that this is not true. He then launches into a devastating critique of Mandeville's audience, using a second person address: "ȝee cristne me*n* ne recche right noght how vntrewly to s*er*ue god; ȝee scholde ȝeue*n* ensample to the lewed peple for to do wel & ȝee ȝeue*n* he*m* ensample to don euyll."[61] The Sultan then lists numerous offenses of Christians, including gluttony, violence against other Christians, fickleness in newfangled dress, and greed. Moreover, the Sultan declares that the sinful nature of Christians translated into military defeat: "þ*us* for here synnes han þei lost all this lond þ*at* wee holden. For for hir*e* synnes her*e* god hath taken he*m* in to our*e* hondes, noght only be strengthe of our*e*self, but for her*e* synnes."[62] The Holy Land, the "right heritage" of the readers in the prologue, was, according to the Sultan, lost due to Christianity's own discord.

Mandeville then offers, in the guise of the Sultan, a stinging critique of his audience, one which asks them to simultaneously act more piously and strive to retake the Holy Land. This is another of the contradictions of the text. Mandeville correlates a piety in individual life, which should provide the personal reward of salvation, with military conquest, which is an apparently earthly, temporal benefit. This is, of course, the paradoxical rhetoric of the Crusades: the earthly, financially rewarding conquest is meant, really, for the glory of God; yet this combination is at odds with Mandeville's relatively tolerant attitude toward Islam and other forms of devotion. The contradiction highlights the conflicting cultural elements that Mandeville tries to string together. He wants both religious devotion and military conquest, and the contradictions of such a combination are apparent in passages such as this one.

Mandeville himself joins the critique when the Sultan finishes, further questioning his fellow Christians. Mandeville laments,

> Allas þ*at* it is gret sclaundr*e* to oure feith & to our*e* lawe, whan folk þ*at* be*n* w*ith*oute*n* lawe schull rep*re*ue*n* vs & vnd*er*neme*n* vs of oure synnes, And þei þ*at* scholden be*n* conu*er*ted to crist & to the law of Ih*es*u be oure gode ensamples & be our*e* acceptable lif to god, & so conu*er*ted to the lawe of Ih*es*u crist, be*n* þorgh our*e* wykkedness & euyll lyuynge fer fro vs & straungeres fro the holy & verry beleeve schull þus appele*n* vs & holde*n* vs for wykkede lyu*e*res & cursede.[63]

Here, Mandeville demands that his community note its own faults and its responsibility for the fact that the Saracens are not Christians. In a strange rhetorical combination, Mandeville immediately follows his outrage that "people with no law" can so criticize them with a testament to their veracity: "And treuly þei sey soth, For the sarazines be*n* gode & feythfull, For þei kepen entierly the co*m*mandement of the holy book ALKARON."[64] This passage highlights another paradoxical combination in *The Book*, one of a dominant idea of Islam as a non-religion (having no laws) and an emergent understanding that Muslims are quite devout, in a separate religion.

This is one of the oldest satiric tricks, to have an outsider expose the foibles of your society so that the author appears to have critical distance. As such, this scheme confirms for us that Muslims are outsiders for the audience of *The Book*. Moreover, the satire gains added weight because the character is Islamic. Christians are being upbraided by a person who could be equated with a pagan. In addition, the ease with which Muslims may be converted emphasizes the impotency of Islam as a religion.

On the whole, the portrait of Islam could not be wholly positive for the medieval audience. Not surprisingly, Mandeville's discussion also includes a number of more negative aspects. Mandeville focuses on the sexual nature of the Islamic idea of Paradise, calling attention to polygamy as a tenet of Islam: "Also Machomet co*m*manded in his ALKARON þ*a*t eu*er*y ma*n* scholde haue .ij. wyfes or .iij. or .iiij. but now þei taken vnto .ix. & of le*m*ma*n*nes als manye as he may susteyne."[65] Mandeville highlights the Saracens' trampling of their own law, exceeding the "allowed" number of wives and having other women for purely sexual purposes. In addition, Mandeville relates that Saracens allow divorce.[66] For the readers, who believe marriage to be sacrament, this laxness opposes "true" marriage.

Mandeville also reports that Muslims, though they recognize the three elements of the trinity, deny that they are one God: "wha*n* me*n* speke*n* to he*m* of the fad*er* & of the sone & of the holy gost þei seyn þ*a*t þei be*n* .iij. p*er*sones, but not o god, For here Alkaron speketh not of the trynyte."[67] The negation of this core belief of Christianity keeps any religious connection to a minimum.

Most significantly, Mandeville relates that the Saracens do not accept another central tenet of Christianity, that Jesus was crucified to redeem humankind. Mandeville states that they believe that Jesus "was neu*er*e crucyfyed as [the Jews] seyn, but þ*a*t god made hi*m* to stye vp to hi*m* w*ith*oute*n* deth & w*ith*oute*n* anoye, But he t*r*ansfigured his lykness into IUDAS SCARIOTH & hi*m* crucifyeden the Iewes & wende*n* þ*a*t it had be*n* Ihe*sus*."[68] Although Mandeville explains that the Saracens believe so because God, as they understand Him, would never allow an innocent Jesus to die, this justification does not carry much weight against the accepted theology in England. Mandeville, addressing his original audience, need not add, but does, "And in this fayleth her*e* feyth."[69]

In addition, Mandeville does not completely erase the memory of the Crusades; after all he does argue for a new crusade in the prologue. Tyre, for example, used to be a "gret cytee & a gode of crystenme*n* but sarazins ha*n* destroyed it a gret p*ar*tye."[70] The Saracens, for all their positive features, are still the enemy.[71] The Saracens will not allow either Christians or Jews to enter the graves of the patriarchs "For þei holden cristene me*n* & Iewes as dogg*es* And þie sey*n* þ*a*t þei scholde no entr*e* into so holy place."[72] Few positive feelings are engendered by such an admission.

And in addition, in one passage, Muslims are anachronistically included in the betrayal of Jesus. According to Mandeville, next to the tree where Judas hanged himself, "was the synagoge where the bysschoppes of Iewes &

the sarrazins camen togidere and helden her*e* conseill And þer*e* caste Iudas the .xxx. pens before he*m* and seyde þ*at* he hadde sy*n*ned bet*r*ayenge oure lord."[73] Hamelius claims that the text should read "Pharisees" instead of Saracens and that this is a scribal error.[74] However, this could very well be a willful scribal "error"; Muslims were often anachronistically involved in the death of Jesus.[75] Whatever the source of the attribution, the reading audience of *The Book* would have an additional cause for distrust of Muslims.

But the most negative feature of Islam in *The Book* is Mandeville's contention that the Muslims themselves know that Islam shall be superseded in the end by Christianity. Mandeville explains that "þei sey þ*at* þei knowe*n* wel be the p*ro*phecyes þ*at* the lawe of Machomete schall fayle as the lawe of the Iewes dide And þ*at* the lawe of cristene peple schall laste to the day of doom."[76] This admission allows for some comfortable room for Mandeville to critique Christianity through the eyes of Muslims, and also explains the absence of overt invective, because ultimately Islam is powerless. Muslims are portrayed in *The Book* as living a lie. Their religion, albeit described in often sympathetic terms, ultimately becomes an exercise in futility.

If the text's treatment of Muslims and Islam is relatively sympathetic, and, at the least, occasionally informed, *The Book*, in its treatment of the Jews, provides nothing new, evincing the most virulent strains of medieval anti-Semitism. Even the Muslims presume that the Jews are cursed.[77] Higgins explains that Jews exist only in the past and future in *The Book*,[78] yet Mandeville also alludes to the idea that current Jews are a constant threat in the present. As does the Hereford map, Mandeville distinguishes between "Jews" and "Israelites." Moses led the "peple [*sic*] of Israel,"[79] but Jews are always mentioned in the most negative of terms. For Mandeville, they are the killers of Christ and instruments of the Antichrist.

The Jews are definitely not part of the collective the text posits. Although mentioned nominally when Mandeville states that Jesus called himself "kyng of Jewes" in the prologue,[80] Jews first show up in the second chapter as the killers of Christ, when Mandeville notes that the Cross is in Constantinople, accompanied by "the spounge & the reed of the whiche the Jewes ȝaue oure lord eysell & galle in the cros."[81] The Jews become a "they" who killed "our" Lord. Moreover, not only are Jews saddled with the blame for the death of Christ, Mandeville highlights their cruelty. Asserting that the Cross was made of cypress, palm, cedar, and olive, Mandeville explains that "the Jewes maden the cros of theise .iiij. man*er*e of trees for þei trowed þ*at* our*e* lord Jh*es*u crist scholde han honged on the cros als longe as the cros myghte last & þ*er*fore made þei the foot of the cros of Cedre. For Cedr*e* may not in erthe ne in wat*er* rote & þ*er*fore þei wolde þ*at* it schold haue lasted longe."[82] So, not content with mere death, the Jews in Mandeville's account want suffering in perpetuity. Thus early in the narrative, Mandeville fashions the Jews as exceedingly hateful and malicious.

In line with many other instances of medieval Christian paranoia, he also accuses them of having conspired to eradicate all Christians. Mandeville notes, for instance, that on an island called Pathen near Java, trees grow poison for which there is no cure. Mandeville asserts that the Jews have used this poison for sinister purposes: "Of this venym the Iewes had let sechen of on of here frendes for to enpoysone all cristiantee as I haue herd hem seye in here confessioun before here dyenge. But thanked be all myghty god þei fayleden of hire purpos but allweys þei maken gret mortalitee of poeple."[83] This story is an allusion to the Black Death as a plot of the Jews. More frightening for Mandeville's audience, the ominous "allweys" suggests that the Jews were still capable and amenable to other attempts.

In addition to the Black Death conspiracy, a recent, contemporary allusion for his audience, Mandeville asserts that all Jews learn Hebrew to assist the Antichrist, stating that the Jews are the enclosed nations of Gog and Magog in the Scythian mountains: "Betwene þo mountaynes the Iewes of .x. lynages ben enclosed þat men clepen GOTH & MAGOTH."[84] In contrast to the Hereford map, which associates Turks and other peoples with the races of Gog and Magog, for Mandeville all the enclosed "nations" are Jews. Mandeville specifically notes the connection these enclosed Jews have to the Antichrist as well as all living Jews:

> *And þogh it happene* sum *of hem be fortune to gon out, þei conen no maner of langage but EBREW, so þat þei can not speke to the peple. And ȝit natheles men seyn þei schull gon out in the tyme of ANTECRIST And þat þei schull maken gret slaughter of cristene men, And þerfore all the Iewes þat dwellen in all londes lernen all weys to speken EB REW, in hope þat whan the oþer Iewes schull gon out, þat þei may vnderstonden hire speche & to leden hem in to cristendom for to destroye the cristene peple.*[85]

Every Jew, therefore, was suspect. The conspiracy was worldwide, and Jews everywhere in the world, even those far from the enclosure, were equally as guilty.

The Hereford map had erased Jews from Europe and placed them in Asia, connecting them to Islam and separating them from "Israelites." Mandeville is not even so lenient as that; he attests to his audience that only the enclosure of Gog and Magog is the true home of the Jews until they emerge during the Apocalypse: "ȝee schull vnderstonde þat the Iewes han no propre lond of hire owne for to dwellen jnne in all the world, but only þat lond betwene the mountaynes."[86] Jews, therefore, have no place anywhere on earth; this statement supports the exile of Jews from England and indeed anywhere in Europe. This type of rhetoric could obviously easily coexist with pogroms in times of economic scarcity or religious fervor, when "they" were living in "our" land.

The Book of John Mandeville is a book of many contradictions; it is both tolerant and vindictive, religious and secular. These contradictions may be an indictment of aesthetic merit for some modern critics who expect all parts of a narrative to be unified, yet they are more fruitfully interpreted as intersections of different cultural currents. The "Renaissance" ideas did not emerge fully formed in an instant. *The Book*, early as it is, reveals many of these ideas: curiosity in the "secular world," an emphasis on experience as a legitimate vehicle to find the truth, and an interest in commodities from around the world. They are contradictions that point to the changing perspectives in late medieval England.

The Hereford map and *The Book of John Mandeville* are texts which made the world for their readers. The connection of identity and geographic proximity is both assumed and fostered by these texts. The treatment of Jews and Muslims, however, reveals the tenuous nature of this connection. Actually living in England or Europe was a necessary but not sufficient requirement to be "English" or "European." Although these texts efface numerous other differences in the name of communal identity, they are unable to overcome the alterity that accompanied those who practiced, and were thereby identified by, Judaism and Islam. At the end of the late medieval period, when nationalism will become more important and more visible, the Hereford *mappamundi* and *The Book of John Mandeville* attest to the inability to limit the idea of geographic identity to mere geography. Those who do not meet further requirements could be defined as foreigners in their homeland.

Notes

1. *William Shakespeare: The Complete Works*, ed. Alfred Harbage (New York: Penguin, 1969; New York: Viking, 1977), I.i.14–15.
2. I will use this title for "Mandeville's Travels" following the Mandeville-critic Iain Higgins, who adopts the medieval rather than modern editorial title in his recent study *Writing East*. Throughout, however, my quotations will be from *Mandeville's Travels*, ed. P. Hamelius, 2 vols. O.S., 153 and 154 (London: Early English Text Society, 1919).
3. Nelson Goodman, *Ways of Worldmaking* (Indianapolis: Hackett, 1978), 8.
4. Thorlac Turville-Petre, *England the Nation: Language, Literature, and National Identity, 1290–1340* (Oxford: Oxford University Press, 1996), 7.
5. Benedict Anderson, *Imagined Communities: Reflections of the Origin and Spread of Nationalism*, rev. ed. (London: Verso, 1991), 7.
6. Benedict Anderson, *Imagined Communities*, 6.
7. Nelson Goodman, *Ways of Worldmaking*, 14.
8. Hastings Rashdall, *The Universities of Europe in the Middle Ages*, ed. F. M. Powicke and A. B. Emden, vol. 3 (Oxford: Clarendon, 1936), 58.
9. Raymond Williams, *Marxism and Literature*. Marxist Introductions (Oxford: Oxford University Press, 1977), 123.

10. Thorlac Turville-Petre, *England the Nation*, 6.
11. This nationalism does not at all points resemble the often militaristic nineteenth-century nationalism, which has led many historians to deny the existence of any nationalism in the medieval period. Yet these texts do connect geographic space in ways similar to the operation of nationalism. The terminology is imprecise and, for some historians, anachronistic. "Until we can sort out what the medieval idea of a people did and did not have in common with modern nationalism," argues Susan Reynolds, "it is better to avoid the words nation and national altogether" [*Kingdoms and Communities in Western Europe, 900–1300* (Oxford: Oxford University Press, 1997), 254]. However, I will use the term nationalism, albeit always under advisement, to refer to that imagined community posited in these texts rather than some kind of natural division.
12. Salo Wittmayer Baron, *Citizen or Alien Conjurer, A Social and Religious History of the Jews: Late Middle Ages and Era of European Expansion, 1200–1650*, vol. 11. 2d ed. (New York: Columbia University Press, 1967), 201
13. Pierre de Langtoft, *The Chronicle in French Verse from the Earliest Period to the Death of King Edward I*, vol. 2, ed. Thomas Wright. Rerum Britannicarum medii aevi scriptoes 47 (London: Longmans, Green, Readem, and Dyer, 1868), 87.
14. P. D. A. Harvey, "Medieval Maps: An Introduction," J. B. Harley and David Woodward, *Cartography in Prehistoric, Ancient, and Medieval Europe and the Mediterranean, The History of Cartography* 1 (Chicago: University of Chicago Press, 1987), 284.
15. Charles Beazley, for example, maintained, "The non-scientific maps of the later Middle Ages . . . are of such complete futility . . . that a bare allusion to the monstrosities of Hereford and Ebsdorf should suffice." [C[harles] Raymond Beazley, *The Dawn of Modern Geography: A History of Exploration and Geographical Science, vol. 3: From the Middle of the Thirteenth to the Early Years of the Fifteenth Century (c. A.D. 1260–1420),* (Oxford, Clarendon Press, 1906. New York: Peter Smith, 1949), 528.
16. John Kirtland Wright, *The Geographical Lore of the Time of the Crusades: A Study in the History of Medieval Science and Tradition in Western Europe*, intro. Clarence J. Glacken (1925; New York: Dover, 1965), 248.
17. John Kirtland Wright, *The Geographical Lore*, 248.
18. For more information about medieval mapping in general and/or the Hereford *mappamundi* in particular see also: W. L. Bevan and H. W. Phillott *Mediæval Geography: An Essay in Illustration of the Hereford Mappa Mundi* (London: E. Stanford, 1873. Amsterdam: Meridian, 1969); Valerie Flint, *The Imaginative Landscape of Christopher Columbus* (Princeton: Princeton University Press, 1992); P.D.A. Harvey, *Mappa Mundi: The Hereford World Map*, (Toronto: University of Toronto Press, 1996); and Rudolf Simek, *Heaven and Earth in the Middle Ages: The Physical World Before Columbus*, trans. Angela Hall (Woodbridge, Suffolk: The Boydell Press, 1996).
19. David Woodward, "Medieval *Mappaemundi*," *Cartography in Prehistoric, Ancient, and Medieval Europe and the Mediterranean*, 286.

20. David Woodward, "Medieval *Mappaemundi*," 326.
21. Marcia Kupfer, "Medieval World Maps: Embedded Images, Interpretive Frames," *Word & Image* 10 (1994): 262–88.
22. Paul Zumthor, "Mappa Mundi und Performanz. Die mittelalterliche Kartographie," >*Aufführung*< und >Schrift< in Mittelalter und Früher Neuzeit, ed. Jan-Dirk Müller. Germanistische Symposien. Berichtsbände XVII (Stuttgart and Weimar: Verlag J. B. Metzler, 1996), 317–27; here 317, argues: "Die Karte ist in der Tat alles zusammen: Objekt und Figur, Schrift und Bild, Diskurs und Performanz" [The map is, indeed, everything in one: object and figure, writing and picture, discourse and performance].
23. Rudolf Wittkower, "Marvels of the East: A Study in the History of Monsters," *Journal of the Warburg and Courtland Institutes,* 5 (1942): 177.
24. In *The City of God Against the Pagans*, Augustine ends a section answering "Whether certain monstrous races of men sprang from the seed of Adam or the sons of Noah" without much resolution: "Let me then tentatively and guardedly state my conclusion. Either the written accounts of certain races are completely unfounded or, if such races do exist, they are not human; or, if they are human, they are descended from Adam" [*The City of God Against the Pagans*, trans. Eva Matthews Sanford and William McAllen Green. The Loeb Classical Library 5 (Cambridge: Harvard University Press, 1965), Book XVI.viii, 49]. He is unable to distinguish where such creatures, if they do exist, belong.
25. John Block Friedman, *The Monstrous Races in Medieval Art and Thought* (Cambridge: Harvard University Press, 1981), 37.
26. Although southern Africa was unknown to Europeans at the time, the southern region of the continent on the map is populated with very large representations of monstrous peoples.
27. Joyce E. Salisbury, *The Beast Within: Animals in the Middle Ages* (New York: Routledge, 1994), 153.
28. Cf. Michael Goodich's contribution to this volume.
29. Kathleen Biddick, "The ABC of Ptolemy: Mapping the World with the Alphabet," *Text and Territory: Geographical Imagination in the European Middle Ages*, ed. Sylvia Tomasch and Sealy Gilles (Philadelphia: University of Pennsylvania Press, 1998), 291.
30. For a different view in a medieval text, see Albrecht Classen, "Multiculturalism in the German Middle Ages? The Rediscovery of a Modern Concept in the Past: The Case of *Herzog Ernst*, *Multiculturalism and Representation: Selected Essays*," ed. John Rieder, Larry E. Smith. Literary Studies East and West 10 (Honolulu: College of Languages, Linguistics and Literatures, University of Hawaii, 1996), 198–219. See also David Tinsley's contribution to this volume.
31. Kathleen Biddick, "The ABC of Ptolemy," 269.
32. The quotations from the map presented here follow a semi-diplomatic transcription. Between some words appears a raised dot "·" which I have reproduced. Abbreviations have been expanded and the added letters appear in italics. Superscript letters have silently been lowered to the baseline. Rubricated words are not specified in this transcription. The symbol for "et" resembles a

European 7 (one with a line through the stem) which I have transcribed as "&." The suffix "-us" often appears looking very much like a yogh ("$_3$").

33. For the present examination, I am not concerned with the question of who is/are the author[s] but what kind of reading a medieval English audience would have given a text in which they had no reason to doubt its authorship by an English knight. Therefore, I will use "Mandeville," without quotation marks, specifically to mean the persona of the story, making no claim that he is a real author.
34. Mandeville, 210.
35. Mandeville, 105.
36. Mandeville, 2.
37. Mandeville, 146.
38. Mandeville, 210.
39. Mandeville, 4.
40. Iain Macleod Higgins, *Writing East: The "Travels" of Sir John Mandeville* (Philadelphia: University of Pennsylvania Press, 1997), 42.
41. Mandeville, 181.
42. Mandeville, 146.
43. Mandeville, 146.
44. *The Book* does not limit designation of "Christian" to Latin Christendom or even the Eastern Church. In every continent, Mandeville locates and describes "cristen men." The text notes the differences, but Mandeville does not polemicize about errors in any direct way. Higgins avers that Mandeville offers the belief that "piety and devotion are said in effect to compensate for theological error" (Iain Macleod Higgins, *Writing East,* 80). Christians are mentioned throughout the text and their differences are noted, thereby accentuating the distinction between the constructed audience of *The Book* and the entity of "Christendom," but still, I think, connecting them to the entire unknown world.
45. Donald Roy Howard, *Writers and Pilgrims: Medieval Pilgrimage Narratives and Their Posterity,* (Berkeley: University of California Press, 1980), 67.
46. See also the introduction to this volume and John Victor Tolan, ed., *Medieval Christian Perceptions of Islam: A Book of Essays*, Garland Medieval Casebooks 10 (New York: Garland, 1996).
47. Mandeville, 21.
48. Iain Macleod Higgins, *Writing East*, 112.
49. Mandeville, 21.
50. Norman Daniel, *The Arabs and Mediaeval Europe*, (London: Longman, 1975), 233.
51. Mandeville, 84.
52. Mandeville, 47.
53. Mandeville, 86.
54. Norman Daniel, *The Arabs and Mediaeval Europe*, 33.
55. Mandeville, 88.
56. Mandeville, 84.
57. Mandeville, 85.
58. Mandeville, 85.

59. Mandeville, 87.
60. Mandeville, 88.
61. Mandeville, 88.
62. Mandeville, 89.
63. Mandeville, 89–90.
64. Mandeville, 90.
65. Mandeville, 87.
66. Mandeville, 87.
67. Mandeville, 87.
68. Mandeville, 86.
69. Mandeville, 86.
70. Mandeville, 18.
71. For a parallel case, see the conclusion of Konrad von Würzburg's *Partonopier und Meliur*, discussed by Albrecht Classen in this volume.
72. Mandeville, 43.
73. Mandeville, 61–62.
74. P. Hamelius, *Mandeville's Travels: Translated from the French of Jean d'Outremeuse*, vol. 2. (London: Oxford University Press, 1923), 65.
75. For evidence of this in medieval English drama, see David Leshock, "The Representation of Islam in the Wakefield Corpus Christi Plays," *Medieval Perspectives* 11 (1996): 195–208.
76. Mandeville, 87.
77. Mandeville, 86.
78. Iain Macleod Higgins, *Writing East*, 42.
79. Mandeville, 37.
80. Mandeville, 1.
81. Mandeville, 6.
82. Mandeville, 6.
83. Mandeville, 126.
84. Mandeville, 176.
85. Mandeville, 177–78.
86. Mandeville, 177.

13
Foreigners in Konrad von Würzburg's *Partonopier und Meliur*

ALBRECHT CLASSEN

One of the reasons for the renewed excitement which Medieval Studies create today rests in the many new and diverse interpretive approaches and theoretical concepts applied for the critical analysis of medieval literature, historical documents, and other cultural artifacts that often invite us to consider heretofore ignored or neglected dimensions of medieval ideology, belief systems, values, morality, and ethics.[1] Modern research tracing medieval *Mentalitätsgeschichte,* in particular, has proven to be highly productive in many respects as many traditionally marginalized texts such as sermons, poenitentials, confessors' handbooks, as well as paintings, sculptures, popular ballads, and law books have suddenly revealed a treasure of new information about how medieval people thought about their environment, society, religious customs, economic aspects, traditions, other peoples, the body, and the foreign.[2] Although medieval cathedrals, castles, houses, chronicles, stained glasses, and the like have not changed much over the centuries (except that time took its toll) a renewed investigation of the hidden messages contained in them about medieval people promises to unearth "Neuigkeiten aus dem Mittelalter" (news from the Middle Ages). Instead of limiting ourselves to the lives of medieval royal families, chivalric adventures, religious and philosophical debates, and so on, modern medievalists from many different disciplines have discovered everyday life in the Middle Ages, that is, aspects such as work, death, fear, urban communities, sexuality, and such, and fundamental existential concepts, attitudes, behavioral patterns, rituals, customs, and traditions.[3]

One particular aspect of this new research interest has been the interaction between medieval Europeans and outsiders, foreigners, non-Christians, and other people of different religion, skin color, sexual orientation, culture, and so forth.[4] Quite obviously, homogenous societies almost always have striven to establish a close-knit community by excluding others who are different from them in a variety of ways. This was also the case with medieval society.[5] For instance, almost everywhere within medieval Europe, Jews were (by and large) the primary target of xenophobia, but apostates, converts, and homosexuals, among others, experienced hatred, racism, and marginalization as well.[6] At the same time the foreign world of the Orient which from the eleventh and twelfth centuries on increasingly opened its doors to curious European travelers, missionaries, pilgrims, and diplomats, represented both the absolute Other and also a peculiar familiarity.[7] From very early on the distant East was allegedly populated by monsters of many different kinds, as is well documented by travel accounts such as the famous pan-European narratives about Alexander the Great's conquest of the Persian empire and India—based on several Latin sources such as the Historia de preliis—and the fabulous Middle High German account of the goliardic *Herzog Ernst* ("Spielmannsepos"). The collective consciousness was deeply influenced by ancient Greek teratology, and medieval literature happily reflected on the same myths for centuries to come.[8]

Nevertheless, despite the many medieval voices which projected horrible and fearful images of the distant East and also maligned outsiders, marginal figures, heretics, and nonconformists within medieval society,[9] medieval literature also knows of a number of alternative voices which represent quite different views of the Other. In Marie de France's lai of "Bisclavret" (ca. 1200), in Wolfram von Eschenbach's Willehalm (ca. 1220), in Johann von Würzburg's *Wilhelm von Österreich* (1314), and in the anonymous *Sir Gawain and the Green Knight* (end of the fourteenth century) surprising elements of open-minded, perhaps even "tolerant" thinking emerged which sharply contradicted the prevalent opinion of the general audience and sensitized readers to the multiplicity of creatures here on earth which all enjoy the same privilege of human existence.[10] Both contacts during crusades and pilgrimages to the East, and mercantile and cultural exchanges between East and West opened significant windows on another culture and created a variety of "Bewußtseinssyndrome," as Volker Rittner calls them—'syndromes of consciousness.' One of them he describes as positive, utopian, and nostalgic, projecting dreams and desires into the distant world of the Orient. The other one he identifies as negative, reactionary, hysteric, and the consequence of deep-seated fears. Nevertheless, despite these contrasts, both syndromes share common elements:

> *Die Externvorstellungen konzipieren in beiden Fällen Inhalte, die sich dem Maß des Lokalen und Normalen entziehen. Verheißungen wie auch Gefährdungen sind in ihrer Qualität überdimensional, exzeptionell. Sie haben Außerordentlichkeitscharakter.*[11]

> [The external imagination in both cases conceives contents which are beyond the familiar and the normal. Promises and endangerments are beyond any grasp, exceptional in their nature. They are of an extraordinary character.]

Rittner adds that both negative and positive concepts of the Foreign or Other require the notion of distance from one's own world and the temporary incursion into it and subsequent disappearance of the Foreign into the distance.[12] Consequently, depending on the context, the experience of the Other either undermined or stabilized medieval society and was both feared and sought.

To explore this topic further and to shed new light on the intriguing question whether the medieval world ever really had a clear notion of the meaning of tolerance,[13] here I want to discuss some curious narrative elements in Konrad von Würzburg's courtly romance Partonopier und Meliur which he composed, on the basis of the Old French *Partonopeus de Blois* (ca. 1180), sometime around 1270. The basic element of the romance is deeply steeped in an old folkloric myth of the "Martenehe," that is, of the marriage between a human being and a ghost-like person, perhaps best represented by the equally popular theme of "Melusine."[14] Although Konrad does not specifically explore any peculiar "pre-modern" tolerant attitudes and ideas in his romance—it remains to be seen how far this concept was even feasible for the Middle Ages—he presented his material in a surprisingly refreshing fashion which indicates that he harbored a remarkably open-minded attitude toward foreigners, the world of the Orient, and other social outsiders. Although Partonopier und Meliur relies, in part, as it so often happens in medieval literature, on the almost worn-out theme of the conflict between Christianity and Islam, opening the well-known Pandora's box of the crusade motif,[15] there is sufficient evidence that the author did not really care about the religious tensions of his time and was fully prepared to accept Muslims, that is, visitors from the exotic East, as fellow human beings with the same virtues and vices as any Christian European knight. From the narrator's point of view the ancient conflict between both religions had to be dealt with in a military fashion, almost as a lip service to the audience's expectations, but in fact throughout the romance the heathens are welcomed in just as friendly a fashion as any other knights and are invited to compete for the hand of the emperor's daughter. In other words, the focus of the subsequent examination will rest on how Konrad refers to the Saracens, how he has them interact with the Christians, and how they are viewed within the courtly context.

Before we consider specific aspects supporting our thesis, however, let us first examine the basic content of the romance. Partonopier, the son of the Count of Blois, gets lost while on a hunt and comes to a completely deserted but beautifully decorated city. Exhausted, he lies down in a bed and is surprised by an invisible woman who wants to marry him within two years, although he won't be allowed to see her until then. Partonopier immediately falls in love with this woman. She, as we will learn later, is Meliur, the daughter of the Emperor of Constantinople, and he willingly stays in the empty city, enjoying the nights with Meliur. After six months Partonopier departs to visit his mother, who tries in vain to warn him against the seemingly dangerous love of Meliur, whom she suspects of being an evil spirit. When Partonopier returns home a second time, the Archbishop, upon the mother's urging, convinces him at least to test Meliur and make her appear in front of his eyes with a magical lantern. As soon as the young man has broken the taboo and hence has destroyed his mistress's magic, he is forced to leave her and, not being strong enough to commit suicide, he turns into a hermit. Soon after, when Meliur must decide on a husband, she calls for a tournament in which, after many turns of events, the revived and once-again hopeful Partonopier proves his absolute superiority and is finally able to marry Meliur after all. A contender, the Sultan of Persia, whom Partonopier had defeated in the jousts, returns with an army and tries to take Meliur with force, but he is met with a strong chivalric opposition led by Partonopier. The text breaks off in the middle of the battle descriptions.[16]

Although this voluminous romance has often been the object of critical studies,[17] the particular aspect to be examined here has never been considered by Konrad von Würzburg scholars.[18] In his doctoral dissertation W. Obst primarily discusses the question of Konrad's French sources and his adaptations.[19] Ursula Peters emphasizes the intriguing phenomenon that Konrad specifically reveals the name of his patron and hence the sociological background of his audience living in the city, arguing that the romance must be considered a literary document reflecting urban culture.[20] Rüdiger Brandt has detailed the text's sources, the European distribution of the original narrative long before Konrad put his hands on it, described the romance's style and structure, and attempted to provide a comprehensive interpretation. He particularly focuses on the protagonist's psychological development, the education process, the concept of the hero, the virtues of a ruler, the overarching ideal of loyalty ("triuwe"), and on the way in which Konrad projects nature.[21] Hartmut Kokott makes another attempt to reevaluate Konrad von Würzburg and studies all of his works in depth and outlines in detail critical approaches to a full understanding of his poems, a "Gesamtdarstellung" (total interpretation).[22] In contrast to earlier scholarship Kokott distances himself from the attempts to relate Konrad's Partonopier to the old literary and mythical tradition of a human being marrying a member of the world of spirits (*Martenehe*), not because these connections might be irrelevant from a global perspective but because they do not shed significant light on Konrad's version and blind us to his actual intentions and messages in the text (222).

It is important for our understanding that Partonopier is at first portrayed as a child who still needs parental supervision and guidance, but the actual conflict in his life will soon result from competing forces coming both from outside and inside which influence him. Partonopier at first struggles to free himself from his mother's control, but eventually he also needs to distance himself from Meliur in order to find his own self and to gain independence in his decisions and evaluations. The romance demonstrates the protagonist's maturation process and illustrates how he eventually, successfully, accepts the position of a highly respected ruler who is capable of defending both his own family and his country from external intruders and enemies. Kokott also considers the personal interaction of the men during the tournament at which Meliur's future husband will be determined and briefly mentions the presence of heathen contenders (242), but he does not pay any particular attention to their unique evaluation, as his focus is always directly aimed at the protagonist Partonopier and his comportment (244–45).

Several aspects of Konrad's romance deserve mention before we focus on the treatment of heathens in his narrative. Initially, Partonopier's primary challenge consisted of coming to terms with a magical apparition and in sustaining his belief in the human nature of Meliur whom he loves dearly although he is not allowed to see her for one and a half years. Similar to Herzog Ernst in the eponymous "Spielmannsepos" (ca. 1170/1220), young Partonopier enters a seemingly completely deserted city after a ship has taken him to a foreign shore. Awestruck, the hero wanders through the splendid streets and marvels at the exotic beauty of the houses, walls, and towers.[23]

mit rôten und mit wîzen
mermelînen steinen
wâren si nâch reinen
siten wol gezieret
gequâdert und gevieret,
alsam ein schâchzabelspil.
(810–815)[24]

[They were delicately decorated, built, and layered with red and white marble stones like a chess set.]

Moreover, he is treated to an exquisite dinner without knowing its origin and who might have served it, which makes him worried that "ez dûhte in allez gar ein troum/und ein gespenste, daz er sach" (1054f.; he thought it was a dream and he was seeing a ghost). Partonopier, however, sets aside his worries because he appreciates the wonderful food and drinks and rather wants to believe that "got selbe in sînem trône/mache dirre wirtschaft" (1064f.; that God himself on his throne had prepared this dinner). Partly due to his childish naivité, but partly because of his pragmatic and realistic thinking he is not overcome by superstitious fear and blithely takes what is offered him. Nevertheless, deadly fear threatens to overcome him at night when an invisible woman approaches his bed: "er zittert als ein espen loup/und hæte nâ den sin verlorn" (1234f.; he trembled like a leaf and almost would have lost his mind), lies down next to him (1254f.), and pretends to be surprised about his presence in "her" bed. The narrator paints a highly vivid picture of the psychological process which the young protagonist is going through and presents an almost classical case of how a person experiences an encounter with an apparition. The woman, Meliur, appeals to the Virgin Mary for help, thus soothing Partonopier's fears (1350f.),[25] and soon he falls in love with her and touches and embraces her body, until she finally accepts him as her lover and joins him in the "minne spil" (1709; game of love). Subsequently we learn that Meliur had previously manipulated Partonopier's life in a way to bring him to her without anybody noticing it: "ouch schuof daz mîner künste list,/daz du bist komen in daz lant" (1874f.; with the help of my art I made you come to this land). Although she explicitly identifies herself as a Christian, she nevertheless commands magical arts and is able to influence people to obey her orders. She has used this craft to secure for herself a beloved husband, but not to gain any wealth because her social status has made this aspect unnecessary: "wan ich gedâhte, daz ein wîp/verkoufen niht solt umbe guot/ir minne, frîheit unde muot" (1812–1814; as I thought that a woman should not sell her love, freedom, and spirit for valuable objects). Meliur has set up a concrete plan for them both eventually to get married, but this requires that he abstain from any effort to make her visible: "ez sol dir werden wilde/biz an die zît und ûf den tac/daz ich dich offenlîche mac/erlesen unde erkiesen" (2018–2020; you will not see me until the time and the day will have come that I will be allowed to choose and select you [as my husband] in public).

Konrad is not only concerned with the protagonists' learning process, with their trials and tribulations, he also confronts us with the hero's dilemma to live in the real world of chivalric society during the day and to enter the world of magic at night.[26] Partonopier's love for the invisible princess compensates all his fear of the unknown and unexplainable although Meliur also threatens him with dire consequences in case he might break the taboo: "ob du niht wilt verliesen/dîn leben und die sælde mîn,/sô lâ dir niemer werden schîn/mîn schœne antlitze wünniclich" (2022–2025; if you do not want to lose your life and my grace, never try to call forth an image of my beautiful and delightful face). He does not have to doubt her Christian belief and does not need to suspect that she might be marred by any kind of physical disfiguration or ugliness (2059–2065). The magical framework serves as a test of his loyalty and constancy, even though the entire situation might seem strange and uncanny to him.[27] Partonopier immediately assures his beloved of his unswerving service and commitment to keep his promise and never to try to make her appear in front of his eyes: "ich lâze iuch unbeschouwet" (2091; I will not try to see you). The catastrophe, however, awaits them both soon, not because the young man is distrustful and reveals weakness of character, but because his jealous and insecure mother Lucrête intervenes and eventually manages with the help of the archbishop to convince her son that Meliur might have signed a pact with the devil and has to be exposed.[28]

Walter Haug has pointed out that Konrad von Würzburg here projects a new dimension of the courtly world where the clear dividing line between the idealized court and the dangerous and threatening world of the Other has become blurred and evil proper has gained a new dimension: "es erscheint unter der Kategorie des Unheimlichen" (it figures within the category of the uncanny).[29] This observation requires some further elaborations as neither Meliur nor Partonopier's mother emerge as evil in any real sense of the word. The mother might be criticized for being overly protective of her son, and of being a victim of her own motherly instincts, but in reality Meliur's magical manipulations also fail to evoke the outsiders' trust, as the entire situation leaves a strange and uncanny impression on ordinary people. Partonopier, however, fully confides in Meliur because he loves her, and does not question her particular skills and powers until his mother has the archbishop infuse fear in his heart with religious arguments; the latter thus debilitates the strength of his love for the ghostly woman. We can concur with Haug: "An die Stelle der Integration des Negativen treten Mechanismen des Bösen und des Guten: sie drängen den Helden immer wieder in eine passive Position" (mechanisms of evil and of good replace the integration of the negative: they force the hero again and again into a passive position).[30] His observation, however, needs to be modified as Meliur does not represent evil and does not have any improper intentions with her lover. Partonopier fully agrees with all conditions set by the princess, and he would have happily spent the required time in her magical kingdom until the long awaited moment when Meliur would have been able to reveal herself to him, if the very young man had not have felt a need to visit his mother and hence to return to his previous childish existence.

The problem for the lovers arises from the clash between the mysterious kingdom of Schiefdeire, where Meliur rules more or less independently with her father's consent, and Blois, where Partonopier's mother governs, in other words, from the significant difference between the familiar and the unfamiliar in political and cultural terms—a fundamental element of the experience of the Other.[31] The erotic attraction between the two lovers quickly builds bridges between them and helps to compensate for the mysterious framework of their encounter. Lucrête, however, incapable of comprehending the magical arts practiced by Meliur, makes every effort to draw her son away from this allegedly dangerous person because she is basically afraid of her and worries that she might lose Partonopier to diabolic forces (6818f.).[32]

Undoubtedly, Konrad also presents the conflict between two women separated by a generation, the one being Partonopier's mother, the other being his mistress and future wife, but the narrator clearly stresses Lucrête's fear of the evil spirit as the major motivational factor: "Ir angest was daz aller meist, / daz ez wære ein übel geist, / der ir sun mit zouber trüge / und in mit wîbes bilde züge" (7467–7470; her biggest fear was that it was an evil spirit which deceived her son with magic and the image of a woman).[33] Because she does not understand the nature of Meliur's conditions and is afraid of losing her son to the devil, she has the archbishop intervene, who indeed succeeds in creating a wall in Partonopier's mind separating him from the world of his beloved and (for a time) forces him to trust his old family more than Meliur: "Von dirre predigunge / der hôchgeborne junge / in alsô grimme vorhte viel, / daz im sîn edel herze wiel / dar inne als ein zerlâzen blî" (7647–7651; as a consequence of the sermon the high born young man experienced such a fear that his heart melted like liquid lead). Significantly, the narrator does not agree with Lucrête's decision, even harshly criticizes the archbishop's sermon, and laments the disaster which befalls Partonopier: "owê daz im die ræte / sîn eigen muoter ie gebôt" (7820f.; oh, what a pity that his own mother ever gave this advice). As soon as the young man has accepted the plan, has taken his mother's magical lamp (7760–7769; white magic versus seemingly black magic which, however, proves to be white magic as well), and so eventually destroys Meliur's secret, that is, makes her appear in physical form, he learns the full truth about his beloved. Instead of a devil, Partonopier discovers an angel, that is, the most beautiful woman he has ever seen who altogether proves to be as much a Christian as he is, although she had used her particular "scientific" power to make herself invisible. Partonopier immediately realizes the crime which he has committed against Meliur and knows that he will lose her for good. Utterly distraught he condemns the evil advisors:

> nu var enwec in gotez haz!
> mîn muoter, diu dich ie gemaz
> und dich ze samene brâhte,
> die werde in tiuvels âhte
> versenket iemer und begraben.
> der bischof müeze unsælde haben,
> der mich daz ie gelêrte,
> daz ich sô gar verkêrte
> die triuwe und die gelübede mîn.
> (7925–7933)

> [Now go away in God's hatred; my mother who brought me to this world should be thrown into and buried in the devil's world. The bishop must experience misfortune who once gave me this advice through which I destroyed my loyalty and broke my oath.]

The narrator indicates, through Partonopier's words, that neither immediate family members nor representatives of the church are necessarily in the right position to advise others about the interaction with the Other. Meliur is not a monster or a ghost and does not emerge as a Melusine-like figure, even though she uses (white) magic and occult powers to test her lover and to hide him from the court of Constantinople.[34] Konrad does not portray these particular skills as negative and does not characterize Meliur in any sense as an evil figure, although her harsh condemnation of Partonopier and her previous intentional manipulations of his life, forcing him to become her lover, might detract somewhat from her otherwise highly positive image. Nevertheless, she represents the Other and uses her peculiar abilities to achieve her personal goals in love, without the narrator ever criticizing her for associating with or simply being the Other. Instead, Meliur explains that she received a thorough education in many different disciplines from "die besten meister" (8080; from the best teachers) and eventually earned the degree of a "houbetmeisterîn" (8086; chief master) with a solid knowledge acquired by way of a careful study of many books. Some of these also included information about "nigrômancîen" (8096) which she utilized as a means to provide entertainment ("kurzewîle," 8101) for her father by way of conjuring illusionary images in front of his eyes: "vil manic wunder spæhe" (8108; many miraculous images).

Despite all her magical powers, however, Partonopier's ill-fated attempt, prompted by his mother, to make Meliur reveal herself in physical terms, suddenly destroys the "zouberîe" (8160; magic) and makes it impossible for her to use this astonishing art ever again: ". . . , daz nu niemer kan / mîn kunst getragen für als ê" (8204f.; that from now on I will never be able again to practise my art). The Other, here represented by Meliur's magical skills, turns out to be nothing but a learned art which has no bearing on her religion and is never described as an evil element. At the end, when Partonopier has eventually overcome all odds and defeated his opponents, and consequently has gained Meliur's love and hand as his rightful wife, the narrator returns to this topic and emphasizes once again that Meliur was never again able to employ her magical powers: "doch wizzent, daz diu keiserîn / niht zoubers kunde mêr dô pflegen: / die liste wâren dô gelegen, / der si mit ganzer stæte wielt, / daz si Partonopieren hielt" (17464–468; be informed that the emperess could no longer apply her magic: those arts were lost with which she had held on to Partonopier). On the one hand her necromancy ("nigrômancîen," 8096) is not viewed negatively, instead proves to be a simple art learned in school; on the other, Meliur had employed her necromancy to control and test Partonopier and so, indirectly, had endangered her own happiness. At this late point in the narrative at least, the marriage is described as a happy one, although, or rather because, Meliur has lost her occult powers: "si lebten bêde sunder leit / in ganzer wünne bî der frist / ân allen zouberlichen list" (17474–476; they both lived without sorrow, filled with happiness realized without any magical art).

In a way, as Kokott has suggested, the romance discusses the male protagonist's path from childhood to adulthood on which he has to free himself from his mother and also from the dangerous influence of his future wife. Only when he has gained full independence in intellectual, political, and ethical terms is he ready for the marriage with Meliur.[35] His confrontation with the Other, here represented by the Byzantine princess, serves as a catalyst to bring about the necessary maturation process. At the same time, Konrad has uncovered a new attitude toward the occult arts and necromancy, and demonstrated that their fearful components simply rest on the spectator's ignorance (see also Ackermann, ch. 26). In other words, the romance illustrates a fundamental aspect of xenophobia prevalent in the Middle Ages and concurrently undermines its operating mechanisms.

In the second part of Konrad's romance, the narrative makes a major shift, away from Partonopier's childhood and youth, and suddenly presents to us a young knight who is taking the best way to prove his leadership qualities and his chivalric superiority over all other contenders for Meliur's hand.[36] Surprisingly, many of the potential husbands do not come from Christian countries, but instead have arrived from the Islamic world and prove to be highly impressive characters. These include, among others, the king of Lybia, the king of Barbaria, the king of Arabia, the king of Syria, and the kings of Baldac and Zazamanc (13348–369). They all compete on the same ground, with the same equipment, the same courage and bravery, for the same goal, and for that reason they are fully accepted among the participants in the international tournament. Konrad also includes long lists of European royalty and provides us with a geographical map of the medieval world here represented by rulers of practically all the powerful kingdoms and dukedoms.[37] Drawing from the genre of mappamundi, the narrator projects a world view which was no longer limited by the extension of Christianity, but also incorporated many North African countries and the entire region of the Middle East.[38] Whereas the first part of Konrad's romance treats the Other as an integral part of medieval society, the second part turns to representatives of the Other coming from the outside world to enter courtly European society.

A courtly romance such as Partonopier und Meliur which places such emphasis on the tournament where the happiness of the two protagonists will be decided traditionally requires a key opponent who is here represented by the heathen king Floridanz, "von Persîâ der soldân" (13510; the Soldan of Persia). As we will see, this man exerts a tremendous appeal on all participants and quickly emerges as the central competitor against Partonopier because he excels in every aspect, except that he is a heathen:

veste alsam ein marmelstein
was er an ritters muote.
sîn edel herze bluote
gar in keiserlicher tugent.

er hete dar von kindes jugent
getragen ie der êren kranz.
(13525–531)

[He was as stout in his chivalric spirit as a marble stone. His noble heart had blood with the virtues of an emperor. From early childhood on he had worn the wreath of honor.]

Quite similar to the heathen knights in Wolfram von Eschenbach's *Willehalm* who battle against the Christians in the name of their ladies, Floridanz is lavishly decorated and armed, not simply out of hubris, but because he wants to serve his lady: "wolte ein vrouwen ritter wesen" (13567; he wanted to be a lady's knight).[39] His ultimate narrative function, however, proves to be to serve as Partonopier's only serious challenger by demonstrating, through his personal defeat, that the latter indeed deserves the full recognition as the best knight of them all and is truly worthy of Meliur's hand. Whereas nobody in the tournament dares to cross arms with Floridanz—"kein ritter dâ justieren / getorste mit dem fieren" (13579f.; no knight dared to joust with the bold one)—Partonopier, together with his friend Gaudîn, breaks the spell, accepts the challenge and eventually defeats the heathen king: "dô kâmen ouch die frechen, / Gaudîn und Partonopier. / die riten alsam wildiu tier / tobend allez umbe sich" (13584–587; then the bold Gaudîn and Partonopier arrived who rode like wild animals hewing at all around them).

The narrative pattern is easily identifiable, as Konrad has these two heroes fight each other over and over again until the "Soldan" is finally crushed by his Christian opponent and has to give up his dream to gain the prize of the tournament, Meliur herself. Partonopier's triumph, however, is not related to the religious conflict which here does not play any significant role, even though some of the courtiers warn of Floridanz's heathendom and the danger that he might impose his religion on their country, causing profound damage to Christianity once he would have married Meliur.

Significantly, during the tournament all the Saracen kings and other non-Christian rulers are given the same opportunity to vie for Meliur's love, and Konrad presents the clearly observable option that a marriage between Meliur and Floridanz, or any other heathen king, might be within reach for the latter.

At one point during the tournament when the knights band together to fight in groups against each other, the master of the ceremony makes the decision to split heathens and Christians up and mix them to new groups to avoid any conflict along religious lines which could, after all, still erupt and endanger the peacefully organized tournament:

der turnei dô geteilet wart,
daz kristen unde heiden

beliben ungescheiden,
wan man si mischet under ein,
durch daz kein strît dâ von in zwein
sich hüebe noch kein slahte,
(14054–059)

[The participants of the tournament were divided in such a way that Christians and heathens were not separated, because they were all mixed so that no fight or quarrel could arise among them.]

Consequently it is possible, for instance, that the Persian ruler and the King of Spain fight on the same side:

den turnei muoste halten
der soldân zeinre sîten,
und wielt sîn an den zîten
mit im ein künec ûz erkorn,
der was ûz Spangen lant geborn.
(14088–092)

[The Soldan had to fight in the tournament on the same side as the the outstanding king of Spain.]

Since all the descriptions of the individual fights follow fairly standard imagery of weaponry, skills in jousting, and general chivalric equipment, ignoring any cultural characteristics which might, for instance, differentiate the Saracens from the Europeans, the traditional conflict between Christians and non-Christians does not play any significant role during this scene and only surfaces at a later point after Partonopier's victory and his marriage with Meliur. At that time Floridanz primarily acts as a jealous lover who feels deeply frustrated and hurt because of the defeat in the battle for the princess, and tries once again with military might to defeat his opponents, not realizing that he would never be able to convince Meliur in this way that he might be a better husband than Partonopier.

During the tournament the protagonist even credits the Soldan for his excellence in chivalry and virtue: "von Persîâ der Soldân / der koufet ûf dem grüenen plân / ouch vil maneger êren hort" (15075–077; the Soldan of Persia purchased many treasures of honor on the green meadow). Floridanz, in turn, also publicly acknowledges Partonopier's chivalric achievements and rejects any attempts by other knights to create an artificial rift between the two heroes who display many curious similarities. At one point Herman of Thenadôn is unhorsed by Partonopier and pretends, while talking to Floridanz, that the former had insulted the Persian ruler, trying to incite him to take revenge against the young man on his behalf:

Der soldân hübesch unde wîs
gap im der rede in spottes wîs
antwürte, wande er sich verstuont,
same die sinneclichen tuont, . . .
mich dunket, er hab iuch geleit
ûz dem satel ûf daz lant.
(15765–773)

[The Soldan mockingly answered him in a courtly and intelligent manner, since he understood things as reasonable people do, . . . I think he threw you out of the saddle to the ground.]

Partonopier repeatedly emphasizes his admiration for the Soldan, echoing the narrator's own opinion:

ouch hete dâ sô wol gestriten
von Persîâ der soldân
nâch hôhen êren ûf dem plân,
daz im holdez herze truoc
Partonopier der grâve kluoc
und in begunde vaste loben.
(15956–961)[40]

[The Soldan from Persia had fought so valiantly for high honors on the field that the wise count Partonopier admired him in his heart and praised him in public.]

Nevertheless, at the end Partonopier proves to be the uncontested winner as he is even able to defeat Floridanz: "biz Partonopier mit kraft / den soldân küene und ellenthaft / betwanc ân underscheide" (16287–289; until Partonopier forcefully defeated the bold and strong Soldan without any doubt).[41] The young man, however, does not trust his good fortune and continues to worry that possibly Meliur might like the Soldan better than him: "daz der vil werde soldân / geviele baz der frouwen sîn" (16332f.; that the very honorable Soldan might please his lady more), a fear likewise shared by Floridanz who equally worries about Meliur's attraction to Partonopier (16347–349). Whereas the individual conflicts and chivalric struggles are certainly of great importance for the narrative development of the romance, what truly matters for our investigation proves to be the fact that Konrad presents two very similar, very likable characters whose physical strength, fighting abilities, virtues, and emotions are remarkably comparable. Although the Soldan is obviously presented as an enemy of Christian belief, this conflict is generally ignored by Konrad who instead has simply pitted two outstanding knights against each other. Partonopier gains the victory in the tournament not because of his Christian faith, instead he wins simply because of his physical superiority, his passionate love for Meliur, and the latter's return of his feelings. Floridanz, on the other hand, does not lose simply because of his adherence to a pagan belief, rather he loses because his opponent proves to be the best knight of them all and because Meliur does not love him—and neither argument is related to his religion.

Nevertheless, Konrad does not hesitate to present the possibility that Meliur might marry Floridanz, completely ignoring the the latter's different religious orientation: "daz er dâhte wider sich, / daz diu frouwe keiserlich / dem Sarrazîne ûf erden / ze teile solte werden" (16585–588; he thought to himself that the imperial lady should marry the Saracen here on earth). He also observes that many heathens would have not have been opposed to accepting baptism if this would have guaranteed Meliur's love for them (16604–607). Moreover, while one of Meliur's advisors presents to her the penultimate selection of possible marriage partners, he stresses that they all have demonstrated excellence in character, chivalric virtues, and outstanding fighting skills during the tournament, and could be seriously considered as marriage partners for the princess. This group includes "vier kristen und drî heiden" (16622; four Christians and three heathens), and depending on the final outcome of the competitions one of them would indeed be the chosen one, irrespective of the religious background:

> swer under den hie brichet für
> und er gelît den sehsen obe,
> beide an êren unde an lobe,
> dem ist daz heil gevallen,
> daz er iuch vor in allen
> triuten unde haben sol.
>
> (16624–629)

> [He who excels among the six in honor and public praise will win the glory to become your lover (husband) to the exclusion of the rest.]

These seven wooers are subsequently introduced once again and praised for their outstanding qualities, that is, the king of France (16634ff.); the king of England (16646ff.); Gaudîn from Spain, formerly a Saracen, but now a converted Christian and a close friend of Partonopier (16670ff.); Partonopier (16700ff.), Floridanz of Persia, the Soldan (16738ff.); Margalî, another heathen king (16772ff.); and Appatrîs, king of Nubîe (16782ff.). Insofar as Partonopier is the predestined husband, and the protagonist of Konrad's romance, his highly positive characterization by the narrator does not need any further elaboration. Gaudîn only plays the second fiddle, has already reached the age of 50 (16683), and would never be considered as a serious contender for Meliur's hand. The Soldan outshines the other heathen kings, who eventually defer to him voluntarily acknowledging his supreme rank and esteem. The same applies to the Christian kings who do not want to contend with Partonopier for the princess. In other words, here the dramatic climax has been reached because among all competitors the truly best warriors have been identified who are worthy to be selected by Meliur. The narrator pays especially close attention to Floridanz and offers us a detailed character portrait which provides us with intriguing clues as to how—at least in this context—Konrad viewed members of non-Christian societies, subtly revealing his general attitude toward the foreign as such. Instead of stereotyping and castigating the Persian king as an evil person who deserves to die at the hand of a crusader because of his pagan belief, we are told the following:

Floridanz excels in his manly virtues: "mit hôher mannes krefte" (16740; much outstanding manly strength); but he also has demonstrated enormous generosity toward his fellow men: "kein heiden wart sô milte nie" (16742; no heathen ever was so generous). His wealth and powers are unheard of, and no other Saracen king would be his equal (16743–745). As part of his education he has learned the art of astronomy and astrology and hence knows how to anticipate the future (16748f.), a skill which here does not carry any negative connotations as Meliur herself had previously explored the occult arts through a formal education process and also had learned to read the stars and planets (8094f.).[42]

Astrology played a major role in the Middle Ages and was rarely viewed negatively by the Church, unless it was directed against biblical teachings. Some of the greatest writers such as Wolfram von Eschenbach confirm in their texts (Parzival) that knowledge gleaned from the stars about the future events of humanity deserves full attention and must be regarded as divine information.[43] Moreover, Floridanz gains further recognition through his physical attractiveness and his knowledge and experience in wooing courtly ladies (16750–752). In short, he emerges as an almost picture-perfect knight, only the lack of baptism mars this impression slightly:

> sîn hant vil manecvalten
> prîs hie hât gewunnen.
> wan daz er in dem brunnen
> des toufes niht gereinet ist
> und daz er niht erkennet Krist,
> son ist kein wandel mêr an im.
> (16757–762)

[With his hand he has won much praise, except that he is not cleansed in the fountain of baptism and that he does not recognize Christ; otherwise there is no blemish on him.]

Since his childhood he had striven toward honor and had gained an astonishing reputation: "er hete dar von kindes jugent / getragen ie der êren kranz" (13530f.; since childhood he has worn the wreath of honor) which is here, during the tournament, vividly reflected, as one of the advisors points out: "vil maneger êren bürde / lît an ime, daz ist wâr" (16770f.; many honors are placed on him, that is true). Meliur's marriage would even convince him to accept Christian baptism and to convert his people as well: "daz er sich durch die keiserîn / und alle sîne Sarrazîn / vil gerne toufen lieze, / ob man im daz gehieze" (16763–765; he would happily accept baptism for himself and all his people the Saracens on behalf of the empress if he were asked to do so).

However, since Konrad paints a glorious picture of Partonopier, the young hero of course outshines the Persian ruler in every respect: "Der soldân hete schœne vil: / diu dûhte gar ein kindes spil, / dô man den grâven het ersehen" (17259–261; the Soldan possessed much beauty, yet it was nothing but a child's game when the count was seen). In fact, Clarîn's advice regarding the selection of the Soldan is quickly dismissed as the narrator comments: "der sich unrehtes vleiz" (16825; who strove for evil things), indicating that this positive evaluation of Floridanz's desire to accept baptism in order to gain Meliur's hand (16842–847) cannot be trusted. As Arnolt of Malbriûn explains, the heathen wooer only pretends his interest in Christianity and would, soon after the marriage, return to his old belief: "sô kêrte er sîne sinne / an sînen alten orden wider / und leite den gelouben nider, / die wâren kristenlichen ê" (16968–971; he will remember his old religion, will reject the true belief, the true Christian bond). Indeed, right after Partonopier has been declared the winner and gained Meliur as his wife, Floridanz reveals his true character and attacks his opponent to force the princess to be turned over to him as he believes that he was cheated and dishonored by Partonopier (18751ff.). Major battles ensue and once again pit the Christians against the heathens, just as in the beginning of the romance when Partonopier, on his first return from Meliur's kingdom, had helped the French king to defend his country against the Saracens. At this point the narrative returns to the traditional evaluation of the heathens as dangerous, perhaps even devilish creatures who must be opposed at any costs in the name of Christianity.

Nevertheless, Konrad demonstrates that he harbored quite positive feelings toward the heathen kings and allowed them to compete for Meliur's hand without being cast as monstrous people during the tournament. On the contrary, Floridanz almost would have defeated Partonopier in many respects as he displays an extraordinary character, great chivalric virtues, and royal dignities. The Persian Soldan eventually fails, however, because his arrogance and hubris replaces his previous chivalry and thus casts him as a less than desirable marriage partner for Meliur. Partonopier valiantly fights against his enemy and probably was supposed to gain victory over the heathens, as the narrator points out at the end: "sö was eht ie Partonopier / der beste vor in allen" (21750f.; in truth Partonopier was always the best of them all). Nevertheless, throughout the romance Floridanz is unequivocally represented as a worthy hero who deserves the audience's respect and admiration. Both his heathendom and his failure to defeat Partonopier physically bring about the decision against him, but for a long time Konrad makes us believe that Floridanz might have had a very good chance of winning the tournament and hence could have been chosen as Meliur's husband in spite of his heathen religion.

To conclude, despite the conventional depiction in literary and visual documents of heathens as not worthy of respect and recognition by their Christian contemporaries, Konrad here presents quite a different impression of the world of heathens within the European context. In his romance all of the heathen kings emerge as impressive warriors, attractive, courtly knights, and highly virtuous and admirable characters. Certainly, the narrative framework forces Konrad to make Floridanz lose in the end, but not without leaving us with the impression that heathens are human beings as well, that they share the same social, ethical, and moral values, and that they should be considered as members of a universal community. Floridanz could have married Meliur, but the circumstances of the tournament prevented it. The heathens' lack of baptism undermines, of course, all the positive values attributed to them once again and, after all forces the narrator to dismiss them as worthy marriage partners for Meliur.[44] Nevertheless, both here and early in the romance the discussion of the young princess's necromancy and the tolerant presentation of heathens indicate that Konrad pursued unusually idiosyncratic ideas about other cultures, other peoples, other sciences, and perhaps even other types of religions. This does not make him to a tolerant thinker as such—actually, almost impossible in the Middle Ages—but he must certainly be credited for his open-minded characterization of the heathen rulers and his acceptance of their knightly honors. Much more than Wolfram von Eschenbach in his Willehalm with his positive comments about brave and virtuous heroes from the world of heathendom, Konrad has opened intriguing perspectives, taking us from the European center to the heathen margin and suggested that the audience would certainly encounter peoples there with similar values, morals, and ethics.[45] In addition, it is worth pointing out that the marriage of Meliur and Partonopier unites two people representing the Eastern and the Western Church. An Archbishop and a Byzantine patriarch jointly perform the wedding ceremony (17398f.) reflecting historically well-documented efforts of both churches to build bridges and perhaps even to reunite, as illustrated by the decisions reached during the Council of Lyon in 1274.[46]

Apparently, Konrad used his romance as a public forum to discuss means and measures to bring together people of different beliefs and convictions. At first the concept of the Other is intriguingly developed with the figure of the mysteriously learned and skilled Meliur. Her activities force the reader to acknowledge that alterity does not automatically mean a danger for the individual; in fact it might prove to be a rather ordinary ability with which, unexpected illusions are created. Next, the heathens' participation in the tournament and their positive characterization indicate that a peaceful interaction of Christians and Saracens might well be within the reach of political possibilities for thirteenth-century Europeans. Finally, Konrad obviously strongly supported the attempt by the Western Church to heal the rift with the Eastern Church and to establish a new unity.

Unfortunately, none of the three approaches comes to full fruition, as Meliur simply loses her magical powers and skills through Partonopier's breaking of the taboo; the heathen knights are defeated and are eventually reduced again to their traditional stereotypes; and the unification of the Eastern and Western Church is not fully developed and is quickly lost out of sight within the narrative development. Overall, however, in all three areas Konrad offered remarkable alternatives to dominant and traditional medieval thinking and suggested to his audience new concepts of how to deal with the Other in a constructive, almost rational, at least reasonable manner.

Interestingly, almost the identical observations could be made with regard to the anonymous verse novella "Die Heidin" from about the same time period (late thirteenth century) and where the protagonist's opponent, a heathen king, is presented to the audience as a virtuous, ideal knight, as a courageous and intelligent warrior, and a warm, supportive husband, who will eventually be tricked by the Christian count and loses his wife to the latter, not because of any inferiority resulting from his paganism, but because the protagonist cunningly succeeds in the secret battle for the wife's love and manages to make her hate her husband.[47] This, however, would be the topic of another paper, although it sheds significant light on the overall theme of this paper and the other contributions to this volume.[48]

Notes

I would like to express my thanks to Dr. Aline G. Hornaday and Prof. Hubert Heinen, University of Texas at Austin, for reading my article and making valuable suggestions.

1. For various modern approaches to medieval German literature, see *Medieval German Voices in the 21st Century: The Paradigmatic Function of Medieval German Studies for German Studies*, Internationale Forschungen zur Allgemeinen und Vergleichenden Literaturwissenschaft 46 (Amsterdam and Atlanta: Editions Rodopi, 2000).
2. Aaron J. Gurjewitsch, *Mittelalterliche Volkskultur*, trans. from the Russian by Matthias Springer (Munich: Beck, 1987); *Europäische Mentalitätsgeschichte: Hauptthemen in Einzeldarstellungen*, ed. Peter Dinzelbacher,

Kröners Taschenausgabe 469 (Stuttgart: Kröner, 1993); Hans-Henning Kortüm, *Mensch und Mentalitäten: Einführung in Vorstellungswelten des Mittelalters* (Berlin: Akademie Verlag, 1996); Jean-Claude Schmitt, *Ghosts in the Middle Ages: The Living and the Dead in Medieval Society*, trans. Teresa Lavender Fagan (Chicago and London: The University of Chicago Press, 1998).

3. Gerd Althoff, Hans-Werner Goetz, Ernst Schubert, *Menschen im Schatten der Kathedrale: Neuigkeiten aus dem Mittelalter* (Darmstadt: Primus Verlag, 1998); Harry Kühnel, ed., *Alltag im Spätmittelalter*. 3rd ed. (Graz, Vienna and Cologne: Verlag Styria, Edition Kaleidoskop, 1986).
4. M. J. Ailes, "The Medieval Male Couple and the Language of Homosociality," David M. Herlihy, ed., *Masculinity in Medieval Europe* (London and New York: Longman, 1999), 214–237; Albrecht Diem, "*nu suln ouch wir gesellen sîn*—Über Schönheit, Freundschaft und mann-männliche Liebe im *Tristan* Gottfrieds von Straßburg," *Tristania* 19 (1999): 45–95.
5. Bronisław Geremek, "The Marginal Man," *The Medieval World*, ed. Jacques Le Goff, trans. Lydia Cochrane (London: Collins and Brown, 1990), 347–73; see also the introduction to *Other Middle Ages: Witnesses at the Margins of Medieval Society*, ed. Michael Goodich, The Middle Ages Series (Philadelphia: University of Pennsylvania Press, 1998).
6. *The Stranger in Medieval* Society, ed. F. R. P. Akehurst and Stephanie Cain Van D'Elden, Medieval Cultures 12 (Minneapolis and London: University of Minnesota Press, 1997); *Other Middle Ages,* ed. Michael Goodich, 1998; for the history of medieval Jewry, see Leonard B. Glick, *Abraham's Heirs. Jews and Christians in Medieval Europe* (Syracuse: Syracuse University Press, 1999).
7. Mary B. Campbell, *The Witness and the Other World: Exotic European Travel Writing, 400–1600* (Ithaca and London: Cornell University Press, 1988); *Orient und Okzident in der Kultur des Mittelalters*. Ed. Danielle Buschinger et Wolfgang Spiewok, Wodan 68 (Greifswald: Reineke, 1997).
8. Jeffrey Jerome Cohen, "The Limits of Knowing: Monsters and the Regulation of Medieval Popular Culture," *Medieval Folklore* III (1994): 1–37; for German monster literature, see Claude Lecouteux, *Les monstres dans la littérature allemande du moyen âge: Contributions à l'étude du merveilleux médiéval*, Göppinger Arbeiten zur Germanistik 330, 1–3 (Göppingen: Kümmerle, 1982).
9. Albrecht Classen, "Monsters, Devils, Giants, and other Creatures: 'The Other' in Medieval Narratives and Epics, with Special Emphasis on Middle High German Literature," *Canon and Canon Transgression in Medieval German Literature*, ed. Albrecht Classen, Göppinger Arbeiten zur Germanistik 573 (Göppingen: Kümmerle, 1993), 83–121; Ruth Mellinkoff, *Signs of Otherness in North European Art of the Late Middle Ages*, 2 vols., California Studies in the History of Art 32 (Berkeley, Los Angeles, and Oxford: University of California Press, 1993).
10. Albrecht Classen, "Die guten Monster im Orient und in Europa: Konfrontation mit dem 'Fremden' als anthropologische Erfahrung im Mittelalter," *Mediaevistik* 9 (1996): 11–37.

11. Volker Rittner, *Kulturkontakte und soziales Lernen im Mittelalter: Kreuzzüge im Licht einer mittelalterlichen Biographie*, Kollektive Einstellungen und sozialer Wandel im Mittelalter 1 (Cologne and Vienna: Böhlau, 1973), 79.
12. Rittner, 80f.
13. Ulrich Müller, "Toleranz zwischen Christen und Muslimen im Mittelalter? Zur Archäologie der Beziehungen zwischen dem christlich-lateinischen Okzident und dem islamischen Orient," *Kulturthema Toleranz: Zur Grundlegung einer interdisziplinären und interkulturellen Toleranzforschung*, ed. Alois Wierlacher, Kulturthemen 2 (Munich: Iudicium, 1996), 307–353.
14. Konrad von Würzburg, *Partonopier und Meliur*. Aus dem Nachlasse von Franz Pfeiffer herausgegeben von Karl Bartsch. Mit einem Nachwort von Rainer Gruenter, Deutsche Neudrucke. Reihe: Texte des Mittelalters (Berlin: de Gruyter, 1970; rpt. of the 1871 edition).
15. For the global theme in medieval German literature, see Friedrich-Wilhelm Wentzlaff-Eggebert, *Kreuzzugsdichtung des Mittelalters: Studien zu ihrer geschichtlichen und dichterischen Wirklichkeit* (Berlin: de Gruyter, 1960); unfortunately the author does not consider Konrad's romance.
16. Joachim Bumke, *Geschichte der deutschen Literatur im hohen Mittelalter* (Munich: DTV, 1990), 239–41.
17. Most recently, Jutta Eming, "Partonopiers Mutter," *Schwierige Frauen—schwierige Männer in der Literatur des Mittelalters*, ed. Alois M. Haas and Ingrid Kasten (Bern, Berlin, et al.: Peter Lang, 1999), 53–70, offered a critical reading of the relationship between Partonopier and his mother. See also the courtly romance *Mai und Beaflor*, contemporary to Konrad's narrative (*Mai und Beaflor: Eine Erzählung aus dem dreizehnten Jahrhundert*, Dichtungen des deutschen Mittelalters 7 [Leipzig: G. J. Göschen'sche Verlagshandlung, 1848]) where the bitter conflict between mother and son over the daughter-in-law leads to a point at which Mai executes his mother as a punishment for her murderous plotting against Beaflor.
18. See the many different contributions to Konrad von Würzburg's verse novellas and romances in the *Jahrbuch der Oswald von Wolkenstein Gesellschaft* 5 (1988/1989); Susanne Rikl, *Erzählen im Kontext von Affekt und Ratio: Studien zu Konrad von Würzburg 'Partonopier und Meliûr*,' Mikrokosmos 46 (Frankfurt am Main–New York: Peter Lang, 1996).
19. W. Obst, *Der Partonopier-Roman Konrad von Würzburg und seine französische Vorlage*. Ph.D. thesis Universität Würzburg 1976.
20. Ursula Peters, "*Roman courtois* in der Stadt: Konrad von Würzburg Partonopier und Meliur," *Zeitschrift für Literaturwissenschaft und Linguistik* 48 (1982): 10–28.
21. Rüdiger Brandt, *Konrad von Würzburg*, Erträge der Forschung 249 (Darmstadt: Wissenschaftliche Buchgesellschaft, 1987), 152–73.
22. Hartmut Kokott, *Konrad von Würzburg. Ein Autor zwischen Auftrag und Autonomie* (Stuttgart: Hirzel, 1989), 9.
23. Hartmut Kugler, *Die Vorstellung der Stadt in der Literatur des deutschen Mittelalters*, Münchener Texte und Untersuchungen zur deutschen Literatur des Mittelalters 88 (Munich: Artemis, 1986), 131–38, refers to Konrad von

Würzburg's *Der trojanische Krieg* as an example of a exotic description of a city, but has ignored *Partonopier*.

24. *Herzog Ernst: Ein mittelalterliches Abenteuerbuch*, herausgegeben, übersetzt, mit Anmerkungen und einem Nachwort versehen von Bernhard Sowinski (Stuttgart: Reclam, 1970), vv. 2212–2250.
25. Melusine in Thüring von Ringoltingen's eponymous chapbook also appeases her husband Reymund's fear with specific references to the Christian religion in which she believes.
26. Jutta Eming, "Geliebte oder Gefährtin? Das Verhältnis von Feenwelt und Abenteuerwelt in *Partonopier und Meliur*," *Die Welt der Feen im Mittelalter*. Hg. von Danielle Buschinger und Wolfgang Spiewok, Wodan 47 (Greifswald: Reineke, 1994), 43–58.
27. Once again, the parallels to Thüring of Ringoltingen's *Melusine* (1456) are striking and would require a further investigation of the experience with 'the Other' in late-medieval literature; see Albrecht Classen, "Geschlechts- und Ehebeziehungen im 15. Jahrhundert: Der Fall *Melusine* von Thüring von Ringoltingen. Eine sozial- und literarhistorische Studie aus mentalitätsgeschichtlicher Sichter," *German Studies Review* XVII, 2 (1994): 233–268.
28. Jutta Eming, "Partonopiers Mutter," 1999, 53–70.
29. Walter Haug, "Der Teufel und das Böse im mittelalterlichen Roman," here quoted from: W. Haug, *Strukturen als Schlüssel zur Welt: Kleine Schriften zur Erzählliteratur des Mittelalters* (Tübingen: Niemeyer, 1989; originally printed in *Seminar* [1985]): 67–85; here 79.
30. W. Haug, "Der Teufel," 79.
31. Dietrich Krusche, "Die Kategorie der Fremde. Eine Problemskizze," D. Krusche, Alois Wierlacher, ed., *Hermeneutik der Fremde* (Munich: iudicium, 1990), 13–23.
32. Partonopier's mother is not opposed to his marrying a noble lady worthy of his social status, as she even finds an acceptable partner for her son and treats him with a love potion. In other words, it would be erroneous to characterize the relationship with her son as incestuous, rather she proves to be overly protective and incapable of accepting his independent decision regarding his own future wife.
33. Gisela Werner, *Studien zu Konrads von Würzburg Partonopier und Meliur*. Sprache und Dichtung (Bern and Stuttgart: Haupt, 1977), 149ff.; Lydia Miklautsch, *Studien zur Mutterrolle in den mittelhochdeutschen Großepen des elften (sic! meant: zwölften) und zwölften (sic! meant: dreizehnten) Jahrhunderts*, Erlanger Studien 88 (Erlangen: Palm & Enke, 1991), 163–167; disappointingly, Miklautsch limits herself mostly to a paraphrases of the text and does not gain a full interpretive perception.
34. Bea Lundt, "Schwestern der Melusine im 12. Jahrhundert: Aufbruchs-Phantasien und Beziehungs-Vielfalt bei Marie de France, Walter Map and Gervasius von Tilbury," B. Lundt, ed., *Auf der Suche nach der Frau im Mittelalter. Fragen, Quellen, Antworten* (Munich: Fink, 1991), 233–253.
35. Kokott, 235.
36. James A. Schultz, *The Knowledge of Childhood in the German Middle Ages, 1100–1350*, Middle Ages Series (Philadelphia: University of Pennsylvania Press, 1995), 222.

37. This interest in a "Länderkatalog" is not uncommon in the Middle Ages and reflects an increased fascination with the real world far and wide; see, for instance, the didactic poet Boppe's "Swelch hôhe vürste nû hât hôhes küniges namen" (I, 9), quoted from Heidrun Alex, *Der Spruchdichter Boppe. Edition—Übersetzung—Kommentar*, Hermaea N.F. 82 (Tübingen: Niemeyer, 1998), 46, for further examples see 128.
38. Hartmut Kugler, "Imago Mundi. Kartographische Skizze und literarische Beschreibung," *Mediävistische Komparatistik: Festschrift für Franz Josef Worstbrock zum 60. Geburtstag*, ed. Wolfgang Harms and Jan-Dirk Müller (Stuttgart and Leipzig: Hirzel, 1997), 77–93; see also David B. Leshock's contribution to our volume.
39. This observation regarding Wolfram's treatment of heathens has been made several times, see, for instance, Werner Schröder, "Der Markgraf und die gefallenen Heidenkönige in Wolfram's 'Willehalm'," here quoted from W. Schröder, *Wolfram von Eschenbach: Spuren und Werke. Kleinere Schriften 1956–1987*, vol. 1 (Stuttgart: Hirzel, 1989), 340–72; Karl Bertau, "Das Recht des Anderen. Über den Ursprung der Vorstellung von einer Schonung der Irrgläubigen bei Wolfram von Eschenbach," K. Bertau, *Wolfram vonn Eschenbach: Neun Versuche über Subjektivität und Ursprünglichkeit in der Geschichte* (Munich: Beck, 1983), 241–258; for a theological interpretation, now see David A. Wells, "Medieval Religious Disputation and Theology," *Stvdi Medievali*. Serie Terza XLI (2000): 591–664.
40. See also 16062–065; 16250–259, et passim.
41. H. Kokott, *Konrad von Würzburg*, 235: "Das Turnier ist dann die Gelegenheit, bei der sich Partonopier glanzvoll bewährt, indem er sich gegen die ganze ritterliche Welt, vom römischen Kaiser bis hin zum heidnischen Sultan, durchsetzt. Welch großer Wert darauf gelegt wird, daß Partonopier die Bewährungsprobe allein besteht, zeigt sich daran, daß er inkognito auftritt . . ." [The tournament then offers the opportunity for Partonopier to prove his outstanding qualities by defeating the entire chivalrous world, from the Roman emperor to the heathen Sultan. The fact of his appearance incognito demonstrates that Partonopier has to prove himself all alone].
42. For a general overview of medieval astrology, see Pearl Kibre, *Studies in Medieval Science: Alchemy, Astrology, Mathematics and Medicine*, History Series 19 (London: Hambledon Press, 1984); Anthony F. Aveni, *Behind the Crystal Ball: Magic, Science, and the Occult from Antiquity through the New Age* (New York: Times Books, 1996).
43. See Arthur Groos, *Romancing the Grail: Genre, Science, and Quest in Wolfram's Parzival* (Ithaca and London: Cornell University Press, 1995), 174ff.
44. A similar case proves to be Johann von Würzburg's *Wilhelm von Österreich*, which also found its way into the fifteenth century when a prose version was printed ("Volksbuch" or chapbook); see my studies "The Heathen World in the *Volksbuch Wilhelm von Österreich*. An Anthropological Revision of the Crusade Epics," *Neuphilologische Mitteilungen* XCIII, 2 (1992): 145–61, and: "Emergence of Tolerance: An Unsuspected Medieval Phenomenon. Studies on Wolfram von Eschenbach's *Willehalm*, Ulrich von Etzenbach's

Wilhelm von Wenden, and Johann von Würzburg's *Wilhelm von Österreich*," *Neophilologus* 76 (1992): 586–99.

45. H. Kokott, *Konrad von Würzburg*, 245–53, resolutely rejects the traditional opinion that Konrad's *Partonopier* reflected the poet's turn toward urban culture and urban interests. On the contrary, the romance exclusively idealizes the aristocratic world and renews the fundamental concepts of courtly romances; see also U. Peters, "*Roman courtois*," 26.
46. H. Kokott, *Konrad von Würzburg*, 253.
47. Quoted from *Novellistik des Mittelalters: Märendichtung*, ed. and trans. Klaus Grubmüller, Bibliothek des Mittelalters 23 (Frankfurt a.M.: Deutscher Klassiker Verlag, 1996), 364–468; for a commentary, see ibid., 1153–171.
48. See also the contribution by David B. Leshock, "Religious Geography: Designating Jews and Muslims as 'Foreigners' in Medieval England" to this volume, who also highlights the dialectics of tolerance and xenophobia so characteristic of medieval mentality.

14

The Intimate Other:

Hans Folz's Dialogue between "Christian and Jew"

WINFRIED FREY

I

In 1479 the Nuremberg barber, surgeon and poet Hans Folz published a text in his own print shop,[1] giving it the following title:

> Item ein krieg den der dichter dises spruchs gehapt / hat wider einen iuden mit dem er wandret vnd wie / er im all sein frag verantwurt vnd yn inn seiner eygen / schrift überwant vnd beschloß als das nachfolgent / gedicht clar erzelt vnd aus weyst / Gedruckt von hansen volczen von wurmß barwirer / wonhafft zu nurmberg Im Mcccc vnd lxxix Iare.[2]

> [Concerning a combat that the author of this work had with a Jew with whom he was traveling, and how he answered all the latter's questions and defeated him with the aid of his own scriptures, thus bringing the combat to an end, as the following poem clearly narrates and demonstrates. Printed by Hans Folz, Barber of Worms, domiciled in Nuremberg, in the year 1479]

In Hanns Fischer's edition of Folz's works in rhyming couplets, which gives the texts' modern short titles, this poem is laconically entitled "Christian and Jew." This is justified, inasmuch as the text actually presents us with a dialogue between a Jew and a Christian (even if the opponents are depicted as being far from equals). Nevertheless, it is well worth looking more closely at the Nuremberg author's own title.

In that period, the word "Krieg" [war] still does not unequivocally mean an armed conflict, but still also has the original German meaning of a determined effort, a war of words, even in court.[3] Thus Folz intends to document a combat which he supposedly fought with a Jew who was his traveling companion. This refers to the artisan Hans Folz's years as a journeyman, which took him, among other places, to Spain. Before their expulsion in 1492 there were still Jews in Spain who were allowed to confess their religion and culture openly and actively. The text could therefore have an autobiographical background (even if a fictitious one) which was intended to indicate to his public in Nuremberg, who were surely familiar with his biography, the veracity of his account. In any case, Folz takes up with his war of words a literary tradition that had long been of great importance for the development of the relationship between Christians and Jews in the West. In their debates with the Jews, which were mostly total fiction, Christian theologians had tried for centuries to prove Christianity's claims to the possession of truth in the face of Judaism (and as a deterrent in the face of possible doubts or doubters within Christianity itself) by refuting the Jewish opposition to the teachings of the Christian Church point for point. They were aided by the methods of Christian exegesis, which was not satisfied with the lexical meaning of the sacred Scriptures (which, they insinuated, was all that Jewish exegesis was able to do with its *sensus Judaicus*), but sought a sense that lay beyond and above this—and which found it, because, in accordance with their basic assumptions, it had to be there.[4] Since the Christian side was firmly convinced that it possessed a higher truth than the Jews, and that it could prove this by means of the holy Scriptures, such fictional debates (like the very few that actually took place) could only end with the defeat of the Jewish opposition. Therefore Folz, who can assume this prior knowledge on the part of his readers (among whom there were obviously members of the "upper strata of Nuremberg society"),[5] can say in his title (which at this time and for a long time to come had the function of a book advertisement or blurb) that he defeated the Jew with his interpretation of the Hebrew Bible (for Christians, this meant the Old Testament) without any shadow of doubt. Since no one would have expected anything else, no one would have accepted anything else, certainly not the guardians of the eternal truth.

Thus in terms of the content of the title and the tradition implicitly adopted in it, this text can be taken as evidence of what at the end of the fifteenth century, "when people in the almost unanimous judgment of modern research were more pious and more loyal to the Church than they had ever been in the Middle Ages before this time,"[6] a regular Christian, not a theologian, but a layman who was interested in religious matters and engaged in his community[7] knew about his own religion as distinguished from the 'other' religion of the Jews, and what conclusions he drew from this.

II

In accordance with long-standing tradition, Folz's poem begins with a two-part prologue. First we have the *prologus praeter rem* (vv 1–21), in which the author introduces the theme in a quite general way (and often using *sententiae*). Folz tells us about the usefulness of traveling, and the fact that in the process one can learn about "Der welde lauff und auch ir syt" (v. 3; the way of the world and the behavior of mankind). Thus the reader is meant to understand that the narrator is an experienced man who knows his way around in the world and in whom we can place our trust. In the *prologus ante rem* (vv.22–53) Folz gives a detailed account of the circumstances which led to the battle of words which he narrates. For this purpose, he creates a classical communication situation: he once came upon a group of travelers, among whom was a Jew "der sich daucht gar weys" (v. 27; who thought himself very wise), and who was holding forth because there was no one there who was able to refute him with words, and because they could not, as they would have liked to, forcibly silence him, since the Jew was protected by an armed man, his "gleytzman" (v.34; escort). The narrator, however, although "auch ein ley newr" (v.39; also nothing but a simple layman), considered himself superior to the Jew in terms of knowledge and felt confident enough to defeat him in a debate. He challenged the Jew to a duel of words, and their fellow travelers swore on oath that they would not get involved unless they were requested to do so by one of the combatants.

One should certainly not interpret this description as the report of an event that occurred in reality. Nonetheless, the second part of the prologue gives some indication of the circumstances (and power relations) under which the Jewish minority had to live at that time.

In order to protect himself on his journey from the aggression of his fellow travelers (which is taken as real and obviously accepted by the narrator), the Jewish traveler needs an armed escort. This escort was originally conceived as a protection for the unarmed traveler on the public highway. After the Jews had lost the right to bear arms (codified in the Saxon and German Law Codes [*Sachsenspiegel* and *Deutschenspiegel*]),[8] they had, like other groups in need of protection, to avail themselves of a protective escort when traveling, which was naturally never provided without payment but became a valued source of income for the Protectors, who were usually the territorial lords. This enforced need for an escort developed into the discriminatory *Leibzoll* (body tax) which was only abolished with the emancipation of the Jews in the late eighteenth and nineteenth centuries.[9] What had once been intended as a protection, in the anti-Semitic polemic of the later Middle Ages developed into a begrudged privilege unjustly claimed by the Jews. In his infamous advice to the princes and lords about how one should deal with the Jews, published in 1543 only a few decades after Folz, Martin Luther demanded, in his fifth point, "das man den Jüden das Geleid und Strasse gantz und gar auffhebe, Denn sie haben nichts auff dem Lande zu schaffen, weil sie nicht Herrn noch Amptleute noch Hendeler, oder des gleichen sind, Sie sollen da heime bleiben" [that the Jews should be deprived of their escorts, and the right to travel on the public highway, since they have nothing to seek in the country, because they are neither lords nor officials nor merchants, or the like, but should rather stay at home]. Otherwise, and here Luther is directly threatening them with lynch law, groups of armed riders might assemble to attack the Jews, since they would learn from his pamphlet what the Jews were and that they should not be protected.[10] This call to take justice into one's own hands (and its justification in advance) can already be sensed as a subliminal threat in Folz's brief description.

Another indication of the accepted image of "the Jew" is to be found in the remark that the Jew was able to boast of himself as all-knowing in contrast to the others—and was obviously well able to do so, as long as no one who was better educated stood up to him. Of course, it is an old literary cliché (it is only the defeat of someone who is superior—or at least appears to be so—that is honorable and proves one's bravery), but the matter-of-course way in which it is used is evidence of the actual superiority of many Jews in disputations about religious matters. Traditional Jewish education requires—at least for boys—an intensive training in reading and interpreting the holy Scriptures,[11] which made them considerably more secure in their understanding of the teachings of their religion than was normally the case with Christians. Christian preachers, in total agreement with theologians and Church councils, were well aware of the consequences of this. Berthold of Regensburg, for example, the great thirteenth-century German Franciscan preacher, says in a sermon that the authorities should protect believers against unbelievers, against Jews, Heathens, and Heretics, and in particular forbid the Jews "daz si von ir gelouben iht reden, offenlich noch heimlich. Ir cristen, ir sult ouch niht reden mit in von iwerm gelouben, ez sî denne ein meister der schrift. Ez sol ouch kein kristen mit in wonen noch ir brôt ezzen"[12] [to talk of their religion in any way, either in public or in their homes. You Christians, you should not talk with them about your religion, that is only permitted to the theologians. Nor should any Christian live with them or be their servant]. By making his narrator appear to be a learned person of the kind that is permitted to join in these debates, he demonstrates his own claim to be respected for his learning and at the same time locates himself and his text in the tradition of the dispute (which always, of course, resulted in a Christian victory). The dispute begins with an impressive image: the antagonists open the sacks in which their knowledge is contained, and tip out all that they contain (vv. 54f.).

In response to the question of who is to begin, the Jew insists on the natural prerogative of age. We must, however, always keep in mind that here we are dealing with a fictitious Jew created for polemic purposes by the Christian Hans Folz and who always has to do what the narrator wishes him to do! Consequently, the Jew begins with the question of questions in all disputes between mother and daughter religions: why did you Christians break away from us? In so doing the Jew implies that his religion is the only justified one, and that it is of superior value. But there he meets his match in Folz's narrator figure. In a detailed historical-theological interpretation of the image of the chairs and the number of their legs (here we are presumably more likely to be thinking of stools or milking stools) he replaces the parallelism of the triad "Pagan—Jew—Christian", as it appears in Berthold of Regensburg for example, with a teleological and thus hierarchically ordered sequence of the three "Laws."

But first he skillfully puts his Jewish opponent, and by implication the whole of Jewry, in the wrong (including in terms of linguistic technique) by pointing out to him that the Jews themselves had after all changed their religion when they accepted the ten commandments from Moses, by which he is trying to suggest that they had previously been semi-pagan ("natürlich heyden," v. 68; heathen by nature), and that the Torah actually represented a progress that the Jews had been glad to accept. In this way Folz has already anchored his theoretical construction in history. Humanity had at first been subject only to natural law, or, to put it more precisely, to their own nature (corrupted by original sin). That is, chaos ruled, as there was no "ordinancz" (v. 86) as yet, no generally binding law to regulate the way human beings behaved toward one another.

Folz's Christian protagonist claims that the pagans still remain on this first level of human socialization even today, and in a "gleichnus" (v. 81; allegory, parable) he compares this level to a one-legged stool, which can only remain upright when it is rammed firmly into the earth, that is, still firmly anchored in nature (here still interpreted in a totally medieval way). Jewry, for its part, remained in an unstable state after receiving the Law, like a two-legged stool, which can only stand upright when it is leaning against something stable. Therefore, the Jews—and here the Jewish diaspora is used as historical and theological evidence—have no fixed abode anywhere, and always had to beg for something to lean on (vv. 97–99), they had no state of their own, and were also incapable of having their own order. This was the consequence of their alleged character traits of envy, gluttony, greed, and pride (v. 95), which developed out of their obstinacy and blindness in the face of the truth of the Christian religion (v. 79), to which the Jews were earnestly "gefordert und gepeten" (v. 76; requested and invited) to convert. In turn, these traits made them "stet wacklen hin und heer" (v. 96; constantly waver this way and that).[13]

In Folz's allegory, Christianity is a three-legged stool, a perfect stool, and as a perfect religion it is also the last in the historical sequence:

> Also ist cristenglaub der lest
> Durch alle schrifft so confirmirt,
> Das fürbas mer kein ander wirt.
> Dan het der stul der peyne vyr,
> er stünt hart gleich, glaub worlich myr;
> Wan es wer überflüssig ym:
> Hiepey die keczrisch art vernim.[14]
>
> (vv. 102–108)

[Thus the Christian religion is the last, and all the Scriptures confirm that there will never be another. For if the stool had four legs, it would stand in exactly the same way, believe me truly, because the fourth leg would be superfluous, and this you can comprehend as a symbol of heresy.]

Folz summarizes the significance of the allegory once more: it is reason alone that raises man above the beasts at the first level of social and religious development, on which the pagans lived. However, reason commands humanity to strive for perfection. But this striving would have remained without a goal, if God had not, on the second level, in the second Law of the Hebrew Bible, given directions to humanity, which Folz, in accordance with longstanding Christian exegetic tradition calls "figur" (v. 110, 123; lat. *figura*).[15] The third level, the third Law, is "der zweyer concordancz" (v. 111; the harmonization of the two of them), the unity of all Laws in Christ.

Here Folz proves his familiarity with contemporary views of the history of salvation. While it is true that the old divisions of the history of the world and salvation into six or four ages were still valid in the later Middle Ages, a threefold scheme for the *aetates mundi*, often subjected to a trinitarian exegesis, had developed in the course of the medieval period (perhaps following the tendency of European culture to divide the world into "three orders").[16] This schema, originating in Augustine and later extended by Hugo of St. Victor, divides the history of salvation into the time *ante legem* (before Moses), the time *sub lege* (from Moses to the birth of Christ), and the time *sub gratia* (from the birth of Christ to the end of the world at the Last Judgment).[17] By making use of this popular schema, he exploits its dignity in the Christian world not only for the purpose of arguing against the Jew in his story, but also to present him and his religion in general as inferior in comparison with the perfection of Christianity.

Folz also proceeds in a similar manner when he discusses the next theme, the problem of the Trinity, where the Jew as a doubter (and sophist) is used to give the cues. The conception of the threefold nature of God was an age-old subject of disagreement between Judaism and Christianity, since Judaism, which was committed to the belief in One God,[18] could only see in the Christian belief in the trinitarian God the "service" of "false Gods":[19]

Do sprach der jüd: "mein crist, sag an:
Wie sol ich trey persan verstan,
Den vater, sun und auch den geist,
Die du die leüt anpeten heist?
Seyt newr ein got ist und nit me,
Als uns verkünt Moises e.[20]
Bescheid mich auch, wie sich das schick:
Sint sie nun all drey allmechtick?
Sag, was ist dan der zweyer not?
Ob dan newr einr die allmacht hot,

So hon die zwen der gotheyt nicht.
Sag, was weer mit in ausgericht?
Darumb so mus ein got newr wesen,
Durch den all creatur genesen."
(vv. 131–144)

[Then the Jew said: "Tell me, my Christian, how am I to understand the Trinity, the Father, the Son and the Holy Ghost, which you order believers to adore? There is, after all, only one God and no more, as Moses' law revealed to us. Make clear to me how that is to be understood: are they all three omnipotent? If so, then why is there a need of the two other? And if only one is omnipotent, then the two other are not divine. Tell me then what function they have. For this reason there can only be one God, by whom all creation is saved."]

Folz and his fictional "I"[21] answer in this text in the same way as theologians throughout the centuries had replied to questions and doubts that were really expressed by the Jews, or as those that were only attributed to them for Christian catechistic purposes. Since he as a Christian (who has just narrated the allegory of the milking stool) is convinced that he can interpret the Hebrew Bible better than any Jew, he quotes to his opponent ("jud, lys dein eigen schrifft," v. 145; Jew, read your own Bible!) several passages from the Old Testament and interprets them in a trinitarian sense in accordance with the Christian exegetic tradition. For reasons of brevity, I will select only one passage from Folz's text here and then summarize the rest.

Mer aus deinr schriftt ich dich bericht.
Do in dem anefang[22] "got spricht:
Einen menschen den machen wir
Nach unserm pilde": jud, merck mir,
Hat nit pey dieser red, "got spricht"
Seines wesens eynikeit pflicht,
Und so darnach "wir machen" stat,
Rürt das nit gnug die trinitat?
Dan stet alspald "nach unserm pild":
Künt hie nit klerlich got der mild
Yn dem Wort "unserm" die dreiheyt
Und in dem wort "pild" die einikeyt?
So aber stunnd "gott spricht: ich mach
Ein menschen meinem pilde nach':
Yüd merck, so hestu recht geseyt,
So weer in got pur einikeyt
Und weer nit mer dan ein persan.
Solt aber allso gschriben stan
"Die göter sprechen: wir weln machen
Ein mensch nach unser pildung sachen,"

So weer in got allein dreiheyt
Und nicht des wesens einikeyt.
Doch ich dir teütscher das erzel.
Nim gleichnus pei deinr eigen sel,
Do will, gedechtnuß und vernunfft
Auch treu sint in geeynter zunfft.
(vv. 151–176)

[I will present you with more passages from your Bible. When it says in Genesis: "God says: we will make a man in our own image," then, Jew, take note: is not the unity of God's being expressed in the words "God says", and when this is followed by "We will make", does that not sufficiently demonstrate the Trinity? Directly after this stands the phrase "in our own image": is our merciful God not revealing in the word "our" the Trinity and in the word "image" unity? If the text had: "God says: I will create a Man in my own image," then, Jew, you would be right, then there would only be unity in God and He would be no more than one person. If it had been written: "The Gods speak: we will make a Man in our own image," then there would be in God only plurality, and not the Unity of His being. But I will explain it to you in German: consider your own soul as a comparison, in which Will, Thought and Reason are inextricably combined with one another.]

Folz did not invent this line of argument. Genesis 1,26[23] is the "*Locus classicus* of the Christian argument for the Trinity"[24] and the "most frequently quoted Biblical passage in the *adversus Judaeos* literature."[25] While Jewish exegesis sees in this plural an address by God to angels or other beings accompanying Him, Christian exegesis from very early on—for example in the apocryphal Epistle of Barnabas, written at the beginning of the second century[26]—saw in it a revelation of the Trinity ("obstinately denied" by the Jews), in that they understood the plural as an address by the Father to the Son as "sharing in the creation with the Father."[27] This interpretation was maintained against the arguments of the Jewish side,[28] which were occasionally also brought forward by fictitious Jews in dialogues,[29] by practically all Christian authors: the list includes almost all the important names in early Christian and medieval theology: Origen, Silvester I, Eusebius, Basil the Great, Chrysostom, Isidor of Seville, Peter Damian, Rupert of Deutz, Abelard, Walter of Châtillon, Alanus ab Insulis, Joachim of Fiore, as well as those named above—and naturally also Jewish converts like Petrus Alfonsi or William of Bourges. From the thirteenth century onward these discussions and arguments which had previously been confined more or less to theological circles were promulgated and thus popularized in the vernacular by the Mendicant orders above all. The most frequently used Biblical passages and their exegesis became part of the general religious knowledge of many lay people as well—including the Nuremberg author Hans Folz.[30] When he argues like many social authorities before him, and like other authors of popular vernacular literature, for example the legendary known as the *Passional* from which he borrowed some material, then he not only evokes an impressive legitimizing tradition, but also takes it for granted that his audience already has foreknowledge—and will approve—of the material, which will enable his readers/audience to follow his line of argument. From the outset they will not only expect that he can defeat his Jewish opponent, but will support him in so doing. By rebutting and confuting "the Jew" as a representative of the whole of Jewry, as the title of the pamphlet already proclaims as its main theme, he can create a feeling of togetherness among the Christians and at the same time use the feeling of superiority that is derived from this to stabilize the coherence of his own group.

The other passages are also directed to this goal. They deal with (after a number of other Christian proofs of the Trinity which also follow traditional lines of argument) the Messianic quality of Jesus and his nature (vv. 213–414), the virginity of Mary (vv. 415–450), Christ's redemptive action on the Cross, the Resurrection, and the Eucharist (vv. 451–568), the question of the Justified in the Old Testament (vv. 569–595)—and Jewish doubts about all these basic Christian convictions. The arguments themselves and the passages from the Prophets which are used to support them could all be easily found in Christian writings *adversus Judaeos*. More important for our theme is the way by which this is brought about and how the portrait of "the Jew" as the Other is delineated.

III

Here, too, Folz is following and making use of an old tradition. I will use several passages to illustrate this point. Folz ends the dispute, after "defeating" the Jew ("Der jud sprach: 'crist, ich mus nun sweygen." v. 569; The Jew said: Christian, now I must be silent), with a general reproach to the Jews that they have been led astray by their "plöder sin" (v. 604; their inferior understanding) so that they cannot see what has been revealed. Christ, the divine human being, has redeemed 'us,' Christ "Deen all figur hant figuriert / Und all profeten profetiert, / Die er vor im her hat gesent, / und nomen nach im pald ein ent" (vv. 599–602; whom all prefigurations have prefigured and all the prophets, whom he sent before him and who have not subsequently appeared, have prophesied.) Judaism is thus depicted, as it is commonly done in the late fifteenth-century, in the image of Synagoga whose eyes are blindfolded so that she cannot see, and it is clear that Folz is directly referring to this, since he also uses the theme in his *Fastnachtspiel* (Shrovetide Play) "die alt und neu ee, die synagog, von uberwindung der Juden in ir Talmut etc" (The Old and the New Law, the Synagogue, of the Defeat of the Jews with their Talmud, etc.).[31]

The blindness of the Jews is a consequence of something else and it, in turn, has its own consequences. According to Folz's narrator, who here too stands in a long, now almost two thousand-year-old tradition, it is a consequence of the deed "Die ir an Cristo hapt getan" (v. 414; that you did to Christ). Folz's protagonists hold the fifteenth-century Jews, irrespective of space and time which separate them from the past, responsible for that alleged murder, which Christians throughout the centuries described as deicide. Both the deicide and the continuing guilt are claimed to be responsible for the present state and status of the Jews, as a punishment pronounced by God Himself:

Wer worn anders sein feinde doch
Dan ir juden, alls ir seyt noch.
Des seyt ir von im ausgegeten
Und gancz unter sein füß getreten,[32]
Zeytlichen hie und ewig dort.

(vv. 521–525, cf. vv. 327–329)

[Who else but you Jews were then his enemies, as you still are. That is why you are eradicated like weeds by him, and he tramples you underfoot in this secular world and eternally in the world to come.]

God has this deprivation of rights and the subjection carried out by earthly powers on His behalf, as it were. In response to the Jew's statement that the Jews are under the protection of the Emperor, the Christian replies scornfully, but in total agreement with a long-standing tradition[33] and also in line with the contemporary attitude toward this question[34]: the Emperor's claim to rule is derived from Titus, the destroyer of Jerusalem, who was so contemptuous of the Jews that thirty of them were worth less to him than a single penny.[35] They are still kept in Emperor Titus's captivity "Zu yds römischen keysers zeyt" (v. 314; in the reign of every Roman Emperor cf. vv. 370–372), therefore also at the end of the fifteenth century.[36]

As proof that Jesus is the Messiah, the Christian uses the often quoted statement in Isaiah 9, 5–6. In response to the Jew's remark, which is as skeptical as it is logical, that if this was so, then Isaiah's prophecy of peace on earth (9, 6–8) ought also to have been fulfilled, his Christian opponent replies with a reference to the Christian exegetical tradition: this had been said "peyspils weis" (v. 278; in a metaphorical sense):

Die wilden und heimischen thir,
Das sint ir juden und auch wir:
Wan als die schaff sint ane meyl,
Also piten wir umb ewr heyl;
So hapt ir gen uns wolfes mut,
Wiewol ir würcklich uns nicht dut.

Desgleich mag man auch exponirn
Die kind pey den gifftigen thirn,
Die kinder gottes sint nun wir[37] Und die vergifften würm seyt ir:
Wan het ir uns in ewrm gewallt
Als ir in unserm seyt gezallt,
Kein crist erlebet jares frist.
Das weistu, das im also ist.
(vv. 281–294)

[You Jews are the wild animals and we are the tame. For just as the sheep are spotless, so we pray for your salvation, but you think of us like wolves, even though you cannot actually harm us. In the same way we can interpret the image of the child with the poisonous serpents: we are now the children of God, and you are the poisonous snakes. Because if you had the same power over us as we have over you, no Christian would survive for even a year. You know that this is so.]

In an underhand way—but one that is totally intentional on Folz's part—the lachrymose self-justification of apologetic Christian exegesis develops into a deadly frontal attack on the Jewish minority, the enemies of Christ become enemies of the Christians. This is where the appeal in the structure of the whole text becomes obvious. It is not just a matter of disproving the Jewish interpretation of the holy scriptures, nor is it just a matter of Christian didactics, it is an attempt to transform the familiar other into an enemy who is so dangerous that he can no longer be tolerated. The last sentence of the text before the author is named is: "Und ret fürbas mit im nit mer" (v. 609; and spoke with him no more). This signifies not only the end of this noteworthy dialogue, but also the rejection of any conceivable Judeo-Christian *concivilitas*, a rejection which is ultimately religiously based, but nonetheless obviously also has other causes. Folz formulates this rejection in the same way as in other texts, for example in the *Fastnachtspiel* of *Kaiser Constantinus*[38] which has a similar content, and in the didactic poem *Jüdischer Wucher* (Jewish usury)[39] so that it can be regarded as the basic ideological program of his anti-Semitic texts.[40] This rejection aims at consequences which no longer pertain to the literary field alone.

IV

When Hans Folz published his dialogue "A Christian and A Jew" in 1479, Jews had already been living in the East Frankish and later the German Empire for more than half a millennium,[41] and in Nuremberg (with involuntary interruptions) for about four hundred years.[42] During these centuries Christians and Jews had lived next to one another in the cities of the Empire, had built up intensive economic relationships, but few social and hardly any religious relationships. Rules had been formulated for the religious practices of both groups, especially after the First Crusade, which made absolute demands on the individual and the family in religious and social life; demands that of necessity led to the exclusion of the Others from each of the communities; demands that led to the paradoxical consequence that Christians and Jews who for generations had lived in neighboring parts of the towns, even in neighboring houses, who were themselves therefore neighbors and knew each other, were at one and the same time strangers. Not that closer social, cultural, and even personal contacts and relationships were always impossible, but they were always linked to power relationships and the exercise of power, and thus were subject to the changing interests and intentions of the more influential group—the Christians—and their political, economic, and religious protagonists. Apparently "normal" times of good neighborly coexistence could change overnight, as it were, to times of confrontation, oppression, expulsion, or even extermination.[43] There were many kinds of reasons for such spontaneous or deliberate transformation, political, religious, economic, legal, and often several of these combined—every history book of Judeo-Christian relations in the Middle Ages and the early modern period is full of them. The Jews had been expelled from Nuremberg during the plague period in the fourteenth century, though this was mainly for topographical, economic, and political reasons: 562 people lost their lives in that expulsion.[44] A short time later the Jews were allowed to settle in Nuremberg again—on the site of their former cemetery![45] In 1352 the agreement between the City and the Jews allowing them entrance was confirmed by the king. Nevertheless, the second Jewish community was hardly more than a tenth the size of the earlier community, and by the end of the fifteenth century it consisted of only twelve to fifteen families.[46] These were harassed and oppressed, and as they were less economically necessary for the city the longer they stayed, they became visibly impoverished.[47]

The earliest texts debating the possibility of the expulsion of Nuremberg's Jews appear in the 1470s, although efforts to bring about an expulsion in concert with the neighboring territorial princes failed. It was not until 1498 (and then after the payment of a large sum of money by the city) that the king was prepared to accede to the Nuremberg City Council's wish to expel "his" Jews. It is striking that the Council made every effort to create the impression that the expulsion was the result of a royal decision and order. They were obviously doing this to avoid conflict with the king and the princes, as Toch rightly says.[48] But they also did so to ensure the legitimization of its actions for posterity. If the Council acted independently, that might appear to be arbitrary since they only had "their" Jews by royal grant. If the king acted in his capacity as Emperor, then he placed himself in the tradition of the Emperor Titus, and was acting in accordance with his autochthonous right.[49] The Jews were "captives" in their eyes (and not just in the eyes of their traditionally-thinking contemporaries), according to the tradition of "Kammerknechtschaft" (the idea that the Jews were *servi nostrae camerae speciales*, serfs of the royal court), unfree people with whom the Emperor could dispose of as he wished. In Folz's text, too, the Emperor is the person who acts as the successor of Titus.

Authorities, especially those of the later Middle Ages who were committed to the ideal of harmony and peace,[50] always tried to make their interests and decisions appear as if they had been decided and carried out in agreement with their townspeople and the superior powers (King, Emperor, God). The "simple" townspeople were less interested in legal or economic details than in direct, clear reasoning which accorded with their way of thinking and traditions. It was not only in the twentieth century that an attempt was made to produce this agreement by polarization, marginalization, and exclusion of the minority. In order to legitimize the expulsion within the city and in front of the neighbors it was necessary to stigmatize the familiar minority in the city as the "evil other." Preachers and writers such as Hans Folz took care of this task.

In 1452, when the Franciscan friar Johannes Capistrano[51] preached daily for four months in Nuremberg, the Jews were compelled to listen to the sermons, though nothing is known of any disputation. In 1474/75 the Dominican Petrus Nigri[52] became known in public (in Regensburg at first) and preached to the local Jews, as well as others who had been sent from the whole Empire. He challenged them to a disputation in which they, however, refused to take part. After a year he proclaimed that they had been defeated. In 1475 the Nuremberg Dominicans imitated their role model Nigri so zealously that the Nuremberg City Council had to step in for fear of riots. In 1478 Nigri himself came to Nuremberg to preach to the Jews and challenge them to a disputation. Here, too, the Jews refused to engage in a dispute, which Nigri interpreted as a victory. Nevertheless he was able to move two Jews to convert. It is perfectly possible that Folz, inspired by Capistrano, returned to the theme he had already dealt with in his *Fastnachtspiel* of *Kaiser Constantinus*[53] which was probably produced in 1475, the year of the Dominican's preaching, that is, one year after Capistrano's partial success, in order to support the activities of the preachers and to present himself (Folz) to the Nuremberg council as a loyal and useful (new) citizen.[54]

His writings are evidence of the way the Nuremberg Jews (and with them all other Jews as well) were transformed into the Other in the way that had been traditional practice since the time of the church father Origen at the latest, by expropriating them and representing them as being incapable of understanding their own Scriptures, as heretics to their own religion, as they were frequently reproached.[55] As Christianity—and here Folz makes his Christian figure appear as its universal embodiment—appropriates the holy Scriptures of Judaism, the Jews become intimate others, who are not allowed to know themselves, but are, as a people to be taught and converted, permitted to lead a marginalized existence, though even this could be taken from them when "needed" by the majority.

Michael Toch[56] has described the Nuremberg politicians' preparations for the expulsion of "their" Jews most impressively. The dates (1474, 1475, 1477, 1478) correspond strikingly with the activities of the preaching orders and with those texts by Hans Folz which have been presented here. The result must have pleased the Council, the preachers and the writer: in 1498 and 1499 the Jews were banned from the city and its territory in accordance with "Law and Justice." What happened may have been legal, but it was definitely not just.[57]

Translated by Bill McCann

Notes

1. "Unique of its kind is the form of publication Hans Folz preferred: Nearly all of his literary works—except for most of his—were published in his own printing house, which he ran from 1479 to 1488, probably only to print his own works." Johannes Janota, "Folz, Hans," *Die deutsche Literatur des Mittelalters, Verfasserlexikon*, second edition, ed. Kurt Ruh et al., vol. 2 (Berlin and New York: de Gruyter, 1979), col. 769–93; here 770 f. A short survey of Folz's life and works can be found.
2. Hans Folz, *Die Reimpaarsprüche*, ed. Hanns Fischer. Münchener Texte und Untersuchungen zur deutschen Literatur des Mittelalters 1 (Munich: C. H. Beck'sche Verlagsbuchhandlung, 1961), no. 27. Of particular relevance to "Antisemitism in the plays of Hans Folz" cf. Edith Wenzel, *'Do worden die Judden alle geschant': Rolle und Funktion der Juden in spätmittelalterlichen Spielen*, Forschungen zur Geschichte der älteren deutschen Literatur 14 (Munich: Wilhelm Fink Verlag, 1992), 189–265.
3. Cf. the article "Krieg" in Hermann Paul, *Deutsches Wörterbuch*, 9th ed. Helmut Henne and Georg Objartel (Tübingen: Niemeyer, 1992), 490.
4. For the development of Christian exegesis and the tradition of the polemic texts in dialogue, cf. Heinz Schreckenberg, *Die christlichen Adversus-Judaeos-Texte und ihr literarisches und historisches Umfeld (1.–11. Jh.)*, Europäische Hochschulschriften, Series XXIII: Theologie 172 (Frankfurt am Main–et al.: Peter Lang, 1982, 4th. ed. 1999), see particularly the section on Origen; ibid., *Die christlichen Adversus-Judaeos-Texte (11–13. Jh.), Mit einer Ikonographie des Judenthemas bis zum 4. Laterankonzil*. Europäische Hochschulschriften, Series XXIII: Theologie 335 (Frankfurt am Main et al.: Peter Lang, 1988, 3rd ed. 1997); ibid., *Die christlichen Adversus-Judaeos-Texte und ihr literarisches und historisches Umfeld (13.-20. Jh.)*, Europäische. Hochschulschriften, Reihe XXIII: Theologie 497 (Frankfurt a. M. et al.: Peter Lang, 1994), 587. There is also a good survey in Jeremy Cohn, ed., *Essential Papers on Judaism and Christianity in Conflict: From the Late Antiquity to the Reformation*. Essential Papers on Jewish Studies (New York and London: New York University Press, 1991). One of the most important

and momentous real disputes was that between Paulus Christiani and Moses ben Nachman in Barcelona in 1263. There is a detailed report with bibliography in Schreckenberg, *Die christlichen Adversus-Judeos-Texte*, 1982, 208–19; see also Winfried Frey, "'*Synagoga dialogo exclusa.*' Über das Scheitern des jüdisch-christlichen Dialogs von Anfang an," Ulrich Lilienthal und Lothar Stiem, eds. *Den Menschen zugewandt leben, Festschrift für Werner Licharz* (Osnabrück: secolo, 1999), 39–51.

5. Cf. Janota (see note 1), col. 771 f.
6. Hartmut Bookmann, *Einführung in die Geschichte des Mittelalters*. Beck-'sche Elementarbücher (Munich: Beck, 1978), 117. Bookmann's statement, which has since been frequently repeated and cited, can be regarded as a description of the general scholarly consensus!
7. Cf. Johannes Janota, "Hans Folz in Nürnberg, Ein Autor etabliert sich in einer stadtbürgerlichen Gesellschaft," Heinz Rupp and Eberhard Lämmert, eds., *Philologie und Geschichtswissenschaft:* Demonstrationen literarischer Texte des Mittelalters (Heidelberg: Quelle & Meyer, 1977), 74–91.
8. Cf. Guido Kisch, *Forschungen zur Rechts- und Sozialgeschichte der Juden in Deutschland während des Mittelalters* (Zürich: Europa Verlag, 1955), 20–40.
9. Cf. Friedrich Battenberg, *Das europäische Zeitalter der Juden, Zur Entwicklung einer Minderheit in der nichtjüdischen Umwelt Europas*, vol II: From 1650 to 1945 (Darmstadt: Wissenschaftliche Buchgesellschaft, 1990), ch. 4.
10. D. Martin Luthers Werke, 67 vols.(Weimar: Hermann Böhlaus Nachfolger, 1883–1997), vol. 53, 524; see note 57.
11. Cf. Ephraim Kanarfogel, *Jewish Education and Society in the High Middle Ages* (Detroit: Wayne State University Press, 1992).
12. Berthold von Regensburg, *Vollständige Ausgabe seiner deutschen Predigten*, ed. Franz Pfeiffer, vol. II ed. Joseph Strobl. Die deutschen Neudrucke, Reihe: Texte des Mittelalters (Vienna: Wilhelm Braumüller, 1880; rpt. Berlin: de Gruyter, 1965), 238.
13. A whole arsenal of anti-Semitic clichés is here dealt with in just a few lines; cf. the appendices in Schreckenberg, note 4, especially on "Jewish" *infirmitas*, which collects the "arguments" against the Jews down to the present day. On the Catholic tradition, see Michael Langer, *Zwischen Vorurteil und Aggression: Zum Judenbild in der deutschsprachigen katholischen Volksbildung des 19. Jahrhunderts*. Lernprozess Christen Juden 9 (Freiburg et al.: Herder 1994), and Urs Altermatt, *Katholizismus und Antisemitismus, Mentalitäten, Kontinuitäten, Ambivalenzen: Zur Kulturgeschichte der Schweiz 1918–1945* (Frauenfeld et al.: Verlag Huber, 1999).
14. As to the orthography, I follow the printed edition of Hans Folz and not the editor Hanns Fischer. Folz is here, entirely in the traditional spirit of such disputations, polemicizing against doubters within the Christian religion: anyone who hopes for a (perhaps more perfect) time after Christendom, as many groups did, particularly in the later Middle Ages, is a heretic.
15. "Ea, quae in veritate gesta sunt, alterius sacramenti formam praefigurasse dicuntur. Hrabanus Maurus," quoted from Friedrich Ohly, *Vom geistigen Sinn des Wortes im Mittelalter*. Libelli CCXVIII (Darmstadt: Wissenschaftliche Buchgesellschaft, 1966), 6.

16. Cf. Georges Duby, *Les trois ordre ou l'imaginaire du féodalisme* (Paris: Editions Gallimard , 1978).
17. Cf. Arnold Angenendt, *Geschichte der Religiosität im Mittelalter* (Darmstadt: Wissenschaftliche Buchgesellschaft, 1997), ch. 8. The schema also influenced graphical representations, as for example the representation of the Holy Family on the *Tondo Doni* (1504), today in the Uffizi (cf. Pier Luigi de Vecchi, *Michelangelo: Der Maler* (Darmstadt: Wissenschaftliche Buchgesellschaft, n.d. [1984]), plates 21–24 and 14 f.).
18. The proclamation of the single nature of God is the hallmark of Judaism. According to one Talmudic concept, anyone who professes this is a Jew. Schalom Ben-Chorin, *Jüdischer Glaube: Strukturen einer Theologie des Judentums anhand des Maimonidischen Credo*. Tübinger Vorlesungen, 2. ed. (Tübingen: Mohr (Siebeck), 1979), ch. 2: "Die Einzigkeit Gottes," 59. Cf. the importance of the Shema Jisrael in the daily services in the synagogue: Ismar Elbogen, *Der jüdische Gottesdienst in seiner geschichtlichen Entwicklung*. Olms Paperbacks 30 (Frankfurt am Main: Kauffmann, 1931; rprt. of the third, improved ed. Hildesheim et al.: Olms, 1995), § 7.
19. Johann Maier, *Geschichte der jüdischen Religion: Von der Zeit Alexanders des Großen bis zur Aufklärung, mit einem Ausblick auf das 19./20. Jahrhundert*. de Gruyter Lehrbuch (Berlin and New York: de Gruyter, 1972). "The origin of the dogma of the Trinity" is clearly presented in *Ökumenische Kirchengeschichte I: Alte Kirche und Ostkirche*. Raymund Kottje and Bernd Moeller, eds., 3rd ed. (Mainz and Munich: Matthias-Grünewald-Verlag, Chr. Kaiser Verlag, 1980), 173–179. On the Christian-Jewish controversy about the Trinity, cf. Schreckenberg (note 4), Index.
20. Dt 6, 4–9; 11, 13–21.
21. In v. 134 it is very clearly indicated as the embodiment of Christian teaching, as Ecclesia herself, and accordingly demands agreement!
22. Folz, who is said to have a good acquaintance with Judaism (cf. Edith Wenzel, note 2, 203 ff.), here uses a translation of the Hebrew title 'Bereshit' (In the Beginning) for the Book of Genesis.
23. Buber and Rosenzweig translate the passage as "God said: Let us make Man in our image after our likeness!" *Die fünf Bücher der Weisung*, trans. into German by Martin Buber together with Franz Rosenzweig, *Die Schrift*, trans. into German by Martin Buber together with Franz Rosenzweig, twelfth reprint of the revised edition of 1954 (Gerlingen: Lambert Schneider im Bleicher Verlag, 1997).
24. Schreckenberg II (note 4), 382.
25. Schreckenberg I (note 4), 62.
26. Schreckenberg I (note 4), 175. The letter influenced Justinus Martyr, Irenaeus, Clemens of Alexandria, Tertullian, and Origen!
27. In an anonymous work of c. 1300 ascribed to the Byzantine Emperor Andronicus I. Comnenos. (Schreckenberg II, note 4) 271.
28. E.g. Raschi (Schreckenberg II, note 4, 38), Jehuda ben Samuel Halevi (Schreckenberg II, note. 4, 127), Joseph ben Isaak Kimchi (Schreckenberg II, note 4, 211), Maimonides (Schreckenberg II, note 4, 382).

29. Tryphon, Justinus Martyr's fictitious opponent in the dispute interprets the plural as God speaking to himself (Schreckenberg I, note 4, 185).
30. On his sources for the text, cf. Helmut Lomnitzer, "Das Verhältnis des Fastnachtsspiels vom 'Kaiser Constantinus' zum Reimpaarspruch 'Christ und Jude' von Hans Folz," *Zeitschrift für deutsches Altertum und deutsche Literatur* 92 (1963): 277–291, and Edith Wenzel (note 2), 218 ff.
31. Adelbert von Keller, ed., *Fastnachtspiele aus dem 15. Jahrhundert,* Teil 1–3 und Nachlese. 4 vols. (Stuttgart: Bibliothek des Litterarischen Vereins, 1853–58; rpt. Darmstadt: Wissenschaftliche Buchgesellschaft, 1965, 1966), no. 1; cf. Edith Wenzel (note 2), 193–217.
32. Images from as early as the twelfth century correspond to this statement. They depict Christ on the throne with the Christian Church next to Him, and with Synagoga lying before him on the floor with the goat as a (defamatory) symbol of her religion in her arms. (Montalcino, Biblioteca Communale, twelfth century; Herbert Jochum, ed., *Ecclesia und Synagoga, Das Judentum in der christlichen Kunst*. Ausstellungskatalog Alte Synagoge Essen, Regionalgeschichtliches Museum Saarbrücken (n.p., n.d. [1993]), plate 11); or they place the victorious Ecclesia with banner and goblet in the middle of a letter 'Q,' standing on the blindfolded Synagoga, who forms the tail of the 'Q.'
33. A summary of the tradition can be found in Schreckenberg I (note 4), 76–81.
34. On the contemporary. view, cf. for example, Martin Luther, "Predigt am Sonntag nach Laurentii, 13. August 1525," Martin Luther, *Werke*. Weimarer Ausgabe, 17, I, 380–399. (Thirteen prints of this sermon survive, the last from 1621! Ibidem, XLVIII-LI). On its further influence, see Wilhelm Stählin's Introduction to the tenth Sunday in Trinity (1955): "On the tenth Sunday in Trinity the Church remembers the judgment that came upon the community of the old covenant, the Jewish people, with the destruction of Jerusalem in A.D. 70, and in remembrance of this reads the lament of Christ over Jerusalem and the story of the cleansing of the Temple. The hymn of the weak exhorts the people not to bring a similar judgment down upon themselves by scorning God's beneficence" ([. . .]. Jerusalem und die Geschichte von der Reinigung des Tempels. Das Lied der Woche mahnt das eigene Volk, nicht durch Verachtung der Wohltaten Gottes das gleiche Gericht auf sich herabzubeschwören [. . .]"), Agende I, 160.
35. Folz also uses this comparison in his didactic poem *Jüdischer Wucher*, ed. Hanns Fischer (note 2), no. 37, vv. 40–42.
36. Folz is here referring to the *servitus camerae*, the "Kammerknechtschaft," which had been imposed on the Jews since the thirteenth century, making them people of inferior rights as the "property" of the financial administration first of the king and then later of their relevant territorial or urban ruler. Cf. Friedrich Battenberg (note 9), vol I: *Von den Anfängen bis 1650*, 2nd. ed. (Darmstadt: Wissenschaftliche Buchgesellschaft, 2000), 104–113.
37. A reference to the belief, found as early as in the early Christian period, that the Jews, because of their rejection of Christ as the Messiah, were no longer the chosen people of God, but had been replaced by the (pagan) Christians. Cf. Schreckenberg I (note 4), 97–110.

38. Keller (note 31), no. 106. See also Edith Wenzel (note 2), 218–236.
39. No. 35; for this tradition, see Winfried Frey, " 'Zehen Tunne Goldes', Zum Bild des 'Wucherjuden' in deutschen Texten des späten Mittelalters und der frühen Neuzeit," Carla Dauven-van Knippenberg and Helmut Birkhan, eds., *'Sô wold ich in fröiden singen', Festgabe für Anthonius H. Touber zum 65. Geburtstag*. Amsterdamer Beiträge zur Älteren Germanistik 43–44 (Amsterdam and Atlanta: Editions Rodopi, 1995), 177–194.
40. Cf. Edith Wenzel (note 2), part II, passim.
41. Cf. Michael Toch, "Die Juden im mittelalterlichen Reich," *Enzyklopädie Deutscher Geschichte*, vol. 44 (Munich: R. Oldenbourg Verlag, 1998), 5.
42. Cf. Arnd Müller, *Geschichte der Juden in Nürnberg 1146–1945*. Beiträge zur Geschichte und Kultur der Stadt Nürnberg 12 (Nuremberg: Selbstverlag der Stadtbibliothek, 1968), 14.
43. For a summary, see Toch (note 41), 33–68; on the scholarly debate, cf. Alfred Haverkamp, " 'Concivilitas' von Christen und Juden in Aschkenas im Mittelalter," Robert Jütte and Abraham P. Kustermann, eds., *Jüdische Gemeinden und Organisationsformen von der Antike bis zur Gegenwart*. ASCHKENAS Beiheft 3 (Vienna et al.: Böhlau, 1996), 103–136, which describes the fragile normality of the Middle Ages, which "finally collapses with the end of the Middle Ages," 135, and Friedrich Battenberg, "Zwischen Integration und Segregation: Zu den Bedingungen jüdischen Lebens in der vormodernen christlichen Gesellschaft," *ASCHKENAS, Zeitschrift für Geschichte und Kultur der Juden* 6 (1996): 421–454, who in general terms confirms the outline of the collapse described by Haverkamp, but interprets it in a different way, thus opening the way to the possibility of a new attempt at *concivilitas* in modern times.
44. Arnd Müller (note 42), 30–35.
45. Cf. plate 1 in Arnd Müller (note 42).
46. Michael Toch, " 'Umb gemeyns nutz und nottdurfft willen.' Obrigkeitliches und jurisdiktionelles Denken bei der Austreibung der Nürnberger Juden 1498/99," *Zeitschrift für Historische Forschung* 11 (1984): 1–21; here 7.
47. This was not just the case for the Jews in Nuremberg, but also for the majority of Jewish communities in the German Empire; cf. Markus J. Wenninger, *Man bedarf keiner Juden mehr: Ursachen und Hintergründe ihrer Vertreibung aus den deutschen Reichsstädten im 15. Jahrhundert*. Beihefte zum Archiv. für Kulturgeschichte 14 (Vienna et al.: Böhlau, 1981).
48. As in note 47, 4.
49. This was also confirmed by Thomas Aquinas, cf. Friedrich Battenberg (note 9), vol. I, 112.
50. For a survey, cf. Eberhard Isenmann, *Die deutsche Stadt im Spätmittelalter, 1250–1500: Stadtgestalt, Recht, Stadtregiment, Kirche, Gesellschaft, Wirtschaft*. UTB für Wissenschaft: Große Reihe (Stuttgart: Ulmer, 1988), 74–106.
51. *Lexikon des Mittelalters*, vol. 5 (Munich and Zürich: Artemis 1980–1999), 560 f.
52. Benedikt K. Vollmann, "Nigri, Petrus OP," *Die deutsche Literatur des Mittelalters, Verfasserlexikon*, second edition, ed. Kurt Ruh et al., vol. 6 (Berlin and New York: Walter de Gruyter, 1987), cols. 1008–1013.

53. Keller (note 31), no. 106.
54. Cf. Janota (note 7).
55. Evidence is provided by Schreckenberg I und II (note 4), Index. In the *Hortus deliciarum* by Herrad von Landsberg, Synagoga and Heresis are represented together on folio 60v! Cf. Schreckenberg II, 602. How much this way of proceeding still affects the relationship between Jews and Christians right down to the present day is shown by Erich Zenger, *Das Erste Testament: Die jüdische Bibel und die Christen*. 5th ed. (Düsseldorf: Patmos 1995; 1st ed. 1991): "With such a way of dealing with the Old Testament this is appropriated for Christianity in such a way that the Jews are dispossessed." 135, while discussing theological statements made after 1970!
56. See note 47, 14; among other things, the "conditions for escorting alien Jews" were made more severe in 1477.
57. Cf. ibid., 16.

Contributors

LOURDES MARÍA ALVAREZ is Assistant Professor of Spanish at The Catholic University of America in Washington, DC, and currently Fulbright Senior Scholar (Morocco) 2000–2001. She received her Ph.D. in Spanish from Yale University (1994). Her soon to be completed book, *The Bilingual Heart: Songs of Love, Nostalgia of Songs in Islamic Spain,* examines Andalusian strophic poetry and its symbolic role in Andalusî identity and memory. She is currently doing research for a book on the Andalusian Sufi poet Abū al-Hasan ᶜAlī al-Shushtarī. Her publications include "Hunger of Spirit: Petrus Alfonsi and the Twelfth-Century Renaissance" (in *Cambridge History of Arabic Literature: Al-Andalus*) and articles and numerous entries in the *Routledge Companion to Arabic Literature.*

ALBRECHT CLASSEN is Professor of German Studies at the University of Arizona. He has published books on Oswald von Wolkenstein (1987) and Wolfram von Eschenbach (1990), autobiographical lyric poetry of the late Middle Ages (1991), the German chapbook (1995), fifteenth- and sixteenth-century German women's songs (Amsterdam and Atlanta: Editions Rodopi, 1999), and German songbooks (Münster and New York: Waxmann, 2001). In 1999 he edited the volume *The Book and the Magic of Reading* (New York and London: Garland), and in 2000 he published a textbook of German women's literature from ca. 1000 to ca. 1800 (New York: Peter Lang). A new monograph on "Despair and Hope: Communicative Strategies in Medieval German Literature" (in German) is forthcoming.

LEONA F. CORDERY is Senior Lecturer in the Department of English at the University of Innsbruck, Austria, where she received her Ph.D. with a dissertation on "The Picture of the Saracens in Middle English Literature." She recently published the article "A Medieval Interpretation of Risk: How Christian Women Deal with Adversity as Portrayed in *The Man of Law's Tale, Emaré* and *The King of Tars,*" in *The Self at Risk in English Literature and Other Landscapes, Honoring Brigitte Scheer-Schätzler on the Occasion of Her Sixtieth Birthday* (Innsbruck: Institut für Sprachwissenschaft, Universität Innsbruck, 1999).

WINFRIED FREY is Professor of German at the Johann Wolfgang Goethe University in Frankfurt am Main, Germany. He edited (1983) and translated *Der Eraclius des Otte* (1990), and was the coeditor of the literary history *Einführung in die Deutsche Literatur des 12. bis 16. Jahrhunderts* (3 vols., 1979–1983). He is currently the director of two research projects, promoted by the DFG (German Research Association): The Lexikon deutsch-jüdischer Autoren (9 vols) and *The Image of the Jews in German Pamphlets of the Sixteenth Century.*

MICHAEL GOODICH is Professor of Medieval History at the University of Haifa, Israel, and the author of *Other Middle Ages: Marginal Groups in the Medieval Period* (Philadelphia: University of Pennsylvania Press, 1998) and *Violence and Miracle in the Fourteenth Century: Private Grief and Public Salvation* (Chicago: University of Chicago Press, 1995).

ALINE G. HORNADAY earned her Ph.D. from the University of California, San Diego, in 1984, after a long business career in newspaper publishing. She is the founding copublisher and coeditor with Dr. Ann Elwood of *Journal of Unconventional History* and was so from 1989 until it ceased publication in 2000. Her articles deal with topics such as "Les Saints du 'Cycle de Maubeuge' et la conscience aristocratique dans le Hainaut médiéval," (1991), "Early Medieval Kinship Structures as Social and Political Controls" (1996), and "Toward a Prosopography of the 'Maubeuge Cycle' Saints" (1996).

JEAN E. JOST is Professor of English at Bradley University. She has published a number of articles on Chaucer, the *Morte Darthur, Amis and Amiloun,* and Gottfried von Strasbourg's *Tristan.* She is the author of *Ten MiddleEnglish Arthurian Romances: A Reference Guide* (Boston, Mass.: G. K. Hall, 1986) and *Chaucer's Humor: Critical Essays* (New York: Garland Press, 1994). She serves as coeditor of the *Chaucer Yearbook* and is currently editing the *Southern Recension of the Pricke of Conscience.*

DAVID B. LESHOCK received his doctorate in English from Duquesne University in Pittsburgh, PA. He has taught at Duquesne University and Indiana University of Pennsylvania and is currently employed with a publishing company. He has published articles on the representation of Islam in medieval English cycle drama (*Corpus Christi Plays*) and on Marie de France's *lai* "Bisclavret." His current project explores the scientific, philosophical, and literary examinations of humor, mostly in the Middle Ages.

JESUS MONTAÑO is Assistant Professor of English at Hope College in Holland, Michigan. He holds a Ph.D. from The Ohio State University, where he wrote a dissertation entitled "Writing a Nation: Figuring Community in Late Medieval England." Professor Montaño currently is working on a book examining nationalism and race in the Middle Ages.

CARY J. NEDERMAN, until recently an instructor at the University of Arizona, is currently Professor of Political Science at Texas A&M University. He has published numerous books, including, most recently, *Worlds of Difference: European Discourses of Toleration, c. 1100–c. 1550* (University Park: Pennsylvania State University Press, 2000). He also translated John of Salisbury's *Policraticus* (1990) and is the author of many articles in political science, history, and medieval studies journals.

ALEXANDER SAGER, received his Ph.D. in German literature from Cornell University in 2000 with the thesis *Von osten allenthalben: Imageologies of Eastern Europe in German and Hungarian Literary Culture, 1050–1300.* In the fall of 1999, he joined the faculty of the Department of Germanic and Slavic Languages at the University of Georgia, Athens, where he teaches courses in medieval German language, literature, and culture, as well as business/political German. His research focuses on historical, literary, and cultural relations between Germany and eastern Europe (especially Hungary) in the Middle Ages, courtly love poetry, and Wolfram von Eschenbach.

DAVID F. TINSLEY, Professor of German at the University of Puget Sound, just completed a booklength manuscript in which he explores spiritual implications of extreme asceticism in fourteenth-century Dominican convent culture. Recent publications include articles on Julian of Norwich, Elsbeth von Oye, Ulrich von Liechtenstein, and Wolfram von Eschenbach.

MICHAEL UEBEL is Assistant Professor of English at the University of Kentucky, where he teaches medieval literature and cultural studies. He coedited, together with Harry Stecopoulos, *Race and the Subject of Masculinities* (Durham, NC, and London: Duke University Press, 1997), and is currently working on a book on the inception of utopia in the twelfth century. He has published articles on fantasies of alterity in the Prester John legend and in crusade apologists, male masochism in cyberpornography and in the strip club scene, and masculinity (medieval and modern).

LISA WESTON is Professor of English at California State University, Fresno. Her publications have appeared in a number of journals, including *Modern Philology* and *Neuphilologische Mitteilungen.* Her article "Gender without Sexuality: Hrotsvitha's Imagining of a Chaste Female Community" appeared in *The Community, the Family and the Saint: Patterns of Power in Early Medieval Europe,* ed. Joyce Hill and Mary Swan (Turnhout: Brepols, 1998).

Index